CANTATE DOMINO

An ecumenical hymn book
Ein ökumenisches Gesangbuch
Psautier œcuménique

new edition · neue Ausgabe · nouvelle édition

published on behalf of the
veröffentlicht im Auftrag des
publiée sous le patronage de

World Council of Churches
Ökumenischen Rates der Kirchen
Conseil œcuménique des églises

BÄRENREITER
KASSEL · BASEL · TOURS · LONDON
BA 4994

© by Bärenreiter-Verlag Kassel 1974
Alle Rechte vorbehalten / Printed in Germany
ISBN 3-7618-0500-4

Table of Contents · Inhaltsverzeichnis
Table des Matieres

Foreword

Christianity was born in song. The songs of Mary, Elizabeth, the angels and Simeon heralded the birth of Christ. On that fateful evening when Jesus had his last supper with the disciples they sang a hymn before going out to face the final encounter with betrayal and death. After Pentecost the new Christian community shared their life together 'with glad and generous hearts, praising God'. Throughout its history the vigour of the Church's life and of its renewal has been marked by Christians 'addressing one another in psalms and hymns and spiritual songs, singing and making music to the Lord' (Ephesians 5:19).

'Singing and making music to the Lord' is an act of thanksgiving, acknowledging the mighty acts of grace of the God and Father of our Lord Jesus Christ. It is something we can delight in doing together, a demonstration of our common life in one Body, reconciled and held together by Christ the Head through the Holy Spirit. No wonder the modern ecumenical movement should find its most popular expression in Christians singing each other's hymns.

Already in 1924, the World Student Christian Federation, that pace-setter of the ecumenical movement, published a first edition of *Cantate Domino*, which remained for fifty years its most widely used publication. Noble efforts were made in successive editions, especially that of 1951, to make the book more adequately representative of the world Christian community. Yet, despite the inclusion of some Asian hymns, it was found impossible properly to adapt such music to an 'international' style, and this was considered 'an unsolved problem of ecumenical hymnody'.

As Chairman of the W. S. C. F. in the 1960s, when the pressure was felt for a new edition, I was involved in the discussions and the eventual decision, in 1968, that the task of revision was beyond the time, competence and resources of a mainly student organisation. Since *Cantate Domino* had also become in practice the hymn book of the World Council of Churches, it was appropriate to ask the Uppsala Assembly of the Council to take on the responsibility, which it bravely did, entrusting the project to its Faith and Order Commission. I am therefore delighted to greet this new edition and commend it for use around the world.

'Cantate Domino canticum novum – Sing to the Lord a new song' (Psalm 96:1). This is literally true of this edition. As Editorial Consultant Dr. Erik Routley explains in his preface, an attempt has been made to produce a

new kind of hymn book with songs and hymns from all the main streams of the Church – Orthodox, Roman Catholic and Protestant – and from a wide variety of cultures. This hymn book has also the great merit of expressing the faith and aspirations of people in modern idiom and in terms of their real concerns today. Special thanks are due to Dr. Routley and his team of editors for the mastery with which they have accomplished their extremely difficult but exciting task. We now have an instrument whereby we can joyfully fulfil that other call of the Psalmist: 'Sing to the Lord, all the earth' (Psalm 96:2).

Philip Potter
General Secretary
World Council of Churches

Zum Geleit

Seit den Anfängen hat das Lied die Christenheit begleitet. Die Lieder Marias, Elisabeths, Simeons und der Engel kündigten die Geburt Christi an. An jenem schicksalsschweren Abend, als sie das letzte Abendmahl hielten, sangen Jesus und die Jünger ein Lied, bevor sie hinausgingen und Verrat und Tod auf sich nahmen. Nach Pfingsten entstand die erste Gemeinde, in der die Gläubigen zusammenlebten „mit Freuden und lauterem Herzen, und sie lobten Gott". Solange die Kirche besteht, haben die Christen immer wieder ihre Beständigkeit und ihre Kraft, sich zu erneuern, in Liedern zum Ausdruck gebracht, indem sie „untereinander in Psalmen und Lobgesängen und geistlichen Liedern redeten und dem Herrn sangen und spielten" (Epheser 5,19).

„Dem Herrn singen und spielen" ist ein Akt der Danksagung für die unendliche Gnade Gottes, des Vaters unseres Herrn Jesus Christus. Ihm gemeinsam zu singen und zu spielen kann uns zur Freude werden, zum Ausdruck unserer Gemeinschaft in Einem Leib, versöhnt und vereint im Herrn Jesus Christus durch den Heiligen Geist. Es erstaunt uns daher nicht, daß die moderne ökumenische Bewegung ihren volkstümlichsten Ausdruck dort findet, wo Christen die Lieder ihrer Brüder aus aller Welt singen.

Der Christliche Studentenweltbund, einer der Schrittmacher der ökumenischen Bewegung, veröffentlichte bereits im Jahre 1924 eine erste

Ausgabe des *Cantate Domino*. Sie sollte für die nächsten 50 Jahre seine erfolgreichste Publikation bleiben. In den späteren Neuauflagen – vor allem in der von 1951 – hat man sich dann sehr darum bemüht, die Auswahl der Lieder wenigstens annähernd repräsentativ für die Weltgemeinschaft der Christen zu gestalten. Doch obwohl einige asiatische Lieder aufgenommen wurden, erwies es sich als unmöglich, die asiatische Musik adaequat in „internationale" Musik zu übertragen; dies blieb ein ungelöstes Problem ökumenischer Hymnologie.

Als in den 60er Jahren eine Neuauflage dringend erforderlich wurde, nahm ich als Vorsitzender des Christlichen Studentenweltbundes an der Diskussion teil, die dann 1968 damit beendet wurde, daß wir uns als vorwiegend studentische Organisation aus zeitlichen und finanziellen Gründen, sowie wegen mangelnder Kompetenz nicht in der Lage sahen, eine Neubearbeitung vorzunehmen. Da *Cantate Domino* inzwischen praktisch zum Gesangbuch des Ökumenischen Rates der Kirchen geworden war, lag es nahe, den Rat zu bitten, diese Aufgabe zu übernehmen. Gern akzeptierte er diesen Vorschlag und betraute die Kommission für Glauben und Kirchenverfassung mit der Ausführung. Ich freue mich, Ihnen hiermit die neue Ausgabe vorstellen zu können und darf sie zur Benutzung in allen Teilen der Welt empfehlen.

„*Cantate Domino canticum novum* – Singet dem Herrn ein neues Lied" (Psalm 96, 1). Genau dies wollen wir mit der neuen Ausgabe erreichen. Wie Dr. Erik Routley im Namen seiner Mitherausgeber in der Einführung feststellte, ist hier der Versuch gemacht worden, ein ganz neues Gesangbuch zusammenzustellen, indem man Lieder aus allen großen christlichen Traditionen – orthodoxe, römisch-katholische und protestantische – und aus den verschiedensten Kulturen aufnahm. Darüber hinaus ist es als sehr positiv zu betrachten, daß die ausgewählten Lieder den Glauben und die Bestrebungen des heutigen Menschen in eine zeitgemäße sprachliche Form bringen, daß sie auf seine wirklichen Probleme eingehen. Besonderer Dank gilt Dr. Routley und seinen Mitherausgebern für die Sorgfalt, mit der sie diese außerordentlich schwierige und doch höchst interessante Aufgabe bewältigt haben. Mit diesem Buch in den Händen können wir nun freudig dem Ruf des Psalmisten folgen – „Singet dem Herrn, alle Welt." (Psalm 96, 2).

Philip Potter
Generalsekretär
Ökumenischer Rat der Kirchen

Avant-propos

Le christianisme est né dans le chant. Les cantiques de Marie, d'Elisabeth, des anges et de Siméon annonçaient la naissance du Christ. Le soir du jour fatidique où Jésus prit la dernière Pâque avec ses disciples, le groupe chanta un cantique avant de s'en aller pour assister à la rencontre finale avec la trahison et la mort. Après la Pentecôte, les membres de la nouvelle communauté chrétienne ont vécu en commun 'avec joie et simplicité de cœur, louant Dieu'. Tout au long de l'histoire de l'Eglise, la vigueur de sa vie et de son renouveau a été marquée par le chant de chrétiens qui 's'entretenaient par des psaumes, par des hymnes et par des cantiques spirituels, chantant et célébrant de tout leur cœur les louanges du Seigneur' (Ephésiens 5:19).

'Chanter et célébrer les louanges du Seigneur', c'est exprimer notre reconnaissance devant les actes puissants de la grâce de Dieu, Père de notre Seigneur Jésus-Christ. C'est quelque chose que nous pouvons pendre plaisir à faire ensemble, une démonstration de notre vie commune dans un seul corps, reconcilié et uni par le Christ qui en est la tête, grâce à l'action du Saint-Esprit. Il n'est donc pas étonnant que l'expression la plus populaire du mouvement œcuménique moderne réside dans l'échange de cantiques entre communautés chrétiennes.

En 1924 déjà, la Fédération universelle des Associations chrétiennes d'Etudiants, pionnier du mouvement œcuménique, a publié une première édition du *Cantate Domino* qui est demeurée pendant cinquante ans la plus largement utilisée de ses publications. Des efforts louables ont été entrepris dans les éditions ultérieures, en particulier dans celle de 1951, pour rendre ce livre plus représentatif de la communauté chrétienne mondiale. Cependant, bien qu'on eût introduit quelques cantiques asiatiques, il se révéla impossible d'en adapter la musique de manière satisfaisante à un style 'international' et on considéra que c'était là un 'problème non résolu de l'hymnologie œcuménique'.

En tant que président de la FUACE dans les années soixante, j'ai participé, au moment où le besoin d'une nouvelle édition se faisait sentir, aux discussions qui ont abouti, en 1968, à la conclusion qu'une organisation essentiellement estudiantine ne disposait pas du temps, des compétences et des ressources nécessaires pour se charger de cette révision. Puisque le *Cantate Domino* était devenu en fait le recueil de cantiques du Conseil œcuménique des Eglises, il semblait logique de demander à l'Assemblée du

Conseil à Upsal d'en assumer la responsabilité, ce qu'elle accepta courageusement en chargeant la Commission de Foi et Constitution de ce projet. C'est donc avec un vif plaisir que je salue cette nouvelle édition et que j'en recommande l'usage dans le monde entier.

'*Cantate Domino canticum novum* – Chantez à l'Eternel un cantique nouveau' (Psaumes 96:1). Voilà qui caractérise bien cette édition. Comme l'explique au nom du comité de rédaction M. Erik Routley, on s'est efforcé de produire un recueil de cantiques d'un genre nouveau, contenant des chants et des hymnes représentant tous les courants de l'Eglise – orthodoxe, catholique romain et protestant – ainsi qu'un large éventail de cultures. Ce recueil possède aussi le grand mérite d'exprimer la foi et les aspirations des hommes dans un langage moderne, qui va dans le sens de leurs véritables préoccupations aujourd'hui. C'est ainsi que nous devons des remerciements tout particuliers à M. Routley et à son équipe de rédacteurs pour la maîtrise avec laquelle ils se sont acquittés d'une tâche extrêmement difficile, mais combien passionnante. Nous disposons désormais d'un instrument qui nous permettra de répondre joyeusement à l'appel du psalmiste: 'Chantez à l'Eternel, vous tous, habitants de la terre' (Psaumes 96:2).

Philip Potter
Secrétaire général
Conseil œcuménique des églises

Editor's Introduction

'How will Christians of the future sing? As members of the universal Church, or not at all.' That was said at one of the editorial consultations which led to the making of this book; and it could be regarded as the book's governing principle. It is with such a sentiment as that in mind that we now offer it to Christians of all races and opinions, so that we may all share each other's praises.

History of the Book. Cantate Domino was first published in 1924 as a book of 64 hymns taken from many national sources, each appearing in several languages. In 1930 a revised edition, with 82 hymns in 23 languages, was published and in 1951 a further revision appeared, containing 120 hymns. All these were published by the World Student Christian Federation in Geneva.

The present book is therefore the fourth edition of *Cantate Domino,* but it is much more than a revision of the third. It reflects radical changes of policy and outlook which themselves reflect the needs of a new age.

In the first place, the book has been prepared by a special committee convened by the World Council of Churches. In the second, it is nearly twice the size of the third edition, with a much wider coverage of cultures, styles and languages. In the third place, there has been active participation in its editing from within the Roman Catholic and Orthodox churches.

The Making of the Book. In December 1968 a meeting was called by the World Council of Churches in Geneva to explore the question whether a new *Cantate Domino* was practicable. As a consequence of this working parties were organized in several national centres and a list of some 200 correspondents was compiled; these were approached for material and advice. In May 1970 a consultative committee met in the Russian Orthodox House in the Rue Beaumont, Geneva, to report on the first stages of progress. There an editorial board was appointed. This consisted of Fr Joseph Gelineau, Professor Dmitri Stefanovic, Propst Dr. Dieter Trautwein and Mr Erich Weingärtner, who represented respectively the Roman Catholic, Orthodox, European Protestant and American Lutheran traditions, with Dr. Erik Routley as General Editorial Consultant and chairman of the board. To these were added, from among those permanently in Geneva, Dr. Konrad Raiser, staff member of the Faith and Order Secretariat especially charged with responsibility for the project, Mrs Doreen Potter, wife of Philip Potter, herself a composer with special interest in contemporary hymns, the Reverend Fred Kaan of the staff of the World Alliance of Reformed Churches and a celebrated hymnwriter, and, until April 1972, Miss Margot Toplis. Miss Toplis, who was appointed to take special responsibility for the secretarial work, left for other work in April 1972, and Mr Weingärtner moved out of direct involvement in the Board's work when he finished his period of service with the Lutheran World Federation in the same year. When Miss Toplis left Geneva her secretarial work was taken over by Miss Sally Woolston, and at a later stage Mrs Potter gave substantial assistance with the preparation of the fair copy for the publisher. This is an appropriate place to thank these three especially for their very great contribution to the work which is now in the reader's hands.

We also gratefully acknowledge here the support given to the World Council in this project by several member churches. Financial contributions were made in particular by churches in the Federal Republic of Germany, Sweden, the USA and the Netherlands. The Evangelical Lutheran Church in Finland made a most welcome gift of paper.

It was the task of this editorial Board to gather together the findings of the various working parties and to prepare the manuscript of the book. A consultation in June 1971 made a first attempt to find a way through the enormous mass of material that already lay before us. The Board met again in October 1971 with certain invited guests, including Bishop F. Pagura, formerly of Panama and Costa Rica, and Fr Christopher Coelho of India (some of whose work is in this book), and a new draft of the book was prepared. After much correspondence, a final meeting of the Board was held in October 1972. During this consultative period eight separate drafts of the book were assembled, and the last of these was abridged at a late stage on the publisher's advice; this is what you now have in your hand. The editors are deeply grateful to the publishers, Bärenreiter-Verlag, not only for their readiness to invest in such an unusual book but also for the open-hearted collaboration they have brought to so many of the awkward details.

The Purpose of the Book. At an early stage it was agreed that the purpose of the book was to serve the church at its 'growing points'. The Church is at present growing, we believe, through the meeting of cultures and races, as well as through experiments in text-writing, music and liturgy; an international hymn book with an experimental emphasis was clearly called for, and we have sought to include in the book material in many styles. Not only hymns of the familiar kind will be found here, but also antiphonal canticles and folk songs. We hope to make available not only the hymnody of the west to the east, and of the north to the south, as did the older missionary enterprises, but some of the new and vital hymnody of the southern hemisphere to the north, and of the east to the west.

Translations. This has meant that we have had to be much more flexible in our use of translations than were the earlier editors. On the one hand, it is not now felt to be so necessary that members of an international congregation should sing each in his own language: on the other hand, it has been found that not all our material can be satisfactorily translated into a standard number of languages. So we do not now present all the material in English, French and German, as in the earlier editions. The principle has been to present everything in its original language and in English (although even this we have not followed pedantically), and in such other languages as seemed to carry it best. A few hymns appear in one language only; while a small number of the more familiar classics are given in up to eight languages.

To avoid, however, undue difficulty of presentation, we have retained the tradition of using French, German and English as the basic languages for translation. In each of these language areas a panel of translators has chosen hymns to be translated, and has made or selected the versions we now present. In certain cases, especially in the French versions, we were quite content that the versions should emerge as paraphrases: in one or two cases, indeed, they are new compositions which have nothing but the melody in common with the originals. In such cases, and where there is a different number of stanzas in the different versions, we have indicated that it would be inadvisable to sing these versions concurrently with the originals.

The Use of the Book. You have, then, a quite new kind of hymn book in your hand. It is not the first multilingual book to appear, but it is different from its contemporaries and predecessors to an extent that makes it necessary to recommend some care in its use.

We envisage its use in two ways. On the one hand it is, we feel, uniquely appropriate to international gatherings, large or small. It will find a natural place in any conference centre, retreat house, tourist centre, ocean liner, or other meeting place where people of different languages and cultures gather. But also – especially perhaps in areas where French, German or English are major languages – it can be used as a supplement to a parish hymnal, or to that of a university chapel or a school, in order to enrich the religious experience of those who use it in exactly those directions in which the Church is growing most energetically at present.

In either case, much of the contents will be unfamiliar. Many of the texts and tunes we have selected are unknown outside the communities which have used them up to now; some are altogether new. We offer songs in styles that encourage accompaniment on other instruments than the pianoforte or organ, and songs that invite antiphonal treatment. Whatever its context, we urge that the use of the book be assisted, and usually preceded, by its informal use for practice and for the improvement of people's acquaintance with its various styles. Do not confine yourself to the five or six hymns in it with which you are already familiar. Use whatever talents are available to teach, from the beginning, those new pieces, and thus to introduce those new ecumenical experiences, which only this book makes available in a single collection.

We commend this book to all Christians who care to make use of it. For us, the editorial board and consultants, it is a celebration of that friendship between the nations, and between the different Christian bodies, which the World Council of Churches was founded to promote, and for which our Faith requires us constantly to work and pray. It is, in itself, no more than a chapter in a much longer story, a stage in a long, arduous and rewarding pilgrimage. But such as it is, it represents our effort to serve the churches which we love, and the Lord under whose judgment and promise we all stand.

For the Editorial Board,
ERIK ROUTLEY
Newcastle upon Tyne, England
St Andrew's Day 1973

Vorwort des Herausgebers

„Wie werden die Christen in Zukunft singen? Sie werden entweder als Glieder der universalen Kirche singen oder gar nicht mehr". Diese These wurde in einer Redaktionsbesprechung für eine neue Ausgabe von *Cantate Domino* aufgeworfen und könnte als Leitthema zu diesem Buch betrachtet werden. Im Blick auf diese und ähnliche Fragen bringen wir das neue *Cantate Domino* jetzt für Christen aller Rassen und Überzeugungen heraus, damit wir alle unsere Lieder und Lobgesänge miteinander teilen können.

Vorgeschichte des Buches. Die erste Ausgabe von *Cantate Domino* erschien 1924 mit 64 Liedern aus vielen Ländern, die jeweils in mehreren Sprachen vorgestellt wurden. 1930 wurde eine erste überarbeitete Auflage mit 82 Liedern in 23 Sprachen, 1951 eine zweite Auflage mit 120 Liedern herausgegeben. Als verantwortlicher Herausgeber für alle drei Ausgaben zeichnete der Christliche Studentenweltbund in Genf.

Das vorliegende Buch stellt zwar die dritte neu bearbeitete Auflage von *Cantate Domino* dar, ist aber im Grunde weit mehr als eine Überarbeitung der letzten Ausgabe. Das neue *Cantate Domino* läßt grundlegende Veränderungen in Methodik und Gestaltung erkennen, die ihrerseits die Ansprüche eines neuen Zeitalters widerspiegeln: Zunächst einmal wurde das Buch von einem durch den ÖRK einberufenen Sonderausschuß vorbereitet; dann ist es beinahe doppelt so umfangreich wie die vorherige Ausgabe und stellt eine weit größere Zahl von Kulturen, Vertonungsarten und Sprachen vor; und schließlich ist es in Zusammenarbeit mit Mitgliedern der römisch-katholischen und der orthodoxen Kirche entstanden.

Entstehung des Buches. Im Dezember 1968 berief der Ökumenische Rat der Kirchen eine Tagung in Genf ein, auf der die Teilnehmer sich in erster Linie mit der Frage auseinandersetzten, ob für eine neue Ausgabe von *Cantate Domino* realistische Aussichten bestünden. Als Antwort auf diese Frage wurden in mehreren Ländern Arbeitsgruppen eingerichtet und wurde eine Liste von 200 Korrespondenten zusammengestellt. Gruppen und Korrespondenten wurden anschließend um Material und Rat gebeten. Im Mai 1970 trat im Haus der Russisch-Orthodoxen Kirche in der Rue Beaumont in Genf ein Beratungsausschuß zusammen, um über die ersten Arbeitsergebnisse zu berichten. Auf dieser Tagung wurde auch ein Redaktionskomitee aus folgenden Mitgliedern ernannt: Pater Joseph Gelineau (römisch-katholische Kirche), Prof. Dimitri Stefanovic (orthodoxe Kirche), Propst Dr. Dieter Trautwein und Erich Weingärtner als Vertreter der europäisch-protestantischen, bzw. der amerikanisch-lutherischen Tradition; Reverend Dr. Erik Routley wurde zum mitverantwortlichen Herausgeber und Vorsitzenden des Redaktionskomitees ernannt. Der Redaktionsstab schloß außerdem noch folgende Mitarbeiter ein, die ihren Wohnsitz und Arbeitsplatz in Genf haben: Pfarrer Dr. Konrad Raiser vom Sekretariat für Glauben und Kirchenverfassung, dem die Verantwortung für das Projekt übertragen wurde, Frau Doreen Potter, die selbst komponiert und sich speziell für moderne Kirchenlieder interessiert, Pfarrer Fred Kaan vom Reformierten Weltbund, der bereits als Verfasser von Kirchenliedern bekannt ist, sowie Fräulein Margot Toplis, die die Verantwortung für die Sekretariatsarbeit übernahm. Erich Weingärtner hat den Lutherischen Weltbund nach Ablauf seines Vertrages 1972 verlassen und seine aktive Mitarbeit im Redaktionskomitee einstellen müssen. Auch Fräulein Toplis hat sich im April 1972 anderen Aufgaben zugewandt, und ihre Arbeit wurde von Fräulein Sally Woolston weitergeführt. In einem späteren Stadium hat auch Frau Potter bei der Vorbereitung des druckfertigen Manuskripts intensiv mitgeholfen. Diesen drei Mitarbeiterinnen möchten wir an dieser Stelle besonderen Dank aussprechen für ihren unschätzbaren Beitrag zu dem Werk, das sie jetzt in Händen halten. Dem Bärenreiter-Verlag sei an dieser Stelle gedankt, nicht nur für seine Bereitschaft, ein so ungewöhnliches Werk zu publizieren, sondern gleichermaßen für die vertrauensvolle und geduldige Zusammenarbeit, die die Lösung manch schwieriger Detailfrage ermöglicht hat.

Wir wollen hier auch unsere große Dankbarkeit für die Unterstützung dieses Projektes von Seiten mehrerer Mitgliedskirchen zum Ausdruck bringen. Geldspenden kamen in erster Linie aus der Bundesrepublik Deutschland, aus Schweden, aus den USA und den Niederlanden. Die Evangelisch-lutherische Kirche Finnlands gab eine höchst willkommene Papierspende.

Es war Aufgabe des Redaktionskomitees, die Arbeitsergebnisse der verschiedenen Gruppen zusammenzustellen und das Manuskript des Buches vorzubereiten. Auf einer Redaktionssitzung im Juni 1971 wurde mit der Durchsicht des bis dahin eingegangenen umfangreichen Materials begonnen. Das Komitee trat im Oktober desselben Jahres zu einer weiteren Sitzung zusammen, zu der u. a. Bischof F. Pagura früher Panama jetzt Costa Rica und Pater Christopher Coelho aus Indien (einige seiner Werke sind in das neue *Cantate Domino* aufgenommen) geladen waren. Auf dieser Sitzung wurde ein neuer Entwurf ausgearbeitet. Die Arbeit ging anschließend auf dem Korrespondenzweg weiter, und im Oktober 1972 fand eine abschließende Redaktionssitzung statt. Insgesamt waren acht verschiedene Entwürfe zusammengestellt worden; den letzten Entwurf, der auf Anraten des Verlegers noch etwas gekürzt wurde, legen wir Ihnen hiermit als endgültige Ausgabe vor.

Sinn und Zweck dieses Buches. Schon bei den ersten Vorbereitungen war man übereingekommen, daß das neue *Cantate Domino* den 'Experimentierfeldern' der Kirche dienen sollte. Wir glauben, daß die Kirche gegenwärtig durch die Begegnung verschiedener Kulturen und

Rassen wie auch durch Experimente in Textdichtung, Vertonung und Liturgie in völlig neue Bereiche hineinwächst. Damit lag es auf der Hand, ein neues internationales Gesangbuch herauszubringen, das viele Experimente und neue Sing- und Spielarten vorstellt. So finden Sie neben den traditionellen Liedern auch eine Reihe von antiphonischen Gesängen und volkstümlichen Liedern. Zudem ist es uns gelungen, nicht nur das Liedgut des Westens dem Osten und das des Nordens dem Süden nahezubringen (was dem früheren missionarischen Ansatz entspricht): wir versuchen auch neue ausdrucksstarke Lieder der südlichen Hemisphäre dem Norden und einiges Liedgut des Ostens dem Westen vorzustellen.

Übersetzungen. Die Frage der Übersetzungen haben wir weit flexibler gehandhabt als die früheren Herausgeber: Zum einen wird es heute nicht mehr als absolut notwendig empfunden, daß alle Mitglieder einer internationalen Gemeinde in ihrer Muttersprache mitsingen können, und zum anderen stellte sich heraus, daß sich nicht alles vorliegende Material zufriedenstellend in eine genormte Anzahl von Sprachen übertragen ließ. Wir sind daher davon abgegangen, alle Lieder wie in den früheren Ausgaben auch in englischer, französischer und deutscher Sprache zu bringen. Grundsätzlich – wenn auch nicht mit pedantischer Genauigkeit – stellen wir jedes Werk in der Originalsprache und in Englisch vor (einige Lieder erscheinen somit nur im englischen Original); Übersetzungen in andere Sprachen haben wir nur dann vorgenommen, wenn die fremde Sprache dem spezifischen Charakter eines Liedes auch gerecht werden konnte. Zwar erscheint eine kleine Auswahl bekannterer Lieder in bis zu acht Sprachen, doch ist bei dem genannten Verfahren keine einzelne Sprache systematisch vertreten.

Um den Gebrauch des Buches nun aber nicht unnötig zu komplizieren, haben wir im großen und ganzen Französisch, Deutsch und Englisch als Grundsprachen für die Übersetzungen beibehalten. In jedem dieser Sprachgebiete hat sich eine Gruppe von Übersetzern zusammengesetzt, um die übersetzbaren Lieder auszusuchen und zu übertragen, bzw. bereits vorhandene Versionen auszuwählen. In manchen Fällen, und das gilt besonders für die französischen Versionen, sind freie Wiedergaben entstanden, was wir sehr begrüßen. Ein- oder zweimal sind sogar völlig neue Alternativen dabei herausgekommen, die mit dem Original nur noch die Melodie gemein haben. In diesen Fällen wie auch dort, wo die verschiedenen Versionen in der Anzahl der Strophen differieren, haben wir angemerkt, daß diese Fassungen nicht simultan mit der Originalfassung gesungen werden sollten.

Gebrauch des Buches. Ihnen liegt somit ein völlig neues Gesangbuch vor. Gewiß, es ist nicht das erste mehrsprachige Buch auf dem Markt, doch unterscheidet sich das neue *Cantate Domino* von seinen Vorgängern und Zeitgenossen in einer Weise, daß wir Ihnen empfehlen möchten, es aufmerksam und aufgeschlossen in Gebrauch zu nehmen. Wir sehen insbesondere zwei Gebrauchsmöglichkeiten: Einmal ist es unserer Ansicht nach das Buch für alle großen und kleineren internationalen Zusammenkünfte und sollte daher in jedem Konferenzzentrum, in Stätten der Besinnung und Begegnung, in touristischen Zentren, auf großen Passagierschiffen, kurz, überall dort zu finden sein, wo Menschen verschiedener Sprachen und Kulturen zusammenkommen; darüber hinaus aber kann das Buch – vielleicht besonders in Gebieten, wo in erster Linie Französisch, Deutsch oder Englisch gesprochen wird – genauso gut als Ergänzung zum traditionellen Gesangbuch verwendet werden, das in der Gemeinde oder bei Gottesdiensten in Universität und Schule benutzt wird, und kann so die Erfahrung des einzelnen Christen um die Dimension bereichern, in die die Kirche heute dynamisch hineinwächst.

Wo immer das neue *Cantate Domino* auch benutzt wird, es wird viel Neues und Ungewohntes bringen. Viele Texte und Melodien, die wir Ihnen vorstellen, sind außerhalb der Gemeinschaften, in denen sie gesungen und gespielt werden, nicht bekannt; einige sind völlig neu. Wir bringen auch Stücke, die zur Begleitung auf anderen Instrumenten als Klavier und Orgel anregen sollen, sowie antiphonisch zu singende Lieder. Bitte beschränken Sie sich nicht auf die fünf oder sechs Lieder, die Ihnen bekannt sind, sondern versuchen Sie sich auch gleich an allem Neuen, das *Cantate Domino* zu bieten hat. Es wäre vielleicht zu empfehlen, daß Sie Ihre Gemeinde schon vor dem offiziellen Gebrauch mit allem Ungewohnten vertraut machen, so daß sie sich in die verschiedenen Sing- und Spielarten einüben kann. Setzen Sie alle verfügbaren Talente ein, um diese Stücke bekannt zu machen und zu üben und so Ihre Gemeinde in neue ökumenische Experimente einzuführen, die Ihnen dieses Buch in seiner einzigartigen Ausgabe vorstellt.

Wir möchten dieses Gesangbuch allen Christen empfehlen, die ökumenisch aufgeschlossen sind und die Freude daran finden können. Für uns, d. h. das Redaktionskomitee und die Berater, stellt das neue *Cantate Domino* eine Feier der Freundschaft zwischen den Nationen und zwischen den verschiedenen christlichen Gemeinschaften dar; jener Freundschaft, die zu fördern der Ökumenische Rat der Kirchen gebildet wurde und für die beständig zu wirken und zu beten uns unser Glauben gebietet. Dieses Buch ist an sich nur ein kleines Kapitel in einer viel längeren Geschichte, nur eine kurze Strecke auf einer langen und beschwerlichen Pilgerfahrt, die aber nicht umsonst sein wird. Doch stellt es als solches unser Bemühen dar, den Kirchen, die wir lieben, und dem Herrn, von dessen Verheißung wir alle leben, zu dienen.

Für das Redaktionskomitee:
Erik Routley
Newcastle upon Tyne
Großbritannien
St. Andreas – Tag 1973
(30. November — Missionsfest)

Préface

,De quelle manière les chrétiens chanteront-ils demain? En tant que membres de l'Eglise universelle – ou pas du tout'. Tels sont les propos entendus lors de l'une des réunions de rédaction qui ont conduit à la publication du présent ouvrage; on pourrait ajouter qu'ils en constituent le principe de base. C'est dans cet esprit que nous offrons aujourd'hui ce recueil aux chrétiens de toutes races et de toutes opinions, afin que chacun puisse connaître et partager les chants de louanges des autres fidèles.

Historique. Le premier *Cantate Domino,* publié en 1924, comprenait 64 cantiques présentés en plusieurs langues et issus de nombreuses traditions nationales. En 1930 parut une première édition revue, composée de 82 cantiques en 23 langues et suivie, en 1951, d'une deuxième qui comptait 120 cantiques. Ces trois recueils ont été publiés par la Fédération universelle des Associations chrétiennes d'Etudiants à Genève.

Le présent recueil est donc la quatrième édition du *Cantate Domino.* Mais, bien plus qu'une révision des éditions précédentes, il représente un changement radical d'orientation et de perspective, reflet des exigences d'une ère nouvelle.

C'est ainsi que, préparé par un comité ad hoc réuni sous les auspices du Conseil œcuménique des Eglises, il est près de deux fois plus volumineux que la troisième édition et il représente un éventail beaucoup plus large de cultures, de styles et de langues. En outre, les Eglises catholique romaine et orthodoxes ont participé activement au travail de rédaction.

Elaboration. En décembre 1968, une réunion était organisée à Genève par le Conseil œcuménique des Eglises pour discuter de l'éventuelle publication d'un nouveau *Cantate Domino.* A la suite de cette réunion, des groupes de travail furent établis dans plusieurs pays et on dressa une liste de quelque 200 correspondants qui furent invités à fournir documents et conseils. En mai 1970, un comité consultatif se réunit au Centre orthodoxe russe de la rue de Beaumont à Genève afin d'enregistrer les premiers résultats obtenus. Au cours de cette réunion fut créé un comité de rédaction composé du père Joseph Gelineau, du professeur Dmitri Stefanovic, du pasteur Dieter Trautwein et de M. Erich Weingärtner, qui représentaient respectivement les traditions catholique romaine, orthodoxe, protestante européenne et luthérienne américaine; Dr. Erik Routley fut nommé président du comité de rédaction. A ces membres vinrent s'ajouter des personnes travaillant de manière permanente à Genève, à savoir le pasteur Konrad Raiser, alors membre du personnel de Foi et Constitution, spécialement responsable du projet, Mme. Doreen Potter, compositeur portant un vif intérêt au cantique contemporain et femme du pasteur Philip Potter, le pasteur Fred Kaan, de l'Alliance réformée mondiale, auteur de cantiques des plus appréciés et enfin, jusqu'au mois d'avril 1972, Mlle. Margot Toplis. Cette dernière, qui assumait les tâches administratives du comité, a quitté cet emploi pour d'autres fonctions en avril 1972; pour sa part, M. Weingärtner a cessé de participer directement aux travaux du comité dans le courant de la même année, son engagement au service de la Fédération luthérienne mondiale étant arrivé à son terme. Lorsque Mlle. Toplis a quitté Genève, son travail de secrétariat a été repris par Mlle. Sally Woolston; par la suite, Mme. Doreen Potter a collaboré activement à la mise au net du manuscrit destiné à l'éditeur. Nous tenons à exprimer ici notre profonde reconnaissance à ces trois collaboratrices pour l'aide précieuse qu'elles ont apportée à la préparation du présent ouvrage. Les rédacteurs tiennent à exprimer à la maison d'édition Bärenreiter-Verlag toute leur reconnaissance pour avoir accepté de se charger d'éditer un livre de caractère aussi particulier et pour l'esprit de franche collaboration qui a présidé à la mise au point de nombreux détails.

Nous tenons aussi à exprimer notre reconnaissance aux Eglises membres qui ont aidé le COE pour ce projet. Des Eglises d'Allemagne fédérale, de Suède, des Etats-Unis et des Pays-Bas notamment, ont apporté leur aide financière. L'Eglise évangélique luthérienne de Finlande pour sa part a fait un don très apprécié de papier.

Recueillir les matériaux réunis par les divers groupes de travail et mettre au point le manuscrit de l'ouvrage, telle était la double tâche du comité de rédaction. Lors d'une réunion en juin 1971, une première tentative fut faite en vue de dépouiller l'énorme masse de documents reçus. Le comité se réunit à nouveau en octobre 1971, en présence de plusieurs invités parmi lesquels F. Pagura, ancien evêque méthodiste de Panama et Costa Rica, et le père Christopher Coelho (Inde), dont certains travaux figurent dans ce recueil; un nouveau projet fut alors élaboré. Après de longs échanges de correspondance, le comité tint une dernière réunion en octobre 1972. Au cours de cette période de concertation, huit projets furent mis au point; c'est le dernier d'entre eux, élagué par la suite sur les conseils de l'éditeur, que vous avez en main.

Objectif. Dès le début, chacun fut d'accord pour dire que l'objectif du recueil était de servir l'Eglise dans ses 'expériences nouvelles'. L'Eglise se développe aujourd'hui, croyons-nous, aux points de rencontre des cultures et des races ainsi que par les innovations apportées dans les domaines de la composition littéraire, de la musique et de la liturgie; la publication d'un recueil international de cantiques mettant l'accent sur l'évolution expérimentale s'imposait donc à l'évidence, et nous avons cherché à faire coexister dans ce recueil les styles les plus divers. C'est ainsi qu'on n'y trouve pas seulement des hymnes classiques, mais aussi des cantiques antiphonés et des chansons populaires. Nous avons voulu non seulement que les chrétiens du Sud et de l'Est aient accès au patrimoine de ceux du Nord et de l'Ouest – ce qu'avaient déjà permis les entreprises missionnaires –, mais surtout que ceux-ci s'ouvrent à l'univers musical nouveau et vivant de ceux-là.

Traductions. Tout cela implique que, dans la présente édition, nous avons dû nous montrer beaucoup plus souples quant à la traduction des cantiques que dans les trois précédentes. D'une part en effet, on ne juge plus indispensable que les chrétiens de diverses nationalités réunis pour célébrer Dieu chantent chacun dans sa propre langue. D'autre part, il est apparu impossible de traduire tous les cantiques de manière satisfaisante dans un nombre déterminé de langues usuelles. Tous ne sont donc pas présentés en anglais, en français et en allemand, comme c'était le cas dans les éditions précédentes. Nous avons adopté le principe de publier chaque œuvre dans sa langue originale et en anglais (sans nous en tenir cependant à une règle par trop systématique), ainsi qu'en toute autre langue nous

XXII

semblant apte à en communiquer fidèlement le sens. Si quelques cantiques sont en anglais seulement, aucune langue n'est présente d'un bout à l'autre du recueil; un petit nombre de 'classiques' sont traduits en plusieurs langues (jusqu'à un maximum de huit).

Toutefois, pour éviter de trop grandes difficultés de mise en page, nous avons retenu de manière générale les langues de base traditionnelles, à savoir l'anglais, le français et l'allemand. Dans chacune des régions linguistiques intéressées, un groupe de traducteurs a choisi les cantiques à traduire, et a élaboré ou choisi les versions que nous présentons ici. Dans certains cas, surtout en ce qui concerne les textes français, ces versions sont la paraphrase plus que la traduction de l'œuvre originale. Parfois même, ce sont des œuvres entièrement nouvelles qui n'ont de commun avec l'original que la mélodie. Dans ce cas, et lorsque le nombre de strophes n'est pas le même dans les différentes langues, nous signalons simplement qu'il est préférable de ne pas chanter ces versions en même temps que les cantiques originaux.

Usage. Vous avez donc en main un ouvrage d'un genre tout à fait nouveau. Certes ce n'est pas le premier recueil de cantiques multilingue qui soit publié, mais il diffère de ses prédécesseurs comme de ses contemporains dans une mesure assez importante pour nous inciter à formuler quelques recommandations quant à son usage.

Cette quatrième édition du *Cantate Domino* est conçue dans une double perspective: au niveau international, le recueil conviendra parfaitement à toutes sortes de réunions, grandes ou petites; il trouvera tout naturellement sa place dans les centres de conférences, maisons de retraite, centres touristiques, paquebots et autres lieux où s'assemblent des hommes et des femmes de langues et de cultures différentes. En outre, surtout peut-être dans les régions linguistiques dominées par l'anglais, le français ou l'allemand, il pourra servir de complément au recueil paroissial ou à celui d'une communauté universitaire ou scolaire, enrichir l'expérience religieuse de ceux qui l'utilisent et les sensibiliser aux perspectives dans lesquelles l'Eglise se développe avec le plus de dynamisme à l'heure actuelle.

De toute manière, beaucoup de ces cantiques seront sans doute peu familiers aux fidèles. Plusieurs des textes et mélodies que nous avons choisis sont en effet inconnus en dehors des communautés qui les chantaient jusqu'ici; certains même sont entièrement nouveaux; les uns impliquent un accompagnement faisant appel à des instruments autres que le piano ou l'orgue, d'autres demandent à être chantés dans une forme antiphonée. Dans tous les cas, nous insistons pour que l'utilisation du recueil soit facilitée, et en règle générale précédée, par un effort de répétition et d'amélioration des connaissances des fidèles quant aux différents styles représentés. Ne vous limitez pas aux cinq ou six cantiques que vous connaissez déjà. Ayez recours à tous les talents disponibles pour enseigner ces nouvelles pièces dès le début, et pour vivre ainsi les nouvelles expériences œcuméniques que seul ce recueil est à même d'offrir en un seul ouvrage.

Nous recommandons ce recueil à tous les chrétiens qui prendront la peine de s'en servir. Pour tous les membres du comité de rédaction et ceux qui les ont aidés, il célèbre cette amitié entre les nations et entre les traditions chrétiennes au service de laquelle le Conseil œcuménique a été créé et pour laquelle nous devons œuvrer et prier sans cesse, en obéissance à notre foi. Ce recueil n'est qu'un chapitre d'une très longue histoire, une étape d'un pèlerinage long et difficile, mais combien enrichissant! Tel qu'il est, il incarne notre tentative de servir les Eglises que nous aimons et le Seigneur, notre juge et espérance à tous.

Pour le comité de rédaction,
Erik Routley,
Newcastle upon Tyne (R.-U.)
Saint-André (30. novembre) 1973

Psalms · Psalmen · Psaumes

1 Psalm 99 (100)

Octante-trois Pseaumes
Geneva 1551

1. All peo - ple that on earth do dwell, sing to the Lord with
1. Vous qui sur la terre ha - bi - tez, chan - tez à plei - ne
1. Nun jauchzt dem Her - ren al - le Welt, kommt her, zu sei - nem
1. Tut - ta la ter - ra can - ti a te, Di - o dell' u - ni -

cheer - ful voice; Him serve with mirth, his
voix, chan - tez, Ré - jou - is - sez - vous
Dienst euch stellt, kommt mit Froh - lok - ken,
ver - so; tut - to il crea - to

praise forth tell; come ye be - fore him and re - joice.
au Sei - gneur, é - gay - ez - vous à son hon - neur.
säu - met nicht, kommt vor sein hei - lig An - ge - sicht.
vie - ne a te an - nun - cia la tua glo - ri - a.

2. The Lord ye know is God indeed; / without our aid he did us make; /
we are his folk, he doth us feed, / and for his sheep he doth us take.

3. O enter then his gates with praise; / approach with joy his courts
unto; / praise, laud, and bless his name always, / for it is seemly so to do.

4. For why, the Lord our God is good; / his mercy is for ever sure; / his
truth at all times firmly stood, / and shall from age to age endure.

William Kethe 1560

2. Lui seul est notre souverain, / c'est lui qui nous fit de sa main: / nous le peuple qu'il mènera, / le troupeau qu'il rassemblera.

3. Dans sa maison dès aujourd'hui, / tous présentez-vous devant lui; / célébrez son nom glorieux, / exaltez-le jusques aux cieux.

4. Pour toi, Seigneur, que notre amour / se renouvelle chaque jour: / ta bonté, ta fidélité, / demeurent pour l'éternité.

R. Chapal 1970

2. Erkennt, daß Gott ist unser Herr, / der uns erschaffen ihm zur Ehr, / und nicht wir selbst; durch Gottes Gnad / ein jeder Mensch sein Leben hat.

3. Die ihr nun wollet bei ihm sein, / kommt, geht zu seinen Toren ein / mit Loben durch der Psalmen Klang, / zu seinem Vorhof mit Gesang.

4. Er ist voll Güt und Freundlichkeit, / voll Lieb und Treu zu jeder Zeit; / sein Gnade währet dort und hier / und seine Wahrheit für und für.

Nach Cornelius Becker (1561–1604)
und David Denicke (1603–1680)

2. Unico Dio sei per noi, / fatti dalla tua mano; / Padre, noi siamo figli tuoi, / popolo che tu guidi.

3. Nella tua casa accoglierai / l'inno delle nazioni; / a chi ti cerca tu darai / di lodarti per sempre.

4. Si, ogni uomo lo dirà: / Buono è il Signore Dio; / l'amore suo è verità, / nei secoli fedele.

E. Costa 1973

1. Oh pue-blos to-dos a-la-bad, en al-ta voz a Dios can-tad, re-go-ci-já-os

1. En-yi m-ka-a-o n-chi, mwim-bi-e-ni Mu-ngu sa-na, msi-fu-ni kwa sa-

1. Hai bu-mi Tu-han, so-rak-lah! Bak-ti-kan di-ri pa-da-Nya: da-tang meng-ha-dap

1. よ る ず の く に び と わ が 主 に む か い て て て ろ の か

2

en su ho-nor,   ser - vid   a - le - gres   al   Se - ñor.
u - ti kuu,   mbe - le   za - ke mwa - ku - ta - na.
Yang Ku - dus,   nya - nyi ber - su - ka - ri - a t'rus!

ぎ　り　に　　　よ　ろ　こ　び　た　た　え　よ

2. El soberano Creador / de nuestra vida es el autor; / el pueblo suyo somos ya, / rebaño que El pastoreará.

3. A su santuario pues entrad, / y vuestras vidas ofrendad; / al nombre augusto dad loor, / que al mundo llena de esplendor.

4. Incomparable es su bondad, / y para siempre su verdad; / de bienes colma nuestro ser / su gracia no ha de fenecer.

Federico J. Pagura 1960

2. Mungu mwamjua, kwani / aliyetuumba ndiye, / atuchunga malishani, / na tu kundi lake Yeye.

3. Haya! malangoni mwake, / hata nyuani, imbeni; / mulikuze Jina lake, / Jina la Bwana si duni.

4. Kwani, Jehova ni mwema / ana rehema milele; / kweli yake yasimama / leo na kesho vivile.

2. Akuilah dengan teguh: / Tuhanmu ini Allahmu! / OlehNya kita adalah / dan jadi kawan dombaNya.

3. Masukilah gapuraNya, / puji-syukurma naik serta: / halaman Tuhan b'ri penuh / alunan haleluyamu!

4. Kar'na Tuhanmu mahabaik; / kasihNya pun kekal ajaib / dan setiaNya 'kan teguh / turun-temurun bagimu!

Yayasan Musik Gerejani 1973

2. 主こそはかみなれ、　　　主はわがかいぬし、
　　われらはその民、　　　　みまきのひつじぞ。

3. もろこえあわせて　　　　大御名はめつつ、
　　みかどに入りゆき、　　　みまえに近づかん。

4. めぐみはゆたかに、　　　あわれみつきせず、
　　こよなきまことは　　　　ときわにかわらじ。

2 Psalm 89 (90)

Attributed to William Croft
1678 - 1727

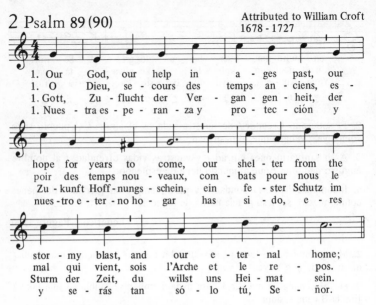

1. Our God, our help in a - ges past, our
1. O Dieu, se - cours des temps an - ciens, es -
1. Gott, Zu - flucht der Ver - gan - gen - heit, der
1. Nues - tra es - pe - ran - za y pro - tec - ción y

hope for years to come, our shel - ter from the
poir des temps nou - veaux, com - bats pour nous le
Zu - kunft Hoff - nungs - schein, ein fe - ster Schutz im
nues - tro e - ter - no ho - gar has si - do, e - res

stor - my blast, and our e - ter - nal home;
mal qui vient, sois l'Arche et le re - pos.
Sturm der Zeit, du willst uns Hei - mat sein.
y se - rás tan só - lo tú, Se - ñor.

2. Under the shadow of thy throne / thy saints have dwelt secure; / sufficient is thine arm alone, / and our defence is sure.

3. Before the hills in order stood, / or earth received her frame, / from everlasting thou art God, / to endless years the same.

4. A thousand ages in thy sight / are like an evening gone, / short as the watch that ends the night / before the rising sun.

5. Our God, our help in ages past, / our hope for years to come, / be thou our guard while troubles last, / and our eternal home.

Isaac Watts 1719 (from Ps. 90)

2. En ton amour, comme des fous, / les saints se sont jetés; / ce même amour, saignant pour tous, / est notre vérité.

3. Avant le ciel, avant le feu, / avant la terre et l'eau, / le mouvement se nommait Dieu, / Dieu la vie, Dieu le mot.

4. L'espace où s'évanouit le temps / nous mène à notre fin. / Mais tu nous tiens hors du néant, / dans l'éternel matin.

5. O Dieu, secours des temps anciens, / espoir des temps nouveaux, / combats pour nous le mal qui vient, / sois l'Arche et le repos.

G. de Lioncourt 1972

2. Wenn deines Thrones Schatten fällt, / auf unsres Weges Not, / und wenn dein Arm uns trägt und hält, / ist nichts, was uns bedroht.

3. Bevor der Berge Ordnung stand, / die Erde Form gewann, / das Weltall ward, war deine Hand, / dein Sein, das nie begann.

4. Du bleibst, und ein Jahrtausend gleicht / vor dir dem Tag, der war, / der Nacht, die bald der Sonne weicht. / Du, Herr, bist immerdar!

5. Gott, Zuflucht der Vergangenheit, / der Zukunft Hoffnungsschein, / du wolltest bis in Ewigkeit / uns Burg und Heimat sein!

Theodor Werner 1952

2. Aún no habías la creación / formado con bondad / más desde la eternidad / tú eras sólo Dios.

3. Delante de tus ojos son / mil años, al pasar / tan sólo un día que fugaz / fenece con el sol.

4. El tiempo corre arrollador / como impetuoso mar; / y así, cual sueño ves pasar / cada generación.

5. Nuestra esperanza y protección / y nuestro eterno hogar, / en la tormenta o en la paz, / sé siempre tú, Señor.

F. J. Pagura

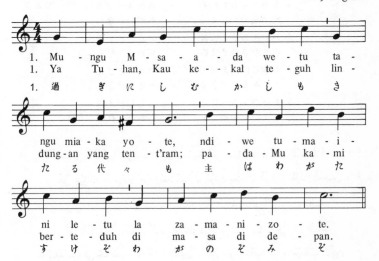

2. Kivuli cha kiti chako / ndiyo Ngome yetu. / Watosha mkono wako / ni ulinzi wetu.

3. Kwanza havi jakuwako / nchi na milima, / ndiwe Mungu; chini yako / twakaa salama.

4. Na myaka elfu ni kama / siku moja kwako; / utaltulinda daima / tu wenyeji wako.

5. Ila Wewe Mingu wetu / ndiwe wa kudumu, / ndiwe bora, Ngome yetu / twakaa dawamu.

2. Dahulu naungan tahtaMu / menjaga kaum kudus; / lengan perkasaMu perlu / mengawal kam t'rus.

3. Seb'lum terlahir dunia / dang gunung terbentuk, / Engkaulah Allah yang baka, / rencanaMu tentu.

4. Seribu tahun di mataMu / sehari yang benam, / sesingkat gilir jaga pun / antara g'lap dan t'rang.

5. Ya Tuhan, Kau kekal teguh / lindungan kaum kudus; / di bawah naungan kasihMu / b'ri kami tinggal t'rus.

Yayasan Musik Gerejani 1973

2. あめつちわかれぬ 　　　世のさきより
　　かわらぬかみてそ 　　　わがかみなれ。

3. わが主のまえには 　　　いくちとせも、
　　みじかきひとよの 　　　ゆめにひとし。

4. あさ日に消えゆく 　　　つゆのごとく、
　　ひとみなうせさり 　　　あとだになし。

5. あめつちうつれど、　　　とこしなえに
　　うごかぬ御座てそ 　　　わがかくれが。

١. يَاعَوْنَنَا فِي مَا مَضَى ۞ رَجَاءَنَا الْوَطِيدْ ۞ مَلْجَأُنَا فِي ضِيقِنَا ۞ مَوْطِنَنَا الْمَجِيدْ

٢. فِي ظِلِّ عَرْشِكَ احْتَمَيَ ۞ كُلُّ الْمُقَدَّسِينَ ۞ عَوْنُكَ بِكُفِينَا أَبَّا ۞ مَعْقِلَنَا الْحَصِينَ

٣. مِنْ قَبْلِ إِبْدَاعِ الْثَّرَى ۞ أَوْ مَنْشَاءِ الْجِبَالْ ۞ أَنْتَ إِلَهُ الْمَجْدِ وَالْ ۞ عِزَّةِ وَالْجَلَالْ

٤. نَظِيرُ أَمْرِ الْمُنْقَضَ ۞ لَدَيْكَ أَلْفُ عَامْ ۞ وَكَهَزِيعِ اللَّيْلِ يَا ۞ حَيُّ عَلَى الَّدَوَامْ

٥. يَاعَوْنَنَا فِي مَا مَضَى ۞ رَجَاءِ نَا الْمَتِينْ ۞ كُنْ حَارِسًا دَوْمًا لَتَا ۞ مَوْطِنَنَا الْأَمِينْ

Translator: Amin Faris (*1938)

3 Psalm 135 (136)

Chinese traditional chant

1. Let us, with a glad - some mind, praise the
1. A mon Dieu, je me con - fi - e, sa clé -
1. Brü - der, macht die Her - zen weit, eu - ren
1. Al Se - ñor, con a - le - grí - a, su ban

Lord for He is kind; for His mer - cies
mence est in - fi - ni - e. Ta pen - sée, ô
Mund zum Lob be - reit! Got - tes Gü - te,
nues - tras me - lo - dí - as, por - que in - men - sa es

shall en - dure, e - ver faith - ful, e - ver sure.
Dieu d'a - mour, est fi - dè - le, é - ter - nel - le.
Got - tes Treu sind an - je - dem Mor - gen neu.
su bon - dad, fir - me por la e - ter - ni dad.

2. He with all-commanding might, / filled the new-made world with light; / For His mercies . . .

3. He His chosen race did bless / in the wasteful wilderness; /

4. He hath, with a piteous eye, / looked upon our misery; /

5. Let us then with gladsome mind / praise the Lord for He is kind: /

after John Milton (1608–1674)

2. La lumière radieuse / est ton œuvre merveilleuse. / Ta pensée, ô Dieu . . .

3. Tu consoles, tu pardonnes, / ta bonté, sur tous, rayonne. /

4. Par ta grâce prévenante / l'âme s'ouvre à l'espérance. /

5. Tout à toi je me confie, / ta clémence est infinie. /

S. Bidgrain 1924

2. Gottes Hand erschafft die Welt, / Finsternis sein Wort erhellt. / Gottes Güte . . .

3. Je und je sein Segen war / über der erwählten Schar. /

4. Und sein Blick aus Himmelshöh'n / hat das Elend angeseh'n. /

5. Macht darum die Herzen weit, / euern Mund zum Lob bereit! /

Johann Christoph Hampe 1950

7

2. A su voz omnipotente / fué la luz respandeciente, / porque
inmensa . . .

3. Dió a su pueblo bendiciones / en sus peregrinaciones, /

4. El con ojos paternales / se apiadó de nuestros males, /

5. Demos pues, con alegría, / gloria a Dios, en este día, /

F. J. Pagura 1960

1. Vin - de, a - le - gres, a - do - re - mos. Ao Se -
1. 全 當 歡 樂 讚 美 主 因 主

nhor_,que é bom, lou - ve - mos. Por - que e - ter - no é
恩 典 多 難 數 上 帝 恒 懷

seu a - mor, por - que e - ter - no é seu fa - vor___.
慈 悲 念 慈 悲 長 久 不 改 變

2. Nosso Deus o sol radiante / faz erguer-se do Levante. / Porque
eterno . . .

3. Junto ao povo do concêrto / acampou-se no deserto. /

4. Estendeu o seu olhar bondoso, / e salvou-nos, generoso. /

5. Vinde, pois, e o exaltemos. / ao Senhor, que é bom, louvemos. /

Jorge Cesar Mota 1949

2. 主之權能甚奇異、造光照滿新天地、
　　副歌

3. 選民在野遭危險、昔蒙主佑恩非淺、
　　副歌

4. 今我既然在苦處、我主慈目仍看顧
　　副歌

5. 所以我當樂讚主、因主恩典多難數
　　副歌

8

1. よろこびあふれ　　はめうたささげん、
　めぐみはとわに　　たゆることなし。

2. かみのかみなる　　あめつちの主の
　めぐみはとわに　　たゆることなし。

3. 世のものすべて　　はぐくみたもう
　めぐみはとわに　　たゆることなし。

4. あらののたびも　　みちびきたもう
　めぐみはとわに　　たゆることなし。

5. われらのよわき　　かえりみたもう
　めぐみはとわに　　たゆることなし。

6. よろこびあふれ　　はめうたささげん、
　めぐみはとわに　　たゆることなし。

4 Psalm 41 (42) 42 (43)

Octante-trois Pseaumes
Geneva 1551

1. Comme un cerf al - té - ré bra - me pour - chas -
1. Seek - ing wa - ter, seek - ing shel - ter gasps the
1. Co - me un cer - vo al - la sor - gen - te as - se -
1. Co - mo el cier - vo an - sio - so bra - ma fres - cas
1. Ca - ri a - ir, ca - ri su - ngai, ru - sa

sant le frais des eaux, O Sei - gneur, ain -
thirs - ty, wea - ry decr. So my soul, in
ta - to ven - go a te. Il tuo vol - to, o
a - guas por be - ber, Así sien - te to -
haus men - j'rit te - rus - ti dak ku - rang

si mon â - me sou - pire a - près tes ruis - seaux.
days of trou - ble, longs for God's re - fresh - ment here.
Dio vi - ven - te, not - te e gior - no cer - che - rò.
da mi al - ma del Dios vi - vo gran - de sed;
ku - per - lu - kan Al - lah, Sum - ber hi - dup - ku!

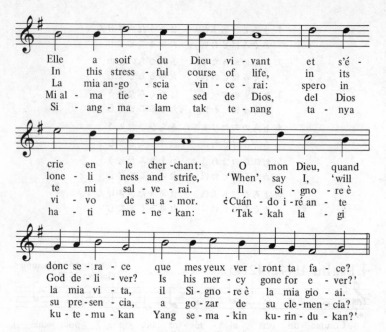

Elle a soif du Dieu vi - vant et s'é -
In this stress - ful course of life, in its
La mia an-go - scia vin - ce - rai: spero in
Mi al - ma tie - ne sed de Dios, del Dios
Si - ang - ma - lam tak te - nang ta - nya

crie en le cher -chant: O mon Dieu, quand
lone - li - ness and strife, 'When', say I, 'will
te mi sal - ve - rai. Il Si - gno - re è
vi - vo de su a - mor. ¿Cuán - do i -ré an - te
ha - ti me - ne - kan: 'Tak - kah la - gi

donc se - ra - ce que mes yeux ver - ront ta fa - ce?
God de - li - ver? Is his mer - cy gone for e - ver?'
la mia vi - ta, il Si - gno -re è la mia gio - ai.
su pre -sen - cia, a go -zar de su cle -men - cia?
ku - te - mu - kan Yang se - ma - kin ku- rin - du - kan?'

2. Tu es seul ma forteresse; / comment peux-tu m'oublier, / quand tu vois
ceux qui me pressent, / ne cessant de me railler? / Montre-toi mon
défenseur / contre tous mes oppresseurs; / me faut-il marcher sans
trêve / dans un deuil que rien n'achève?

3. Dans ma nuit mets ta lumière, / dans mon cœur ta verité, / pour
guider jusqu'à son père / le retour de l'exilé. / A nouveau Dieu de ma
joie, / je ferai monter vers toi / avec tous ceux qui te chantent, / ma
ferveur reconnaissante.

4. Mais pourquoi mon âme encore / frémis-tu d'un tel effroi, / quand
déjà paraît l'aurore / et que Dieu est près de toi? / Tourne-toi vers ton
Sauveur, / il apaisera ton cœur; / et tes chants loueront encore / le
Seigneur que tu adores.

R. Chapal 1970

2. No! he is my soul's true fortress; / though I hear those voices wild, /
'Where's your God, perchance he sleepeth!' / he will not forget his
child. / Come, then, be my advocate; / come, your servant vindicate: /
then no more in fruitless sorrow / will I face a barren morrow.

3. Send your light and truth to lead me, / then the path shall I discern / to my father's house, where welcome / greets the prodigal's return. / Then new songs shall fill my days, / every moment full of praise / with the faithful who surround him, / with the blest ones who have found him!

4. So, my soul, why such disquiet? / Why such mourning, why such fear? / Day already breaks on darkness; / God has sought you. God is near. / Hope in God, and you shall live; / all delight he waits to give, / peace and power and every blessing / you shall know, this faith possessing.

Erik Routley 1972

2. Ogni uomo che mi chiede: / Il tuo Dio ti salverà? / mette a prova la mia fede; / sei nascosto, o Dio, per me. / Il mio pianto ascolterai: / grido a te, risponderai. / Il Signore è la mia vita, / il Signore è la mia gioia.

G. Sobrero 1973

2. Pan de lágrimas amargas / constituye mi porción. / Búrlanse los enemigos, / 'Dinos, dónde está tu Dios?' / Mi recuerdo, con dolor / vuelve al templo del Señor / donde con tu grey un día / te alabé con alegría.

3. No te abatas, alma mía, / ni te turbes en tu fe; / cantarás a Dios un dia, / el que vela por tu bien; / tu clamor escuchará / el Señor, y enviará / su clemencia y consuelo, / el que cambia en gozo el duelo.

4. Solamente en Dios espera, / no te canses de esperar; / pon el El confianza entera, / pues aún lo has de alabar. / Que no hay otra salvación / ni otro Dios; oh, corazón, / canta lleno de alegría / a tu Padre noche y día.

M. Gutiérrez Marin
and F. J. Pagura

2. Namun Kau tetap penyantun / dan tempat suakaku, / walau suara berkecamuk: / 'Mana kini Allahmu?' / Pembela perkaraku, / pertahankan hambaMu! / Maka tiada besok hari / 'ku percuma susah lagi!

3. B'ri cahaya setiaMu, / maka jalanka terang / Yang menuju bait Bapaku: / anak hilang 'kan tent' ram! / Hidup baru kutempuh, / baru pula kidungku / di antara saudaraku / yang t'lah masuk ke rumahMu!

4. Kar'na itu, hai jiwaku, / tak perlu belisahmu; / tiada patut kau berkabung: / kau dicari Tuhanmu! / Yang kauharap mendekat: / damai, kuat dan berkat / 'kan selalu mengiringi / kau dengan imanmu ini!

Yayasan Musik Gerejani 1973

5 Psalm 137 (138)

Pseaulmes cinquante de David
Lyon, 1547

1. Que tout mon cœur soit dans mon chant,
2. Tu me ré - ponds dès que je crie;
1. Thee will I love, my God and King,
2. Set in my heart thy love I find;

qu'il soit brû - lant de tes lou - an - ges.
tu é - lar - gis mon es - pé - ran - ce.
thee will I sing, my strength and to - wer:
my wander-ing mind to thee thou lead - est.

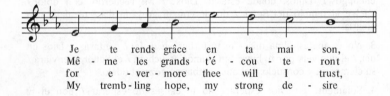

Je te rends grâce en ta mai - son,
Mê - me les grands t'é - cou - te - ront
for e - ver - more thee will I trust,
My tremb - ling hope, my strong de - sire

je loue ton nom de - vant les an - ges.
et bé - ni - ront ta Pro - vi - den - ce.
O God most just of truth and po - wer.
with heaven - ly fire thou kind - ly feed - est.

Tu es ve - nu pour e - xal - ter
Ton saint a - mour, ô roi des cieux,
Thou all things hast in or - der placed,
Lo, all things fair thy path pre - pare,

12

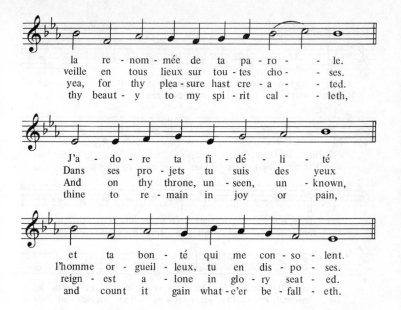

la re - nom - mée de ta pa - ro - le.
veille en tous lieux sur tou - tes cho - ses.
yea, for thy plea - sure hast cre - a - ted.
thy beaut - y to my spi - rit cal - leth,

J'a - do - re ta fi - dé - li - té
Dans ses pro - jets tu suis des yeux
And on thy throne, un - seen, un - known,
thine to re - main in joy or pain,

et ta bon - té qui me con - so - lent.
l'homme or - gueil - leux, tu en dis - po - ses.
reign - est a - lone in glo - ry seat - ed.
and count it gain what - e'er be - fall - eth.

3. Ta paix, mon Dieu, dure à toujours; / c'est ton amour qui me délivre / quand je suis le plus éprouvé / ton bras levé me fait revivre. / Et quand je suis au désespoir / c'est ton pouvoir qui me relève. / Ce qu'il t'a plu de commencer / sans se lasser ta main l'achève.

R. Chapal 1970

3. O more and more thy love extend, / my life befriend with heavenly pleasure; / that I may win thy paradise, / thy pearl of price, thy countless treasure; / since but in thee I can go free / from earthly care and vain oppression, / this prayer I make for Jesu's sake / that thou me take in thy possession.

Robert Bridges 1899

6 Psalm 97 (98)

Octante-trois Pseaumes
Geneva 1551

1. En - ton - nons un nou-veau can - ti - que pour cé -
1. New songs of ce - le - bra - tion ren - der to him

lé - brer le Dieu sau - veur; ce qu'il a fait est ma -
who has great won - ders done; awed by his power his foes

gni - fi - que le - vant pour nous un bras vain-queur.
sur - ren - der and fall be - fore the might - y One.

Le sa - lut de Dieu se ré - vè - le et tous les
He has made known his great sal - va - tion which all his

yeux l'ont re - con - nu; de proche en pro - che la
friends with joy con - fess; he has re - vealed to eve -

nou - vel - le jusqu' au bout du monde a cou - ru.
ry na - tion his e - ver - last - ing right - eous - ness.

2. Chantez pour lui vos chants de fête; / psalmodiez! criez de joie! / Au son du cor et des trompettes, / acclamez tous le Roi des rois. / Le Seigneur vient juger la terre, / sa vérité va s'imposer. / Que tous les peuples qui espèrent / en l'apprenant soient apaisés.

3. Que tous les océans mugissent; / fleuves aussi, battez des mains: / et que les montagnes bondissent / pour acclamer le Roi qui vient. / Le Seigneur va juger le monde / avec droiture et vérité, / et partout sa justice fonde / son éternelle royauté.

R. Chapal 1970

2. Joyfully, heartily resounding, / let every instrument and voice / peal out the praise of grace abounding, / calling the whole world to rejoice. / Trumpets and organs set in motion / such sounds as make the heavens ring: / all things that live in earth and ocean / make music for your mighty King.

3. Rivers and seas and torrents roaring, / honour the Lord with wild acclaim; / mountains and stones look up adoring / and find a voice to praise his name. / Righteous, commanding, ever glorious, / praises be his that never cease: / just is our God, whose truth victorious / establishes the world in peace.

Erik Routley 1972

7 Psalm 1

Thai Traditional Melody

1. Hap - py is he who walks in God's wise way, hap - py who shuns the sin - ful choice: hap - py who finds his plea - sure in God's law,

2. His is the life where du - ty and de - light nou - rish each o - ther bliss - ful - ly; as when be - side a broad and gen' - rous stream

15

เดิน ใน มรร คา ปวง สา ธุ ชน
ไม้ ดอก ออก ผล ตาม กาล เว ลา

hap - py who heeds God's righ - teous voice.
proud - ly stands e - ver - green the tree.

3. Fretful and anxious are the sinner's days, / barren and lonely is his path; / like wind on dust the judgment of the Lord / scatters his pride in sudden wrath.

4. Lord, in your mercy spare me, keep me still, / let me not choose the sinner's way: / promise and law you equally have given: / let them be my delight today.

Erik Routley 1972

3. ฝ่าย ทาง คน ชั่ว หา เป็น ดั่ง เช่น นั้น ไม่ เหมือน แกลบ กระจาย ตาม สาย

ลม พา ดัง นั้น คน ชั่ว จะ ต้อง ทน เวทนา วัน เมื่อ ราชา พิพากษา คน

4. กิจการ คน ชั่ว ย่อม วิบัติ ย่อย ยับ ไป ทำ ไว้ อย่าง ไร ย่อม ได้ แก่ ตน

แต่ ความ ชอบ ธรรม ย่อม นำ คน ให้ ได้ ดล บรรล ยัง ผล ดัง ตน มุ่ง ปอง

8 Psalm 8

Margot Toplis 1972
(Composed for C. D.)

1. Lord, how ma - jes - tic is your name;
1. Dieu, que ton nom est lu - mi - neux!
1. Dein Na - me, Herr, ist groß und gut,

the earth and sky a - dore you,
Le monde en - tier t'a - do - re,
zu dir fleht Erd und Him - mel.

the mouth of ba - bies sings your praise
le mon - de dan - se pour ta joie
Der Schrei des Säug - lings singt dein Lob,

and child - ren dance_____ be - fore you.
mais ne peut dire as - sez ta gloi - re.
und Kin - der tan - - - - zen vor dir.

2. When I look up and see the stars / and think of space unending, / I marvel that you care for man, / and with your love befriend him.

3. You lift him to the very height / of your creative likeness, / just as you raised your Son from death / to Easter's wideawakeness.

Fred Kaan 1968

2. Quand je contemple l'univers, / ton infini royaume, / O la merveille de ton cœur: / tu donneras ton nom à l'homme!

3. Et tu l'élèves jusqu'à toi, / et fais de lui ta gloire; / tu te relèves pour la Vie / dans l'éternel réveil de Pâques.

Claude Rozier 1972

2. Und seh' ich nach den Sternen hin, / bedenk des Weltalls Weite, / dann wundert mich, dass du uns kennst / und liebst und unser Freund bist.

3. Du hebst uns nah zu dir empor, / verleihst uns Schöpferkräfte, / holst uns wie deinen Sohn vom Tod / in deinen Ostermorgen.

Dieter Trautwein 1972

9 Psalm 33(34)   Finnish Traditional Melody

1. Her - ras - ta   vei - saa___   kie - le - ni,
1. O sing, my   soul,   your___ Ma - ker's   praise
1. Ich will dem   Her - ren___   al - le - zeit
1. Je bé - ni - rai   le Sei - gneur en tous   temps,

y - lis - tää   ar - mo - an - sa   Ei un - hot -
in grate - ful hymns as - cend - ing,   whose stead - fast
Lob sin - gen   und ihn prei - sen,   und sei - nen
sous le so - leil, l'o - ra - ge.   Et j'é - cri -

taa voi___   sie - lu - ni   hy - vi - ä
love has___ crowned thy days   with heav'n - ly
Ruhm ver - kün - den weit   in im - mer
rai sur les murs de mes jours   son Nom pour

te - ko - jan - sa.   Mä et - sin ja____ hän
gifts un - end - ing. I sought the Lord___, he
neu - en Wei - sen, daß, wer in Not___, mich
mieux le di - re.   J'al - lais ma route, é - tran -

vas - ta - si.   Ja nöy - rät kuu - li
heard___ my   cry; his ho - ly an - gels
hö - ren kann und sich ge - trö - stet
ger, sans ap - pui; sou - dain j'ai su que

rie - mu - ni   ja loh - du - tuk - sen sai - vat.
ho - ver nigh   the tents of those who love him.
freu - en kann, wie groß des Her - ren Gü - te.
c'é - tait lui   qui as - su - rait ma   gar - de.

18

2. Ne, jotka häntä etsivät / saa avun hältä armaan. / Ne, jotka häntä pelkäävät, / hän varjeleepi varmaan. / Ja ahdingonkin aikana / he tuntea saa iloa, / kun Herra heitä hoitaa.

3. Kasvoihin Herran katsokaa, / ne loistaa suloisesti. / Ja hyvyyttänsä maistakaa, / mi vuotaa iäisesti. / On autuas se ihminen, / ken turvas yksin hänehen, / ei mitään hältä puutu.

Julius Krohn 1835-1888

2. The Lord is good to those who seek / his face in time of sorrow; / he giveth strength unto the weak, / and grace for each tomorrow. / Though grief may tarry for the night, / the morn shall break in joy and light / with blessings from his presence.

3. The Lord will turn his face in peace / when troubled souls draw near him; / his loving kindness ne'er shall cease / to them that trust and fear him. / Our God will not forsake his own, / eternal is his heav'nly throne; / his kingdom stands for ever.

E. E. Ryden and Toivo Harjunpää 1962

2. Wer ihn gesucht von Herzensgrund, / hat Hilfe bald erfahren. / Tut allen, die ihn fürchten, kund, / daß Gott will sie stets bewahren. / Auch wer in Anfechtungen steht, / darin doch nicht zugrunde geht. / Er darf im Herrn sich freuen.

3. Schaut in das Angesicht des Herrn, / es leuchtet euch voll Güte. / Schmeckt seine Freundlichkeit, / die gern euch füllet das Gemüte. / O selig, selig jedermann, / der nur dem Herren trauen kann, / an nichts wird es ihm fehlen.

Käthe Siegfried 1962

2. Ferme les yeux pour goûter qu'il est bon, / c'est le soleil pour l'âme. / Me voilà riche et je sais la chanson, / pour vous je la proclame. / »Cherchez la paix et prenez son parti, / sans crainte alors, aimez la vie / et bannissez la haine.«

3. Dieu me connaît, il me prend au sérieux, / il ne perd pas ma trace. / Les cœurs brisés, le Seigneur est près d'eux / dans les moments d'angoisses. / Et Dieu, quand je côtoierai le tombeau, / se fait comptable de mes os; / mon âme lui rend grâce.

D. Hameline 1972

10 Psalm 35 (36)

Rolf Schweizer 1964

1. Herr, dei - ne Gü - te reicht so weit der Him - mel ist, und dei - ne Wahr - heit so weit die Wol - ken ge - hen. Dei - ne Ge - rech - tig - keit steht wie die Ber - ge, und dein Ge - richt ist tief __ wie das Meer. Men - schen und Tie - ren willst du ein Ge - hil - fe sein.

1. Your lov - ing kind - ness is as wide as noon - day sky, your faith - ful love goes as high as clouds in sum - mer. Your righ - teous judg - ments stand strong as the moun - tains and your pro - nounce-ments deep __ as the sea. Men and the crea - tures live in your pro - tec - ting love.

2. Laßt mich begreifen, Herr, was deine Güte ist, / und deine Wahrheit, von der ich nichts verstehe. / Täglich umgeben mich Worte und Stimmen; / aber ich höre gar nicht mehr hin, / weil sie vom vielen Reden ganz verdorben sind.

3. Gib du doch Sinn, Herr, allem, was ich sag und tu, / Heilgen Geist gib in hilflose Gedanken, / daß ich dich rufen kann, wenn ich nichts höre, / daß ich dich höre, wenn du mich rufst, / daß ich gehorche, wenn du mich berufen willst.

4. Herr, deine Güte reicht so weit der Himmel ist, / und deine Wahrheit, so weit die Wolken gehen. / Dein Flügelschatten ist unsre Bewahrung, / aus deinem Leben, leben wir auch; / und wir erkennen erst in deinem Licht das Licht.

Gerhard Valentin 1964

2. Give me to know, Lord, what your lovingkindness is, / your faithful guidance of which I know but nothing. / Voices and words, O Lord, surround me daily, / but I no longer hear what they say. / They are confused by talking and the strife of tongues.

3. O Lord, give meaning in all that I say and do, / your Holy Spirit in all my helpless thinking, / that I may call on you when I hear nothing, / that I may hear your voice when you call, / and be obedient when you call me to your work.

4. Your lovingkindness is as wide as noonday sky, / your faithful love goes as high as clouds in summer. / Your wings outspread above are our protection, / your life, our Father God, is our life; / and it is only in your light we see the light.

Emily Chisholm 1972

11 Psalm 102 (103)

Malagasy Melody 1818

nto - l'i - zao.
mem - ber his word.
dich noch er - hält.
Di - a___ man -
He will for - give all
Denn er ver - gibt all

ka___ la - za___ A - - - - zy
your in - i - qui - ty and heal all___ your dis - ease.
dei - ne Sün - de, und er hilft dir___ in Ge - fahr.

F'an - to n'i - zao___ re - he - tr'i - zao.
Bless the Lord, my soul, and all that is with - in me.
O du mei - ne See - le, prei - se Gott den Her - ren.

2. Izay zavatra nomeny / mahafaly mahasoa / toy ny andro fararano / to'ny andro mipoaka.

3. Di' ampitomboy ny sainay / hahalala ny teninao. / Hahafantatra marina / Izay sitraky ny fonao.

2. For the Lord is merciful and ever gracious, / slow to anger on his folk, but abounding in love. / He will not always chide nor will he keep his anger evermore. / For the Lord is merciful and ever gracious.

3. As a Father, so the Lord pities his children, / those who keep his holy word, and remember his will. / He has established his kingdom over heav'n and over earth. / As a Father, so the Lord pities his children.

U.S. Leupold 1969

2. Denn der Herr ist gnädig und er ist barmherzig. / Er gedenket seiner Gnad' und erweiset Geduld. / Er hadert nicht auf immer, noch hält er den Zorn auf immerdar. / Denn der Herr ist gnädig und er ist barmherzig.

3. Gott der Herr erbarmt sich derer, die ihn fürchten, / wie ein Vater sich erbarmt über seine Kinder. / Sein Reich gilt denen, die gedenken seines Wirts und danach tun. / Gott der Herr erbarmt sich derer, die ihn fürchten.

U.S. Leupold 1969

12 Psalm 112 (113)

Barry Chevannes 1971

Praise, praise the Lord___, all you sis - ters___ of the
Jauch - zet dem Herrn___, al - le die ihr zu ihm ge -

Lord; may his name be blest for___ ev - er - more.
hört, lo - bet sei - nen Na - men___ ü - ber - all.

Praise, praise the Lord___, all you bro - thers of the
Jauch - zet dem Herrn___, al - le die ihr zu ihm ge -

Lord; praise his name from sun - rise, praise him through the
hört, lo - bet sei - nen Namen vom Mor - gen bis zur

night; Al - le - lu - - - ia___. Who is there that's
Nacht. Hal - le - lu - - - ja___. Wer ist hö - her

high - er than the heavens, high - er than the earth,
als al - le Him - mel, grö - ßer als die Welt?

God a - lone, and there___ is none like him___
Gott al - lein und kei - - ner ist ihm gleich___

23

—! Yet he hung - ers with the poor, he knows our
—! Mit den Ar - men hun - gert er, unsre Sor -

ev' - ry need, Al - le - lu - ia ___. Ev' - ry
gen kennt er, Hal - le - lu - ja ___. Je - der -

poor man will have a house up - on a ___
mann wünscht sich sein ___ Haus am si - che - ren

hill, ev' - ry child will sure - ly know ___ a mo - ther's
Ort. Je - des Kind sucht Ruhe wie an ___ der Mut - ter ___

breast ___, for God swears to lift the low man
Brust ___. Und Gott hilft auch dem Nie - dri - gen

from the dust, Al - le - lu - ia ___.
aus dem Staub. Hal - le - lu - ja ___.

Barry Chevannes 1971
D: Ursula Trautwein 1972

13 Psalm 112 (113)

Heinz Werner Zimmermann 1970

1. Praise the Lord _! Praise, you ser - vants of the Lord,
1. Lou - ez Dieu _! Tous les hom - mes, lou - ez - le ___!
1. Lobt den Herrn _! Got - tes Knech - te, lobt den Herrn!

24

praise the name of the Lord___! Bles-sed___ be the
Chan-tez l'hymne de Dieu___! Bé-ni___ soit le
Lobt den Na-men des Herrn___! Hei-lig___ ist der

name of the Lord__! Bles-sed___ be the
nom du Sei - gneur__, bé - ni___ soit le
Na - me des Herrn__, hei-lig___, hei-lig,

name of the Lord__ from this time forth and for
nom du Sei - gneur__, de - puis ce jour jus-qu'à
na - he und fern___, von An - be - ginn und in

e - ver - more! Praise the Lord, Praise the Lord!
tou-jours, Dieu! Loù - ez Dieu! Chan-tez Dieu!
E - wig - keit! Lobt den Herrn! Lobt den Herrn!

2. Praise the Lord! / Thanks and praises sing to God, / day by day to the Lord! / High above the nations is God, / high above the nations is God, / his glory high over earth and sky. / Praise the Lord! / Praise the Lord!

3. Praise the Lord! / Praise and glory give to God! / Who is like unto him? / Raising up the poor from the dust, / raising up the poor from the dust, / he makes them dwell in his heart and home. / Praise the Lord! / Praise the Lord!

4. Praise the Lord! / Praise, you servants of the Lord! / Praise the love of the Lord! / Giving to the homeless a home, / giving to the homeless a home, / he fills their hearts with new hope and joy. / Praise the Lord! / Praise the Lord!

Marjorie Jillson 1970

2. Louez Dieu! / Rendez grâce, chantez Dieu! / Chaque jour louez-le! / Plus haut que la terre et le ciel, / plus haut que la terre et le ciel, / plus grand que tous les univers, Dieu! / Louez Dieu! / Chantez Dieu!

3. Louez Dieu! / Rendez gloire, chantez-le! / Qui est pareil à Dieu? / Il vient délivrer l'opprimé, / il vient délivrer l'opprimé. / Il dit: prenez place avec moi, Dieu! / Louez Dieu! / Chantez Dieu!

4. Louez Dieu! / O ses œuvres, louez-le! / Chantez l'amour de Dieu, / mendiants qui peuplez sa maison, / mendiants qui peuplez sa maison, / c'est vous qu'il accueille en sa joie, Dieu! / Louez Dieu! / Chantez Dieu!

Claude Rozier 1972

2. Lobt den Herrn! / Tag für Tag lobt Gott, den Herrn, / der den Atem uns gab. / An die rechte Stelle uns stellt, / uns in seiner Gnade erhält, / uns helfen kommt und uns helfen hilft. / Lobt den Herrn! / Lobt den Herrn!

3. Lobt den Herrn! / Auch die Nacht lobt Gott, den Herrn, / und das ferne Gestirn. / Wo auch immer Unheil geschah: / auch im Dunkel bleibt er uns nah, / spricht Mut uns zu, macht uns unverzagt. / Lobt den Herrn! / Lobt den Herrn!

4. Lobt den Herrn! / Gottes Knechte, lobt den Herrn! / Lobt den Namen des Herrn! / Heimatlose bringt er nach Haus, / führt sie aus dem Elend heraus, / erfüllt ihr Leben mit neuem Sinn. / Lobt den Herrn! / Lobt den Herrn!

Heinz Werner Zimmermann 1972

14 Psalm 136 (137)

Latvian Melody
arr. by John Ylvisaker 1964

1. By the Ba - by - lo - nian ri - vers we sat
1. Sur des ri - ves é - tran - gè - res notre ex -
1. Und wir sa - ßen da und klag - ten an den

down in grief and wept; hung our harps up - on a
il nous a con - duits; no - tre cœur songe à la
Flüs - sen Ba - by - lons. Die Gi - tar - ren hat - ten

wil - low, mourn'd for Zi - on while we slept.
Ter - re où notre Arbre at - tend son fruit.
Pau - se. Un - ser Jam - mer schlief nicht ein.

2. There our captors, in derision, / did require of us a song; / so we sat with staring vision / and the days were hard and long.

3. How shall we sing the Lord's song / in a strange and bitter land? / can our voices veil the sorrow? / Lord God hear your lonely band.

4. Let your cross be benediction / for men bound in tyranny; / by the power of resurrection / loose them from captivity.

Ewald Bash 1964

2. On exige sur nos lèvres / un sourire et des chansons, / mais je garde mon poême / pour l'amour de toi, Sion.

3. Que la langue se dessèche / si je chante loin de toi; / en toi seule est notre fête, / ton bonheur fait notre joie.

4. Pour savoir que Dieu nous aime, / nos bourreaux paieront le prix, / ils sauront de Dieu lui-même / qu'il nous tient à sa merci.

Daniel Hameline 1972

2. Die Bewacher sprachen höhnisch: / Leute singt das Zions-Lied! / Und wir starrten in die Ferne, / hart der Tag und hoffnungslos.

3. In Gefangenschaft zu singen: / Herr, dein Lied fällt uns zu schwer. / Unser Kummer lähmt die Stimme, / hol' uns raus aus diesem Land.

4. Herr, befreie die Gefangnen / und zerbrich die Tyrannei. / Gib uns Hoffnung, wenn wir weinen / und zum Singen neuen Mut.

Friedrich Karl Barth, Sabine Leonhard und Otmar Schulz 1972

15 Psalm 148

Elisabeth Poston 1971

1. All things that are praise God by what they are,
1. En tou - te vie le si - len - ce dit Dieu,
1. Al - les, was lebt, lobt Gott, schon weil es lebt.

their be - ing speaks to us of God who is;
tout ce qui est tres - sail - le d'être à lui!
Was er auch schuf, sagt: Gott ist für uns da.

so may we call on them to praise his name,
So - yez la voix du si - lence en tra - vail,
Drum bit - ten wir: Macht Got - tes Tun be - kannt,

to give with us the ho - nour that is his.
cou - vez la vie, c'est elle qui lou - e Dieu!
ehrt ihn mit uns und dankt ihm für sein Ja.

2. Praise God, all angels, made by him to be / forever in the service of his throne; / shine, sun and moon, all stars whose light we see, / and by your shining make his great light known.

3. Praise God, all earthly things which he has made, / come, cold of winter, heat of summer sun; / come, spring and autumn, change and change again, / show in your changing how his will is done.

4. Praise God, all lands and seas, all living things, / all trees and plants that he has made to grow; / all birds and beasts, praise, each in your own way, / his greatness, which all things created show.

5. Praise God, all men and women, young and old: / creation's highest praise is yours to sing / to honour God, to praise with every praise / His Being, everywhere, in everything.

Brian Foley 1971

2. Pas un seul mot, et pourtant c'est son Nom / que tout secrète et presse de chanter; / n'avez-vous pas un monde immense en vous? / Soyez son cri, et vous aurez tout dit.

3. Il suffit d'être, et vous vous entendrez / rendre la grâce d'être et de bénir; / vous serez pris dans l'hymne d'univers, / vous avez tout en vous pour adorer.

4. Car vous avez l'hiver et le printemps, / vous êtes l'arbre en sommeil et en fleurs; / jouez pour Dieu des branches et du vent, / jouez pour Dieu des racines cachées.

5. Arbres humains, jouez de vos oiseaux, / jouez pour Lui des étoiles du ciel / qui sans parole expriment la clarté; / jouez aussi des anges qui voient Dieu.

P. de la Tour du Pin 1972

2. Preist ihn, ihr Boten, die zum Thron er rief. / Für immer dient ihm, folgt ihm, wenn er spricht. / Scheint, Sonne, Mond, erleuchtet unsre Welt, / macht uns vertraut mit Gottes hellem Licht.

3. Alles, was irdisch ist, preist Gott den Herrn. / Komm, Kälte! Komm und wärm uns, Sommerwind! / Frühling und Herbst, kommt, wechselt Jahr um Jahr! / Wechselt und zeigt, was Gott für uns ersinnt.

4. Länder und Meere und was Atem holt, / Bäume und Pflanzen, was das Erdreich deckt, / Vögel und Vieh, preist Gott auf eure Art. / Preist seine Grösse: Er hat euch erweckt.

5. Preist, Männer, Frauen, ob alt oder jung. / Gebt höchstes Lob Gott mit der Stimme Schall. / Dank sei dem Schöpfer, aller Ruhm gilt ihm. / Er lebt für alle und wirkt überall.

Dieter Trautwein 1972

16 Psalm 91 (92)

Rolf Schweizer 1966

Das ist ein köst - lich Ding, dem Her - ren dan - ken,
How good to of - fer thanks to God our Fa - ther,

und lob - sin - gen dei - nem Na - men, das ist ein
to play in ho - nour of th'Al - migh - ty! How good to

köst - lich Ding, dem Her - ren dan - ken, und lob -
of - fer thanks to God our Fa - ther, to play in

sin - gen dei - nem Na - men, du Höch - ster. 1. Des
ho - nour of th'Al - migh - ty Re - deem - er! 1. To
2. Du
2. You

Mor - gens dei - ne Gna - de und des Nachts dei - ne
läßt uns fröh - lich sin - gen von den Wer - ken, die,
sing your love at day - break, and your mer - cy and
make us shout in tri - umph, and with joy ce - le -

Wahr - heit ver - kün - - di - gen auf den zehn
Herr, dei - ne Hand___ ge - macht. Wie tief sind
faith - ful - ness ev' - - ry night; with ten - stringed
brate all your migh - ty works; your thoughts are

Sai - ten und Psal - ter, mit spie - len auf der Har - fe.
dei - ne Ge - dan - ken; du, Höch - ster, blei - best e - wig.
lute and with zi - ther, with mer - ry harp to praise you!
past un - der - stand - ing, your deeds be - yond con - ceiv - ing!

E: Emily Chisholm 1972

30

17 Psalm 107 (108)

Paul Ernst Ruppel 1964

Ich will dir dan - ken, Herr, un - ter den Völ - kern. Ich will dir lob - sin - gen un - ter den Leu - ten. (3) - ten. 1. Denn dei - ne Gna - de reicht, so weit der Him - - mel ist, und dei - ne Wahr - heit, so____ weit die Wol - ken gehn.

I want to thank____ you, God, a - mong the peo - ples, play mu - sic to____ you a - mong all the na - tions. (3) - tions. 1. For your un - fail - ing love high in the hea - - ven spreads, and your great faith - ful - ness____ ran - ges to the clouds.

2. Herr Gott erhebe weit / über den Himmel dich, / und deine Ehre weit über alle Lande.

3. Ehr sei dem Vater Gott, / Ehr sei dem Sohne Gott. / Ehr sei dem Heilgen Geist, Gott in Ewigkeit.

Paul E. Ruppel 1964

2. Rise up on high, O Lord, / fill all the universe, / and let your glory encompass all the earth.

3. To Father and to Son, / to Spirit, Three in One, / glory be given, now and to eternity.

Ivor Jones 1972

18 Psalm 148

Malawi wedding song

1. O praise the King of hea - ven: O praise the Lord of hea - ven, all ye who are his peo - ple! O praise the King of hea - ven, Ye prin - ces! O praise the King of hea - ven, the ho - ly gra - cious King.

1. Lou - ez le Dieu du mon - de, lou - ez le Dieu du mon - de, vous tous a - mis, son peu - ple! Lou - ez le Dieu du mon - de, les prin - ces! Lou - ez le Dieu du mon - de, le Dieu de tout a - mour!

32

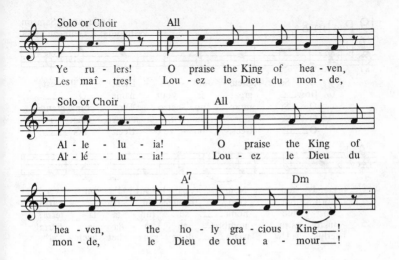

Solo or Choir — All

Ye ru - lers! O praise the King of hea - ven,
Les maî - tres! Lou - ez le Dieu du mon - de,

Al - le - lu - ia! O praise the King of
Al - lé - lu - ia! Lou - ez le Dieu du

hea - ven, the ho - ly gra - cious King___!
mon - de, le Dieu de tout a - mour___!

2. O tell abroad his glory: / O tell abroad his glory, / and publish it to all men. / O tell abroad his glory / Ye fathers! / O tell abroad his glory, / the holy gracious king. / Ye mothers! / O praise the king of heaven, / Alleluia! / O praise the king of heaven, / the holy gracious king.

3. O shout aloud his praises: / O shout aloud his praises / in mountain, hill and valley. / O shout aloud his praises / Young warriors! / O shout aloud his praises, / the holy gracious king. / Ye maidens! / O praise the king of heaven, / Alleluia! / O praise the king of heaven, / the holy gracious king.

E. Maweleva Tembo 1959

2. Chantez partout sa gloire, / chantez partout sa gloire, / partout, à tous les hommes! / Chantez partout sa gloire! / Les pères! / Chantez partout sa gloire, / le Dieu de tout amour! / Les mères! / Louez le Dieu du monde, / Alléluia! / louez le Dieu du monde, / le Dieu de tout amour!

3. Redites ses merveilles, / redites ses merveilles, / par monts, par vaux et plaines! / Redites ses merveilles! / Les jeunes! / Redites ses merveilles, / le Dieu de tout amour! / Les filles! / Louez le Dieu du monde, / Alléluia! / Louez le Dieu du monde, / le Dieu de tout amour!

Claude Rozier 1971

19 Psalm 8

Antienne: J. Samson
Psalmodie: J. Gelineau 1953

O Sei - gneur no - tre Dieu, qu'il est
How___ great is your name O___
O Si - gnore no - stro Dio com'è grande
O___ Heer, on - ze Heer, hoe___

grand ton Nom___, par tout l'u - ni - vers!
Lord our God___, through all the___ earth!
il tuo nome___, su tut - ta la terra!
lustre es tu nombre___ en to - da la tierra!
heerlijk is Uw naam___, door gans het heel - al!

a 1 temps = o

Solo 1. Ta majes - té su - - prême est chan - tée
2. A voir ton ciel, ou - vrage de tes doigts,
3. A peine le fis - tu moindre qu'un dieu,
4. Bre - bis et bœufs tous en - semble,
5. (Rendons gloire au Père tout puis - sant,

par des lèvres d'en - fants, de tout pe - tits;
la lune et les é - toiles que tu fi - xas,
le couron - nant de gloire et de splen - deur;
les bêtes même sau - - vages,
à son Fils, Jésus Christ, le Sei - gneur,

tu op - - poses ton lieu fort à l'agres - seur
qu'est-ce que l'homme que tu en gardes mé - moire,
tu l'éta - blis sur l'œuvre de tes mains,
oiseaux du ciel et pois - - sons de la mer
à l'Es - - prit qui ha - - bite en nos cœurs,

34

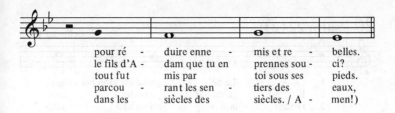

pour ré - duire enne - mis et re - belles.
le fils d'A - dam que tu en prennes sou - ci?
tout fut mis par toi sous ses pieds.
parcou - rant les sen - tiers des eaux,
dans les siècles des siècles. / A - men!)

Your majesty is praised above the heavens;
When I see the heavens, the work of your hands,
Yet you have made him little less than a god;
All of them, sheep and cattle,
Give glory to the Father Al - - mighty,

on the lips of children and of babes
the moon and the stars which you ar - ranged,
with glory and honour you crowned him,
yes, even the savage beasts,
to his Son, Jesus Christ, the Lord,

you have found praise to foil your enemy,
what is man that you should keep him in mind,
gave him power over the works of your hand,
birds of the air, and fish
to the Spirit who dwells in our hearts,

to silence the foe and the rebel.
mortal man that you care for him?
put all things under his feet.
that make their way through the waters. [Ant. 1]
both now and for ever. A - - men.

35

20 Psalm 22 (23)

J. Gelineau 1953

A

1.   Le Sei -   gneur est mon ber -   ger,
2. Il   me   guide par le   juste che -   -   min
3. Devant   moi tu ap -   prêtes une   table
4.   Grâce et bon -   heur m'accom -   pagnent
5.   Gloire au   Père, au   Fils, au Saint Es -   prit

B   **C**

   je   ne   man - que de   rien.
   pour l'a -   mour   de   son   nom.   Pas - se -
   fa -   -   ce à mes ad - ver -   saires;   d'une onc -
   tous les   jours   de   ma   vie;   ma de -
   main - te -   nant et à   ja -   mais;   au Dieu qui

⊕**D**

   Sur des   prés d'herbe   fraîche,   il me   fait   re - po -
   rais - je un ra -   vin de té -   nèbres,   je ne   crains au - cun
   tion tu me par -   fumes la   tête *_____
   meure est la mai - son du Sei -   gneur *_____
   est, qui é -   tait et qui   vient *_____

E

1. ser;   vers les   eaux du re -   pos, il me   mène
2. mal;   près de   moi, ton bâ -   ton, ta hou -   lette

⊕**F**

1. pour y   re -   fai -   re mon   â -   me.
2.   sont là   qui me con -   so -   lent.
3.   et ma   cou -   pe dé -   bor -   de.
4.   en la lon -   gueur___ des___   jours_____.
5.   dans les   siè - cles des   siè -   cles.

36

Antienne

Le Sei - gneur est mon ber - ger, rien ne sau-rait me man-quer.
Il Si - gnore è il mio pas - tor: null - a manc-ar-mi po - trà.
El Se - ñor es mi Pas - tor, na - da me pue-de fal - tar.
O Se - nhor é meu pas - tor, na - da me po-de fal - tar.
Want mijn Her - der is de Heer: nooit zal er mij iets ont - breken.

Texte: de la Bible de Jérusalem
* Le Psaume a cinq strophes. Les strophes 3, 4, 5 omettent les incises D et E:
sauter de ✚ à ✚.

21 Psalm 23 (24)

J. Gelineau 1953

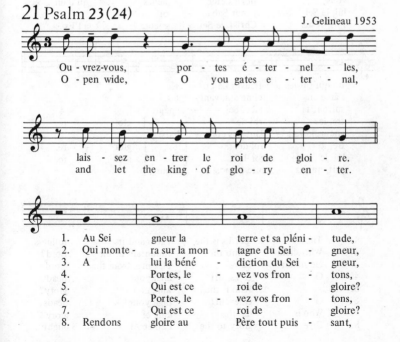

Ou - vrez-vous, por - tes é - ter - nel - les,
O - pen wide, O you gates e - ter - nal,

lais - sez en - trer le roi de gloi - re.
and let the king of glo - ry en - ter.

1. Au Sei	gneur la	terre et sa pléni -	tude,
2. Qui monte -	ra sur la mon -	tagne du Sei -	gneur,
3. A	lui la béné -	diction du Sei -	gneur,
4.	Portes, le -	vez vos fron -	tons,
5.	Qui est ce	roi de	gloire?
6.	Portes, le -	vez vos fron -	tons,
7.	Qui est ce	roi de	gloire?
8. Rendons	gloire au	Père tout puis -	sant,

37

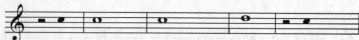

1. le monde et tout son peuple- ment, c'est
2. et qui se tien- dra dans son lieu saint? l'homme
3. la jus - tice du Dieu son Sau - veur; c'est la
4. élévez -
5. C'est le Sei -
6. élévez -
7. C'est
8. à son

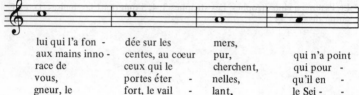

lui qui l'a fon - dée sur les mers,
aux mains inno - centes, au cœur pur, qui n'a point
race de ceux qui le cherchent, qui pour -
vous, portes éter - nelles, qu'il en -
gneur, le fort, le vail - lant, le Sei -
vous, portes éter - nelles, qu'il en -
lui, le Sei - gneur Saba - oth,
Fils, Jésus Christ, le Sei - gneur, à l'Es - -

lui qui sur les fleuves l'a po - sée.
l'âme en - cline aux vani - tés.
suivent ta face, Sei - - gneur.
tre, le roi de [ ] gloi - re.
gneur, le vail - lant des com - bats.
tre, le roi de [ ] gloi - re.
lui, le roi de [ ] gloi - re.
prit, qui ha - bite en nos cœurs.

1. The Lord's is the earth and its fullness,
2. Who shall climb the mountain of the Lord?
3. He shall re - ceive blessings from the Lord
4. O gates, lift high your heads;
5. Who is the king of glory?
6. O gates, lift high your heads;
7. Who is he, the king of glory?
8. Give glory to the Father Al - - mighty,

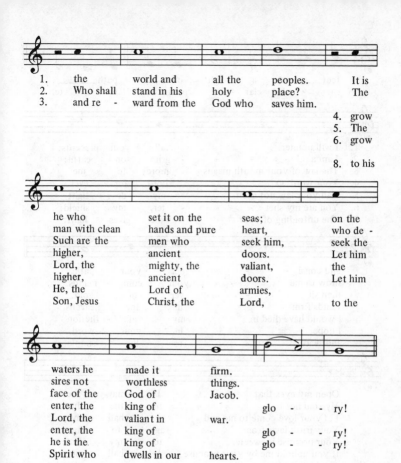

1.	the	world and	all the	peoples.	It is
2.	Who shall	stand in his	holy	place?	The
3.	and re -	ward from the	God who	saves him.	

4. grow
5. The
6. grow

8. to his

he who	set it on the	seas;	on the
man with clean	hands and pure	heart,	who de -
Such are the	men who	seek him,	seek the
higher,	ancient	doors.	Let him
Lord, the	mighty, the	valiant,	the
higher,	ancient	doors.	Let him
He, the	Lord of	armies,	
Son, Jesus	Christ, the	Lord,	to the

waters he	made it	firm.
sires not	worthless	things.
face of the	God of	Jacob.
enter, the	king of	glo - ry!
Lord, the	valiant in	war.
enter, the	king of	glo - ry!
he is the	king of	glo - ry!
Spirit who	dwells in our	hearts.

22 Psalm 118 (119)

Christopher Coelho 1968

1. Your word, O Lord, is a lamp to my
1. Sei - gneur, mon Dieu, quel é - clat ta pa -

39

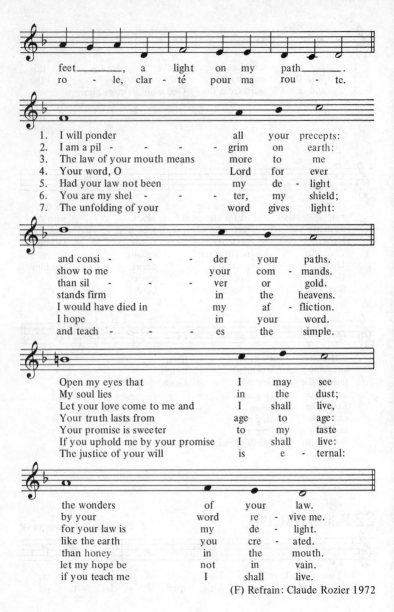

feet_____, a light on my path_____.
ro - le, clar - té pour ma rou - te.

1. I will ponder all your precepts:
2. I am a pil - - - - grim on earth:
3. The law of your mouth means more to me
4. Your word, O Lord for ever
5. Had your law not been my de - light
6. You are my shel - - - ter, my shield;
7. The unfolding of your word gives light:

and consi - - - der your paths.
show to me your com - mands.
than sil - - ver or gold.
stands firm in the heavens.
I would have died in my af - fliction.
I hope in your word.
and teach - - - es the simple.

Open my eyes that I may see
My soul lies in the dust;
Let your love come to me and I shall live,
Your truth lasts from age to age:
Your promise is sweeter to my taste
If you uphold me by your promise I shall live:
The justice of your will is e - ternal:

the wonders of your law.
by your word re - vive me.
for your law is my de - light.
like the earth you cre - ated.
than honey in the mouth.
let my hope be not in vain.
if you teach me I shall live.

(F) Refrain: Claude Rozier 1972

40

23 Psalm 24 (25)

Christopher Coelho 1968

Refrain %

Re-mem-ber me, O Lord, re-mem-ber me, O
Rap-pel - le - toi, Sei-gneur, rap-pel - le - toi, Sei -

Lord, when you come___ in-to your king-dom, when you
gneur, ne m'ou - bli - e pas, mon Dieu, quand tu vien -

Fine

come in-to your kingdom, re-mem-ber me___, re-mem-ber me.
dras ___ dans ton Roy - au-me, rap-pel - le - toi ___, ne m'ou-blie pas!

Solo

1. To you O Lord I lift up my soul, I

trust you, let me not be dis - ap-point - ed.

D. S.

Lord, make me know your ways, Lord teach me your paths. (Refrain)

Solo

2. Make me walk in your truth and teach me, for

you are my God, my Sa - viour; in you I hope all the

D. S.

day long, be - cause of your good-ness O Lord. (Refrain)

Solo

3. Do not re-mem-ber the sins of my youth, re-mem-ber your mer-cy Lord, and the love you have shown from of old; in your love re-mem-ber me. (Refrain) **D. S.**

4. Lord for the sake of your name, for-give my guilt___ for it is great. Turn to me and have mer-cy for I am lone-ly and poor. (Refrain) **D. S.**

5. Re-lieve the ang-uish of my heart and set me free___ from my dis-tress. See my af-flic-tion and my toil and take all my sins a-way. (Refrain) **D. S.**

24 Psalm 102 (103)

Antienne: J. Langlais
Psalmodie: J. Gelineau 1953

Le Sei - gneur est ten - dresse et pi - tié,
For the Lord is com - pas - sion and love,

lent__ à la co - lè - - re et plein d'a - mour.
slow to an - ger and rich_____ in mer - cy.

1. Bé - nis le Sei - gneur, ô mon âme, et du
2. Lui qui par - donne toutes tes of - fenses, qui te gué -
3. Le Sei - gneur qui fait œuvre de ju - stice, qui fait
4. Le Sei - gneur est ten - dresse et pi - tié,

fond de mon être, son saint nom, bé - nis le Sei -
rit de toute ma - la - die, qui ra - chète à la
droit à tous les op - pri - més, révé - la ses des -
lent à la co - lère et plein d'a - mour; elle n'est pas jusqu'à la

gneur, ô mon âme, n'ou - blie au - cun de ses bien -
fos - se ta vie, qui te cou - ronne d'a - mour et de ten -
seins à Mo - ïse, aux en - fants d'Isra - ël, ses hauts -
fin, sa que - relle; elle n'est pas pour tou - jours, sa ran -

faits. *(fin)*
dresse, qui rassa - sie de biens tes a - nnées,
faits. *(fin)*
cune; il n'agit pas envers nous selon nos fautes,

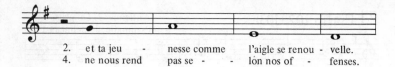

2. et ta jeu - nesse comme l'aigle se renou - velle.
4. ne nous rend pas se - lon nos of - fenses.

1. My soul, give thanks to the Lord, all my
2. It is he who for - gives all your guilt, who
3. The Lord does deeds of justice gives
4. The Lord is com - passion and love, slow to

being, bless his ho - ly name. My soul, give
heals every one of your ills, who re - deems your
judgment for all who are op - pressed. He made known his
anger and rich in ___ mercy. His wrath will

thanks to the Lord and never for - -
life from the grave, who crowns you with
ways to Moses and his deeds to
come to an end, he will not be

get all his blessings.
love and com - passion, who fills your life with good
Israel's sons.
angry for ever. He does not treat us ac - cording to our

2. things, re - newing your youth like an eagle's.
4. sins, nor re - pay us ac - cording to our faults.

44

25 Psalm 116 (117)

Joseph Samson

Semi-chorus / All

Lou - ez le Sei - gneur, tous les peu-ples, Al - lé - lu -
O sing to the Lord, all you peo-ples: Al - le - lu -

ia! fê - tez - le, tous les pa - ys, Al - lé - lu - ia!
ia! Ev' - ry na - tion, ho-nour him, Al - le - lu - ia!

Fort est son a - mour pour nous, Al - lé - lu - ia!
Strong is his love for us, Al - le - lu - ia!

pour tou - jours sa vé - ri - té, Al - lé - lu - ia!
e - ver - !as - ting is his truth, Al - le - lu - ia!

Gloire au Père, au Fils, au Saint-Es - prit, Al -
Praise the Fa - ther, the Son, the Ho - ly Spi - rit, Al -

lé - lu - ia! main - te - nant et à ja - mais, Al -
le - lu - ia! Praise to - day and e - ver more, Al -

lé - lu - ia! Au Dieu qui est, qui é -
le - lu - ia! The God who is, and who

tait et qui vient, Al - lé - lu - ia! dans les
was and is to come, Al - le - lu - ia! through the

45

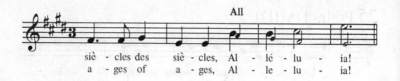

siè - cles des siè - cles, Al - lé - lu - ia!
a - ges of a - ges, Al - le - lu - ia!

26 Psalm 129 (130)

J. Gelineau 1953

Je mets mon es - poir dans le Sei -
En Dios pon - go mi es - pe ran - -
Io metto la spe - ran - za nel Sig -
Con - fi - a mi - nha alma no Se -
I place all my trust in you my
Ik roep uit de diep - ten tot U,

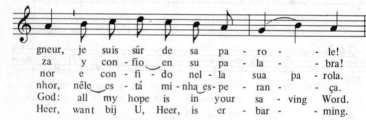

gneur, je suis sûr de sa pa - ro - - le!
za y con - fio en su pa - la - - bra!
nor, e con - fi - do nel - la sua pa - rola.
nhor, nêle es - tá mi - nha es - pe - ran - - ça.
God: all my hope is in your sa - ving Word.
Heer, want bij U, Heer, is er - bar - - ming.

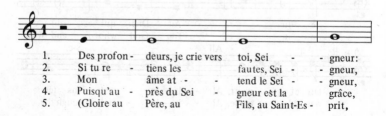

1. Des profon - deurs, je crie vers toi, Sei - - gneur:
2. Si tu re - tiens les fautes, Sei - - gneur,
3. Mon âme at - - tend le Sei - - gneur,
4. Puisqu'au - près du Sei - gneur est la grâce,
5. (Gloire au Père, au Fils, au Saint-Es - prit,

46

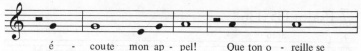

é - coute mon ap - pel! Que ton o - reille se
qui donc sub-sis - te - ra? Mais près de toi se
je suis sûr de sa pa - role; c'est lui qui rachète-
l'abon - dance du ra - chat, c'est lui qui rachète-
mainte - nant et à ja - mais; au Dieu qui est, qui é -

fasse atten - tive au cri de ma pri - è - re.
trouve le par- don: je te crains et j'es - pè - re.
ment le Sei - gneur qu'un veil - leur n'at -tend l'au - ro - re.
ra Isra - ël de tou - tes ses fau - tes.
tait et qui vient dans les siè - cles des siè - cles.)

1. Out of the depths I cry to you, O Lord,
2. If you, O Lord, should mark our guilt,
3. My soul is waiting for the Lord, I
4. Be - cause with the Lord there is mercy and
5. To the Father Al - mighty give glory, give

Lord, hear my voice! O let your
Lord, who would sur - vive? But with you is
count on his word: My soul is
fullness of re - demption, Israel in -
glory to his Son, to the Spirit most

ears be at - tentive to the voice of my plead - ing.
found for - giveness: for this we re - vere you.
longing for the Lord more than watch-man for day - break.
deed he will re- deem from all its in - iqui - ty.
Holy give praise, whose reign is for ev - er.

27 Psalm 135 (136)

J. Gelineau 1953

Solo

1. Ren - dez grâce au Sei - gneur car il est bon,
2. Lui seul a fait des mer - veilles,
3. Il a fait les grands lu - mi - naires,
4. Il frap - pa les premiers - nés des E - gyp - tiens,
5. Il fen - dit la mer Rouge en deux parts,

All   **Solo**

Car é - ter - nel est son a - mour! Rendez
Por - que su a - mor no tie - ne fin! Il
Sim, pa - ra sempre é seu a - mor! Le so -
Great is his love, love with - out end! Et d'E -
     Et fit pas -

All

grâce au Sei - gneur le Dieu des dieux, Car é - ter -
fit les cieux a - vec sa - gesse, Por - que su a -
leil pour gouver - ner sur le jour, Sim, pa - ra
gypte fit sor - tir Is - ra - ël, Great is his
ser Isra - ël en son mi - lieu,

Solo

nel est son a - mour! Rendez grâce au Sei -
mor no tie - ne fin! Il affer - mit la
sempre é seu a - mor! La lune et les é -
love, love with - out end! A main forte et à
     Y culbu - tant Phara -

All

gneur des sei - gneurs, Car é - ter - nel est son a - mour!
terre sur les eaux, Por - que su a - mor no tie - ne fin!
toiles sur la nuit, Sim, pa - ra sempre é seu a - mour!
bras é - ten - du, Great is his love, love with - out end!
on et son ar - mée,

6. Il me - na son peuple au dé - sert,
7. Il don - na leur terre en hé - ri - tage,
8. Il nous sau - va de la main des op - pres - seurs,

Car é - ter - nel est son a - mour! Il frap -
Por - que su a - mor no tie - ne fin! En héri -
Sim, pa - ra sempre é seu a - mor! A toute
Great is his love, love with - out end!

pa des prin - ces puis - sants, Car é - ter -
tage à Isra - ël son ser - vi - teur, Por - que su a -
chair il don - ne le pain, Sim, pa - ra
Great is his

nel est son a - mour! Fit pé - rir des
mor no tie - ne fin! Il se sou - vint de son
sempre é seu a - mor! Rendez grâce au Dieu du
love, love with - out end!

rois re - dou - tables, Car é - ter - nel est son a - mour!
peuple hu - mi - lié, Por - que su a - mor no tie - ne fin!
ciel. A - men! Sim, pa - ra sempre é seu a - mor!
Great is his love, love with - out end!

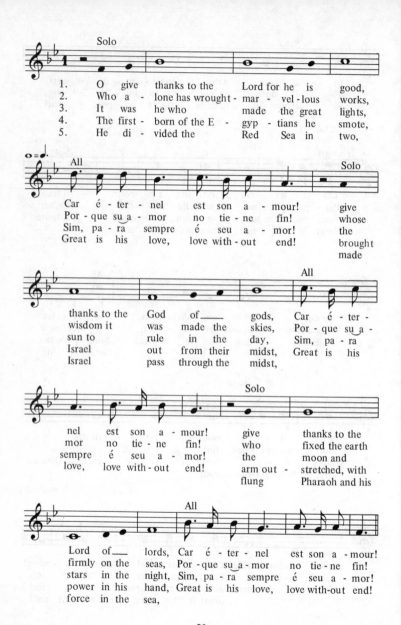

1. O give thanks to the Lord for he is good,
2. Who a - lone has wrought - mar - vel - lous works,
3. It was he who made the great lights,
4. The first - born of the E - gyp - tians he smote,
5. He di - vided the Red Sea in two,

Car é - ter - nel est son a - mour! give
Por - que su a - mor no tie - ne fin! whose
Sim, pa - ra sempre é seu a - mor! the
Great is his love, love with - out end! brought
made

thanks to the God of__ gods, Car é - ter -
wisdom it was made the skies, Por - que su a -
sun to rule in the day, Sim, pa - ra
Israel out from their midst, Great is his
Israel pass through the midst,

nel est son a - mour! give
mor no tie - ne fin! who
sempre é seu a - mor! the
love, love with - out end! arm out -
flung

thanks to the
fixed the earth
moon and
stretched, with
Pharaoh and his

Lord of__ lords, Car é - ter - nel est son a - mour!
firmly on the seas, Por - que su a - mor no tie - ne fin!
stars in the night, Sim, pa - ra sempre é seu a - mor!
power in his hand, Great is his love, love with - out end!
force in the sea,

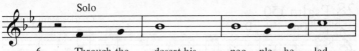

6. Through the   desert his   peo - ple he   led,
7. He   let   Israel in -   he - rit their   land,
8. And   he   snatched us a - way from our   foes,

Car é - ter - nel   est son a   - mour!
Por - que su_a - mor   no tie - ne   fin!   On his
Sim, pa - ra   sempre   é   seu a   - mor!   He gives
Great is   his   love,   love with - out   end!

Nations in their   great - ness he   struck,   Car é - ter -
servants their   land he bes - towed,   Por - que su_a -
food to   all   li - ving   things,   Sim, pa - ra
     Great is   his

nel   est son a   - mour!   kings in their
mor   no tie - ne   fin!   he re - membered
sempre   é   seu a   - mor!   to the   God of
love,   love with - out   end!

splen - dour he   slew,   Car é - ter - nel   est son a - mour!
us in   our dis - stress,   Por - que su_a - mor   no tie - ne fin!
hea - ven give   thanks,   Sim, pa - ra   sempre é   seu a - mor!
     Great is   his   love,   love with-out end!

28 Psalm 150

Charles Mani (Tamil)

Refrain

Um-mai vazh - tu-vom um-mai po - tru-vom um-mai
Praise the Lord _____! Praise the Lord _____! Praise the

e - thu - vom___ i - rai - va um - mai
Lord on___ earth and in the___ heav'ns: let all

e - thu - vom___ i - rai - va - va.
things that breathe praise the___ Lord! Lord!

1. I - rai - va - nin san - ni - dhi - yil.
1. Praise the Fa - ther in his___ ho - ly place:

I - rai - va - nin Il - - - la - thil - thil.
praise him in the fir - ma-ment of his power! power!

I - rai - va - nin se - yal - ga - lu - kai
Praise the Fa - ther for his might - y works:

I - rai - va - nin mat - chi - mai - kai___ - kai.
praise him for his ex - cel - lent great-ness. greatness.

52

2. Ek ka - la tho - ni - yu - da - ne nam
2. Praise him with trum - pet's ro - yal sound: with

i - rai - va - nai po - tru - vom. - vom.
lute and harp and zi - ther praise his name! name!

Math - a - la - thu - da - ne yam nam
Praise him with mer - ry pipes and dan - ces with

i - rai - va - nai e - thu - vom. - vom.
drum and ta - bor beat out his praise. praise.

3. Ya - zho - dum vi - nai - yo - dum
3. Cym - bals high: cym - bals clang - ing:

pul - lan - gu - zha - lo - dum Ya - zho -
praise your cre - a - tor's name! Cym - bals

- dum nam i - rai - va - nai po - tru - vom.
name! Let ev'ry thing that hath breath praise the Lord!

53

The Human Condition
Das Leben des Menschen
La Condition Humaine

29

Henry Purcell 1659 - 1695

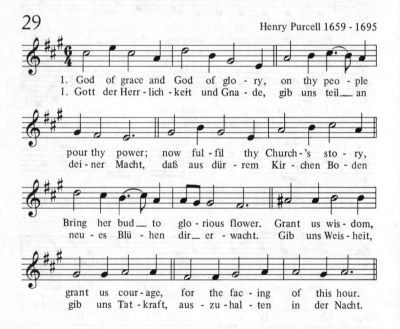

1. God of grace and God of glo - ry, on thy peo - ple
1. Gott der Herr - lich - keit und Gna - de, gib uns teil — an

pour thy power; now ful - fil thy Church - 's sto - ry,
dei - ner Macht, daß aus dür - rem Kir - chen Bo - den

Bring her bud — to glo - rious flower. Grant us wis - dom,
neu - es Blü - hen dir — er - wacht. Gib uns Weis - heit,

grant us cour - age, for the fac - ing of this hour.
gib uns Tat - kraft, aus - zu - hal - ten in der Nacht.

2. Lo, the hosts of evil round us / scorn thy Christ, assail his ways; / from the fears that long have bound us / free our hearts to faith and praise. / Grant us wisdom, grant us courage, / for the facing of this hour.

3. Cure thy children's warring madness, / bend our pride to thy control; / shame our wanton, selfish gladness, / rich in goods and poor in soul, / grant us wisdom, grant us courage, / lest we miss thy kingdom's goal.

4. Set our feet on lofty places, / gird our lives that they may be / armoured with all Christ-like graces / in the fight to set men free. / Grant us wisdom, grant us courage, / that we fail not man nor thee.

Harry Emerson Fosdick 1930

2. Sieh', die bösen Mächte um uns / ächten Christus, suchen Streit. / Reiß' uns aus dem Bann der Ängste, / zum Bekennen mach' bereit. / Gib uns Weisheit, gib uns Tatkraft, / fest zu steh'n in dieser Zeit.

3. Heile unser stolzes Streben; / das vermessen deiner lacht, / das nach Gut und Reichtum fiebert / und die Seele hungrig macht. / Gib uns Weisheit, gib uns Tatkraft, / bis du uns ans Ziel gebracht.

4. Rüste uns mit deinen Gaben, / setze unsern Fuß auf Stein. / Steh' uns bei in unserm Mühen, / deine Menschen zu befrei'n. / Gib uns Weisheit, gib uns Tatkraft, / Täter deines Worts zu sein.

Sabine Leonhard 1973

30

Nick Hodson

1. It's a long, hard jour-ney, and the road keeps
1. Ei - ne lan - ge Rei - se, und der Sand knirscht

turn-ing and we just keep tra-vel-ling on_____; the
lei - se, und wir wan-dern mü - de und stumm_; weil

signs aren't clear e - nough, the ends aren't near e - nough, and
kein Weg mehr da ist, und kein Ziel uns nah ist, und

half our time __ is gone. O, the
der Tag ist schon halb um. Ja, der

Lord sends troub-les, the Lord sends tri-als, the Lord sends a
Herr schickt Fra-gen, der Herr schickt Pla-gen, der Herr läßt uns

hea-vy __ load. But he'll keep on lead-ing us and
schwer be - stehn; doch er will uns Lei-ter sein und

keep on guid-ing us as long as we're trav' ling his
mit uns wei-ter sein, wenn wir sei-ne Stra-ße nur

road __ , as long as we're trav' ling his road.
gehn __ , wenn wir sei-ne Stra-ße nur gehn.

2. With so many days to live, it's hard for life to give a meaning mile after mile. / The roads keep crossing, and the coins we're tossing choose the path in a visionless style. / O, the Lord . . .

3. Though we walk as brothers, still we hurt each other, and our love turns acid and stone, / though we're hand in hand we don't understand that no one's walking alone. / O, the Lord . . .

4. Well, he never told us that the road before us would be smooth or simple or clear. / But he set us singing and our hope keeps springing and we're raised from hating and fear. / O, the Lord . . .

5. Well, the road is ours with its rocks and flowers and mica gleams in the stone. / Well, there's joy awaiting in the celebrating that we're never walking alone. / O, the Lord . . .

2. Soviel Lebenstage hat uns manche Frage nach dem Sinn der Wege berührt, / die sich oft verschränken, bis wir manchmal denken, daß uns nur der Zufall führt. / Ja, der Herr . . .

3. Wir sind Kameraden und tun uns doch Schaden, und die Nächstenliebe wird klein. / Keiner denkt beim Wandern an den Weg des andern, und doch gehn wir nicht allein. / Ja, der Herr . . .

4. Er hat nie verheißen, daß auf unsern Reisen alle Straßen glatt sind und breit; / doch er läßt ein Singen aus der Hoffnung dringen, und wir lassen Angst und Streit. / Ja, der Herr . . .

5. Alle Wege flimmern, wo die Felsen schimmern und die schönen Feldblumen stehn. / Unsre Herzen schlagen, Dank dafür zu sagen, dass wir nie alleine gehn. / Ja, der Herr . . .

Gerhard Valentin 1972

31

Jamaican Folk song, arr. Doreen Potter 1972

1. Take the dark strength of our nights, soft with pee - ny wal - lies' lights. Take the star - signs wheel - ing round, while the steel - drum melts to sound. Take and weave a womb of night that we may live, that we may live.

2. Take the pro - test of our need, what the gar - den? what the weed? Take the orb and break the chain, break the shac - kles of the brain. Take and weave a womb of right that we may live, that we may live.

3. Take the is - lands' hu - man skills, danc - ing seas and wise old hills. Take our Je - sus and his power, match his peo - ple to this hour. Take and weave a womb of light that we may live, that we may live.

John Hoad 1971

32

Hans-Rudolf Siemoneit 1965

1. Die ganze Welt hast du uns überlassen. Doch wir begreifen deine Großmut nicht___. Du gibst uns frei. Wir laufen eigne Wege in diesem unermesslich weiten Raum. Gott schenkt Freiheit. Seine größte Gabe gibt er seinen Kindern___.

1. You gave us all the world for our dominion, but such a gift we could not comprehend___. You set us free. We ran around in circles in this unlimited extent___ of space. God gives freedom; sends his greatest gift to please his adult children___.

1. Le monde entier sera notre domaine, le monde entier que tu nous a donné___. Nous avançons au risque de nous perdre, suivant les voies que nous avons___ libres! C'est le don le plus grand___!

2. Du läßt in deiner Liebe uns gewähren. / Dein Name ist unendliche Geduld. / Und wir sind frei, zu hoffen und zu glauben, / und wir sind frei, zu Trotz und Widerstand. / Gott schenkt Freiheit. Seine größte Gabe gibt er seinen Kindern.

3. Wir wollen leben und uns selbst behaupten. / Doch deine Freiheit setzen wir aufs Spiel. / Nach unserm Willen soll die Welt sich ordnen, / wir bauen selbstgerecht den Turm der Zeit. / Gott schenkt Freiheit. Seine größte Gabe gibt er seinen Kindern.

4. Wir richten Mauern auf, wir setzen Grenzen / und wohnen hinter Gittern unsrer Angst. / Wir sind nur Menschen, die sich fürchten können, / wir brachten selbst uns in Gefangenschaft. / Gott schenkt Freiheit. Seine größte Gabe gibt er seinen Kindern.

5. Wenn du uns richtest, Herr, sind wir verloren. / Auf unsern Schultern lastet schwere Schuld. / Laß deine Gnade, Herr, vor Recht ergehen; / von gestern und von morgen sprich uns los. / Gott schenkt Freiheit. Seine größte Gabe gibt er seinen Kindern.

6. Gib uns die Wege frei, die zu dir führen, / denn uns verlangt nach deinem guten Wort. / Du machst uns frei zu lieben und zu hoffen, / das gibt uns Zuversicht für jeden Tag. / Gott schenkt Freiheit. Seine größte Gabe gibt er seinen Kindern.

Christa Weiss 1964

2. In love, you leave us to our own devices, / whilst your eternal patience suffers long. / And we are free in hoping and believing, / and we are free to trust and to resist. / God gives freedom; sends his greatest gift to please his adult children.

3. We want to live and make our own decisions / but yours the freedom that we put at stake. / We think the world revolves around our wishes; / self-righteously we build the tower of time. / God gives freedom; sends his greatest gift to please his adult children.

4. We build up walls, inventing dismal frontiers, / and live behind the iron bars of fear. / We know this fear because we are but human; / we brought ourselves into captivity. / God gives freedom; sends his greatest gift to please his adult children.

5. If you should judge us, Lord, we are in error. / We're burdened with a sense of heavy guilt. / Let grace have precedence of legal justice; / acquit us daily from the sentence due. / God gives freedom; sends his greatest gift to please his adult children.

6. Make free for us the way that leads towards you, / because we long to hear your gracious Word. / You make us free in loving and in hoping, / which gives us confidence to greet each day. / God gives freedom; sends his greatest gift to please his adult children.

John B. Geyer 1971

2. Tu n'as voulu placer d'autre frontière / que celle d'un amour illimité. / Nous découvrons la joie de ton alliance; / mais nous restons pourtant dans nos refus. / Dieu nous aime, Il nous aime libres! C'est le don le plus grand!

3. Nous façonnons le monde à notre guise, / et nous voulons que règne notre loi. / Nous élevons plus haut nos forteresses, / pour mieux lancer le cri de nos defis. / Dieu nous aime, Il nous aime libres! C'est le don le plus grand!

4. Nous mesurons le champ de nos empires, / et nous dressons la honte de nos murs. / Autant de grilles, autant de barricades, / autant de peurs que nous tenons cachées. / Dieu nous aime, Il nous aime libres! C'est le don le plus grand!

5. Nous oublions le don de ta confiance. / Nous ignorons le prix de ton amour. / Tu es pourtant la source qui redonne / la liberté que nous avons perdue. / Dieu nous aime, Il nous aime libres! C'est le don le plus grand!

6. Que ta lumière éclaire notre route, / quand nous cherchons le seuil de ta maison! / Que ta bonté libère notre force, / quand nous voulons reprendre ton chemin! / Dieu nous aime, Il nous aime libres! C'est le don le plus grand!

Marc Ginot 1972

33 Sven-Eric Johanson 1968

1. 'Vi vil - le dig se', så gre - ker - na bad, och
1. 'It's Je - sus we want', re - quest - ed the Greeks, and
1. 'Wir woll - ten dich seh'n', so ba - ten sie einst, und

Je - sus i dag till dig vi - nu ber. Vi
so, Lord, to - day, it's you whom we seek. We
jetzt kom - men wir und wün - schen das auch. Wir

tror att du finns i - bland oss än - nu. Och
know you are near, be - fore and be - hind; by
glau - ben du bist gar un - ter uns noch. Viel -

kans - ke vårt liv är du, ba - ra du_____.
you, on - ly you, cre - a - tion is signed___.
leicht bist nur du un - ser Le - ben, nur du_____.

2. I strömmen av liv, i gatornas brus / vi skymtar ibland ditt ansiktes
ljus; / en gråt och ett skrik ur ångestens djup, / då rycker vi till; vi hör
det är du.

3. Vi tror du är med bland dem som för fred / och frihet och rätt mot
bergen sej drar, / till djungel och skog, vår broder och vän / tills jorden
igen är mänskornas hem.

4. O sårade kropp som aldrig kan dö, / o kärlek som högt på ett kors
spikas opp, / du eviga ljus och skapade ord, / låt frihetens träd gå i blom
på vår jord.

Anders Frostenson 1971

2. Sometimes in the streets of hurry and haste, / we happen to catch the
light of your face; / a cry and a shout from deepest despair. / We stop
and we know: it's you whom we hear.

3. We know that you live in jungle and wood / with those who are bent
on freedom's pursuit. / You take to the hills, their brother and friend, /
till earth is again a home for mankind.

4. Rejected by men and nailed to a cross, / you die but you rise for ever
with us. / You, light of the age, and formative word, / let freedom spring
up and blossom on earth!

Fred Kaan 1972

2. Im Strome des Tags, im Straßengelärm / wir sehen bisweil deines Antlitzes Strahl; / ein Weinen, ein Schrei aus Tiefen der Angst. / Da horchen wir auf, sind gewiß, das bist du.

3. Wir glauben, du wohnst als Bruder und Freund / bei denen, die jetzt für Freiheit und Recht / auf Berge hinziehn, in Dschungel und Wald, / bis wieder die Welt wird der Menschen Zuhaus.

4. Verwundeter Leib, der niemals erstirbt, / du Liebe, erhöht, am Kreuz aufgespießt, / du ewiges Licht und schaffendes Wort, / der Freiheit gib Raum auf der Erde zu blühn.

Helli Halbe 1972

34

Reginald Barrett-Ayres 1966

1. 'Am I my bro-ther's keep-er?' The
1. „De-vais-je ai-mer mon frère?" Se-
1. „Bin ich des Bru-ders Hü-ter?" Der

mut-tered cry was drowned by A-bel's life-blood
rais-je son gar-dien? Il cou-le sur la
Ein-spruch Kains ver-weht. Denn schwei-gend schreit das

shout-ing in si-lence from the ground. For
ter-re le sang de-puis A-bel. Le
Lei-den des Bru-ders, der ver-geht. Kein

no man is an is-land di-vi-ded from the
glas d'A-bel ré-son-ne tou-jours pour les Ca-
Mensch ist ei-ne In-sel, vom Gan-zen frei, al-

62

main; the bell that toll'd for A - bel toll'd
ins, car nul n'est com - me une île cou -
lein. Als A - bels Stun - de nah - te, da

e - qual - ly for Cain. (3)hands.
peé du con - ti - nent.
schlug sie auch für Kain.

2. The ruler called for water / and thought his hands were clean. / Christ counted less than order / the man than the machine. / The crowd cried 'Crucify him!' / their malice wouldn't budge, / so Pilate called for water / and history's his judge.

3. As long as people hunger, / as long as people thirst, / and ignorance and illness / and warfare do their worst, / as long as there's injustice / in any of God's lands, / I am my brother's keeper, / I dare not wash my hands.

John Ferguson 1966

2. Jugeant qu'on était propre / on s'est lavé les mains; / on a donc sauvé l'ordre / au prix de l'innocent! / En croix, hurlait la foule / et n'en démordait pas. / Voilà devant l'histoire / Pilate scélérat.

3. Tant qu'il y a la guerre, / tant qu'il y a la faim, / le mal et l'ignorance, / l'angoisse des humains, / tant que dure injustice / en tout pays, sans fin, / je dois aimer mon frère / et me salir les mains.

Claude Rozier 1972

2. Der Richter rief nach Wasser, / verleugnete die Tat. / Die Liebe wich der Ordnung, / der Mensch dem Apparat. / Die Menge wollte Blut sehn, / den Menschen sah sie nicht. / Pilatus rief nach Wasser / und spach sich selbst Gericht.

3. Solange Menschen hungern / und dürsten auf der Welt, / solang' die Dummheit Macht hat / und Krieg die Völker quält, / solange Kinder weinen / in irgendeinem Land, / bin ich des Bruders Hüter, / ist Blut an meiner Hand.

Ernst Lange 1972

35

In well-defined rhythm. With majesty.

João Wilson Faustini 1967

1. Nes - ta gran - de ci - da - de vi - ve - mos on - de mui - tos es - tão___ a lu - tar, en - tre a in - sô - nia e o tra - ba - lho cons - tan - te pa - ra o pão co - ti - dia - no ga - nhar.
1. Mo - dern man has the ci - ty for his home___, where his life is walled in by want and dread, pained by nights with - out sleep and days of grind - ing work, in the strug - gle to earn his dai - ly bread.
1. Hoy en gran - des ciu - da - des vi - vi - mos don - de hay mi - les que de - ben lu - char, en - tre in - somnio y tra - ba - jo a go bian - te para el pan co - ti - dia - no lo - grar.
1. Ac - ca - blés de tris - tes - se et de fa - ti - gue, par mi - liers, nous march - ons, foule a - no - nyme, si - len - cieux, nos cœurs d'hommes cri - ent fa - mi - ne: le bon - heur s'est en - fui de nos ci - tés.

2. Nesta grande cidade que cresce / há milhares sem fé, sem amor, / que precisam da graça de Cristo / p'ra viver uma vida melhor.

3. Nesta grande e ruidosa cidade / há milhares sedentos de luz, / multidões sem ouvir a mensagem / do poder salvador de Jesus.

4. Nesta grande cidade onde há crimes, / onde há fome, dinheiro, ilusão . . . / nós, os filhos de Deus fomos postos / como luz, a indicar salvação.

5. Cresce, cresce, cidade gigante, / crescem fábricas e arranha-céus, / mas não podes crescer desprezando / o evangelho do Cristo de Deus!

João Dias de Araujo 1967

2. In our cities, immense and growing out, / there are millions from faith and love estranged, / who need to recapture hope of better things, / and whose hearts, by the grace of Christ, can change.

3. In the dark of our noisy city life, / men and women are groping for the light, / human beings who hunger to see right prevail, / unaware of the liberating Christ.

4. In the great giant cities of our globe, / hollowed out by the ways of greed and crime, / we are set to reflect the likeness of our God / and to act out renewal's great design.

5. Grow then, cities, to house the world of man, / with your skyscrapers blotting out the sun. / Let Christ be the light to shine from human homes / in the high-rising blocks of steel and stone.

Fred Kaan 1972

2. En inmensas ciudades que crecen / hay millares sin fe y sin amor, / que precisan la gracia de Cristo, / la visión de una vida mejor.

3. En modernas, ruidosas ciudades, / hay millones sedientos de luz, / multitudes que nada conocen / del poder redentor de Jésus.

4. En las grandes ciudades modernas, / donde hay crimen, dinero, ilusión, / como hijos de Dios somos puestos / por señal de una nueva creación.

5. Crezcan, crezcan, ciudades gigantes, / rascacielos que cubren el sol: / pero en ellas la luz resplandezca / que por Cristo nos viene de Dios.

F.J. Pagura 1969

2. Enfermés dans nos lourdes solitudes, / par milliers, nous peinons sans espérance, / verrons-nous apparaître dans nos brumes / le Soleil qui nous semble disparu?

3. Aveuglés par des feux qui nous fascinent, / par milliers, nous cherchons la vraie lumière ... / Nous levons vers le ciel nos regards vides, / sans savoir que le Christ est parmi nous.

4. Voici l'heure où surgissent dans nos villes, / par milliers, des brasiers de vie nouvelle: / tous unis, redonnons la joie de vivre / à ceux-là qui ne savent plus aimer.

5. Bâtissons, la justice nous appelle / par milliers, à combattre pour nos frères, / et demain, telle une œuvre qui s'achève, / nous verrons la Cité du Dieu vivant.

Sœur M.-C. Sachot 1972

36

Doreen Potter 1972

1. Can I see the suffer-ing crowd and not ___
2. Can I see the heav-y la-den and not
3. Hand and heart I give you Lord, and not lip

lend ___ a hand ___? Can I hear the hung-ry
help bear the load ___? Can I hear the deep-est
ser-vice to a creed, may I bring new hope and

cry and fail to un- -der-stand ___? Can the
sigh or bro-ken heart -ed groan ___? Can I
joy ___ to a world ___ of need ___; may my

beg-gar's out-stretched hand ___ fail to call forth a res-
hear the cry for help ___ and ___ pass un-heed-ing
days on earth in ser-vice to my fel-low-men be

ponse ___? Then stir my heart, O Lord ___, then stir my heart ___.
by ___? Then stir my heart, O Lord ___, then stir my heart ___.
spent ___; so stir my heart, O Lord ___, so stir my heart ___.

S. Wilfred Hodge 1972

66

Sydney Carter 1962

1. When I need - ed a neigh - bour were you
1. C'é - tait toi, en ce jour où j'é - tais
1. Jag be - höv - de en näs - ta, var du

there, were you there? When I need - ed a
seul, c'é - tait toi l'é - tran - ger qui m'a
där, var du där? Tag be - höv - de en

neigh-bour were you there? And the creed and the
sou - ri ce jour - là? Peu m'im - por - te ta
näs - ta, var du där? Och din tro och din

co - lour and the name won't mat - ter, were you there?
cou - leur ou ton cré-do! Viens! toi qui é - tais là.
ras och ditt namn gör det - sam - ma, var du där?

2. I was hungry and thirsty, were you there, were you there? . . .

3. I was cold, I was naked, were you there, were you there? . . .

4. When I needed a healer were you there, were you there? . . .

5. Wherever you travel I'll be there, I'll be there, . . .

And the creed and the colour and the name won't matter, I'll be there.

Sydney Carter 1962

2. C'était toi, en ce jour où j'avais faim, c'était toi l'étranger qui m'a
nourri, ce jour-là? . . .

3. C'était toi, en ce jour où j'avais froid, c'était toi l'étranger qui m'a vêtu, ce jour-là? . . .

4. C'était toi, en ce jour de maladie, c'était toi l'étranger qui m'a soigné, ce jour-là? . . .

5. Je suis là, maintenant, où que tu sois: je suis là, mon ami: éternel est ce jour-là? . . .

Et c'est moi qui te donnerai mon nom: Viens! Toi qui. étais là.

Nicole Berthet 1972

2. Jag var hungrig och törstig, var du där, var du där? . . .

3. Jag var frusen och naken, var du där, var du där? . . .

4. Jag behövde din hjälp, men var du där, var du där? . . .

5. Du kan resa långt bort, och jag är där, jag är där. . . .

Och din tro och din ras och ditt namn gör detsamma. Jag är där!

Anders Frostenson 1968

38

Doreen Potter 1970

1. Sing we of the mo - dern ci - ty,
1. Singt das Lied der Stadt von heu - te,

scene a - like of joy and stress; sing we of its
Bild des Glan - zes und der Hast. Singt das Lied der

name-less peo - ple in their ur - ban wil - der - ness.
Na - men - lo - sen un - ter - wegs im La - by - rinth.

In - to end - less rows of hou - ses life is
End - los schlie - ßen Häu - ser - ket - ten Le - ben

set a mil - lion - fold, life ex - pressed in
ein mil - lio - nen - fach. Le - ben formt sich

hu - man be - ings dai - ly born and gro - wing old.
aus in Mas - sen, heu - te jung und mor - gen alt.

2. In the city full of people, world of speed and hectic days; / in the ever changing setting of the latest trend and craze, / Christ is present and among us, in the crowd we see him stand. / In the bustle of the city Jesus Christ is ev'ry man.

3. God is not remote in heaven but on earth to share our shame; / changing graph and mass and numbers into persons with a name. / Christ has shown, beyond statistics, human life with glory crowned; / by his timeless presence proving: people matter, people count!

Fred Kaan 1968

2. In der Stadt der Menschen Ballung, in der Welt der schnellen Zeit, / wo die Mode stets sich wandelt immer nach dem letzten Schrei, / ist doch Christus noch zugegen, läßt sich in der Menge seh'n. / Im Getümmel unsrer Städte heißt auch Jesus: Jedermann.

3. Gott bleibt nicht im Himmel sitzen, teilt auf Erden unser Los, / wandelt Pläne, Zeichen, Zahlen in Personen, die du kennst. / Christus zeigt, daß nicht Statistik, sondern Menschlichkeit uns schmückt. / Er beweist zu allen Zeiten: Menschen zählen, sind geliebt.

Dieter Trautwein 1972

39

Doreen Potter 1970

1. Sing we a song___ of high re-
1. Au souffle ar - dent de ce - lui qui
1. Auf, singt das Lied___, das Um-sturz

volt; make great the Lord_, his name ex - alt!
vient, que passe en - core sur le monde an - cien
preist, das Gott al - lein___ den Größ-ten nennt.

Sing we the song___ that Ma - ry sang, of
le chant nou - veau que chan - tait Ma - rie, le
Singt wie Ma - ri - a sang von dem, der

God at war___ with hu - man wrong.
chant des pau - vres que Dieu choi - sit!
fal - scher Macht den Kampf an - sagt.

2. Sing we of him who deeply cares / and still with us our burden bears. / He who with strength the proud disowns, / brings down the mighty from their thrones.

3. By him the poor are lifted up; / he satisfies with bread and cup / the hungry men of many lands; / the rich must go with empty hands.

4. He calls us to revolt and fight / with him for what is just and right, / to sing and live 'Magnificat' / in crowded street and council flat.

Fred Kaan 1968

2. Un long mépris les tenait captifs, / mais Dieu en eux reconnaît son Christ! / Le Fils de l'homme avec eux fait corps, / il boit leur coupe et détruit leur mort!

3. Ouvrez vos cœurs au combat de Dieu, / L'Agneau viendra y jeter son feu; / dépouillez-vous car le temps est court, / suivez la voie qu'a tracée l'amour.

4. Vos biens retiennent vos mains liées, / ne gardez rien, vous serez comblés; / il faut tout perdre et laisser monter / le chant nouveau que chantait Marie.

Sœur Marie-Pierre Faure 1972

2. Auf, singt von ihm, der tief besorgt / die Last der Unterdrückten trägt, / der aus der Bahn die Stolzen wirft / und Größenwahn vom Platz verweist.

3. Er setzt die Armen obenan, / und er versorgt mit Brot und Trank / die hungrig sind und ohne Lohn. / Besitzer läßt er leer ausgehn.

4. Zum Umsturz ruft er und zum Kampf / ihm nach für Menschentum und Recht. / Wo Volk sich drängt und Elend herrscht, / zeigt, was es heißt: Nur Gott ist groß!

Dieter Trautwein 1972

40

Philibert Jambe-de-Fer 1555

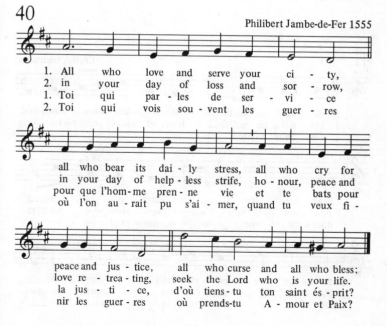

1. All who love and serve your ci - ty,
2. in your day of loss and sor - row,
1. Toi qui par - les de ser - vi - ce
2. Toi qui vois sou - vent les guer - res

all who bear its dai - ly stress, all who cry for
in your day of help - less strife, ho - nour, peace and
pour que l'hom - me pren - ne vie et te bats pour
où l'on au - rait pu s'ai - mer, quand tu veux fi -

peace and jus - tice, all who curse and all who bless;
love re - trea - ting, seek the Lord who is your life.
la jus - ti - ce, d'où tiens - tu ton saint és - prit?
nir les guer - res où prends-tu A - mour et Paix?

3. In your day of wealth and plenty, / wasted work and wasted play, / call to mind the word of Jesus, / 'I must work while it is day.'

4. For all days are days of judgment, / and the Lord is waiting still, / drawing near to men who spurn him, / offering peace from Calvary's hill.

5. Risen Lord! shall yet the city / be the city of despair? / Come today, our Judge, our Glory, / be its name, 'The Lord is there!'

Erik Routley 1966

3. Si tu crois que l'abondance / fait le lit du moindre effort, / souviens-toi de la parole: / Dieu travaille tous les jours.

4. Dieu, Seigneur de tout espace, / l'aujourd'hui de tous les temps, / chaque jour, partout, nous juge / sur mesure de la Croix.

5. Dieu, Seigneur, de notre pâque, / nous passons ... ne passe pas! / Il est tard, la nuit s'avance: / viens en nous, ô Dieu vivant!

Claude Rozier 1973

An alternative tune is in Full Score edition.

41 English traditional

1. O God of earth and al - tar, bow down and hear our cry; our earth - ly ru - lers fal - ter, our peo - ple drift and die; the

1. Toi qui fis naître terre et cieux, penche - toi vers nous mon Dieu; l'uni - vers sans toi n'a plus d'â - me, il mar - che vers sa mort; en trou -

1. Oh Dios de todo el or - be, es - cu - cha nues - tra voz; tor - pie - za el go - ber - nan - te, y mue - re la nac - ión: el

72

walls of gold en - tomb us, the swords of
peaux les hom - mes ac - cla - ment le rè - gne
o - ro cau - sa___ muer - te, el o - dio

scorn di - vide; take not thy thun - der
du plus fort: La faim, la guer - re
di - vi - sión, des - pó - ja - nos de or -

from___ us, but___ take a - way our pride.
sont par - tout, ô Sei - gneur, dé - li - vre - nous!
gu_____ - llo y de - ja o - ir tu voz.

2. From all that terror teaches, from lies of tongue and pen, / from all the easy speeches that comfort cruel men; / from sale and profanation of honour and the sword; / from sleep and from damnation, deliver us, good Lord!

3. Tie in a living tether the prince and priest and thrall, / bind all our lives together: smite us and save us all! / In ire and exultation, aflame with faith and free, / lift up a living nation, a single sword to thee!

G. K. Chesterton 1874–1936

2. De l'ombre où nous parquons nos peurs, nos mensonges, nos tièdeurs / du danger de toute parole qui nous entraîne au mal; / de l'argent tenu pour idole et pour seul idéal, / de ce néant où mène tout, ô Seigneur, délivre-nous!

3. Rassemble-nous dans ton amour, fais pour tous le même jour; / de nos vies ne lie qu'une gerbe, le pauvre avec le roi; / donne-nous le souffle du Verbe, affame-nous de Toi ! / Berger, séduis aussi les loups . . . ô Seigneur, délivre-nous!

G. de Lioncourt 1972

2. De frutos de mentira y de engañosa voz; / de amargas tiranías que siembran el terror; / del dolo y de la espada, del sueño y la traición, / de profanar tu nombre, hoy líbranos, Señor.

73

3. Al príncipe, al esclavo, y a tu ministro, oh Dios, / con fuerte y vivo lazo mantenlos en unión. / Potente se levante, en libertad y en fe, / un pueblo que te alabe, un brazo de tu ley.

S. Jerez 1959

42

Octante-trois Psaumes,
Geneva 1551

1. Turn back, O man, for-swear thy foo-lish ways.
1. Kehr um, o Mensch, vom Weg, den Tor-heit wählt.
1. Sans le Sei-gneur qui s'est le-vé pour nous
1. Vuél-ve-te, hom-bre, de-ja ya tu e-rror;

Old now is earth, and none may count her days,
Hast du die Ta-ge uns'-rer Welt ge-zählt?
quand l'en-ne-mi s'est dres-sé con-tre nous,
vie-ja es la tie-rra que te vió na-cer.

yet thou her child, whose head is crowned with flame,
Du bist ihr Kind und den-noch Gott be-kannt.
ils nous au-raient en-glou-tis tout vi-vants,
Mas tú, que ol-vi-das tu li-mi-ta-ción,

still wilt not hear thine in-ner God pro-claim:
Hat er dich nicht sein Ei-gen-tum ge-nannt?
tant leur co-lère est un feu dé-vo-rant.
la voz de Dios no quie-res a-ten-der.

'Turn back, O man, for-swear thy foo-lish ways.'
Kehr um, o Mensch, vom Weg, der Tor-heit wählt.
Sans le Sei-gneur qui s'est le-vé pour nous.
„Vuél-ve-te, hom-bre, de-ja ya tu e-rror."

2. Earth might be fair, and all men glad and wise. / Age after age their tragic empires rise, / built while they dream, and in that dreaming weep: / would man but wake from out his haunted sleep, / earth might be fair and all men glad and wise.

3. Earth shall be fair, and all her people one; / nor till that hour shall God's whole will be done. / Now, even now, once more from earth to sky, / peals forth in joy man's old undaunted cry. / 'Earth shall be fair, and all her people one.'

Clifford Bax 1916

2. Schön wär die Welt, die Menschheit froh und klug, / doch weiter kämpfen wir mit Macht und Trug, / bauen im Traum und häufen Leid auf Leid: / Würden wir wach aus der Besessenheit – / schön wär die Welt, die Menschheit froh und klug.

3. Schön wird die Welt, wenn wir geeint uns sehn, / dann erst wird Gottes Willen ganz geschehn. / Jetzt schon erschallt von hier zu Gott der Schrei, / daß er die Sehnsucht stillt: Herr, mach uns frei! / Schön wird die Welt, wenn wir geeint uns sehn.

August Sann 1972

2. Alors les eaux nous auraient entraînés, / et les torrents nous auraient submergés, / comme est détruit par le flot écumant / le champ paisible où murit le froment. / Alors les eaux nous auraient entraînés.

3. Béni soit Dieu qui nous a délivrés. / Quand sur leur proie leurs dents étaient serrées, / comme l'oiseau échappe à l'oiseleur, / nous avons vu se rompre le filet. / Notre secours est au nom du Seigneur.

Roger Chapal 1972

2. Podría el mundo venturoso ser, / si despertara vanidad / de sus conquistas y de su poder, / para buscar de Dios la voluntad: / Podría el mundo venturoso ser.

3. Todos los pueblos una gran nación: / Tal el anhelo del Creador y Rey, / tal la esperanza que arde en oración, / en todo tiempo, raza, pueblo o grey: / 'Todos los pueblos, una gran nación.'

F.J. Pagura 1972

God's Promises and Providence
Gottes Verheißung und Vorsehung
Les Promesses de Dieu et sa Providence

43

Geoffrey Laycock 1971

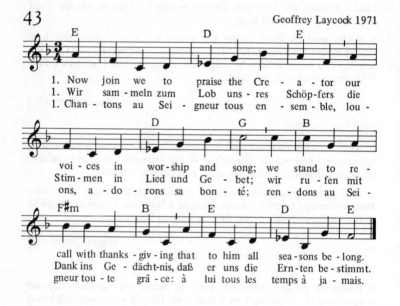

1. Now join we to praise the Cre - a - tor our
voi - ces in wor-ship and song; we stand to re-
call with thanks - giv - ing that to him all sea-sons be - long.

1. Wir sam - meln zum Lob uns - res Schöp-fers die
Stim - men in Lied und Ge - bet; wir ru - fen mit
Dank ins Ge - dächt-nis, daß er uns die Ern-ten be - stimmt.

1. Chan - tons au Sei - gneur tous en - sem - ble, louons, a - do - rons sa bon - té; ren - dons au Seigneur tou - te grâ - ce: à lui tous les temps à ja - mais.

2. We thank you O God for your goodness, / for the joy and abundance of crops; / for food that is stored in our larders, / for all we can buy in the shops.

3. But also of need and starvation / we sing with concern and despair, / of skills that are used for destruction, / of land that is burnt and laid bare.

4. We cry for the plight of the hungry, / while harvests are left on the field, / for orchards neglected and wasting, / for produce from markets withheld.

5. The song grows in depth and in wideness; / the earth and its people are one. / There can be no thanks without giving, / no words without deeds that are done.

6. Then teach us, O Lord of the harvest, / to be humble in all that we claim; / to share what we have with the nations, / to care for the world in your name.

Fred Kaan 1968

2. Wir danken dir, Gott, für das Gute, / für Freude und Fülle der Frucht, / für Vorrat in Schränken und Lagern, / für das, was der Einkauf uns bringt.

3. Doch auch von der Not und vom Hunger, / von Ohnmacht klagt dir unser Lied, / von Gaben, gebraucht zur Vernichtung, / von Land, das verbrannt liegt und brach.

Wir schrei'n für den Hungrigen Notstand: / daß Frucht auf den Feldern verfault, / daß Obstgärten achtlos verkommen, / daß Waren dem Markt man entzieht.

5. Das Lied wächst zur Tiefe und Weite: / Die Erde, die Völker sind eins! / Es gibt keinen Dank ohne Geben, / kein Wort ohne wirksame Tat.

6. Drum hilf uns, du Herr aller Ernte, / daß ehrlich sei unser Protest, / daß wir, was wir haben, euch teilen / und sorgen mit dir für die Welt.

Dieter Trautwein 1971

2. Merci notre Dieu, pour ta grâce, / merci pour nos belles moissons, / merci pour la joie, l'abondance, / merci de combler nos maisons.

3. Merci! . . . mais pourquoi tant de ruines, / de larmes sur tant de régions? / Pourquoi s'ingénier à détruire? / Seigneur, qu'a-t-on fait de tes dons?

4. On laisse pourrir des récoltes, / on jette, on gaspille sans fin, / alors que des cris de famine / réclament l'amour et le pain.

5. Il n'est qu'un pays sur la terre, / qu'un peuple: les hommes, partout, / chacun de chacun solidaire, / chacun au service de tous.

6. Seigneur, apprends-nous la mesure / quand nous demandons la moisson! / Surtout, apprends-nous le partage, / la joie de donner en ton nom!

Claude Rozier 1972

44

Gustaf Bjarnegård 1964 (1970)

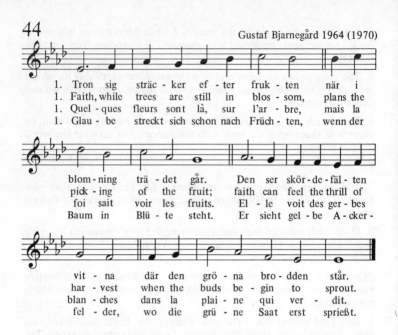

1. Tron sig sträc-ker ef-ter fruk-ten när i
1. Faith, while trees are still in blos-som, plans the
1. Quel-ques fleurs sont là, sur l'ar-bre, mais la
1. Glau-be streckt sich schon nach Früch-ten, wenn der

blom-ning trä-det går. Den ser skör-de-fäl-ten
pick-ing of the fruit; faith can feel the thrill of
foi sait voir les fruits. El-le voit des ger-bes
Baum in Blü-te steht. Er sieht gel-be A-cker-

vit-na där den grö-na bro-dden står.
har-vest when the buds be-gin to sprout.
blan-ches dans la plai-ne qui ver-dit.
fel-der, wo die grü-ne Saat erst sprießt.

2. Innan gryningsljuset ännu / över bergen tänds i brand, / skådar tron den nya dagen / hastar till sin gärning fram.

3. Länge förrän regnet kommit, / hördes Noas hammarslag. / Bortom främlingskap och träldom / Abraham såg Kristi dag.

4. Innan vattnet ännu delats, / lyfte tron sin stav och såg / hur en väg på havets botten / framför Israels fötter låg.

5. Tro är visshet om Guds löfte, / ting som inte syns men finns / svarar honom som oss kallar: / 'Ja, jag kommer. Ja, jag vill'.

Anders Frostenson 1960

2. Long before the dawn is breaking, / faith anticipates the sun. / Faith is eager for the daylight, / for the work that must be done.

3. Long before the rains were coming, / Noah went and built an ark. / Abraham, the lonely migrant, / saw the Light beyond the dark.

4. Faith, uplifted, tamed the water / of the undivided sea / and the people of the Hebrews / found the path that made them free.

5. Faith believes that God is faithful. / - He will be that he will be - / Faith accepts his call, responding: / 'I am willing: Lord, send me.'

Fred Kaan 1972

2. L'aube hésite au bas des pentes / le village dort toujours; / mais la Foi sort de sa tente, / elle voit déjà le jour.

3. Dans le ciel pas un nuage . . . / on entend de sourds échos, / car là-bas Noë se hâte: / c'est le bruit de son marteau.

4. Sur la mer, du haut des rives, / la Foi lève en pain sa main: / elle a vu dans ces abimes / un chemin vers Chanaan.

5. La Foi vive en la Promesse, / éternise le Présent. / A celui qui nous appelle / elle dit, 'Je viens, je viens!'

Père Lorigiola 1972

2. Schon bevor der Dämmrung Schimmer / über Bergeshöhn entbrennt, / schaut den neuen Tag der Glaube, / eilt auf seine Taten zu.

3. Lang bevor die Fluten kamen, / dröhnte Noahs Hammerschlag. / Jenseits Einsamkeit und Knechtschaft / Abraham sah Christi Tag.

4. Noch bevor die See sich teilte, / hob der Glaub' den Stab und sah / einen Weg am Meeresboden / vor den Füssen Israels.

5. Glaube glaubt, was Gott gelobt hat. / Dinge, unsichtbar doch da, / geben dem, der ruft, die Antwort: / 'Ja, ich komme, ja, ich will.'

Helli Halbe 1972

45

Erik Routley 1971
Composed for C. D.

1. God who spoke in the be - gin - ning
1. Dieu, ce monde é - tait en - core ab - sent
1. Gott, der einst - mals sprach: „Es wer - de! ",

for - ming rock and sha - ping spar, set all
que dé - jà, de - puis tou - jours, toi, pa -
form - te Fels und Tal - be - ginn, setz - te

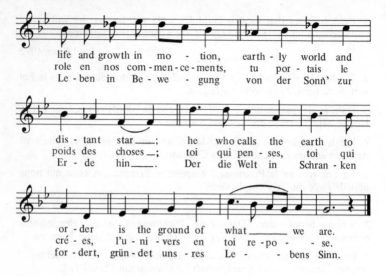

life and growth in mo - tion, earth - ly world and
role en nos com - men - ce - ments, tu por - tais le
Le - ben in Be - we - gung von der Sonn' zur

dis - tant star ___; he who calls the earth to
poids des choses ___; toi qui pen - ses, toi qui
Er - de hin ___. Der die Welt in Schran - ken

or - der is the ground of what ___ we are.
cré - es, l'u - ni - vers en toi re - po - se.
for - dert, grün - det uns - res Le - bens Sinn.

2. God who spoke through men and nations, / through events long past and gone; / showing still today his purpose, / speaks supremely through his Son; / He who calls the earth to order / gives his word and it is done.

3. God whose speech becomes incarnate, / – Christ is servant, Christ is Lord! – / calls us to a life of service, / heart and will to action stirred; / He who uses man's obedience / has the first and final word.

Fred Kaan 1968

2. Dieu, quand l'homme eût habité le temps, / y jetant ses propres cris, / toi, Parole en nos événements, / tu déroules notre histoire, / toi qui juges, toi qui sauves, / Jésus Christ nous dit ta gloire.

3. Dieu, nos fleuves vont charriant leurs eaux, / ignorant des lendemains, / toi, qui tiens déjà le dernier mot, / tu connais le Jour et l'Heure. / Toi qui aimes, qui acceuilles, / tu prépares la Demeure.

Daniel Hameline 1972

2. Gott, der sprach durch Menschen, Völker, / durch vergangne Tradition, / zeigt uns heute noch das Ziel an, / spricht verbindlich durch den Sohn. / Der die Welt in Schranken fordert– / wenn er spricht, geschieht es schon.

3. Gott, das Wort, das selber Mensch wird– / Christus, Knecht und Herr zugleich- / ruft uns alle auch zum Dienen, / will ein Leben tatenreich. / Der der Menschen Dienste annimmt, / hält sein Wort und bleibt sich gleich.

Dieter Trautwein 1972

46

Joseph Gelineau 1966

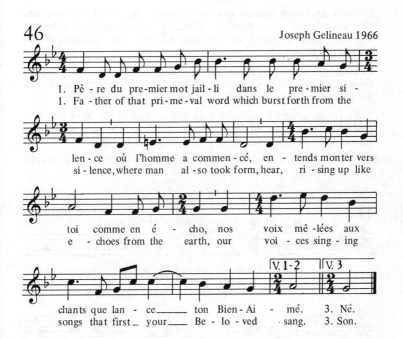

1. Pè - re du pre-mier mot jail - li dans le pre - mier si -
1. Fa - ther of that pri - me - val word which burst forth from the

len - ce où l'homme a commen - cé, en - tends mon ter vers
si - lence, where man al - so took form, hear, ri - sing up like

toi comme en é - cho, nos voix mê -lées aux
e - choes from the earth, our voi - ces sing - ing

V. 1-2 | V. 3

chants que lan - ce____ ton Bien - Ai - mé. 3. Né.
songs that first_ your____ Be - lo - ved . sang. 3. Son.

2. Père du premier jour / levé sur les premières terres / au souffle de l'Esprit, / voici devant tes yeux / comme en retour, / le feu / qui prend au cœur des frères / de Jésus Christ.

3. Père du premier fruit / gonflé de la première sève / au monde ensemencé, / reçois le sang des grains / qui ont mûri, / et viens / remplis les mains qui cherchent / ton Premier-né.

Didier Rimaud

2. Father of that primeval day your Spirit's breath enkindled / across the new-made lands, / see now, as if reflected from that dawn, / the fire which glows within the brothers of Jesus Christ.

3. Father of that primeval fruit by the first sap expanded, / to stock your self-sown world, / receive as sacrifice your ripened grain / and come to fill the hands that seek now your first-born Son.

Caryl Micklem 1972

1. Vater des ersten Wortes, das aus der Stille / des Nichts hervorbrach, als menschliches Leben begann! / Höre, zu Dir steigen unsre Stimmen wie / ein Echo empor! / Sie mischen sich mit den Gesängen deines geliebten Sohnes.

2. Vater des ersten Tages, der über der Erde emporstieg / beim Wehen deines Geistes! / Sieh wie in einem Spiegel das Feuer, / das die Herzen der Brüder Jesu Christi ergreift.

3. Vater der ersten Frucht, die heranreifte / und in die Welt hinein- / gesät wurde: / Nimm an die Kraft des reifen Korns / und komm, die Hände derer zu füllen, / die Dich in deinem Sohne suchen.

Paraphrase: Ursula Trautwein 1972

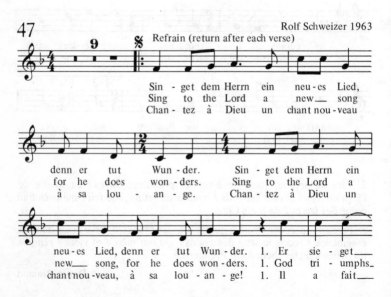

47

Rolf Schweizer 1963

82

2. Du meinst, Gott sei sehr verborgen, / seine Macht sei klein und gering? / Gott sähe nicht das, was dich bedrückt? / Sieh auf dein Leben, er hat es bewahrt!

3. Du kennst oftmals deinen Weg nicht, / und du weißt nicht recht, was du sollst. / Doch da schickt Gott dir Hilfe zu: / den einen Menschen, der dich gut versteht.

4. Du mußt nur zu sehen lernen, / wie er dich so väterlich führt; / auch heute gibt er dir seine Hand, / so greif doch zu und schlage sie nicht aus.

(Strophe 1 wiederholen)

Paulus Stein 1963

2. You think God is the Unknown One, / that his power is of small account? / That God can't see what oppresses you? / Look at your life, how he takes care of it.

3. Often you don't know his purpose, / or what is the right thing to do, / but God sends his help to everyone / who truly seeks to understand him well.

4. You must learn to see him only / as the Father who guides your life; / this very day he holds out his hand: / so seize it now and do not turn away.

(v. 1 may be repeated)

F. Pratt Green 1972

83

2. Ne crois pas que Dieu se cache, / sans pouvoir et sans volonté; / jamais il ne reste indifférent / mais sans relâche il veille sur tes jours.

3. Ton chemin souvent s'égare, / et le bien te reste caché, / mais Dieu vient lui-même à ton secours / comme un ami sur qui tu peux compter.

4. Cet amour qu'il te propose, / c'est celui d'un père pour toi. / Sur toi tous les jours il tient les yeux: / il tend la main, ne la refuse pas!

(on peut chanter à nouveau la Ière strophe)

E. Pidoux 1972

48

Joseph Gelineau 1971
Composed for C. D.

1. Von gu - ten Mäch - ten wun-der-bar ge - bor - gen,
1. By gra-cious pow'rs so won-der-ful-ly shel - ter'd,
1. Sur nous, mer - veil - le! des puis-san-ces veil - lent!

er - war - ten wir ge - trost, was kom-men mag.
and con - fi-dent-ly wai - ting come what may,
Sans peur ____, nous a - van-çons vers l'a - ve - nir!

Gott ist mit uns am A - bend und am Mor - gen
we know that God is with us night and mor - ning
Dieu, près de nous, de l'au - be au soir de - meu - re,

und ganz____ ge - wiß an je - dem neu - en Tag.
and ne - ver fails to greet us each new day.
fi - dè - le cha - que jour qui doit ve - nir!

2. Noch will das Alte unsre Herzen quälen, / noch drückt uns böser Tage schwere Last; / ach Herr, gib unsern aufgescheuchten Seelen das Heil, / das du für uns bereitet hast.

3. Und reichst du uns den schweren Kelch, den bittern, / des Leids, gefüllt bis an den höchsten Rand. / So nehmen wir ihn dankbar ohne Zittern / aus deiner guten und geliebten Hand.

4. Doch willst du uns noch einmal Freude schenken, / an dieser Welt und ihrer Sonne Glanz. / Dann woll'n wir des Vergangenen gedenken, / und dann gehört dir unser Leben ganz.

5. Wenn sich die Stille nun tief um uns breitet, / so lass uns hören jenen vollen Klang / der Welt, die unsichtbar sich um uns weitet, / all deiner Kinder hohen Lobgesang.

Dietrich Bonhoeffer 1944/5

2. Yet is this heart by its old foe tormented, / still evil days bring burdens hard to bear; / O give our frightened souls the sure salvation / for which, O Lord, you taught us to prepare.

3. And when this cup you give is filled to brimming / with bitter suffering, hard to understand, / we take it thankfully and without trembling / out of so good and so beloved a hand.

4. Yet when again, in this same world you give us / the joy we had, the brightness of your Sun, / we shall remember all the days we lived through / and our whole life shall then be yours alone.

5. Now when your silence deeply spreads around us, / O let us hear all your creation says: / That world of sound which soundlessly invades us, / and all your children's highest hymns of praise.

F. Pratt Green 1972

2. Le lourd passé encore nous tourmente. / Nos cœurs en sont restés tout accablés! / Que ton salut s'empare de nos âmes. / Seigneur, puisque tu nous l'as préparé!

3. La coupe amère, si Tu la présentes, / et Tu proposes le calice plein, / nous l'acceptons, sans crainte, rendant grâce, / ô Dieu, de Ta si bonne et tendre main.

4. Si Tu nous donnes Ton soleil encore, / la joie des hommes dans ce monde-ci, / nous en gardons entière la mémoire / afin de Te remettre notre vie!

5. Quand nous oppresse le trop grande silence, / fais-nous entendre au fond du firmament / l'accord puissant du monde de louange / où chantent, invisibles, Tes enfants!

J. F. Frié 1972

49

Lars Åke Lundberg 1968

1. Guds kär - lek är som stran - den och som
1. The love of God is broad like beach and
1. Dieu est a - mour, es - pa - ce, lar - ge
1. Herr, dei - ne Lie - be ist wie Gras und
1. Co - mo la pla - ya, co - mo el pas - to

grä - set, är vind och vidd och
mea - dow, wide as the wind, and
plai - ne, souf - fle du vent plus
U - fer, wie Wind und Wei - te
ver - de, vien - to y re - fu - gio es

ett o - änd - ligt hem. Vi fri - het fick att
an e - ter - nal home. God leaves us free to
loin de l'ho - ri - zon. Nous som - mes libres et
und wie ein Zu - haus. Frei sind wir, da zu
el a - mor de Dios. Li - bres nos hi - zo

bo där, gå och kom - ma __, att __ sä - ga
seek him or re - ject him __, he __ gives us
rien ne nous en - chaî - ne __; l'un __ di - ra
woh - nen und zu ge - hen __, frei __ sind wir,
so - bre el vas - to mun - do __ pa - ra a - cep -

'ja' till Gud och sä ga 'nej'. Guds kär - lek är som
room to an - swer 'yes' or 'no'. The love of God is
oui, un au - tre di - ra non. Dieu est a - mour, es -
ja zu sa - gen o - der nein. Herr, dei - ne Lie - be
tar - le o res - pon - der - le: 'no'. Co - mo la pla - ya,

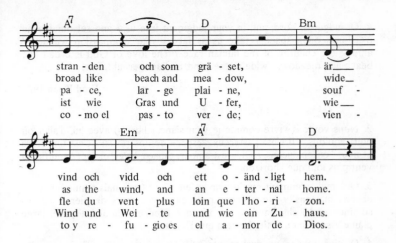

stran - den	och som	grä - set,	är___
broad like	beach and	mea - dow,	wide__
pa - ce,	lar - ge	plai - ne,	souf -
ist wie	Gras und	U - fer,	wie__
co - mo el	pas - to	ver - de;	vien -

vind och	vidd och	ett o - änd - ligt	hem.
as the	wind, and	an e - ter - nal	home.
fle du	vent plus	loin que l'ho - ri -	zon.
Wind und	Wei - te	und wie ein Zu -	haus.
to y re -	fu - gio es	el a - mor de	Dios.

2. Vi vill den frihet där vi är oss själva, / den frihet vi kan göra något av, / som ej är tomhet men än rymd för drömmar, / en jord där träd och blommor kan slå rot. / Guds kärlek är som stranden och som gräset, / är vind och vidd och ett oändligt hem.

3. Och ändå är det murar oss emellan / och genom gallren ser vi på varann. / Vårt fängelse är byggt av rädslans stenar, / vår fångdräkt är vårt eget knutna jag. / Guds kärlek är som stranden och som gräset, / är vind och vidd och ett oändligt hem.

4. O, döm oss, Herre, frisäg oss i domen. / I din förlåtelse vår frihet är. / Den sträcker sig så långt din kärlek vandrar / bland alla mänskor, folk och raser här. / Guds kärlek är som stranden och som gräset, / är vind och vidd och ett oändligt hem.

Anders Frostenson 1968

2. We long for freedom where our truest being / is given hope and courage to unfold. / We seek in freedom space and scope for dreaming, / and look for ground where trees and plants may grow. / The love of God is broad like beach and meadow, / wide as the wind, and an eternal home.

3. But there are walls that keep us all divided; / we fence each other in with hate and war. / Fear is the bricks-and-mortar of our prison, / our pride of self the prison coat we wear. / The love of God is broad like beach and meadow, / wide as the wind, and an eternal home.

4. O, judge us, Lord, and in your judgment free us, / and set our feet in freedom's open space; / take us as far as your compassion wanders / among the children of the human race. / The love of God is broad like beach and meadow, / wide as the wind, and an eternal home.

Fred Kaan 1972

2. Nous voulons vivre comme le vent sème, / libre(s) avec lui, d'aller où nous voulons. / Il n'est pas creux, l'espace de nos rêves; / c'est une terre et nous l'ensemençons. / Dieu est amour, espace, large plaine, / souffle du vent plus loin que l'horizon.

3. Oui, mais comment entr'ouvrir la fenêtre? / Oui, mais comment sortir de nos maisons? / Nous avons peur entre nos murs de pierre. / Nous sommes seuls, chacun dans sa prison. / Dieu est amour, espace, large plaine, / souffle du vent plus loin que l'horizon.

4. O, viens, Seigneur, exauce nos prières: / viens, aujourd'hui, accorder ton pardon; / nous pourrons vivre, enfin, auprès du Père, / libres d'aimer au souffle de son Nom: / Dieu est amour, espace, large plaine, / souffle du vent plus loin que l'horizon.

Nicole Berthet 1972

2. Wir wollen Freiheit, um uns selbst zu finden, / Freiheit, aus der man etwas machen kann. / Freiheit, die auch noch offen ist für Träume, / wo Baum und Blume Wurzeln schlagen kann. / Herr, deine Liebe ist wie Gras und Ufer, / wie Wind und Weite und wie ein Zuhaus.

3. Und dennoch sind da Mauern zwischen Menschen, / und nur durch Gitter sehen wir uns an. / Unser versklavtes Ich ist ein Gefängnis / und ist gebaut aus Steinen unsrer Angst. / Herr, deine Liebe ist wie Gras und Ufer, / wie Wind und Weite und wie ein Zuhaus.

4. Herr, du bist Richter! Du nur kannst befreien, / wenn du uns freisprichst, dann ist Freiheit da. / Freiheit, sie gilt für Menschen, Völker, Rassen, / so weit wie deine Liebe uns ergreift. / Herr, deine Liebe ist wie Gras und Ufer, / wie Wind und Weite und wie ein Zuhaus.

Ernst Hansen 1970

2. La libertad de ser nosotros mismos / para vivir, soñar, crear, servir; / la libertad como una tierra fértil / que se convierte en pródigo jardín. / Como la playa, como el pasto verde, / viento y refugio es el amor de Dios.

3. Y aún así, murallas nos separan, y tras las rejas nos podemos ver / nuestras prisiones son nuestros temores, / fuertes cadenas atan nuestro ser. / Como la playa, como el pasto verde, / viento y refugio es el amor de Dios.

4. Júzganos Padre; y al juzgar perdona, / que en tu perdón hallamos libertad, / y no hay fronteras que tu amor no cruce / por liberar a nuestra humanidad. / Como la playa, como el pasto verde, / viento y refugio es el amor de Dios.

F. J. Pagura 1972

50

James Carley 1969

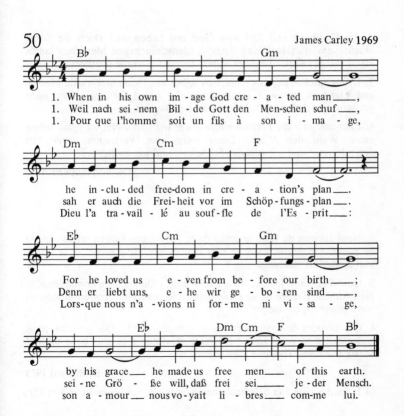

1. When in his own im-age God cre-a-ted man___,
1. Weil nach sei-nem Bil-de Gott den Men-schen schuf___,
1. Pour que l'homme soit un fils à son i-ma-ge,

he in-clu-ded free-dom in cre-a-tion's plan___.
sah er auch die Frei-heit vor im Schöp-fungs-plan___.
Dieu l'a tra-vail-lé au souf-fle de l'Es-prit___:

For he loved us e-ven from be-fore our birth___;
Denn er liebt uns, e-he wir ge-bo-ren sind___,
Lors-que nous n'a-vions ni for-me ni vi-sa-ge,

by his grace___ he made us free men___ of this earth.
sei-ne Grö-ße will, daß frei sei___ je-der Mensch.
son a-mour___ nous vo-yait li-bres___ com-me lui.

2. God to man entrusted life as gift and aim. / Sin became our prison, turning hope to shame. / Man against his brother lifted hand and sword, / and the father's pleading went unseen, unheard.

3. Then in time, our maker chose to intervene, / set his love in person in the human scene. / Jesus broke the circle of repeated sin, / so that man's devotion newly might begin.

4. Choose we now in freedom where we should belong, / let us turn to Jesus, let our choice be strong. / May the great obedience which in Christ we see / perfect all our service: then we shall be free!

Fred Kaan 1966

2. Als Geschenk und Ziel wies Gott uns Leben zu. / Doch die Sorge brachte uns statt Hoffnung Angst. / Menschen gegen Menschen hoben Hand und Schwert. / Und des Vaters Einspruch wurde überhört.

3. Drum mischte, der uns schuf, sich selber ein, / kam und wurde Mensch und Liebe in Person: / Jesus nimmt die Angst fort, die nicht mehr vertraut, / so daß unser Leben wieder neu beginnt.

4. Laßt uns jetzt die Freiheit wählen, wer wir sind. / Nur zu Jesus nehme unsre Wahl den Weg. / Denn wenn sein Vertrauen unser Tun durchdringt, / sind wir Bild des Schöpfers, sind wir endlich frei.

Dieter Trautwein 1973

2. Nous tenions de Dieu la grâce de la vie, / Nous l'avons tenue captive du péché: / Haine et mort se sont liguées pour l'injustice / et la loi de tout amour fut délaissée.

3. Quand ce fut le jour, et l'heure favorable, / Dieu nous a donné Jésus, le Bien-Aimé: / L'arbre de sa croix indique le passage / vers un monde où toute chose est consacrée.

4. Qui prendra la route vers ces grands espaces? / Qui prendra Jésus pour Maître et pour ami? / L'humble serviteur a la plus belle place! / Servir Dieu rend l'homme libre comme lui.

D. Rimaud 1973

(A la fin des vers 1 et 3, la finale féminine tombe sur les mesures 4 et 12)

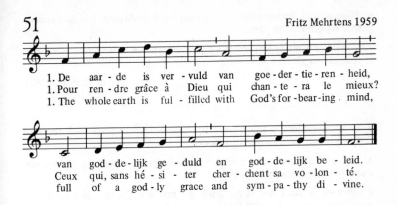

51   Fritz Mehrtens 1959

1. De aar - de is ver - vuld van goe - der - tie - ren - heid,
1. Pour ren - dre grâce à Dieu qui chan - te - ra le mieux?
1. The whole earth is ful - filled with God's for - bear - ing mind,

van god - de - lijk ge - duld en god - de - lijk be - leid.
Ceux qui, sans hé - si - ter cher - chent sa vo - lon - té.
full of a god - ly grace and sym - pa - thy di - vine.

2. Gods goedheid is te groot / voor het geluk alleen, / zij gaat in alle nood / door heel het leven heen.

3. Zij daalt als vruchtbaar zaad / tot in groeve af / omdat zij niet verlaat / wie toeven in het graf.

4. Omdat zij niet vergeet / wie godverlaten zijn: / de wereld hemelsbreed / zal goede aarde zijn.

5. De sterren hemelhoog / zijn door dit zaad bereid / als dienaars tot de oogst / dergoedertierenheid.

6. Het zaad der goedheid Gods, / het hoge woord, de Heer, / valt in de voor des doods, / valt in de aarde neer.

7. Al gij die God bemint / en op zijn goedheid wacht, / de oogst ruist in de wind / als psalmen in de nacht.

W. Barnard 1970

2. Dieu parle en ses travaux: / on peut le prendre au mot, / il a dressé son plan / qu'il mène au long des temps.

3. Le vent souffle où il veut: / il reste aux mains de Dieu. / L'homme a conquis le ciel, / seul Dieu est éternel.

4. Dieu reste le plus fort / quand il vainc notre mort: / pour le Dernier combat, / c'est Dieu qui fait le poids.

5. On peut compter sur lui, / il n'a jamais trahi / ceux qui se sont fiés / à sa fidèlité.

6. Dieu rit des Importants / qui croient en leur Argent: / si tu t'avoues petit, / il prendra ton parti.

7. C'est le Vivant Seigneur / qui nous tient en son cœur / plus vaste que le temps: / sa gloire nous attend.

Daniel Hameline 1972

2. God's goodness is too great / for happiness alone, / it goes through deepest pain, / bred in our very bone.

3. It penetrates as seed / into the furrow's womb / because it does not leave / the sleepers in the tomb.

4. Because it does not rest / until the lost are found, / sky-wide, the world becomes / a fair and fruitful ground.

5. The stars above, sky-high, / are by this seed prepared, / as servants sent to reap / the mercy of the Lord.

6. The seed of godly love, / the Lord, the world of truth, / descends into the earth, / into the soil of death.

7. All you, in love with God, / who for his goodness wait, / the grain waves in the wind / as psalmtunes in the night.

Fred Kaan 1972

52

Bernard Huijbers

1. De Heer heeft mij ge - zien en on - ver - wacht ben
1. The Lord has seen me, and to my sur - prise I'm

ik op - nieuw ge - bo - ren en ge - to - gen.
like a child who's born and raised all - o - ver.

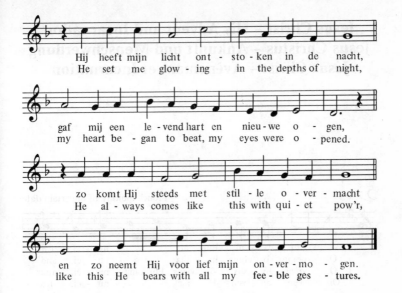

Hij heeft mijn licht ont - sto - ken in de nacht,
He set me glow - ing in the depths of night,

gaf mij een le - vend hart en nieu - we o - gen,
my heart be - gan to beat, my eyes were o - pened.

zo komt Hij steeds met stil - le o - ver - macht
He al - ways comes like this with qui - et pow'r,

en zo neemt Hij voor lief mijn on - ver - mo - gen.
like this He bears with all my fee - ble ges - tures.

2. Hij doet met ons, Hij gaat ons in en uit. / Heeft in zijn handen onze naam geschreven. / De Heer wil ons bewonen als zijn huis, / plant als een boom in ons zijn eigen leven, / wil met ons spelen neemt ons tot zijn bruid / en wat wij zijn, Hij heeft het ons gegeven.

3. Gij geeft het uw beminden in de slaap, / gij zaait uw naam in onze diepste dromen. / Gij hebt ons zelf ontvankelijk gemaakt / zoals de regen neerdaalt in de bomen, / zoals de wind, wie weet waarheen hij gaat, / zo zult Gij uw beminden overkomen.

Huub Oosterhuis

2. He deals with us, goes in and out of us. / Upon his hands our names are clearly written. / The Lord would dwell in us as in his house, / plant in us his life, a tree deep-rooted, / would play with us, and take us for his bride, / all that we are – the Lord alone has given.

3. You come to your belov'd when they're asleep, / implant your name like seed in our deep dreaming. / And you yourself have opened us to you / like rain descending on the thirsty tree-tops, / or like the wind – who knows where it may go? – / so shall you come upon your own beloved.

Redmond McGoldrick

Jesus Christ – His Advent and Incarnation
Jesus Christus – Ankunft und Menschwerdung
Jésus Christ – Avènement et Incarnation

53

French melody of uncertain date

1. Ve - ni, ve - ni Em - ma - - - nu - el, cap -
1. O come, o come Im - ma - - - nu - el, and
1. Ô viens, Jé - sus, ô viens Em - ma - nu - el, nous
1. Oh ven, oh ven E - ma - - - nu - el, res -

ti - vum sol - ve Is - - ra - el, qui
ran - som cap - tive Is - - ra - el that
dé - voi - ler le mon - de fra - ter - nel où
ca - ta ya a Is - - ra - el, que

ge - mit in ex - si - - li - o pri - va -
mourns in lone - ly ex - - ile here un - til
ton a - mour, plus fort que la mort, nous ré -
llo - ra en su de - so - - la - ción Y es - pe -

tus De - i Fi - - li - o. Gau -
the Son of God ap - pear. Re -
gé - nère au sein d'un mê - me corps. Chan -
ra su li - be - - ra - ción. Ven -

94

de,   gau - de!   Em - ma - - nu - el
joice!   Re joice!   Im - ma - - nu - el
tez!   Chan - tez!   Il vient à no - tre ap - pel
drá,   ven - drá   E - ma - - nu - el.

nas - ce - tur pro te Is - - ra - el.
shall come to thee, O Is - - ra - el.
com - bler nos cœurs, Em - ma - - nu - el!
A - lé - gra - te, oh Is - - ra - el.

2. Veni, O Jesse virgula, / ex hostis tuos ungula, / de specu tuos tartari / educ, et antro barathri. / Gaude, gaude, Emmanuel, / nascetur pro te, Israel.

3. Veni, veni O Oriens / solare nos adveniens, / noctis depelle nebulas / dirasque noctis tenebras. / Gaude, gaude, Emmanuel, / nascetur pro te, Israel.

4. Veni Clavis davidica, / regna reclude caelica, / fac iter tutum superum / et claude vias inferum. / Gaude, gaude, Emmanuel, / nascetur pro te, Israel.

18th century Latin tr.

2. O come, thou Rod of Jesse, free / thine own from Satan's tyranny. / From depths of hell thy people save / and give them vict'ry o'er the grave. / Rejoice! rejoice! Immanuel / shall come to thee, O Israel.

3. O come, thou dayspring, come and cheer / our spirits by thine advent here; / disperse the gloomy shades of night / and death's dark shadows put to flight. / Rejoice! rejoice! Immanuel / shall come to thee, O Israel.

4. O come, thou Key of David, come / and open wide our heavenly home; / make safe the way that leads on high, / and close the path to misery. / Rejoice! rejoice! Immanuel / shall come to thee, O Israel.

J. M. Neale 1852

2. O viens, Berger, que Dieu nous a promis, / entends au loin ton peuple qui gémit; / dans la violence il vit son exil, / de ses souffrances, quand renaître-t-il? / Chantez! chantez! il vient à notre appel / combler nos cœurs, Emmanuel!

3. O viens, Jésus, et dans la chair blessée / fleuris pour nous, racine de Jessé: / près de l'eau vive, l'arbre planté / soulève jusqu'à Dieu le monde entier. / Chantez! chantez! il vient à notre appel / combler nos cœurs, Emmanuel!

4. O viens, Jésus, tracer notre chemin, / visite-nous, Etoile du matin; / au fond de nos regards fais monter / l'éclat soudain du jour d'éternité. / Chantez! chantez! il vient à notre appel / combler nos cœurs, Emmanuel!

Frère Pierre-Yves 1972

2. Sabiduría celestial / al mundo hoy ven a morar; / corrígenos y háznos ver / en ti, lo que podemos ser. / Vendrá, vendrá Emanuel. / Alégrate, oh Israel.

3. Anhelo de los pueblos, ven; / en ti podremos paz tener, / de crueles guerras líbranos, / y reine soberano Dios. / Vendrá, vendrá Emanuel. / Alégrate, oh Israel.

4. Ven Tú oh Hijo de David, / tu trono establece aquí: / Destruye el poder del mal. / Visítanos, Rey Celestial! / Vendrá, vendrá Emanuel. / Alégrate, oh Israel.

Federico J. Pagura 1950

1. Oh! vem, oh! vem, E - ma - - nu - el! Rom-
1. Ka - ri - bu, Ee I - ma - nu - e - li, U-
久 し く 待 ち に し 主

pe as ca - dei - as de Is - ra - el, que
wa - kom - bo - e Is - ra - e - li, Wa-
よ と く 末 り て み

ge - me e so - fre em - dis - - per - são, sem fé,
na - o - hu - zu - ni - ka ha - pa kwa ku-
民 の な わ め を と き

sem luz, sem Re - - - den - çâo! E-
wa wa - kung - o - ja We - we. Fu-
放 ち た ま え 主

96

xul - ta,　e - xul - - ta,　ó　Is - ra - el:
rá - - ha kuu!　I - ma - nu - e - li
よ　　　　主　よ　　み　民　　　　　　を

Já　vem　a　ti　o E - ma - - nu - el!
A - ta - ku - ji - a　Is - ra - e - li.
救　　わ　せ　た　ま　　　　　　　え　や

2. Embaixador do Eterno Deus, / do opróbrio livra e exalta os teus; / Da escura cova e do terror / resgata os teus, ó Rendentor!

3. Vem, Emanuel, Senhor Jesus, / banhar nossa alma em santa luz! / Dissipa o medo e a escuridão: / Acalma o nosso coração!

4. Luz de Davi, desfaze o véu / que vela a rota para o Céu: / Aponta aos átrios eternais / e esconde as portas infernais!

Isaac N. Salum 1961

From: Venite Exultemus

2. Karibu, Mwana wake Yese. / Shetani asitukamate, / motoni tusiangamie, / Kaburilisitupoteze.

3. Karibu, Nuru ya subuhi, / kwa kuja kwako tufariji, / tuondolewe giza lote. / Na kusafishwa dhambi zetu.

4. Karibu, Wewe Ufunguo, / na mbingu utufungulie, / onyesha njia ya amani, / uzibe njia ya ouvu.

2. あしたの星なる　　　主よ、とく来りて、
　　お暗きこの世に　　　み光をたまえ。
　　主よ主よ、み民を　　救わせたまえや。

١. هَيَّا لَنَا عَمَانُوئِيل ۰ وَرَدَّ أَسْرَى بَيْتَ إِبِل ۰ مَنْ ذَابَ ذُلًّا فِي مَنْفَاهُ ۰
حَنَّ أَتَاهُ ابْنُ الْإِلَهُ ۰ فَلْتَبْتَهِجْ يَا بَيْتَ إِبِل ۰ هَا قَدْ أَتَى عَمَانُوئِيل

٢. هَيَّا لَنَا يَوْمَ الرَّبِيعْ ۰ وَفَرِّحِ الرُّوحَ الْوَدِيعْ ۰ وَلْتَنْقَشِعْ سُحُبُ الظَّلَامْ ۰
وَلْيَخْتَفِ الْمَوْتُ الزُّوَامْ ۰ فَلْتَبْتَهِجْ يَا بَيْتَ إِيلْ ۰ هَا قَدْ أَتَى عَمَّانُوئِيلْ

٣. هَيَّا يَا ابْنَ دَاوُدْ ۰ وَافْتَحْ لَنَا بَيْتَ الْوُعُودْ ۰ مُمَهِّدًا لَنَا الطَّرِيقْ ۰
وَنَجِّنَا مِنْ كُلِّ ضِيقْ ۰ فَلْتَبْتَهِجْ يَا بَيْتَ إِيلْ ۰ هَا قَدْ أَتَى عَمَّانُوئِيلْ

Dr. Walter Skellie,

54

Dominique Ombrie 1963

Refrain

Viens pour notre at - ten - te, ne tar - de plus. Pour
Come to us who wait here, and tar - ry not! You
Kom-me, weil wir war - ten und säu - me nicht! Komm,

no - tre dé - li - vran - ce, viens, Sei - gneur Jé - sus!
on - ly can de - li - ver us, Lord Je - sus.
ret - te und be - frei - e uns, Herr Je - sus Christ.

Versets

1. Dans no - tre mon - de de dé - tres -
1. Out of our world___, out of its dis -
1. In die - se uns - re Welt voll höch - ster

se, nous t'ap - pe - lons, Sei - gneur Jé - sus.
tress, we call on you, Lord Je - sus.
Not wir ru - fen dich, Herr Je - sus Christ.

2. L'amour, plus fort que nos misères, / nous réunit, Seigneur Jésus.

3. Dans notre angoisse, nos ténèbres, / nous te cherchons, Seigneur Jésus.

4. Dans nos discordes qui te blessent, / nous t'implorons, Seigneur Jésus.

5. Tu es venu chez nous en pauvre / pour nous sauver, Seigneur Jésus.

6. Ta Croix sera notre espérance / dans notre nuit, Seigneur Jésus.

7. Un jour enfin naîtra l'aurore, / nous te verrons, Seigneur Jésus.

Dominique Ombrie 1963

2. A love much stronger than our sadness / has made us one, Lord Jesus (Christ).

3. In all our anguish, all our darkness, / we search for you, Lord Jesus (Christ).

4. And in our discords, though they wound you, / we plead with you, Lord Jesus (Christ).

5. You came among us once, a poor man, / to save us all, Lord Jesus (Christ).

6. And in our night, your Cross of sorrow / shall be our hope, Lord Jesus (Christ).

7. But when, at last, your day is dawning / we shall see you, Lord Jesus (Christ).

F. Pratt Green 1972

2. Die Liebe, die all unser Leid besiegt, / vereinigt uns, Herr Jesus Christ.

3. In unsrer Dunkelheit und großen Angst / wir suchen dich, Herr Jesus Christ.

4. In unsrem Zank, der dich so tief verletzt, / wir fleh'n dich an, Herr Jesus Christ.

5. Du kamst in Armut zu uns in die Welt, / um uns zu retten, Jesus Christ.

6. Weil Du zu Deinen Brüdern uns gemacht, / wir loben Dich, Herr Jesus Christ.

7. Das Kreuz ist unsre Hoffnung allezeit / in unsrer Nacht, Herr Jesus Christ.

8. Wenn eines Tages kommt das Morgenlicht, / dann schau'n wir dich, Herr Jesus Christ.

Marlies Flesch-Thebesius 1972

55

J. Lindemann 19th century

1. Lord Christ when first thou cam'st to men
1. Herr Christ, als du zu Men - schen kamst,
1. Pour nous sau - ver, Sei - gneur Jé - sus,

up - on a cross___ they bound thee,
wardst du ans Kreuz___ ge - schla - gen
tu pris la rou - te des hom - mes.

and mock'd thy sa - ving king - ship then by thorns with
hast, als du uns - re Sün - de nahmst, den Dor - nen -
Au - cun pour - tant ne t'a re - çu a - veu - gles

which_ they crowned thee: and still our wrongs may
kranz_ ge - tra - gen; und uns - re Bos - heit
nés que nous som - mes. Nous t'a - vons mis sur

weave thee now new thorns to pierce that stea -
hat dir jetzt von neu - em das Ge - sicht
u - ne Croix; nous a - vons ri de no -

dy brow, and robe of sor - row round thee.
zer - fetzt, läßt dich von neu - em kla - gen.
tre Roi, mort sur la rou - te des hom - mes.

2. O aweful love which found no room / in life where sin denied thee, / and, doom'd to death, must bring to doom / the power which crucified thee, / till not a stone was left on stone, / and all a nation's pride o'erthrown / went down to dust beside thee!

3. New advent of the love of Christ, / shall we again refuse thee, / till in the night of hate and war / we perish as we lose thee? / From old unfaith our souls release / to seek the kingdom of thy peace / by which alone we choose thee.

4. O wounded hands of Jesus, build / in us thy new creation; / our pride is dust, our vaunt is stilled, / we wait thy revelation; / O love that triumphs over loss, / we bring our hearts before thy cross, / to finish thy salvation.

Walter Russell Bowie 1928

2. Ach, Herr, der keine Stätte fand, / sein Haupt dahin zu legen, / zum Tod verdammt, den Tod noch band / und wandelte in Segen: / du hältst in Händen alle Macht – / was ist der Erde Glanz und Pracht / und Völkerstolz dagegen?

3. Die Liebe Christi kommt noch heut – / wer wollte sie verschmähen / und in der Nacht von Hass und Streit / verloren untergehen? / Unglauben tilg aus unserm Sinn, / führ uns zu deinem Frieden hin, / in dem wir fest bestehen.

4. Ihr wunden Hände Jesu, schafft / das Reich, uns zu bewahren. / Der Stolz wird Staub, und deine Kraft / will sich nun offenbaren. / Den Tod besiegt die Liebe hier, / wir bringen unsre Herzen dir, / um Rettung zu erfahren.

Gerhard Valentin 1972

2. Jour après jour, nos lâchetés / tissent ta robe de peine; / et ton amour n'a pas trouvé / place où se faire fontaine. / Toujours les mêmes, nos abus, / notre mollesse, nos refus / tissent ta robe de peine.

3. Et cependant, Tu nous poursuis / de l'aiguillon de ta Grâce. / Tu nous appelles dans la nuit, / et jamais Tu ne Te lasses. / Peut-être avant la fin des temps / deviendrons-nous des clairvoyants / sous l'aiguillon de ta Grâce.

4. Tu reviendras, Seigneur Jésus, / Soleil de l'aube éternelle. / Mais serons-nous de tes élus, / porteurs de bonne nouvelle? / Ne pèse pas le mal commis / du cœur des hommes prends souci, / soleil de l'aube éternelle.

G. de Lioncourt 1972

56

Johannes Petzold 1939

1. Die Nacht ist vor-ge-drun-gen, der
1. Dé - jà la nuit s'a - chè - ve, le
1. The night is near-ly o - ver, the

Tag ist nicht_ mehr fern. So sei nun Lob ge-
jour n'est plus_ très loin. Voi - ci un chant s'é-
day-light near - ly here. With prai-ses let us

sun - gen dem hel-len Mor-gen - stern. Auch wer zur
lè - ve pour l'as-tre du_ ma - tin. Mal-gré la
wel - come God's bright and mor - ning - star. Who suf-fered

Nacht ge - wei - net, der stim-me froh mit_ ein. Der
nuit a - mè - re ac-cueil-le dans ton_ coeur l'E -
long in dark - ness join in the joy-ful_ strain: the

Mor - gen - stern be - schei - net auch dei - ne Angst und Pein.
toi - le qui é - clai - re ta peur et ta dou - leur.
mor - ning - star is shi - ning on all your fear and pain.

2. Dem alle Engel dienen, wird nun ein Kind und Knecht. / Gott selber ist erschienen zur Sühne für sein Recht. / Wer schuldig ist auf Erden, verhüll nicht mehr sein Haupt. / Er soll errettet werden, wenn er dem Kinde glaubt.

3. Die Nacht ist schon im Schwinden, macht euch zum Stalle auf! / Ihr sollt das Heil dort finden, das aller Zeiten Lauf / von Anfang an verkündet, seit eure Schuld geschah. / Nun hat sich euch verbündet, den Gott selbst ausersah!

4. Noch manche Nacht wird fallen auf Menschenleid und -schuld. / Doch wandert nun mit allen der Stern der Gotteshuld. / Beglänzt von seinem Lichte, hält euch kein Dunkel mehr, / von Gottes Angesichte kam euch die Rettung her.

5. Gott will im Dunkel wohnen und hat es doch erhellt! / Als wollte er belohnen, so richtet er die Welt! / Der sich den Erdkreis baute, der lässt den Sünder nicht. / Wer hier dem Sohn vertraute, kommt dort aus dem Gericht!

Jochen Klepper 1938

2. Celui que tous les anges adorent en tremblant / pour vous se fait esclave et tout petit enfant. / A l'heure où Dieu vous aime et prend déjà sa croix / allez vers lui sans crainte, donnez lui votre foi.

3. L'aurore va paraître: sortez de votre nuit! / Marchez jusqu'à la crèche où Jésus vient sans bruit. / C'est lui le Dieu qui sauve selon qu'il est écrit: / le Fils qui se fait pauvre partage notre vie.

4. Sur toutes vos misères viendront bien d'autres nuits, / mais Dieu dans vos ténèbres vous guide et vous conduit. / Que peut sur vous l'Abîme et son obscurité? / Déjà vous êtes libre car Dieu vous est donné.

5. Splendeur inaccessible tu restes en notre nuit! / O Maître de justice, tu ne sais que bénir! / Tu ouvres à tous les hommes qui t'ont donné leur foi / la porte du Royaume où tout n'est plus que joie!

Armand Ory 1972

2. He who was served by angels, comes as a child to serve; / for God atones in mercy the justice we deserve. / Whoever here is guilty, who knows himself defiled: / Look up! and find salvation, believing in this child.

3. How quickly night is passing – haste to the stable now! There you will find salvation; the reason why and how / God from your guilt's beginning has heard you when you cried. / Now he whom God has chosen is standing at your side.

4. As long as nights are falling on human guilt and pain, / the star of God's good pleasure will shine on travelling men. / In souls lit by its radiance the darkness cannot brood: / look up! for your salvation shines from the face of God!

5. God wants to live in darkness, so he can make it bright: / as though he would reward it he guides the world aright. / He who created all things does not forsake the lost: / Who trusts the Son as Saviour wins discharge at the last.

F. Pratt Green 1972

57

Homero Perera 1960

1. Ben - di - to el Rey que vie - ne en el nom - bre
1. Blest be the King whose co - ming is in the
1. Qu'il soit bé - ni, qu'il vien - ne le Roi no -
1. Ge - lo - bet sei der Kö - nig, den Gott uns

del Se - ñor! Al - zad, al - zad las puer - tas del
name of God! For him let doors be o - pened, no
tre Sei - gneur! Ou - vrez, ou - vrez vos por - tes, ne
hat ge - sandt! Welt, öff - ne ihm die Tü - ren, das

du - ro co - ra - zón! No vie - ne re - ves -
hearts a - gainst him barred! Not robed in roy - al
fer - mez pas vos cœurs! Il vient à nous sans
Herz und den Ver - stand. Er kommt zu uns nicht

ti - do de su ro - pa - je real: su tú - ni -
splen - dour, in power and pomp, comes he: but clad as
fas - te gran - deur ni ma - jes - té, vê - tu com -
präch - tig, im kö - nig - li - chen Kleid, sein Zep - ter

ca es de sier - - vo, tal es su hu - mil - dad.
are the poor - - est, such his hu - mi - li - ty!
me le pau - - vre dans son hu - mi - li - té!
ist die Lie - - be, sein Kron', Barm - her - zig - keit!

2. Bendito el rey que viene en el nombre del Señor! / Atentos los oídos, atentos a su voz! / Pues ay del que orgulloso no quiere percibir / al Cristo prometido que viene a redimir!

3. Bendito el rey que viene en el nombre del Señor! / Que muestre a los humildes la faz del santo Dios; / a quien le han sido dadas la gloria y el poder, / que al fin de las edades los pueblos han de ver.

4. Bendito el rey que viene en el nombre del Señor! / Que ofrece a los cansados descanso y salvación. / Es manso y es humilde y en su servicio está / el yugo que nos lleva a eterna libertad.

Federico J. Pagura 1960

2. Blest be the King whose coming is in the name of God! / By those who truly listen his voice is truly heard. / Pity the proud and haughty, who have not learned to heed / the Christ who is the Promise and has our ransom paid.

3. Blest be the King whose coming is in the name of God! / He only to the humble reveals the face of God. / All power is his, all glory! All things are in his hand, / all ages and all peoples, till time itself shall end!

4. Blest be the King whose coming is in the name of God! / He offers to the burdened the rest and grace they need. / Gentle is he and humble! And light his yoke shall be, / for he would have us bear it so he can make us free!

F. Pratt Green 1973

2. Qu'il soit béni, qu'il vienne, le Roi, notre Seigneur! / Entendez-le qui parle, sortez tous de l'erreur! / Malheur à l'homme riche s'il ne veut écouter / le Christ de la Promesse qui vient nous racheter.

3. Qu'il soit béni, qu'il vienne, le Roi, notre Seigneur! / Il montre à tous les humbles la face du Sauveur! / A lui sont en partage la gloire et le pouvoir, / ce qu'à la fin des âges les peuples pourront voir!

4. Qu'il soit béni, qu'il vienne, le Roi, notre Seigneur! / Il donne aux misérables la paix du Bon Pasteur. / Il est doux. Il est humble. Son joug sera léger! / Et c'est Lui qui nous mène jusqu'à la liberté!

J. F. Frié 1972

2. Gelobet sei der König, den Gott uns hat gesandt! / Vernehmet seine Stimme, das Herz ihm zugewandt! / Kein Mensch soll sich voll Hochmut vom Retter halten fern, / der diese Welt befreit hat. Empfanget diesen Herrn!

3. Gelobet sei der König, den Gott uns hat gesandt! / In seiner Lieb und Demut, wird Gott von uns erkannt! / Ihm ist das Reich gegeben, die Macht, die Herrlichkeit; / so wird die Welt ihn sehen, am Ende aller Zeit!

4. Gelobet sei der König, den Gott uns gesandt! / Er gibt den Müden Stärke, hält uns in seiner Hand. / In Demut ist er mächtig, im Dienen liegt sein Heil, / sein Joch ist das der Liebe, an ihr gibt er uns teil!

Arthur Blatezky 1972

58

1. Cor - de na - tus ex pa - ren - tis an - te mun - di ex - or - di - um, Alpha et Ome - ga cog - no min - a - tus, ip - se fons et clau - su - ra. O - mni - um quae sunt, fu - er - unt, quae - que post fu - tu - ra sunt, Sae - cu - lo - rum sae - cu - lis ___ .

1. Of the Fa - ther's heart be - got - ten ere the world from cha - os rose, he is Al - pha: from that foun - tain all that is and hath been flows; He is O - me - ga, of all ___ things yet to come the mys - tic close, e - ver - more and e - ver - more ___ .

1. Né du Père a - vant les siè - cles Fils de Dieu tu es l'E - ter - nel; tu fais naî - tre la lu - miè - re, ton Es - prit rem - plit l'u - ni - vers! Clef de tout, tu es l'Al - pha, tu es l'O - me - ga! Tou - te vie s'é - veille en toi: Gloire à Dieu et Paix sur ter - re!

2. O beatus ortus ille, / virgo cum puerpera / Edidit nostram salutem / foeta sancto Spiritu, / Et puer redemptor orbis / os sacratum protulit / Seculorum saeculis.

3. Psallat altitudo caeli, / psallant omnes angeli, / Quidquid est virtutis usquam / psallat in laudem Dei, / Nulla linguarum silescat, / voce et omnis consonet / Saeculorum saeculis.

4. Ecce, quem vates vetustis / concinebant saeculis, / Quem prophetarum fideles / paginae spoponderant, / Emicat promissus olim, / cuncta collaudent cum / Saeculorum saeculis.

Prudentius, b. 348

2. By his word was all created; / he commanded and 'twas done; / earth and sky and boundless ocean, / universe of Three in One, / all that sees the moon's soft radiance, / all that breathes beneath the sun: / Evermore and evermore.

3. This is he whom seer and sybil / sang in ages long gone by; / this is he of old revealed / in the page of prophecy; / lo! he comes, the promised Saviour; / let the world his praises cry, / evermore and evermore.

4. Sing, ye heights of heaven, his praises; / angels and archangels, sing! / Wheresoe'er ye be, ye faithful, / let your joyous anthems ring, / every tongue his name confessing, / countless voices answering, / evermore and evermore.

R. F. Davis 1906

2. Quand va l'homme vers sa perte, / Fils de Dieu, tu prends notre chair! / Ta naissance est la merveille / qui redonne vie aux mortels / et les anges dans le ciel annoncent Noël / aux bergers de Bethléem: / Gloire à Dieu et Paix sur terre!

3. Sous les traits de la faiblesse, / Fils de Dieu, tu caches ta vie / pour apprendre à ceux qui peinent / que tu es l'ami des petits! / Chez les pauvres tu seras la source de joie / qui apaise notre soif: / Gloire à Dieu et Paix sur terre!

4. Sur les pas de tes prophètes, / Fils de Dieu, tu es apparu / et les hommes sont en fête / pour chanter ce jour attendu! / Quand ton heure sonnera, tout être verra / le salut qui vient de toi: / Gloire à Dieu et Paix sur terre!

J. Martin 1972

59

Malcolm Stewart 1969

Refrain

When he comes back, when he comes back, our
A son re - tour, à son re - tour, nous
An je - nem Tag, an je - nem Tag, laßt
A su vol - ver, a su vol - ver, ha -
Ri - tor - ne - rà, ri - tor - ne - rà, in

lamps will be bur - ning to wel - come him
é - clai - re - rons de joi - e son che -
bren - nen vor Freu - de die Lam - pen, wenn
re - mos bril - lar mil fa - ro - les en
co - ri can - tia - mo fe - li - ci per -

Fine   Verses
(7)

when he comes back_____!   1. The Ma - ster has
min, son re - tour_____!
er wie - der - kommt__!   1. Der Herr hat ver -
sa - lu - ta - ción_____.
chè ri - tor - ne - rà_____.

promised that he will re - turn on a night when there's
sprochen, er kom - me zu - rück in der Nacht, wenn kein

no one ex - pect - ing to see him at all_____.
einz - ger er - war - tet, daß er wie - der - kommt__.

Keep oil in the lamps so they're rea - dy to
Füllt Öl in die Lam - pen und macht sie be -

108

| burn | on the | night of | the | sec - ret, | when | those who are |
| reit, | zu er - hel - len | die | Nacht, da | er | kommt und die |

Back to Refrain

| wai - ting he'll | call___. |
| War - ten - den | ruft___. |

2. Look not for the Master in heaven's dark space: / by the light of our living on earth we'll discover his face. / The face of the Master is always at hand / in the face of the stranger, the poor, in the face of a man.

3. This stranger will search for his home in the night, / and then how will he find it, unless all the windows are bright? / But if we are waiting, why then, he'll come in – / and there'll be a homecoming, with dancing and singing within!

Malcolm Stewart 1969 (and all refrains)

2. Ihr findet ihn nicht in der Weite des Raums; / wir begegnen ihm dort, wo wir leben, / hier sind wir erkannt. / Er sieht auf uns täglich und sucht unsern Blick / aus den Augen des Fremden, des Armen, des Menschen am Weg.

3. Und sucht dann der Fremde sein Haus in der Nacht, / so wird er es nur finden, / wenn Licht aus den Fenstern erstrahlt. / Wenn wir auf ihn warten, so kommt er herein, / und dann feiern wir alle die Heimkehr mit Singen und Tanz.

Konrad Raiser 1972

60

Gottfried Neubert und Seminargruppe 1964

1. Kommt Gott als Mensch in Dorf und Stadt,
2. Drum sind die Kir - chen viel zu klein,
1. God will, when he comes down to earth,
2. That's why the chur - ches are too small,

hat er nicht viel zu la - chen. Das Chri-sten-
wo die Cho-rä - le klin - gen. Läßt Gott sich
have lit - tle ground for laugh - ter; he'll find the
where hymns are sung on Sun - day. When God's with

volk ist lau und matt, ver - strickt in
mit den Men-schen ein, kann auch die
Christ - ians cold and slack, con - tent with
man, the ve - ry streets will shout for

eig - ne Sa - chen. Doch er zieht ein für
Stra - ße sin - gen. Ho - san - na kommt vom
arch and raf - ter. But he is there for
joy on Mon - day! Ho - san - na from the

je - der-mann, denkt nicht nur an die From-men.
Stra-ßen-rand und von den Kir-chen-bän-ken,
ev' - ry man, his thought is with the low - ly,
pa - ving stones, and from the con-gre - ga - tion!

110

Er will für al - le kom - men.
doch er weiß, was wir den - ken.
not on - ly with the ho - ly.
– He knows our me - di - ta - tion –.

3. Kommt Gott als Mensch in Dorf und Stadt, / hat er nicht viel zu lachen: / Wir setzen ihn am Kreuze matt, / um weiter Krieg zu machen. / Auch Schweigen wird uns zum Gericht / in Kirchen und in Straßen. / Gott läßt nicht mit sich spaßen!

4. Drum sind die Kirchen viel zu klein, / wo die Choräle klingen: / Die ganze Welt muß Schauplatz sein, / wenn wir von neuem singen. / Es fängt mit dem Erschrecken an, / das wir so lieblos leben. / Der Richter hat vergeben.

5. Kommt Gott als Mensch in Dorf und Stadt, / Kann der nur wieder lachen, / der nicht mehr weiter lau und matt / das eigne Spiel will machen. / Wer Gottes Anspiel weiterspielt, / wird dies auch sehen lassen / in Kirchen und in Straßen.

Dieter Trautwein 1964

3. God will, when he comes down to earth, have little ground for laughter; / again we nail him to the cross / and go to war and slaughter. / But even silence spells our guilt / in churches and in cities. / Pray God that he has pity!

4. That's why the churches are too small / with singing congregations: / the world itself must be the stage / for workday celebrations. / It starts when people see with fright / their loveless ways of living. / God knows, we need forgiving.

5. There will, when God comes down to earth, / be only ground for laughter / with those who leave their selfish game / and join to follow after / the God who teaches us the round / from worship on the Sunday / to service on the Monday.

Fred Kaan 1972

61

Gerd Watkinson 1967

Solo (or semi-chorus)

1. Wer kann mir sa - gen, wo Je - sus
1. O who can tell me where Je - sus
1. Qui peut me di - re l'en - droit où

All

Chri - stus ge - bo - ren ist? Dort ist Chri - stus ge -
Christ is born to - day? Christ is born___ to -
Jé - sus le Christ est né? Vois, Jé - sus prend nais -

bo - ren, wo Men - schen be - gin - nen, mensch - lich zu
day___, where men are be - gin - ning to live as
san - ce où l'hom - me com - men - ce d'ou - vrir son

han - deln und sich be - sin - nen, die Welt zu ver -
bro - thers, and aim at win - ning a new world for
cœur et ses mains pour chan - ger la vie de ses

wan - deln. Dort___ ist Chri - stus ge - bo - ren.
o - thers, Christ___ is born___ to - day___.
frè - res. Oui, là Jé - sus prend nais - san - ce.

2. Wer kann mir sagen, wann Jesus Christus geboren ist? / Dann ist
Christus geboren, wenn Menschen beginnen, / menschlich zu handeln und
sich besinnen, die Welt zu verwandeln. / Dann ist Christus geboren.

3. Wer kann mir sagen, wozu Jesus Christus geboren ist? / Dazu ist Christus geboren, daß Menschen beginnen, / menschlich zu handeln und sich besinnen, die Welt zu verwandeln. / Dazu ist Christus geboren.

Kurt Rommel 1967

2. O who can tell me where Jesus Christ is born today? / Christ is born today where men are beginning / to live as brothers and aim at winning / a new world for others – Christ is born that day

3. O who can tell me why Jesus Christ is born today? / Christ is born today that men should *begin* / to live as brothers, and aim at winning / a new world for others – Christ is born for *this*.

Emily Chisholm 1973

2. Qui peut me dire le jour où Jésus le Christ est né? / Vois, Jésus prend naissance quand l'homme commence / d'ouvrir son cœur et ses mains pour changer la vie de ses frères / alors, Jésus prend naissance.

3. Qui peut me dire pourquoi Jésus le Seigneur est né? / Vois, Jésus prend naissance pour toi qui commences / d'ouvrir ton cœur et tes mains pour changer la vie de tes frères / pour toi, Jésus prend naissance.

Nicole Berthet 1972

62

Maluku Popular Tune

My soul doth mag - ni - fy the Lord, my
in God my Sa - viour, for his word de -

spi - rit doth _ re - joice _
clared to me _ , the choice _

of his hand - mai - den

to be - come___ the mo - ther of___ the
Christ_____ that for the Son___ of
God my home___ and hum - ble heart suf - ficed___.

2. Behold, from henceforth to my name / shall generations give / their blessings, for the Lord who came / as man with man to live. / The mercy of our God is great / and great his deeds of love; / he looked upon man's low estate / and lifted him above.

3. The proud he scattered in their pride, / the rich must empty go. / The strong his strength doth set aside, / the mighty are brought low. / The humble are exalted high, / the hungry filled with food. / The God of Israel has drawn nigh / the Lord, our God, is good.

D. T. Niles 1963

63

Adapté du plainchant 'Jésu Redemptor' par C. Geoffray

1. Au - jour - d'hui dans no - tre mon - de le
1. Lo! to - day in - to our world___ the
1. Heu - te noch kommt Got - tes Wort un - ter

Verbe est né pour par - ler du Pè - re aux
Word is born, to de - clare to men the
uns zur Welt und er - zählt vom Va - ter,

114

hom - mes qu'il a tant ai - més. Et le
Fa - ther's deep love and con - cern. Heav'n it -
wie sehr die Men - schen er liebt. Of - fen -

[E. v. 4]

ciel nous ap - prend le grand mys -
self tea - ches us how great the
bar ist uns jetzt das gro - ße

tè - - re. Gloi - re à Dieu et
mys - te - ry: Glo - ry to God, and
Wun - - der. Eh - re sei Gott und

paix sur ter - re, al - lé - lu - ia!
peace on earth___, al - le - lu - ia!
Fried' auf Er - den. Hal - le - lu - ja!

2. Aujourd'hui dans nos ténèbres le Christ a lui / pour ouvrir les yeux des hommes qui vont dans la nuit. / L'univers est baigné de sa lumière: / Gloire à Dieu et paix sur terre, alléluia!

3. Aujourd'hui dans notre mort a paru la Vie / pour changer le cœur des hommes qui sont endurcis, / et l'amour est plus fort que nos misères: / Gloire à Dieu et paix sur terre, alléluia!

4. Aujourd'hui, dans notre chair est entré Jésus / pour unir en lui les hommes qui l'ont attendu. / Et Marie, à genoux, l'offre à son Père: / Gloire à Dieu et paix sur terre, alléluia!

Didier Rimaud 1968

2. Lo! today into our darkness has shone the Light, / to restore eyesight to men who are groping in night. / All his vast universe bathes in his mystery: / Glory to God, and peace on earth. Alleluia!

3. Lo! today into our death the Life breaks in, / to transform the hearts of men who are hardened by sin. / Love shall be stronger far than all our misery: / Glory to God and peace on earth. Alleluia!

4. Lo! today into our flesh the Lord descends / to unite the men who wait to be counted his friends; / offering him to his Father, Mary kneels reverently: / Glory to God and peace on earth. Alleluia!

F. Pratt Green 1972

2. Heute fällt in unsere Dunkelheit großes Licht. / Christus leuchtet hell / den Blinden im Dunkel der Nacht. / Alle Welt ist durchstrahlt von diesem Glänzen. / Ehre sei Gott und Fried' auf Erden. Halleluja.

3. Heute bricht in unsrem Tod sich das Leben Bahn, / wandelt Herzen, die belastet und hoffnungslos sind. / Stärker ist Gottes Macht als unser Elend. / Ehre sei Gott und Fried' auf Erden. Halleluja.

4. Heute kommt in Jesus Gott als ein Mensch zu uns, / um sie alle zu vereinen, die warten auf ihn. / Gott gab ihn durch Marie – mit ihr wir singen: / Ehre sei Gott und Fried' auf Erden. Halleluja.

Ursula Trautwein 1973

64

Mélodie traditionelle d'Auvergne

1. Tout le ciel s'em - plit d'u - ne joie nou -
1. All the sky is bright, fill'd with joy, a
1. Al - les, was Gott schuf, ist er - füllt mit

vel - le: on en - tend la nuit di - re la mer -
new joy. Wai - ting for the night, we will talk of
Freu - de. Mit - ten in der Nacht spre - chen wir vom

veil - le. Fê - te sans pa - reil - le: Le Sau -
won - ders. Ne - ver was a feast like this: Born is
Wun - der. Fest - tag oh - ne - glei - chen: Chri - stus

116

veur est né; l'en - fant Dieu nous est don - né.
Je - sus Christ, born the Child-God giv'n to us!
ist ge - born! Gott kommt als ein Kind zu uns.

2. Le Seigneur parait, verbe de lumière / l'univers connait la bonté du Père. / Dieu de notre terre vient tracer la voie où chemineront nos pas.

3. Avec les bergers, avec tous les sages, / c'est le monde entier qui vers lui s'engage / pour voir le visage de l'Amour vivant qui pour nous s'est fait enfant.

4. Gloire à Jésus-Christ, gloire au Fils du Père! / Gloire à son Esprit dont l'amour éclaire / l'eclatant mystère qui remplit de ciel: Gloire à l'homme-Dieu! Noël!

Claude Rozier 1956

2. Now our Lord appears, he whose word enlightens, / all creation hears of the Father's goodness. / He, the God of this poor earth. He has come to show where our wand'ring steps should go.

3. Not alone they come, simple shepherds, wise men: / all the human race wants to make him welcome, / wants to look upon the face of the Lord of bliss, / who becomes a child for us.

4. Glory be to Christ, glory to the Father's Son, / and the Holy Ghost, he whose love enlightens! / Dazzling is the mystery filling all the sky: / To the Man-God 'Glory' cry!

F. Pratt Green 1972

2. Unser Herr erscheint, läßt sein Wort uns leuchten, / und die ganze Welt sieht des Vaters Güte. / Herr der armen Erde, richte unsern Blick / auf den Weg, der zu dir führt.

3. Mit dem Hirtenvolk und auch mit den Weisen / zeigt die ganze Welt, daß sie dich erwartet, / will das Antlitz sehen, das von Liebe spricht. / Dieses Kind bringt dich uns nah!

4. Lob sei dir, o Herr, dir dem Sohn des Vaters. / Lob sei Gott, dem Geist, der uns liebt und leitet, / Wunder aller Wunder, das die Welt erfüllt. / Lob sei dir, du Mensch und Gott.

Ursula Trautwein 1973

65

Probably by J. F. Wade 1711 - 86

1. Ad - es - te fi - de - les, lae - ti tri - um -
1. O come, all ye faith - ful, joy - ful and tri -
1. Peu - ple fi - dè - le, le Sei - gneur t'ap -
1. Ve - nid, Fie - les to - dos; a Be - lén mar -

phan - tes, ve - ni - te, ve - ni - te in
um - phant, O come ye, O come ye to
pel - le: C'est fê - te sur ter - re, le
che - mos, de go - zo triun - fan - tes, hen -

Beth - le - hem. Na - tum vi - de - te,
Beth - le - hem; come and be - hold him,
Christ est né. Viens à la crè - che
chi - dos de a - mor; y al Rey de los cie - los

re - gem an - ge - lo - rum: Ve - ni - te, ad - o -
born the King of an - gels: O come, let us a -
voir le Roi du mon - de: En lui, viens re - con -
con - tem - plar po - dre - mos: Ve - nid ; a - do -

re - mus, ve - ni - te, a - do - re - mus, ve -
dore him, O come, let us a - dore him, O
naî - tre, en lui viens re - con - naî - tre, en
re - mos, ve - nid , a - do - re - mos; ve -

118

ni - te, a - do - re - mus___ Do - mi - num!
come, let us a - dore him___, Christ___ the Lord!
lui viens re - con - naî - tre ton Dieu, ton Sau - veur!
nid___, a - do - re - mos a Chris - to el Se - ñor!

2. Deum de Deo, Lumen de lumine, / Gestant puellae viscera; / Natum
videte regem angelorum: / Venite, adoremus, venite, adoremus, / Venite,
adoremus Dominum!

3. Cantet nunc 'Io!' Chorus angelorum, / Cantet nunc aula caelestium, /
Gloria in excelsis Deo! / Venite, adoremus, venite adoremus, / Venite,
adoremus Dominum!

4. Ergo qui natus, die hodierna, / Jesu, tibi sit gloria; / Patris aeterni,
Verbum caro factum! / Venite, adoremus, venite adoremus, / Venite,
adoremus Dominum!

(Anonymus)

2. God of God: Light of Light: / Lo! he abhors not the virgin's womb; /
Very God, begotten, not created: / O come, let us adore him, O come, let
us adore him, / O come, let us adore him, Christ the Lord!

3. Sing, choirs of angels, sing in exultation, / sing all ye citizens of heav'n
above! / Glory to God in the highest! / O come, let us adore him, O
come let us adore him, / O come, let us adore him, Christ the Lord!

4. Yea, Lord, we greet thee, born this happy morning, / Jesu, to thee be
glory given: / Word of the Father, now in flesh appearing: / O come, let
us adore him, O come let us adore him, / O come, let us adore him,
Christ the Lord!

F. Oakeley 1841, 1852

2. Verbe, Lumière, et Splendeur du Père, / Il naît d'une mère, petit
enfant, / Dieu véritable, le Seigneur fait homme: / En lui viens
reconnaître, en lui viens reconnaître, / En lui viens reconnaître ton Dieu,
ton Sauveur.

3. Peuple, acclame, avec tous les anges, / Le Maître des hommes qui
vient chez toi, / Dieu qui se donne à tous ceux qu'il aime! / En lui viens
reconnaître, en lui viens reconnaître, / En lui viens reconnaître ton Dieu,
ton Sauveur!

(Pour la veillée ou le jour de Noël)

4. Peuple fidèle, en ce jour de fête, / Proclame la gloire de ton Seigneur. / Dieu se fait homme pour montrer qu'il t'aime. / En lui viens reconnaître, en lui viens reconnaître, / En lui viens reconnaître ton Dieu, ton Sauveur!

C. Rozier 1950

2. El que es hijo eterno del eterno Padre, / Y Dios verdadero que al mundo creó, / Al seno virgineo vino de una madre: / Venid, adoremos, venid, adoremos, / Venid, adoremos a Cristo, el Señor.

3. En pobre pesebre yace reclinado, / Al hombre ofreciendo eternal salvación, / El santo Mesías, Verbo humanado: / Venid, adoremos, venid adoremos, / Venid, adoremos a Cristo, el Señor.

4. Cantad jubilosas, célicas criaturas: / Resuenen los cielos con vuestra canción: / ¡Al Dios bondadoso gloria en las alturas! / Venid, adoremos, venid, adoremos, / Venid, adoremos a Cristo, el Señor.

5. Jésus, celebramos tu bendito nombre / Con himnos solemnes de grato loor; / Por siglos eternos que te adore el hombre: / Venid, adoremos, venid, adoremos, / Venid, adoremos a Cristo el Señor.

Juan B. Cabrera 1837–1916

J. F. Wade 1711 - 86

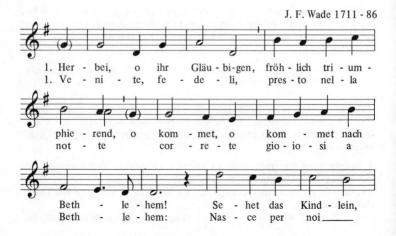

1. Her - bei, o ihr Gläu - bi - gen, fröh - lich tri - um -
1. Ve - ni - te, fe - de - li, pres - to nel - la

phie - rend, o kom - met, o kom - met nach
not - te cor - re - te gio - io - si a

Beth - le - hem! Se - het das Kind - lein,
Beth - le - hem: Nas - ce per noi____

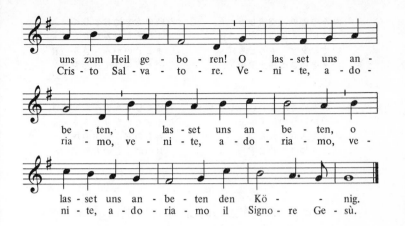

uns zum Heil ge - bo - ren! O las - set uns an -
Cris - to Sal - va - to - re. Ve - ni - te, a - do -

be - ten, o las - set uns an - be - ten, o
ria - mo, ve - ni - te, a - do - ria - mo, ve -

las - set uns an - be - ten den Kö - nig.
ni - te, a - do - ria - mo il Signo - re Ge - sù.

2. Du König der Ehren, / Herrscher der Heerscharen / verschmähst nicht, zu ruhen in Mariens Schoß. / Gott, wahrer Gott, von Ewigkeit geboren! / O laßet uns anbeten, o laßet uns anbeten, / o laßet uns anbeten den König.

3. Kommt, singet dem Herren, / o ihr Engelchöre, / frohlocket, frohlocket, ihr Seligen! / Ehre sei Gott im Himmel und auf Erden! / O laßet uns anbeten, o laßet uns anbeten, / o laßet uns anbeten den König.

4. Dir, der du bist heute / Mensch für uns geboren, / o Jesu, sei Ehre und Preis und Ruhm! / Dir, Fleisch gewordnes Wort des ewgen Vaters! / O laßet uns anbeten, o laßet uns anbeten, / o laßet uns anbeten den König.

aus dem Lateinischen

2. L'eterna Parola viene in questo mondo, / la luce del Padre risplende a noi: / Figlio di Dio, nato di Maria. / Venite, adoriamo, venite, adoriamo, / venite, adoriamo il Signore Gesù.

3. Fratello dell'uomo, debole bambino, / riveli il Mistero ai poveri: / Gloria nei cieli, pace sulla terra! / Venite, adoriamo, venite, adoriamo, / venite, adoriamo il Signore Gesù.

E. Costa

1. かみの御子は今宵しも
ベツレヘムに生れたもう。
いざや友よ、もろともに
いそぎゆきて拝まずや。

2. 賤の女をば母として
生れまししみどりでは、
まことのかみ、きみの君、
いそぎゆきて拝まずや。

3.「かみにさかえあれかし」と、
みつかいらの声すなり。
地なる人もたたえつつ
いそぎゆきて拝まずや。

4. とこしなえのみことばは
今ぞ人となりたもう。
待ちのぞみし主の民よ、
おのが幸をいわわずや。

1. أَيَّامُؤْمِنونا ، أَلَا تَصْحَبُونَا ، بِنَاىْ وَعُودِ ، إِلىَ بَيْتِ لَحْمْ ، طِفْلٌ أَتَانَا ، طَالِبًا فِدَانَا

القرار: لَهُ اسْجُدُوا جَمِيعًا ، لَهُ اسْجُدُوا جَمِيعًا ، لَهُ اسْجُدُوا جَمِيعًا ، هُوَ الْمَسِيحْ

2. جُيُوشُ الْعُلاءِ ، بِأَحْلَى ثَنَاءِ ، تَعَالَوْا وَغَنُّوا ، لِسَيِّدِكُمْ ، لِلهِ مَجْدٌ ، فِى الْعُلَى وَحَمْدٌ

3. لَكَ الشُّكْرُ نَهْدِي ، إِلَهَ الْوُجُودِ ، يَسُوعَ الْمَسِيحَ ، وَحِيدَ الْعَلِى ، فَأَنْتَ جِئْتَ ، وَلَنَا وُلِدْتَ

Khalil Asaad Ghobrial

Jesus Christ – His Ministry and Teaching
Jesus Christus – Dienst und Lehre
Jésus Christ – Ministère et Enseignement

66

Dieter Trautwein and
Hans Rudolf Siemoneit 1964

Refrain

Herr, laß uns hö - ren, was du sagst!
Lord, let us lis - ten when you speak!

Sprich durch die Wor - te, die wir re - den!
Speak through the words that we are u - sing!

Hilf uns, dir ge - hor - sam sein!
Help us to o - bey___ you, Lord!

Herr, laß uns hö - ren, was du___ sagst!
Lord, let us lis - ten when you___ speak!

123

1. Ihr sollt Christi Füße sein heute in der Welt:
1. You are Christ's feet__ here to-day in the world;

geht hin-aus und spürt die Menschen auf in ih-rer Not.
go, dis-co-ver all the peo-ple who are most in need.

2. Ihr sollt Christi Augen sein heute in der Welt: / Blickt auch hinter die Fassaden, wo das Unrecht schreit!

3. Ihr sollt Christi Hände sein heute in der Welt: / Greift nun zu und tut das Gute, wo es Menschen hilft!

4. Ihr sollt Christi Lippen sein heute in der Welt: / Redet von des Menschen Rettung, die durch ihn geschah!

Dieter Trautwein + Kurt Rommel 1964

2. You are Christ's eyes here today in the world: / look behind all our pretences when injustice shouts!

3. You are Christ's hands here today in the world: / so by grasping life do all the good you can and should!

4. You are Christ's lips here today in the world: / speak of that amazing rescue he has carried out!

F. Pratt Green 1972

67

Juhani Forsberg 1969

1. Jee - sus saa-pui Ka - per - nau-miin, ko - ti kau-pun-
1. Je - sus Christ has come in - to Ca - per - na - um, his
1. Je - sus ist in sei - ne Stadt, Ka - per - na - um, ge -

124

kiin - sa   mai - ne kul - ki   juo - rut juok - si
ci - ty,   some   there are who   praise him, but the
kom - men.   Und   die ei - nen   lo - ben ihn, die

koh - ta ym - pä   riin - sä   E - li - aak - si
o - thers shout in   pro - test.   'He   must be   E -
an - dern pro - te - stie - ren.   'Er   ist   der   E -

kut - sut - tiin ja   jos - kus pro - fee - tak - si.
li - jah, or   a - no - ther of the   pro - phets!'
li - as   o - der   ei - ner der Pro   phe - ten!'

Recitativo

Joku kuitenkin   sa - noi: 'Äl - kää menkö sen miehen
And somebo - dy shouts: 'Don't go near that man! He
Und ein and - rer   ruft: 'Geht   nicht hin zu dem Mann,

a tempo

luokse, se on Beelse - bu - li____!'   E - li - aak - si
has Beelzebub   the   de - vil!'   'He   must be   E -
er hat den Beelzebub, den   Teu - fel!'   'Er   ist   der   E -

kut - sut - tiin ja   jos - kus pro - fee - tak - si.
li - jah or   a - no - ther of the   pro - phets!'
li - as   o - der   ei - ner der Pro - phe - ten!'

2. tungoksessa valtavassa Jeesus puhuu sanaa / neljä miestä päällä
halvattua kantaa / ovesta ei sisään pääse, katto täytyy purkaa / joku
sanoi: 'kuka nyt tolla tavalla rupee saarnaa häiritsemään?' / ovesta ei
sisään pääse, katto täytyy purkaa

125

3. paarit maahan laskettiin ja Jeesus sairaan näki / lausui sanan, kohta sitä ihmetteli väki: / 'poikani, sun syntisi on pyyhitty pois kaikki' / joku sanoi: 'onko nyt laitaa puhua synnistä kun toinen on kuolemansairas?' / ja moni mietti: (lausuen) 'kuinka hän voi antaa syntejä anteeksi? hän pilkkaa Jumalaa!' / poikani, sun syntisi on pyyhitty pois kaikki

4. arvoituksen pulmallisen Jeesus heille antaa: / kumpi näistä helpompaa nyt oikein olla mahtaa: / synnit antaa anteeksi vai halvattua auttaa / Jeesus sanoi: 'koska Ihmisen Pojalla on valta anteeksi antaa, niin minä sanon: / nouse, ota vuoteesi ja täältä kotiin lähde'

5. polvin hieman horjuvin hän matkaan lähti sieltä / mennessänsä kiitosvirsi kuului kotitieltä: / 'halleluja halleluja kiitos Jumalalle!' / silloin kaikki sanoivat: 'tämän kaltaista emme ole ikinä nähneet / halleluja halleluja kiitos Jumalalle!'

Juhani Forsberg 1969

2. In the overcrowded house the Lord speaks to the people. / Look, they're bringing in the paralytic on a stretcher. / 'Crowds are blocking up the door. You'll have to break the roofing.' / And somebody shouts: 'You can't disturb a sermon like this!' / 'Crowds are blocking up the door, you'll have to break the roofing!'

3. As he lies before his feet, the Lord looks at the sufferer, / speaks a powerful word to him, and many are offended: / 'Son, your past is washed away, your sins are all forgotten!' And someone calls out, 'Talking of his sins, and the man so ill!' / And many are thinking: 'How can he forgive sins? This is blasphemy.' / 'Son, your sin is washed away. Your sins are all forgiven!'

4. Jesus puts a question now, and asks them for the answer: / 'Tell me, anybody, which is easier to manage, / Sinful man to pardon, or to cure the paralytic?' / And Jesus says to them: 'Since the Son of Man has power to forgive sins, / I say: "stand up straight, take up your bed, and walk home through the city!"'

5. And the man stands up and walks, although his knees are shaking. / All can see that he can walk. They listen to his praises. / 'Alleluia! Alleluia! Thanks to God Almighty!' / And they all are amazed: 'We have never seen anything like it!' / 'Alleluia! Alleluia! Thanks to God Almighty!'

Emily Chisholm 1972

2. Und im überfüllten Haus spricht Jesus zu den Leuten. / Seht, sie bringen ihm den Gichtgelähmten auf der Bahre. / 'Durch die Tür kann niemand rein, ihr müsst das Dach abdecken!' Und ein andrer ruft: 'Stört man auf solche Weise eine Predigt?' / 'Durch die Tür kann niemand rein, ihr müsst das Dach abdecken!'

3. Wie er ihm zu Füssen liegt, sieht Jesus dann den Kranken, / spricht zu ihm ein starkes Wort, daß viele ganz entsetzt sind: / 'Dir sind deine Sünden abgenommen und vergeben!' / Und ein andrer ruft: 'Gehört es sich von Sünde zu sprechen, wenn ein Mensch so krank ist?' / Und viele dachten: 'Wie kann er Sünden vergeben! Er lästert Gott!' / 'Dir sind deine Sünden abgenommen und vergeben!'

4. Da stellt Jesus ihnen eine Frage, läßt sie raten: / 'Kann mir einer sagen, was ist leichter zu vollbringen, / Sünden zu vergeben oder dem Gelähmten helfen?' / Und Jesus sagt zu ihnen: 'Weil der Sohn des Menschen die Macht hat zu vergeben', spreche ich: / 'Stehe auf und nimm dein Bett und geh damit nachhause!'

5. Und der Mann steht auf und geht, es schwanken ihm die Knie. / Alle sehen, daß er geht, und hören, wie er betet: / 'Hallelujah, Hallelujah! Dank sei Gott, dem Herren!' / Da staunen alle Leute: 'So was haben wir noch nie gesehen!' / 'Hallelujah, Hallelujah! Dank sei Gott, dem Herren!'

Dieter Trautwein 1971

68

William Llewellyn 1969

Show us your ways, O Lord,
En - sei - gne - nous tes che - mins,

teach us your paths. Blest are the poor in
gui - de nos pas! A eux le ro - yau - me des

spi - rit: for theirs is the king-dom of heaven.
A eux le ro - yau - me des cieux.

Blest are they that mourn: for they shall be com-for-ted.
car ils se-ront con-so-lés.

Blest are the meek: for they shall in - he-rit the
Ils pos-sé-de-ront l'u-ni-

earth. Show us your ways, O Lord, teach us your
vers. En-sei-gne-nous tes che-mins, gui-de nos

paths. Blest are they that hun-ger and thirst af-ter
pas !

right-eousness: for they shall be filled.
car ils se-ront com-blés.

Blest are the mer-ci-ful: for they shall ob-
car ils ob-tien-

tain mer-cy. Show us your ways, O
dront grâ-ce. En-sei-gne-nous tes che-

128

Lord, teach us your paths _____. Blest are the
mins, gui - de nos pas _____.

Solo

pure_ in heart; for they shall see God. Blest
car ils ver - ront Dieu.

Choir / **Solo**

are___ the peace - ma - kers; for they shall be
car ils se - ront

Choir

called God's sons. Blest are they which are
fils de Dieu.

Solo

per - se - cu - ted for right - eous - ness' sake:

the king - dom of heaven is theirs.
Le Rè - gne de Dieu est là.

Choir

Show us your ways _, O Lord, teach us your paths __.
En - sei - gne - nous tes che - mins, gui - de nos pas___!

All

Scripture, St. Matthew 5, 3 - 10 / Psalm 25, 4
(F) J. Gelineau 1972

129

69

Roland Forsberg 1970

1. Han sat - te sig ner på stran - den, och
1. When Je - sus sat down on the lake - shore, the
1. As - sis sur la berge, il ai - me la
1. Er ließ sich am Stran - de nie - der, die

ska - ror - na kring ho - nom var____. Och
peo - ple flocked round him to hear____. The
foule as - sem - blée a - len - tour____, ses
Scha - ren ver - sam - mel - ten sich____. Das

bru - set från ber - gen och vatt - net hans
surf and the wind from the moun - tains, they
mots pleins de sel et d'é - cu - me sont
Brau - sen der Ber - ge und Flüs - se sein

ord till de lyss - nan - de bar____ om
car - ried his word to their ears____ of
ceux que tout hom - me con - naît____: Les
Wort zu den Lau - schen - den trug____, er -

såd - den, om nä - tet och ska - ten: och
so - wing and fish - ing and trea - sures; and
fi - lets trou - és la for - tu - ne; et
zähl - te von Saat, Netz und Schät - zen: s'ist

allt är när - het och vind långt - i - från____.
all is near - ness and wind from a - far____.
tout est souf - fle et pré - sence à ja - mais____.
al - les Nä - he und Wind von weit - her____.

130

2. Han satte sig ner vid brunnen. / En synderska hos honom stod, en utstött: / ur staden fördriven av rädslan för mänskornas dom. / Han gav henne åter till livet; / och allt är närhet och väg låntifrån.

3. Han satte sig ner i öknen / den sjuke till honom man bar. / Och borta var plågan och döden. / 'Gå hem till de dina i dag!' / De hungriga räckte han bröden: / och alet är närhet och makt långtifrån.

4. Han sitter på högra sidan / om Fadern. Hos alla han är. / På gatan han går och vid bordet / han tjänande böjer sig ner. / Hans röst vi förnimmer ur Ordet: / och allt är närhet. Vår värld är hans värld.

Anders Frostenson 1970

2. When Jesus sat down at the wellside, / a woman came out of the town, / rejected by public opinion / because of her doubtful renown; / but Jesus restored her to living: / and all is nearness and streams from afar.

3. When Jesus sat down in the desert, / they brought to him those who were ill. / He healed their despair and diseases: / 'Arise and go home: you are well!' / And then he broke bread with the hungry: / and all is nearness and strength from afar.

4. And now he is with us for ever: / he sits at the Father's right hand: / he serves us at table, we meet him / in city streets and on the land. / His word is our hope and our challenge: / and all is nearness, for his is the world!

Fred Kaan 1973

2. Assis près du puits, il aime / la femme qui vient en tremblant, / chassée de la cité hautaine, / par honte de ses jugements; / mais lui aussitôt la délivre, / et tout est houle et présence à jamais.

3. Assis au désert, il aime / les malheureux et les souffrants, / le pauvre éclopé qu'on amène / et qu'il guérit en un instant; / l'affamé reçoit nourriture / et tout est force et présence à jamais.

4. Assis à côté du Père, / il est avec tous et partout / en ville comme à notre table / sa parole s'adresse à nous; / on voit dans ses yeux joie ou peine: / présence au cœur de ce monde à jamais.

Edouard Kressmann 1972

2. Er setzte sich hin am Brunnen. / Die Sünderin neben ihm stand, / verstoßen, verjagt aus dem Städtchen / aus Angst vor Menschengericht. / Er gab sie zurück an das Leben: / s'ist alles Nähe und Sturm von weither.

3. Er setzte sich in der Wüste. / Den Kranken trug man zu ihm hin. / Verscheucht waren Krankheit und Qualen. / 'Noch heute geh heim in dein Haus!' / Den Hungrigen gab er die Brote: / s'ist alles Nähe und Macht von weither.

4. Er sitzt nun zur Rechten Gottes. / Bei allen von uns ist er da. / Er geht auf der Straße. Am Tische bückt er sich als Diener herab. / Das Wort seiner Stimme wir hören: / s'ist alles Nähe. Die Welt, sie ist sein.

Helli Halbe 1972

70

Chorus — Indian lyric

1. Main___ pre - ma hun pre - ma ba - na -
1. God is love! God is love! He is love's___
1. Die___ Lie - be bin ich, Schöp - fer der___

ta - hun, su - na pre - ma ka - ra - ga su -
cre - a - tor, lis - ten now, lis - ten now___ to his
Lie - be, hört auf mich, und die Lie - be bleibt

1.
na - ta hun___. Main___
word of love___. God is
ganz in euch___! Die___

2. Fine
-na - ta hun.
word of love.
ganz in euch.

Verses

Is - a ja - ga ke na - hin ji - s(a)
You are in this world of mine, but you
Ihr ge - hört zu die - ser Welt und seid

132

men_____ tu - m(a) ho   I - sa
are not of the world.   All its
nicht_____ mehr von ihr,   denn ich

D. C.

men du - kha hai - du-kh(a) pa - ta hun__.
sor - row I bear__, and you bear it with me.
tra - ge die Sor - ge, die euch be - schwert.

2. Sab(a) dush(a) mano ko tuma piyar(a) karo / Main prem(a) se kashta uthata hun.

3. Main prema ki khushobu sekhush(a) hun / aura prema ka baga lagata hun.

4. Main yesa na hobezarana ho / main teredil(a) men ata hun.

Bantam Ram Banda (Hindustani)

2. You must love all those who are enemies to you: / all your burdens I bear, all your stress and sorrow.

3. I shall sow seeds of love in the garden of love, / and the scent of their flowers will always delight me.

4. Do not weep, do not fear, let your courage burn bright; / for this is my promise: I am with you always.

Erik Routley 1972

2. Euren Freund wie euren Feind sollt ihr lieben wie euch, / denn auf mir liegt die Schuld, welche euch entzweit.

3. Gleich dem Samenkorn das stirbt, um zur Frucht zu gedeih'n. / So soll auch meine Liebe in euch erblüh'n.

4. Kein Verzagen, keine Angst mache schwer euer Herz. / Denn ich bleibe bei euch, bis die Welt vergeht.

Konrad Raiser 1972

71

Melody from Sri Lanka

1. Son of the Fa - ther__, Je - sus, Lord and slave,
1. Dieu, né de Dieu, toi Jé - sus, qui dis, 'Ve - nez!'

born a - mong the cat - tle in the squa - lor of a cave,
En - fant né___ dans une crê - che! Ve - nez voir, ber - gers!

one with God, you made your-self one with man, shun-ning wealth;
Fils de l'hom-me, fils de Dieu, né pour nous, par - mi nous:

Lord, we wor - ship you with heart and mind.
gloire à toi sur terre et dans les cieux!

2. Son of the Father, worker's friend, / you whom Joseph taught the skills of working with your hands, / man, at home in builder's yard, / one with man, toiling hard; / Lord, we worship you with hand and mind.

3. Son of the Father, author of our faith, / choosing men to follow you from every walk of life, / who with them, in boats, on shore, / troubles shared, burdens bore; / Lord, we worship you with hand and mind.

4. Seed of the Father, from life's furrow born, / teaching men in parables from agriculture drawn, / Jesus, lover of the soil, / man of earth, son of toil; / Lord, we worship you with hand and mind.

5. Father and Spirit, Jesus, Lord and Man, / bless us in the work you have appointed to be done. / Lift our spirits, guide our wills, / steer our hands, use our skills; / Lord, we worship you with hand and mind.

Fred Kaan 1972

2. Dieu, né de Dieu, toi, Jésus, qui vis caché, / Ouvrier dans ton village, simple charpentier. / Fils de l'homme, fils de Dieu, / au travail parmi nous: / Gloire à toi sur terre et dans les cieux.

3. Dieu, né de Dieu, toi, Jésus, qui dis: 'Venez, / Laissez vos filets de pêche! Venez et voyez!' / Fils de l'homme, fils de Dieu. / Prends nos peurs, conduis-nous: / Gloire à toi sur la terre et dans les cieux!

4. Dieu, né de Dieu, toi, Jésus qui dis: 'Voyez' / grain qui meurt et blé qui lève pour les affamés, / Fils de l'homme, fils de Dieu, / Verbe né parmi nous: / Gloire à toi sur terre et dans les cieux!

5. Dieu, né de Dieu, Jésus, envoie ton Esprit, / Qu'il nous mène vers le Père, qu'il nous garde unis! / Fils de l'homme, fils de Dieu, / fais nous voir ton amour: / Gloire à toi sur terre et dans les cieux!

Nicole Berthet 1973

72

Carl Nielsen 1917

1. Där - för att Or - det bland oss bor blir
   värl - den ald - rig stum. En lov - sång lyfts. Vi
   väcks till tro i vår för - tviv - lans stund.

1. How can cre - a - tion's voice be still, when
   with us dwells the Word? A song of praise is
   raised from earth; faith ri - ses like a bird.

1. Quand la Pa - ro - le vient chez nous qui
   res - ter - ait sans voix? Un chant s'é - lè - ve
   de par - tout dès que jail - lit la foi.

1. Da un - ter uns noch wohnt das Wort, ver -
   stummt die Welt nicht mehr. Ein Lob - lied klingt, der
   Glaub' er - wacht in der Ver - zweif - lung Stund.

2. I stoft, i gräsens bräcklighet, / hos den som hjälplös böjs / bor Gud i samma majestät / som in sin himmels höjd.

3. Den gode herdens röst blir hörd / ur rop, som tystas ner. / Bland orm och varg Guds hjord blir förd / och intet ont den sker.

4. Den sten som framför graven ställts / är Paradisets port / och hjärtan tänds i pingstens eld / och språken smälts ihop.

5. Därför att ordet bland oss bor / har världen ljus och liv. / Ge oss, o Gud, en lyhörd tro / en öppen, vaksam blick.

Anders Frostenson 1962

2. God dwells as much in grass and dust, / in human souls weighed down, / as in the realm of majesty, / the heavens and their span.

3. The shepherd's voice is heard to call / through voices that are stilled. / The flock is led in danger's face / but shall not come to ill.

4. The stone is rolled away; the tomb / becomes the gate to life. / The earth is warmed by tongues of fire / that speak, and none is deaf.

5. The Word is with us, and the world / is full of light and life. / Lord, give us faithfulness and faith, / alert and seeing eyes.

Fred Kaan 1973

2. Dans la poussière du sentier / cherche les pas de Dieu! / Et dans la fleur d'un jour d'été / vois le Seigneur des cieux!

3. Entends la voix du vrai Berger / parmi les cris des fous, / marche avec lui, le cœur en paix / entre serpent et loup!

4. Langues de feu, parlez encore / embrasez toute vie! / Pierre de Pâques, Porte d'or, / ouvre le paradis!

5. Reste avec nous, Verbe de Dieu, / Lumière sans déclin! / A ta splendeur ouvre nos yeux, / astre du clair matin!

Armand Ory 1972

2. Im Staub, in Feldes schwachem Gras, / bei dem, der niedersinkt, / wohnt Gott in gleicher Majestät / wie in des Himmels Höhn.

3. Des guten Hirten Wort man hört / noch aus ersticktem Schrei, / durch Schlang' und Wolk zieht Gottes Herd, / der Böses nicht geschieht.

4. Die Feuerzungen sprechen noch, / die Sprachen werden eins, / der Stein, der vor dem Grabloch steht, / gibt frei des Himmels Tür.

5. Da unter uns noch wohnt das Wort, / besitzt die Welt noch Licht, / Oh Gott, gib hellen Glauben uns / und einen wachen Blick.

Helli Halbe 1972

73

Gerhard Kloft 1965

Refrain

Wir sind nicht ir - gend - wer___ und nicht nur
We're not just a - ny - one___; we're not just

un - ge - fähr___, son - dern ganz
no - bo - dies___; we're com - plete -

Got - tes Kin - der, Got - tes Kin - der.
ly God's chil - dren, God's___ chil - dren.

1. Ihr sollt nicht irgendwer, sondern Gottes Kinder sein / Kinder Gottes, erkannt am Gehorsam. / Ihr sollt nicht irgendwie wieder die Dummen sein, / haltlos von Selbstsucht getrieben.

2. Er ist nicht irgendwer! Der euch beruft, ist selbst heilig. / Ihr sollt nicht irgendwie, sondern wie Christus sein. / Heilig heißt: Gott ganz zu eigen!

3. Er ist nicht irgendwer. Der Vater, der Taten richtet, / zieht euch nicht andern vor. / Ihr sollt nicht irgendwie, sondern mit Sorgfalt die Tage verbringen.

4. Ihr seid nicht irgendwer, sondern befreiten Sklaven gleich, / los von der Jagd nach dem Leben. / Er war nicht irgendwer, Christus vergab sein Leben, / daß ihr frei sein und leben könnt.

Dieter Trautwein, 1965, based on I Peter 1, 4–19

(Die Verse werden über improvisierter Musik gesprochen, der Refrain zwischen den Strophen gesungen)

1. You're not just anyone, you're God's own children, / yes, children of God, proved so by obedience. / You must not be a stupid person, / always driven anyhow by selfishness.

2. He's not just anyone! He who calls you is himself holy. / You mustn't live just anyhow, but as Christ lived. / Being holy is making God one's own.

3. He's not just anyone: the Father in his actions does not prefer you to others. / You mustn't live just anyhow, but spend the days that are yours with due care.

4. You're not just anyone, but all the same are slaves set free, free from the hue and cry of life. / He wasn't just anyone, for Christ gave up his life so that you might be free and might live.

F. Pratt Green 1972

(Verses spoken above improvised music: the refrain is sung and can be repeated)

74   T. de M. Oyens 1959

1. Zo - lang er Men - sen zijn op aar - de,
1. While still the world is full of peo - ple,
1. So - lang es Men - schen gibt auf Er - den,
1. Sans fin, Sei - gneur, Dieu no - tre Pè - re,

zo - lang de aar - de vruch - ten geeft,
and earth to man her in - crease gives,
so - lang die Er - de Früch - te trägt,
sans fin, Sei - gneur, nous te loue - rons:

zo - lang zijt Gij ons al - ler Va - der, wij
we give our thanks to you, the keep - er and
so - lang bist du uns al - len Va - ter, wir
la terre ex - ul - te d'al - lé - gres - se, bé -

dan - ken U voor al wat leeft.
Fa - ther God of all that lives.
dan - ken dir für das, was lebt.
ni sois - tu, Dieu des vi - vants.

138

2. Zolang de mensen woorden spreken, / zolang wij voor elkaar bestaan, / zolang zult Gij ons niet ontbreken, / wij danken U in Jezus' naam.

3. Gij voedt de vogels in de bomen, / Gij kleedt de bloemen op het veld, / O Heer Gij zijt ons onderkomen / en al mijn dagen zijn geteld.

4. Gij zijt ons licht, en eeuwig leven, / Gij redt de wereld van den dood, / Gij hebt uw Zoon aan ons gegeven, / Zÿn / lichaam is het levend brood.

5. Daarom moet alles U aanbidden, / uw liefde heeft het voortgebracht, / Vader, Gijzelf zijt in ons midden, / O Heer, wij zijn van uw geslacht.

Huub Oosterhius 1965

2. As long as human words are spoken / and for each other we exist, / you give your love as faithful token, / we thank you in the name of Christ.

3. You feed the birds in tree and rafter, / you clothe the flowers of the field. / You shelter us, now and hereafter, / and to your care our days we yield.

4. You are our light and our salvation, / you raise your people from the dead. / You gave your Son for every nation, / his body is the living bread.

5. The world is bound to bow before you, / you brought it by your love to birth, / you live among us, we adore you, / we are your children down to earth.

Fred Kaan 1972

2. Solang die Menschen Worte sprechen, / solang dein Wort zum Frieden ruft, / solang hast du uns nicht verlassen. / In Jesu Namen danken wir.

3. Du nährst die Vögel in den Bäumen. / Du schmückst die Blumen auf dem Feld. / Du machst ein Ende meinem Sorgen, / hast alle Tage schon bedacht.

4. Du bist das Licht, schenkst uns das Leben, / du holst die Welt aus ihrem Tod, / gibst deinen Sohn in unsre Hände, / er ist das Brot, das uns vereint.

5. Darum muß jeder zu dir rufen, / den deine Liebe leben läßt: / Du, Vater, bist in unsrer Mitte, / machst deinem Wesen uns verwandt.

Dieter Trautwein 1972

2. Sans fin, ton Verbe en nos paroles, / sans fin, Seigneur, te chantera; / l'amour s'éveille en nos cœurs d'hommes / au nom du Fils, ton Bien-aimé.

3. L'oiseau reçoit sa nourriture, / la fleur se pare de beauté; / tu aimes toute créature, / tu sais le prix de nos années.

4. Tu es, Seigneur, notre lumière, / toi seul nous sauve de la mort; / ton fils offert à tous les peuples / est pour chacun le Pain vivant.

5. Heureux les hommes qui t'adorent, / le monde ouvert à ton amour; / l'Esprit déjà te nomme Père: / un jour, Seigneur, nous te verrons.

Sœur Marie–Claire Sachot 1972

75

J. B. Fernandes, S. J. 1964

Refrain

This is my com - mand - ment: love one
Voi - ci mon com - man-de - ment: c'est de vous

an - oth - er as I have loved you.
ai - mer com - me je vous ai - me.

1. Charity is	kind	Charity feels	no	envy
2. Charity is	meek	Charity seeks	not	its own
3. Charity is	mild	Charity thinks	no	evil
4. Charity is	just	Charity finds	joy	in truth

Charity	bears up	to	the	end.
Charity has	faith	to	the	end.
Charity can	hope	to	the	end.
Charity is	patient	to	the	end.

T.: Scripture – I Cor. 13 and St. John 15
(F) J. Gelineau 1972

76

José Alves 1970

To - dos sa - be - rão que so - mos de
Ev' - ry - one will know that we are of
L'u - ni - vers sau - ra que le Christ est

Chris - to se nos a - mar - mos, se nos a -
Christ___, if___ we love___, if___ we
là si nous nous ai - mons, si nous nous ai -

mar - mos uns aos ou - tros. 1. Deus habita quem vive a
love___ one an - oth - er. 1. God dwells in him who
mons les uns les au - tres.

ca - ri - da - de: pois Deus é ca - ri - da - de.
lives by love___ because God is___ love___!

2. O pai nos amou com tanto amor / que para nossa vida enviou seu Filho amado.

3. Esta é a maravilha do amor / Foi Deus que nos amou por primeiro.

4. As trevas que sofremos passarão, / e brilhará todos nós a verdadeira luz.

Jo. 13.35: I Jo. 3.3-4.7

2. The Father loved us with so great a love / that for our life he sent his beloved Son.

3. This is the marvel of his love / that it was God who loved us first.

4. The shadows which we suffered have passed / and the true Light shall shine for us all.

arranged by Helena Scott 1973

F: Refrain: J. Gelineau 1973

77

Refrain   José Weber 1970

Em   Am

Pro - va   de   a - mor ma - ior   não   há
Great - er love has   no___   man   than   this:
La   plus gran - de   preu - ve   de   l'a - mour

B7   Em   Fine

que   dó - ar   a   vi - da   pa - lo ir - mão.
that he   give his life___   for   his   friends.
c'est don - ner   sa   vie   pour   ses   a - mis.

Solo   D

1. Eis   que   eu   vos   dou   o   meu
1. Now   I   give___   you   my   new   com -
1. Ce   Com - man - de - ment nou - veau   au - jour -

Bm   Em   Am

nô - vo   man - da - men - to: A - mai vos uns aos
mand - - - ment__: [—] Love___ one an -
d'hui je vous le donne__: Ai - mez - vous en - tre

D   Bm   D   G   D. C.

ou - tros co - mo   eu vos ten - ho a - man - do.
oth - er   as___   I   my - self have loved you.
vous___ com - me moi___ je vous ai - me.

2. Vós sereis os meus amigos, se seguirdes meu preceito: / Amaivos.

3. Como o pai sempre me ama assim também eu vos amei: / Amai-vos . . .

4. Permanecei em meu amor e segui meu mandamento. / Amai-vos . . .

5. E chegando a minha Páscoa vos amei até o fim: / Amai-vos . . .

6. Nisto todos saberao que vós sois os meus discípulos: / Amai-vos . . .

(Scripture)

2. You will be my friends if you follow my precept: / Love one another . . .

3. As the Father loves me always, so also have I loved you: / Love one another . . .

4. Be constant in my love and follow my commandment. / Love one another . . .

5. And approaching my Passover I have loved you to the end. / Love one another . . .

6. By this shall men know that you are my disciples. / Love one another . . .

arr. by Helena Scott 1973

2. Oui, vous êtes mes amis quand vous suivez ma parole: / Aimez-vous. . . .

3. Tel l'amour que j'ai pour vous, tel pour moi l'amour du Père: / Aimez-vous . . .

4. Demeurez dans mon amour, faites ce que je commande: / Aimez-vous . . .

5. O vous tous que j'ai aimés jusqu'à l'heure de ma Pâque: / Aimez-vous. . . .

6. A ceci tous connaîtront que vous êtes mes disciples: / Aimez-vous. . . .

J. F. Frié 1973

Jesus Christ · Jesus Christus
His Atonement, Resurrection and Reign
Sühne, Auferstehung und Herrschaft
Expiation, Resurrection et Règne

78

J. Gelineau 1965

Semi-chorus (men)

1. Par la Croix qui fit mou - rir le fils du
2. Par le Sang dont fut mar - qué le bois des
1. By the Cross which did to death our on - ly
2. By the Blood with which we marked the wood-en

Pè - re, sar - ment bé - ni où la grappe est
por - tes, pour nous gar - der dans la nuit où
Sa - viour, this bles - sed vine from which grapes are
lin - tels, for our pro - tec - tion the night when

All

ven - dan - gée, Jé - sus Christ, nous te bé - nis -
Dieu pas - sait, Jé - sus Christ, nous te bé - nis -
ga - thered in, Je - sus Christ, we thank and bless
God passed by, Je - sus Christ, we thank and bless

Semi-chorus (women or boys)

sons. Par la Croix qui met le feu sur no - tre
Par le Sang qui nous sau - va dans notre ex -
you. By the Cross which casts down fire up - on our
By the Blood which in our Ex - o - dus once

144

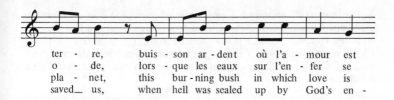

ter - re, buis - son ar - dent où l'a - mour est
o - de, lors - que les eaux sur l'en - fer se
pla - net, this bur - ning bush in which love is
saved— us, when hell was sealed up by God's en -

All

ré - vé - lé, Jé - sus Christ, nous te glo - ri -
re - fer - maient, Jé - sus Christ, we glo - ri - fy
plainly shown, Je - sus Christ, we glo - ri - fy
gul - fing sea,

Semi-chorus (Soprano and / or Tenor)

fions. Par la Croix qui fut plan - tée sur le Cal -
Par le Sang qui rend la vie aux sè - ves
you. By the Cross on Calv'ry's hill se - cure - ly
By the Blood which kills the poi - son in bad

vai - re, ra - meau vi - vant qui gué - rit de tout pé -
mor - tes, en dé - trui - sant le ve - nin du fruit mau -
plan - ted, this li - ving branch which can heal our ev' - ry
frui - tage, and gives new life to the dead sap in the

All

ché, Dieu vain - queur, ton é - gli - se t'ac - cla - me.
vais,
sin, Con - qu'ring God, we your peo - ple pro - claim— you!
tree,

145

3. Par la mort du premier-Né sur la colline / portant le bois et la flamme du bûcher, / Jésus-Christ, nous te bénissons. / Par la mort du Bon Pasteur dans les épines, / Agneau pascal dont le cœur est transpercé, / Jésus-Christ, nous te glorifions. / Par la mort du Bien-Aimé, hors de sa vigne, / pour qu'il changeât l'homicide en héritier, / Dieu vainqueur, ton Eglise t'acclame.

4. Par le Bois qui a chanté le chant des noces / du Dieu vivant épousant l'humanité, / Jésus Christ, nous te bénissons. / Par le Bois qui fait lever en pleine force / le Fils de l'Homme attirant le monde entier, / Jésus Christ, nous te glorifions. / Par le Bois où s'accomplit le Sacerdoce / du seul Grand Prêtre immolé pour le péché, / Dieu vainqueur, ton Eglise t'acclame.

5. Arbre saint qui touche au ciel depuis la terre / pour que le Dieu de Jacob soit exalté, / Jésus-Christ, nous te bénissons. / Grand Vaisseau qui nous arrache à la Colère / en nous sauvant du Déluge avec Noé, / Jésus Christ, nous te glorifions. / Tendre Bois qui adoucit les eaux amères / et fait jaillir la fontaine du Rocher, / Dieu vainqueur, ton Eglise t'acclame.

Didier Rimaud

3. By the Death on Calvary's hill of him the First-born / who bears the wood and the flame for his own pyre: / Jesus Christ, we thank and bless you! / By the Death, amid the thorns, of God's own Shepherd, / the Pascal Lamb who was pierced by our despair: / Christ Jesus, we glorify you! / By the Death of God's Beloved outside his vineyard, / that he might change us from murderer into heir: / Conquering God, we your Church proclaim you!

4. By the Wood which sings a song of nuptial gladness, / of God who takes for bride our human race: / Jesus Christ, we thank and bless you! / By the Wood which raises up in his full vigour / the Son of Man who draws all men by his grace: / Jesus Christ, we glorify you! / By the Wood where he perfects his royal Priesthood / in one High Priest who for sin is sacrifice: / Conquering God, we your Church proclaim you!

5. Holy Tree which reaches up from earth to heaven / that all the world may exult in Jacob's God: / Jesus Christ, we thank and bless you! / Mighty Ship which snatches us from God's deep anger, / saves us, with Noah, from drowning in the Flood: / Jesus Christ, we glorify you! / Tender Wood which gives to brackish water sweetness, / and from the Rock shall strike fountains for our good: / Conquering God, we your Church proclaim you!

F. Pratt Green 1972

79

2. To God and to the Lamb I will sing, I will sing, / to God and to the Lamb I will sing; / to God and to the Lamb who is the great I AM, / while millions join the theme, I will sing, I will sing, / while millions join the theme, I will sing.

3. And when from death I'm free I'll sing on, I'll sing on, / and when from death I'm free, I'll sing on. / And when from death I'm free I'll sing and joyful be. / And through eternity I'll sing on, I'll sing on, / and through eternity I'll sing on.

American folk hymn

2. Pour Dieu et pour l'Agneau, ma chanson, ma chanson, / pour Dieu et pour l'Agneau, ma chanson! / Pour Dieu et pour l'Agneau je chanterai d'amour, / par cent millions de voix, ma chanson, ma chanson, / par cent millions de voix, ma chanson!

3. A ma resurrection, chanterai, chanterai,/ a ma résurrection chanterai,/ a ma résurrection je danserai de joie / et pour l'éternité chanterai, chanterai, / et pour l'éternité chanterai.

Claude Rozier 1972

2. Gott und dem Sohn, dem Lamm, gilt mein Lied, gilt mein Lied, / Gott und dem Sohn, dem Lamm, gilt mein Lied! / Gott und dem Sohn, dem Lamm, dem, der sein „Ich bin" sagt; / Millionen haben teil, darum sing ich mein Lied. / Millionen haben teil, singt mein Lied.

3. Bin ich vom Tod befreit, sing ich weiter mein Lied. / Bin ich vom Tod befreit, klingt mein Lied. / Bin ich vom Tod befreit, sing ich und freue mich. / Und durch die Ewigkeit dringt mein Lied, dringt mein Lied, / und durch die Ewigkeit dringt mein Lied.

Dieter Trautwein 1972

80

John Ireland 1919

1. My song is love un - known, my Sa -viour's love to
2. He came from his blest throne, sal - va - tion to be -
1. Ich sin - ge Lie - be, dir, die du zu mir ge -
2. Mit Gott uns zu ver - ein'n, gab er sein Le - ben

me, love to the love - less shown, that they might
stow; but men made strange, and none the longed - for
bracht, den, der das Le - ben mir hat völ - lig
dran. Doch die da war'n die Sein'n, die nah - men

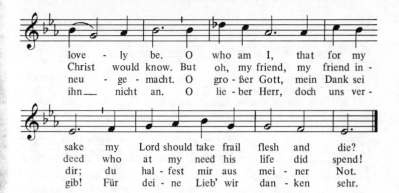

love - ly be. O who am I, that for my
Christ would know. But oh, my friend, my friend in -
neu - ge - macht. O gro - ßer Gott, mein Dank sei
ihn __ nicht an. O lie - ber Herr, doch uns ver -

sake my Lord should take frail flesh and die?
deed who at my need his life did spend!
dir; du hal - fest mir aus mei - ner Not.
gib! Für dei - ne Lieb' wir dan - ken sehr.

3. Sometimes they strew his way and his sweet praises sing; / resounding all the day hosannas to their King. / Then 'Crucify!' is all their breath, / and for his death they thirst and cry.

4. Why, what hath my Lord done? What makes this rage and spite? / He made the lame to run, he gave the blind their sight. / Sweet injuries! Yet they at these / themselves displease, and 'gainst him rise.

5. They rise, and needs will have my dear Lord made away; / a murderer they save, the Prince of Life they slay. / Yet cheerful he to suffering goes, / that he his foes from thence might free.

6. Here might I stay and sing. No story so divine; / never was love, dear King, never was grief like thine! / This is my friend in whose sweet praise / I all my days could gladly spend.

S. Crossman 1664

3. 'Gelobet sei der Herr', so grüßen sie ihn heut'. / 'O daß er tot erst wär', so schreiet bald die Meut'. / Am Kreuze stirbt er ohne Schuld. / Des Heilands Huld so um mich wirbt.

4. Was hat mein Herr getan? Er hieß die Lahmen gehn. / Gern half er jedermann und macht die Blinden sehn. / Ihr Zorn und Neid rafft ihn dahin, / zu töten ihn sind sie bereit.

5. Er stirbt, -es sollt so sein- am Kreuz an meiner Statt. / Den Mörder sie befrein, der Straf' verdienet hat. / Sein Leiden erst, sein Sterben dann / öffnen die Bahn zum Leben mir.

6. Solch große Liebestat besing ich Tag und Nacht, / die Liebe, die mir hat das Leben neu gemacht. / Mein Freud du bist, dir Dank ich bring, / dein Lob ich sing, Herr Jesu Christ.

Erich Griebling 1969

81

Verner Ahlberg 1933

1. De såg ej dig, blott tim - mer - man - nens
1. They saw you as the lo - cal buil - der's
1. Tu les sau - vais, mais ils ne t'ont pas
1. Sie sahn dich nicht — nur Zim - mer - man - nes

son. De såg ej dig, när de dig drev med
son, and there-fore out of house of prayer and
vu. Qu'é - tait pour eux, le fils du char - pen -
Sohn, so sahn sie dich. Sie jag - ten dich hin -

hån mot klip - pans brant och ut i en - sam
town they chased you, by your pro - phe - cy en -
tier? Sur la col - line ils t'ont a - ban - don -
aus in dun - kle Nacht, bis an der Klip - pe

natt. En falsk pro - fet de såg och en be - satt.
raged, in - to the dark - ness, to the moun-tain edge.
né, toi, Dieu vi - vant, qu'ils nont pas re - con - nu.
Rand, für sie ein Schwär - mer und ein Falsch-pro - phet.

2. De såg ej dig, du världens enda hopp, / när de drev spjut och spikar i din kropp. / Guds kärlek såg de ej, en utstött blott. / De såg ej dig som sonar allas brott.

3. De såg ej dig, din hand kring smärtan krökt, / den hand som världen byggt och syndarn sökt. / De såg ej dig, som under mörknad sol / lät korset blie en evig nådastol.

4. En gång vi alla ser den nåd du gav, / som floden sedd från källan till sitt hav. / Omkring din tron förbundets båge står / och allas sår har läkts i dina sår.

Anders Frostenson 1962

2. They did not see in you the nation's hope, / or see you take and drink the bitter cup. / They did not recognize the love divine / in you, who bore away our guilt and sin.

3. They did not see your hand in anguish curled, / your hand that heals, the hand that made the world. / They failed to see, when darkness came at noon, / that on your cross your saving work was done.

4. The time will come when every man shall see / your grace is like a stream that fills the sea. / You give us of your covenant the sign, / and in your wounds you heal all human pain.

Fred Kaan 1973

2. Ils n'ont su voir qu'un homme rejeté, / ils ont moqué le faux prophète mort. / Ils ont plongé la lance dans ton corps. / Ils n'ont pas vu l'espoir qui se levait.

3. Ils n'ont pas vu le signe sur ta main, / la main crispée du Maitre et créateur / qui bénissait le monde des pécheurs; / ils n'ont pas vu mourir le Saint des Saints.

4. Vienne le jour de toute Vérité / où nous aurons enfin les yeux ouverts / sur cette grâce et cet amour offerts. / Vienne le jour du Christ en majesté!

G. de Lioncourt 1972

2. Sie sahn dich nicht, der Menschen einzger Trost, / sie quälten dich mit Nägeln und dem Speer, / sahn Gottes Liebe nicht, den Ketzer nur. / Sie sahn dich nicht, der du die Schuldlast trägst.

3. Sie sahn dich nicht, sahn nicht den Schmerz der Hand, / die Sünder sucht, einst unsre Welt gebaut. / Sie sahn dich nicht, der du in Finsternis / dein Kreuz zum ewgen Gnadenstuhl gemacht.

4. Wir werden alle deine Gnade sehn / wie einen Fluß vom Quell bis an das Meer. / Das Bundesvolk steht rings um deinen Thron / und aller Wunden sind in dir Geheilt.

Helli Halbe 1972

82a

H. L. Haßler 1601, 1613

1. O Haupt voll Blut und Wun - den, voll Schmerz und vol - ler Hohn, o Haupt, zum Spott ge - bun - den mit ei - ner Dor - nen - kron, o Haupt, sonst schön ge - krö - net mit höch - ster Ehr und Zier, jetzt a - ber frech ver - höh - net: Ge - grü - ßet seist du mir.

1. O sac - red Head, sore wound - ed, with grief and shame weighed down; how scorn - ful - ly sur - round - ed with thorns thy on - ly crown; how art thou pale with an - guish, with sore a - buse and scorn; how does that vis - age lan - guish which once was bright as morn.

1. O dou - lou - reux vi - sa - ge de mon hum - ble Sei - gneur, ô tê - te sous l'ou - tra - ge, ô front sous la dou - leur; plein de beau - tés di - vi - nes dans les cieux in - fi - nis, c'est cou - ron - né d'é - pi - nes que je te vois i - ci.

1. O ca - po in - san - gui - na - to di Cris - to mio Si - gnor, di spi - ne co - ro - na - to, col - pi - to per a - mor. Per - ché so - no spie - ta - ti gli uo - mi - ni con te? Tu por - ti i miei pec - ca - ti: Ge - sù, pie - tà di me.

2. Was du, Herr, hast erduldet, / ist alles meine Last; / ich, ich hab es verschuldet, / was du getragen hast. / Schau her, hier steh ich Armer, / der Zorn verdienet hat; / gib mir, o mein Erbarmer, / den Anblick deiner Gnad.

3. Ich danke dir von Herzen, / o Jesu, liebster Freund, / für deines Todes Schmerzen, / da du's so gut gemeint. / Ach gib, daß ich mich halte, / zu dir und deiner Treu / und, wenn ich einst erkalte, / in dir mein Ende sei.

Paul Gerhardt 1656

2. Thy grief and bitter passion / were all for sinners' gain; / mine, mine was the transgression, / but thine the deadly pain. / Lo, here I fall, my Saviour, / 'tis I deserve thy place; / Look on me with thy favour, / vouchsafe to me thy grace.

3. What language shall I borrow / to thank thee, dearest friend, / for this, thy dying sorrow, / thy pity without end? / O make me thine for ever, / and, should I fainting be, / Lord, let me never, never / outlive my love to thee.

J. W. Alexander 1861

2. C'est toi que ma main blesse / c'est moi qui suis guéri; / c'est moi qui me redresse / c'est toi qui es meurtri; / quel étrange partage / de ma vie et ta mort, / où ta mort est le gage / que la vie est mon sort.

3. Parmi tant de blessures / de la lance et des clous, / parmi tes meurtrissures / la trace de mes coups; / et parmi tant d'offenses / ton seul, ton seul pardon, / et pour seule espérance / la force de ton nom.

(omettre cette strophe en chantant simultanément)

4. De l'humaine misère / tu t'es fait serviteur / de tout homme ton frère / tu portes la douleur. / Seigneur de nos souffrances / et de nos lendemains / garde notre espérance / en tes vivantes mains.

Henri Capieu 1950

2. Nell'ora della morte / il Padre ti salvò. / Trasforma la mia sorte: / con te risorgerò. / Contemplo la tua croce, / trionfo del mio re, / e chiedo la tua pace: / Gesù, pietà di me.

3. Mistero di dolore, / eterna carità! / Tu doni, o Redentore, / la vera libertà. / Fratello di ogni uomo / tu soffri insieme a noi; / speranza di perdono, / Gesù, pietà di me.

E.C.-G.S.

82b

1. O' fron-te en-san-güen-ta - do, em tan-to o-
1. Na - ku-sa-li-mu kich - wa ki - li-cho-

pró-bio e dor: de es- pi - nhos co-ro - a - da, com
jaa da-mu, ki - li-cho-vik - wa ta - ji ya

ó-dio e com fu-ror! Tão glo-rio-sa ou-
mii - ba mi-kub - wa, ki - li-cho-pa - ta

tro - ra, tão be-la, tão vi - ril! Tão a-ba-
en - zi kwa Mu-ngu mbin-gu-ni ki - tu-kan-

ti - da a - go - ra. De afron-te e es-cár-neo vil!
wa-cho sa - sa ma - tu-si ma-ka - li.

2. Estás tão carregado / mas todo o fardo é meu! / Eu só me fiz culpado / e o sofrimento é teu. / Venho aos teus pés, tremente / mereço a punição, / mas olhas-me clemente / com tanta compaixão.

3. Sê meu refúgio forte, / meu Guia e Vida e Luz! / Que eu sinta, vendo a morte / conforto em tua cruz. / Na cruz com fé me abrigo / se eu vir que ao lado estás, / eu me unirei contigo / e hei de dormir em paz!

Isaac N. Salum 1958

2. Mateso yaka Bwana, / yanipasa mimi. / Wewe waadhibishwa / kwa ajili yangu, / Hukumu unapata / iliyonipasa. / Bwanangu nakuomba, / unihurumie!

3. Bwana nayashukuru / masumbuko yako, / sababu ya kuteswa / na kufa kuchungu. / Wewe umenishika, / nami nakushika / mwisho nitakufia / uliyenifia.

1. 至聖之首受重創、希世痛苦難當；遍壓荊冠皆恥辱、
讒評嫌怨、憂傷；仰瞻慈容何慘淡！想見滿懷悽愴！
此刻愁雲掩聖範、當年基督輝光。

2. 眼見我主英勇力、戰爭中間消盡、眼見冷酷的死亡、
剝奪主身生命；嗚呼痛苦又死亡！因愛萬罪身當！懇
求施恩的耶穌、轉面容我仰望。

3. 我用何辭來感謝、如斯高誼奇恩、成仁臨難之悲哀、
無量慈悲憐憫？懇求收我為弟子、忠愛永不變更；千
萬千萬莫容我離開主愛偷生。

4. 將來與世長別時、懇求迅速來臨、賜我自由與安慰、
昭示寶架光明；凡百守信而死者、因愛雖死猶生；願
我微心起大信、與主永遠相親。阿們。

١. إِكْلِيلُهُ مَضْفُورٌ . بِالشَّوْكِ مِنْ أَجْلِي . يُدْمَى بِهِ جَبِينٌ . فَاقَ سَنا النُّبْلِ . قَدْ وَضَعْتُهُ أَيْدٍ . أَثِيمَةٌ لِلْعَارْ . تَاجًا لِرَاْسِ الْفَادِي . رَبِّ السَّمَاءِ الْبَارّْ

٢. قُوَّاكَ تَفْنِي حُزْنًا . بِأَلَمِ الصَّلِيبْ . دِمَاكَ تَجْرِى طُهْرًا . لِلصَّفْحِ يا حَبِيبْ . آلَامُكَ الْعَظِيمَةْ . تُخَفِّفُ الْأَثْقَالْ . وَرُوحُكَ الرَّحِيمَةْ . تُحْيِي بِنَا الآمَالْ

٣. تَحْتَ الصَّلِيبِ أَجْثُو . لِأَرْفَعَ الصَّلَاة . مُخَلِّصِي فَدَانِي . بِسَفْكِهِ دِمَاهْ . يَسُوعُ قَدْ هَدَانِي . فِي ظُلْمَةِ الْوُجُودْ . بِصَلْبِهِ أَحْيَانِي . فَفُزْتُ بِالْخُلُودْ

George Khoury

155

83

arranged by E. Miller 1731 - 1807

1. When I_____ sur - vey the won - drous
1. A l'heu - re dite il s'est dres -
1. Schau ich_____ dein Kreuz, o Hei - land
1. La cruz_____ ex - cel - sa al con - tem -

Cross on which the Prince of glo - ry
sé, clou - é en croix pour nos_____ pé -
an, an dem du star - best, Herr_____ und
plar, do mi Se - ñor por mi_____ mu -

died_____, my ri - chest gain I count_ but
chés_____, ra - meau plan - té sur fond_ de
Held_____, zer - bricht des Reich - tums blin - der
rió_____, Ya na - da pue - do com - pa -

loss and pour con - tempt on all_____ my pride.
ciel: son ombre an - non - ce le_____ so - leil.
Wahn und al - ler Stolz in nichts_ zer - fällt.
rar con las ri - que - zas de_____ su a - mor.

2. Forbid it, Lord, that I should boast / save in the death of Christ my God; / all the vain things I covet most / I sacrifice them to his blood.

3. See from his head, his hands, his feet / sorrow and love flow mingled down; / did e'er such love and sorrow meet, / or thorns compose so rich a crown?

4. His dying crimson like a robe / spreads o'er his body on the tree, / then am I dead to all the globe / and all the globe is dead to me.

5. Were the whole realm of nature mine / it were a present far too small, / love so amazing, so divine, / demands my soul, my life, my all.

Isaac Watts 1674–1748

2. Tu rend courage aux cœurs perdus, / ma vie attend ta mort, Jésus, / pour prendre goût à son destin: / ta croix rend libre le chemin.

3. Tes mains, tes pieds, ton corps charnel / seront marqués des coups mortels / portés pour nous par les soldats: / ton corps glorieux les gardera.

4. Le sang d'un Dieu s'est écoulé / du cœur d'un Homme transpercé! / mon cœur peut battre dans la paix, / la mort est sainte désormais.

5. Voici le monde et son destin / remis au Père par tes mains / où gît le signe de la Croix: / tu viens graver ta marque en moi.

Daniel Hameline 1972

2. Schütz' mich vor falscher Sicherheit! / Mein Ruhm in deinem Tode ruht. / Ich opfre Tand und Eitelkeit, / die mich umgarnen, deinem Blut.

3. Seht, wie von seinen Wunden her / das Blut der Liebe ihm entquillt! / Wo find ich solcher Liebe Meer, / wo solcher Krone Ebenbild?

4. Dich überströmt es scharlachrot, / gleich ein Gewand, am Marterstamm. / Mir ist die ganze Welt wie tot. / Ich sterb ihr an, du Gotteslamm!

5. Wie dank' ich Dir? 's wär' zu gering, / schenkt' ich der Erde Gold und Glanz. / Du, Liebe, die am Kreuze hing, / willst Leib und Seele, willst mich ganz.

Wilhelm Horkel 1950, 1972

2. No me permitas, Dios, gloriar / más que en la muerte del Señor. / Lo que más puede ambicionar / lo doy gozoso por su amor.

3. Ved en su rostro, manos, pies, / las marcas vivas del dolor; / es imposible comprender / tal sufrimiento y tanto amor.

4. Cual vestidura regia allí / la sangre cubre al Salvador, / y pues murió Jesús por mi / por El al mundo muero yo.

5. El mundo entero no será / presente digno de ofrecer; / amor tan grande, sin igual, / en cambio exige todo el ser.

W.T.T. Milham
(1a., 2a., 3a. y 5a. estrofa)
Trad. anónima (4a. estrofa)

1. Ni - mwo - na - po M - ti - bo -
1. Me - man - dang sa - lib yang a -
1. さ　か　え　の　主　イエス

ra Kri - sto a - li - po - ni - fi -
jaib dan wa - fat Ra - ja mu - li -
の　十　字　架　を　あ　お　け

a___, Kwa - ngu pa - to ni ha - sa -
a___, se - ri har - ta - ku ja - di
は　世　の　と　み　は　ま　れ

ra Ki - bu - ri na - ki - chu - ki - a.
aib, ge - nap po - ngah - ku ku - ce - la.
は　ち　り　に　ぞ　ひ　と　し　き

2. Na nisijivune, Bwana, / ila kwa mauti yako; / upuzi sitaki tena, / ni chini ya damu yako.

3. Tangu kichwa hata nyayo, / zamwagwa na hamu, / ndako pweke hamu hiẏo, / pendo zako zimetimu.

4. Vitu vyote vya dunia / si sadaka ya kutosha; / pendo zako zaniwia / nafsi, mali, na maisha.

2. B'ri, Tuhan, jangan 'ku menggah / selain di dalam salibMu; / kubuang hasrat yang fana / demi darahMu yang kudus.

3. Berpadu kasih dan sedih / memancur dari lukaMu / dan dari duri yang pedih / teranyamlah mahkotaMu!

4. Melihat jubah maut telah / melingkup tubuh Tuhanku, / 'ku mati bagi dunia / dan dunia mati bagiku.

5. Sekira jagat milikku, / tak cukup itu kuserah: / kasihMu tuntut hatiku; / diriku, Tuhan, t'rimalah!

Yayasan Musik Gerejani 1973

2. 十字架のほかには　はこりはあらされ、
　この世のものみな　消えなは消えされ．

3. みよ主のみかしら　み手みあしよりぞ、
　めぐみとかなしみ　てもでもながるる．

4. めぐみとかなしみ　ひとつにとけあい、
　いばらはまばゆき　かむりとかがやく．

5. ああ主のめぐみに　むくゆるすべなし、
　ただ身とたまとを　ささげてぬかずく．

1. حِينَ أَرَى صَلِيبَ مَنْ ، قَضَى فَحَازَ ٱلْإِنْتِصَارْ ، رِبْحِي أَرَى خَسَارَةً ،
وَكُلَّ مَجْدِ ٱلْكَوْنِ عَارْ

2. يَا رَبِّى لَا تَسْمَحْ بِأَنْ ، أَفْخَرَ إِلَّا بِالصَّلِيبْ ، مُكَرِّسًا نَفْسِي وَمَا ،
أَمْلِكُ لِلْفَادِي الْحَبِيبْ

3. أَيُّ دَمٍ زَاكٍ جَرَى ، كَدَمِهِ ٱلزَّاكِي ٱلثَّمِينْ ، وَأَيُّ تَاجٍ مِثْلَ تَا جِ
الشَّوْكِ أَحْيَا الْعَالَمِينْ

4. بِمَ أَكَافِي مُنْقِذِي ، مِنْ سُلْطَةِ الْخَطِيئَةْ ، إِلَّا بِتَكْرِيسِي لَهُ نَفْسِي ،
وَكُلَّ قُوَّتِي

Salim Abdel Ahad

159

84

Melchior Vulpius 1609

1. Ge - lobt sei Gott im höch - sten Thron
1. Good Christ - ian men, re - joice and sing!
1. Lou - ange à toi, Sei - gneur Jé - sus,

samt sei - nem ein - ge - bor - nen Sohn,
Now is the tri - umph of our King!
l'hum - ble che - min de ta ve - nue,

der für uns hat ge - nug ge - tan. Hal - le - lu -
To all the world glad news we bring: Al - le - lu -
l'a - mour tri - om - phe par la croix: Al - lé - lu -

ja_____, Hal - le - lu - ja_____, Hal - le - lu - ja.
ia_____, al - le - lu - ia_____, al - le - lu - ia!
ia_____, al - lé - lu - ia_____, al - lé - lu - ia!

2. Er ist erstanden von dem Tod, / hat überwunden alle Not; / kommt, seht, wo er gelegen hat. / Halleluja, halleluja, halleluja.

3. Nun bitten wir dich, Jesu Christ, / weil du vom Tod erstanden bist, / verleihe, was uns selig ist. / Halleluja, halleluja, halleluja.

4. Damit von Sünden wir befreit / dem Namen dein gebenedeit, / frei mögen singen allezeit: / Halleluja, halleluja, halleluja.

Michael Weisse gest. 1534

2. The Lord of life is risen for aye; / bring flowers of song to strew his way; / let all mankind rejoice and say: / Alleluia, alleluia, alleluia!

3. Praise we in songs of victory / that love, that life which cannot die, / and sing with hearts uplifted high: / Alleluia, alleluia, alleluia!

4. Thy name we bless, O risen Lord, / and sing today with one accord, / the life laid down, the life restored: / Alleluia, alleluia, alleluia!

C.A. Alington 1931

2. La mort n'a pu garder sa proie, / l'enfer vaincu s'ouvre à ta voix. / Guide nos pas jusqu'au salut. / Alléluia, alléluia, alléluia.

3. Voici la tombe descellée, / et ses témoins, pour l'annoncer, / sont envoyés au monde entier. / Alléluia, alléluia, alléluia.

4. Tu est vivant, gloire à ton nom! / Hâte le temps où nous pourrons / vivre sans fin dans ta maison. / Alléluia, alléluia, alléluia.

Frère Pierre-Yves 1973

Negro Spiritual
Edited by John W. Work, 1940

85

He is King of kings, he is Lord of lords,
Je - sus Christ the first and last__, no man works like him.

Solo
1. He built his throne up in the air __,
2. He pitched his tents on Ca - naan's ground,

no man works like him, and called his saints from
and broke the Ro - man

ev' - ry - where__, no man works like him.
king - dom down__,

161

86

Traditional melody from Cameroun

3. Dans la Chambre Haute, la Table est dressée; / le pain et le vin y sont partagés. (Refrain A)

4. En lavant les pieds comme un serviteur, / il annonce aux siens son abaissement. (Refrain A)

5. Tous sont avec lui à Gethsemané; / mais devant Pilate seul il s'est trouvé. (Refrain A)

6. Pilate a jugé: il est innocent; / son peuple a crié: ôte et crucifie. (Refrain A)

7. Avant le sabbat tout est terminé; / et dans son tombeau Christ est enfermé. (Refrain A)

8. Où sont les disciples? où sont ses amis? / Le Seigneur est mort, tout est donc fini? / Pause (sans Refrain)

9. Au troisième jour la nouvelle court: / tout n'est pas fini: Jésus est vivant. / (Refrain B, bis)

10. Il est tout amour, il mourut pour nous; / il vainquit la mort, il nous rend vainqueurs. / (Refrain B)

Abel Nkuinji 1965

3. The Table is set in an upper room; / the bread and the wine foretell his doom. (Refrain A)

4. In form of a servant he washes their feet, / and says 'thus humbly each other greet.' (Refrain A)

5. They all go with him to Gethsemane, / but in Pilate's courts there is none but he. (Refrain A)

6. 'Not guilty', says Pilate, and washes his hands. / 'Away with him now!' the crowd demands. (Refrain A)

7. Before evening falls, it all is done; / the tomb receives our Holy One. (Refrain A)

8. Where are the disciples? where now are his friends? / The Lord is dead: and here all hope ends . . . Pause (no Refrain)

9. Two nights and a day, and the news is abroad: / not end but beginning! alive is the Lord! (Refrain B – twice)

10. So praise we God's love for what Jesus has done. / Now death is defeated, and victory won. / (Refrain B)

Erik Routley 1972

87

Joas Kijugo 1964

Solo

(1) 1. Bwa - na   Ye - su   ka - fu -   fu - ka,   a - me -
    1. Christ is   ri - sen, death is   van - quished, he   has
    1. Ve - nez   voir,   la tombe est   vi - de,   Jé - sus

All

to - ka   ka - bu -   ri - ni.
left   the   tomb's dark   pri - son.
vient,   il   res - sus -   ci - te.

Hal - le - lu - ia,   Hal - le - lu - ia,
Al - le - lu - ia,   Al - le - lu - ia,
Al - lé - lu - ia,   Al - lé - lu - ia,

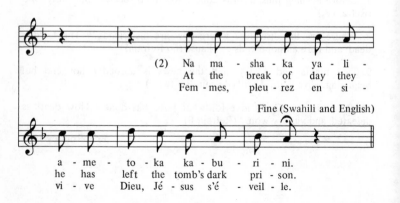

(2) Na ma - sha - ka   ya - li -
    At the   break of   day they
    Fem - mes,   pleu - rez   en si -

Fine (Swahili and English)

a - me -   to - ka   ka - bu -   ri - ni.
he has   left   the tomb's dark   pri - son.
vi - ve   Dieu, Jé - sus s'é -   veil - le.

164

zu - ka, ha - pa - ku - wa tu - ma - i - ni.
doubt-ed; hope had va - nished; life had left them.
len - ce.. plus de foi, plus d'es - pé - ran - ce.

Hal - le - lu - ia, Hal - le -
Al - le - lu - ia, Al - le -
Al - lé - lu - ia, Al - lé -

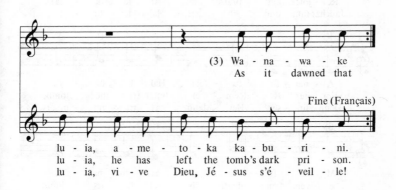

(3) Wa - na - wa - ke
As it dawned that

Fine (Français)

lu - ia, a - me - to - ka ka - bu - ri - ni.
lu - ia, he has left the tomb's dark pri - son.
lu - ia, vi - ve Dieu, Jé - sus s'é - veil - le!

(Sw.) Joas Kijugo 1964
(E.) Erik Routley 1972
(F.) N. Berthet 1972

88

Solo

Tanzanian Melody

1. M- fu - ra - hi - ni, Hal - le - lu - ya,
1. He has a - ri - sen, Al - le - lu - ia!
1. Er ist er - stan - den, Hal - le - lu - ja.

M- ko - mbo - zi a - me - fu - fu - ka.
Re - joice and praise him; Al - le - lu - ia!
Jauchzt ihm und sin - get, Hal - le - lu - ja.

A - me - fu - fu - ka, Hal - le - lu - ya.
For our Re - deem - er burst from the tomb,
Denn un - ser Hei - land hat tri - um - phiert,

M- si - fu - ni sa - sa yu ha - i.
e - ven from death, dis - pel - ling its gloom.
all sei - ne Feind' ge - fan - gen er führt.

All

Tu - mwi - mbi - e so - te kwa fu - ra - ha.
Let us sing praise to him with end - less joy.
Laßt uns froh - lo - cken vor un - se - rem Gott,

Ye - su a - me - to - ka ka - bu - ri - ni.
Death's fear - ful sting he has come to de - stroy.
der uns er - lö - set vom e - wi - gen Tod.

Ka - shin - da Ki - fo, Hal - le - lu - ya,
Our sins for - gi - ving, Al - le - lu - ia!
Sünd' ist ver - ge - ben, Hal - le - lu - ja.

Hal - le - lu - ya, Ye - su yu ha - i.
Je - sus is li - ving, Al - le - lu - ia!
Je - sus bringt Le - ben, Hal - le - lu - ja.

2. Amefufuka Mkombozi, / Halleluya, tushangilie. / Nguvu za mwovu ameshinda. / Ametuondoa kufani. / Tumwimbiesote . . .

3. Malaika aliwaambia / Wanawake, 'Msiogope. / Sasa kaburi lipo tupu, / Kwani Yesu amefufuka.' / Tumwimbiesote . . .

4. 'Amebatilisha Shetani. / Amewaletea wokovu. / Kwa hiyo ninyi mtangaze, / Ni hakika, Yesu yu hai.' / Tumwimbiesote . . .

Bernard Kyamanywa

2. For three long days the grave did its worst, / until its strength by God was dispersed. / He who gives life did death undergo, / and in its conquest his might did show. / Let us sing praise . . .

3. The angel said to them, 'Do not fear, / you look for Jesus who is not here. / See for yourselves, the tomb is all bare: / only the grave-clothes are lying there.' / Let us sing praise . . .

4. Go spread the news, he's not in the grave. / He has arisen, mankind to save. / Jesus' redeeming labours are done. / Even the battle with sin is won. / Let us sing praise . . .

Howard S. Olson 1969

2. Er war begraben drei Tage lang, / ihm sei auf ewig Lob, Preis und Dank; / doch die Gewalt des Tods ist zerstört; / selig ist, wer zu Jesus gehört. / Laßt uns frohlocken . . .

3. Der Engel sagte: 'Fürchtet euch nicht! / Ihr suchet Jesus, er ist hier nicht. / Seht die Stätte, wo er einst lag: / er ist erstanden, wie er gesagt.' / Laßt uns frohlocken . . .

4. 'Geht und verkündigt, daß Jesus lebt, / er lebt in allem, was lebt und webt. / Was Gott geboten, ist nun vollbracht, / Christus hat's Leben wiedergebracht.' / Laßt uns frohlocken . . .

U. S. Leupold 1969

89

Pablo D. Sosa 1960

1. Cris - to vi - ve, fue - ra el llan - to, los la -
1. Christ is ri - sen, Christ is li - ving, dry your
1. Chri - stus lebt, drum laßt das Jam - mern, al - le
1. Le Sei - gneur vit! Plus de lar - mes, plus de

men - tos y el pe - sar! Ni la muer - te ni el se -
tears, be un - a - fraid! Death and dark - ness could not
Kla - gen und das Leid! Denn vom Kreuz, von To - des -
plain - tes, plus de peurs! Ni la mort, ni le sé -

pul - cro lo han po - di - do su - je - tar. No bus -
hold him, nor the tomb in which he laid. Do not
schat - ten ist der Hei - land längst be - freit. Sucht nun
pul - cre, de Lui, n'ont é - té vain - queurs! Il n'est

qué - is en - tre los muer - tos al que
look a - mong the dead for one who
nicht mehr bei den To - ten ihn, der
pas en - tre les morts Ce - lui qui

siem - pre ha de vi - vir. Cris - to vi - ve!
lives for e - ver - more; tell the world that
uns am Le - ben hält. Chri - stus lebt, drum
pour tou - jours vi - vra! Jé - sus vit, et

168

	C	G	Bm	Em

es - tas   nue - vas   por do - quier   de - jad   o - ir.
Christ is   ri - sen,   make it   known he goes   be - fore.
sagt es   wei - ter   al - len   Men - schen in   der   Welt.
la nou - vel - le   par le   mon - de s'en   i - ra!

2. Que si Cristo no viviera / Vana fuera nuestra fe. / Mas se cumple su promesa: / 'Porque vivo, viviréis.' / Si en Adán entró la muerte, / por Jesús la vida entró; / No temáis, el triunfo es vuestro: /¡El Señor resucitó!

3. Si es verdad que de la muerte / El pecado es aguijón, / No temáis pues Jesucristo / Nos da vida y salvación. / Gracias demos al Dios Padre / Que nos da seguridad, / Que quien cree en Jesucristo / Vive por la eternidad.

Nicolas Martinez 1960

2. If the Lord had never risen, / we'd have nothing to believe. / But his promise can be trusted: / 'You will live, because I live.' / As we share the death of Adam, / so in Christ we live again. / Death has lost its sting and terror. / Christ the Lord has come to reign.

3. Death has lost its old dominion, / let the world rejoice and shout! / Christ, the firstborn of the living / gives us life and leads us out. / Let us thank our God who causes / hope to spring up from the ground. / Christ is risen, Christ is giving / life eternal, life profound.

Fred Kaan 1972

2. Wäre Christus nicht am Leben, / wär der Glaube Schall und Rauch. / Doch nun ging es in Erfüllung: / Weil ich lebe, lebt ihr auch, / müssen wir mit Adam sterben, / so mit Jesus aufersteh'n! / Alle Furcht hat nun ein Ende: / Weil wir in das Leben geh'n!

3. Ist die Sünde doch der Stachel, / der zum Tode führt die Welt, / laßt uns alle Angst vergessen, / Jesus hat die Nacht erhellt! / Dank sei dem Herrn gesungen, / er schenkt uns die Sicherheit; / wer schon hier gebaut auf Christus, / lebt mit ihm in Ewigkeit!

Arthur Blatezky 1972

2. Si le Christ ne ressuscite / vaine alors est notre foi! / Mais Il tient cette promesse: / 'Vous vivrez tous comme moi!' / Par Adam nous vient la mort. / La vie, Jésus nous l'a donnée! / Plus de peur! C'est la victoire / du Seigneur ressuscité!

3. La mort tient de notre faute, / du péché, son aiguillon. / N'ayez crainte, Jésus donne / et la vie et le pardon. / Rendons grâces! Dieu le Père / nous veut en sécurité. / En Jésus, si l'homme espère, / il vivra l'éternité!

J.F. Frié 1972

90

Persian Melody

1. Spread the news that＿ our world is re-
1. En - ton - nez un chant nou - veau, tout re -

deemed through and through, each from slum - ber＿ so
vient à la vie; cé - lé - brez des jours plus

deep wakes to bright - ness a - new. See the heav - ens a -
beaux car la mort s'est en - fuie. Le Sei - gneur est plus

blaze with the co - lours＿ of dawn, and the
fort que la mort, il est vi - vant, li - bé -

gar - dens do laugh as their wee - ping is gone.
rés a - vec lui, fê - tons - le en chan - tant.

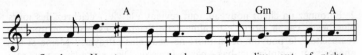

See how Na - ture, once dead, comes a - live out of night,
Tout re - prend un vi - sage au so - leil du ma - tin,

how the sun o - ver land casts a man - tle of light:
re - gar - dons la lu - mière, ou - bli - ons nos cha - grins,

For the Christ, who for us took the place of — a slave,
le Sei - gneur est plus fort que la mort, il est vi - vant.

gave us free - dom and life as he rose from the grave:
Tri - om - phant de la nuit il nous ouvre un che - min,

gave us free - dom and life as he rose from the dead.
il est vie, li - ber - té, pour un jour sans dé - clin.

2. Spread the news! look abroad! He has risen to reign! / Now at last heav'n is open'd to earth once again. / Now that death's power is spent and is vanquish'd for aye, / who should fear any storm, who now cringe in dismay? / Lift your eyes to the hills, greet the bright rising sun; / now our hearts and our souls are renewed all as one! / See, the tomb is found bare; this the work of God's hand; / see our Jesus now ris'n! In this faith may we stand: / see our Jesus now ris'n! In this faith may we stand!

Lewis Johnson 1969

2. Entonnez un chant nouveau, tout revient à la vie; / célébrez des jours plus beaux car la mort s'est enfuie. / Le Seigneur est sorti du tombeau ressuscité; / le pouvoir de la mort ne peut plus effrayer. / Même si nos années sont comptées ici-bas / par la force de Dieu notre chair revivra. / Le Seigneur est sorti du tombeau ressuscité. / La puissance de Dieu nous a tous libérés; / maintenant nous aussi, nous pouvons espérer.

G. Comment 1972

(ویژه پرستش سپیده دم عید قیام)

۱ ــ مژده بادا که نو شد سراسر جهان! گشته بیدار گیتی ز خواب گران! بین چگونه شود رنگ رنگ آسمان! که کند گریه که خنده بر بوستان. بر طبیعت نگر مرده بد زنده شد! در جهان پرتو مهر تابنده شد. آن مسیحی که از بهر ما بنده شد، مرد و برخاست ما را رهاننده شد!

۲ ــ مژده آمد که اینك قیامش ببین! باز شدتا ابد آسمان بر زمین! موت دیگر نبد قدرتش بیش از این. از چه ترسم دگر از چه باشم حزین؟ سر بر آر از افق مهر تابان ما! بین چسان تازه گشته تن و جان ما! قبر خالی نگر! کار یزدان ما؟ زنده عیسی ببین! اصل ایمان ما.

Persian text by Hassan Dehqani (Anglican Church in Iran)

91

Anon. 13 th century

1. Christ ist er - stan - den ___ von der Mar -
2. Wär er nicht er - stan - den, so wär die Welt
1. Christ is now ris'n a - gain ___ from his death
2. Had he not ris'n a - gain ___ we had been
1. Christ res - sus - ci - te ___ hors de tout
2. Les en - fers suc - com - bent, il a vain - cu

ter al - le; des soll'n wir al - le
ver - gan - gen; seit daß er er -
and all his pain; there - fore will we
lost, this is plain; but since he is
sup - pli - ce. Ré - jou - is - sons - nous
la tom - be, il a en - ten -

froh ___ sein ___, Christ will un - ser Trost ___
stan - den ist, so freut sich al - les, was da
mer - ry be ___, and re - joice with him glad -
ris'n in - deed ___ let us love him with all
en - ce jour ___, Christ vi - vant l'est pour tou -
du nos cris. Lou- ange au Pè - re, gloire au

sein. Ky - ri - e - leis!
ist. Ky - ri - e - leis!
ly. Ky - ri - e - leis!
speed. Ky - ri - e - leis!
jours. Ky - ri - e - leis!
Fils! Ky - ri - e - leis!

3. Hal - le - lu - ja!
3. Al - le - lu - ia!
3. Al - lé - lu - ia!

Hal - le - lu - ja! Hal - le - lu - ja!
Al - le - lu - ia! Al - le - lu - ia!
Al - lé - lu - ia! Al - lé - lu - ia!

173

Des soll'n wir al - le froh___ sein, Christ
There - fore will we mer - ry be, and
Ré - jou - is - sons - nous en ce jour, Christ

will un - ser Trost___ sein. Ky - ri - e - leis!
re - joice with him glad - ly. Ky - ri - e - leis!
vi - vant l'est pour tou - jours. Ky - ri - e - leis!

D. Anon. 13. Jh.
E. Miles Coverdale 1538

92

Martin Luther 1524

1. Christ lag in To - des - ban - den, für un -
1. Christ Je - sus lay in death's strong bands, for our
1. Christ est res - sus - ci - té des morts, car Dieu

ser Sünd ge - ge - ben, der ist wie - der er -
of - fen - ces___ gi - ven, but now at God's right
nous est fi - dè - le. Il donne à nos cœurs

stan - den und hat uns bracht das___ Le - ben.
hand he stands and brings us life from___ hea - ven.
et nos corps, la vie en - fin nou - vel - le.

Des wir sol - len fröh - lich sein, Gott lo -
Where - fore let us joy - ful be, and sing
Et voi - ci a - vec son roi l'é - té

- ben und dank - bar sein, und sin - gen
to God right thank - ful - ly loud songs of
du - ra - ble de la joie, Chan-tons tous,

Hal - le - lu - - ja! Hal - le - lu - ja!
Al - le - lu - - ia! Al - le - lu - ia!
Al - lé - lu - - ia! Al - lé - lu - ia!

2. Es war ein wunderlich Krieg, / da Tod und Leben rungen; / das Leben behielt den Sieg, / es hat den Tod verschlungen. / Die Schrift verkündet das, / wie ein Tod den andern fraß, / ein Spott aus dem Tod ist worden. / Halleluja!

3. So feiern wir das hohe Fest / mit Herzensfreud und Wonne, / das uns der Herr scheinen läßt, / er ist selber die Sonne. / Der durch seiner Gnaden Glanz, / erleucht' unsrer Herzen ganz, / der Sünden Nacht ist vergangen. / Halleluja!

Martin Luther 1524

2. It was a strange and dreadful strife, / when death and life contended. / The victory remained with life; / the reign of death was ended. / Stript of power no more he reigns, / an empty form alone remains; / his sting is lost for ever. / Alleluia!

3. So let us keep the festival / whereto the Lord invites us. / Christ is himself the joy of all, / the sun that warms and lights us. / By his grace he doth impart / eternal sunshine to the heart; / the night of sin is ended. / Alleluia!

R. Massie 1854

2. Il efface tous nos péchés / par sa mort en silence. / A tous les siens il vient montrer / l'éclat de sa puissance. / Terre et cieux, il faut chanter / la force de sa vérité. / Chantons tous, alléluia! / Alléluia!

3. Il vient pour nous donner le pain, / le pain, le vin, la grâce. / Prendre les hommes par la main, / sa droite est notre place. / Nous chantons sa royauté, / nous chanterons l'éternité. / Chantons tous, alléluia! / Alléluia!

H. Capieu 1972

93

Georg Friedrich Händel 1746

1. A toi la gloire, ô___ Res - sus - ci - té!
1. Yours be the glo - ry, yours O___ ri - sen friend!
1. Cri - sto è ri - sor - to, a - lle - lu - ia!
1. A tí la glo - ria, o___ nues - tro Se - ñor!

A___ toi la vic - toi - re, pour l'é - ter - ni - té!
You have won for e - ver vic - t'ry with - out end!
Vinta è or - mai la mor - te, a - lle - lu - ia!
A___ tí___ la vic - to - ria, gran li - ber - ta - dor.

Bril - lant___ de lu - miè - re, l'ange est de - scen - du,
O___ how bright an an - gel rolls the stone a - way,
Can - ti l'u - ni - ver - so, a - lle - lu - ia!
Te___ alza - ste pu - jan - te, lle - no de po - der,

il___ rou - le la pier - re du tom - beau vain - cu.
con - quer'd is the tomb in which your bo - dy lay.
Un___ i - nno di gio - ia al nostro Re - den - tor.
más que el sol ra - di - an - te al a - ma - ne - cer.

A toi la gloi - re, ô___ Res - sus - ci - té!
Yours be the glo - ry, yours, O___ ri - sen friend!
Cri - sto è ri - sor - to, a - lle - lu - ia!
A tí la glo - ria, o___ nues - tro Se - ñor!

A___ toi___ la vic - toi - re pour l'é - ter - ni - té!
You have won for e - ver vic - t'ry with - out end.
Vinta è or - mai la mor - te, a - lle - lu - ia!
A___ tí___ la vic - to - ria, gran li - ber - ta - dor.

176

2. Vois-le paraître, c'est lui, c'est Jésus, / ton Sauveur, ton Maître; Ôh! ne doute plus; / sois dans l'allégresse, peuple du Seigneur, / et redis sans cesse que Christ est vainqueur! / A toi la gloire, Ô Ressuscité! / A toi la victoire pour l'éternité.

3. Craindrais-je encore? Il vit à jamais, / celui que j'adore, le Prince de paix; / il est ma victoire, mon puissant soutien, / ma vie et ma gloire, non, je ne crains rien! / A toi la gloire, Ô Ressuscité! / A toi la victoire pour l'éternité.

Edmond Bury 1904

2. See, here is Jesus! who else could it be? / He, your Lord and Saviour, surely it is he! / Happy Church of Jesus, you who doubt no more, / never cease to tell us Christ is conqueror! / Yours be the glory, yours O risen Friend! / You have won for ever vict'ry without end.

3. He lives for ever! Bids me fear no more; / he is Prince of Peace! the one whom I adore. / With him to support me, vict'ry shall be won: / Now, my life, my glory, ev'ry fear is gone! / Yours be the glory, yours O risen Friend! / You have won for ever vict'ry without end.

F. Pratt Green 1971

2. Cristo è risorto, alleluia! / dona a noi la vita, alleluia! / Con la sua morte, alleluia! / ha ridato ·all'uomo la vera libertà. / Cristo è risorto, alleluia! / Vinta è ormai la morte, alleluia!

3. Cristo è risorto, alleluia! / dona a noi l'amore, alleluia! / Segno di speranza, alleluia! / luce di salvezza per questa umanità. / Cristo è risorto, alleluia! / Vinta è ormai la morte, alleluia!

Mario Piatti

2. Gozo, alegría, reinen por doquier, / porque Cristo hoy día muestra su poder; / ángeles cantando himnos al Señor / vanle adorando como vencedor. / ¡A tí la gloria, O nuestro Señor! / ¡A tí la victoria, gran libertador!

3. Libre de penas, nuestro Rey Jesús, / Rompe las cadenas de la esclavitud. / Ha resucitado, ¡ya no morirá! / Quien muera al pecado en Dios vivirá. / ¡A tí la gloria, O nuestro Señor! / ¡A tí victoria, gran libertador!

anónima

94

1. Christ the Lord is ris'n to-day__. Al - le - lu - ia!
1. Un nou-veau ma - tin se lè - ve. Al - lé - lu - ia!
1. Christ, der Herr ist heut er-stan-den. Hal - le - lu - ja!
1. El Se - ñor re - su - ci - tó__, A - le - lu - ya!

Sons of men and an - gels say__: Al - - le -
Pre - mier jour de la se - mai - ne. Al - - lé -
Mensch und En - gel freu - en sich__. Hal - - le -
Muer-te y tum - ba ya ven - ció__. A - - le -

lu - ia! Raise your joys and tri - umphs high:
lu - ia! Re - gar - dez ma joie bril - ler.
lu - ja! Singt von Her - zen un - serm Gott!
lu - ya! Con su fuer - za y su vir - tud

Al - - le - lu - ia! Sing_, ye_heav'ns, and
Al - - lé - lu - ia! C'est Jé - sus qui
Hal - - le - lu - ja! Him - mel_, Er - de
Al - - le - lu - ya! Cau - ti - vó la es -

earth re - ply__. Al - - le - lu - ia!
se re - lè - ve. Al - - lé - lu - ia!
sa - ge Dank_. Hal - - le - lu - ja!
cla - vi - tud__. Al - - le - lu - ya!

178

2. Love's redeeming work is done. / Fought the fight, the battle won; /
Lo, our Sun's eclipse is o'er; / Lo, he sets in blood no more.

3. Vain the stone, the watch, the seal; / Christ has burst the gates of
hell; / Death in vain forbids him rise; / Christ has opened Paradise.

4. Lives again our glorious King; / Where, O Death, is now thy sting? /
Once he died our souls to save; / Where thy victory, O grave?

Charles Wesley 1739

2. Tombeau vide et plus de gardes / Seul les anges me regardent, /
Entonnez de nouveaux chants: / C'est Jésus qui nous fait vivre. /

3. Le jardin est clair et calme, / Le Seigneur est là qui parle, / J'ai cru
voir le jardinier: / C'est Jésus qui est lumière.

4. Il m'envoie vers vous mes frères / Lui déjà il nous précède, / Ecoutez
mes compagnons: / C'est Jésus qui nous appelle.

N. Berthet

2. Christi Werk ist nun vollendet; / aus der Kampf, der Sieg ist da! /
Seht, die Schatten lichten sich, / strahlend geht die Sonne auf.

3. Stein und Wache sind vergebens, / und das Siegel ist zerbrochen. /
Auch der Tod kann ihn nicht halten. / Christus schenkt uns neues Leben.

4. Unser Herr, er lebt auch heute, / Tod, du hast dein Spiel verloren. /
Jesus holt uns aus der Angst. / Singt mit uns das Lied der Freude.

Emil Schaller und Gruppe, 1972

2. El que al polvo se humilló, / Vencedor se levantó: / Canta hoy la
cristiandad / Su gloriosa majestad.

3. Cristo, que la cruz sufrió, / Y en desolación se vió, / Hoy en gloria
celestial / Reina vivo e inmortal.

4. Cristo, nuestro Salvador, / De la muerte triunfador, / Haznos siempre
en tí confiar. / Cantaremos sin cesar.

Trad. J. B. Cabrera

1. E' ri-sor-to il Sal-va-to-re, al - le - lu - ia:
1. Bwa-na a-me-fu-fu-ka___, Al - le - lu - ya!
1. すくいのぬしは ハ レ ル ヤ

ques-to é gior-no di spe-ran-za, al - - - le -
Tu-im-be na-ma-la-i-ka, A - - -le -
よみがえりたもう ハ レ

lu - - ia. Cris-to vi-ve in mez-zo a noi,
lù - - ya. Si-fa ze-tu na shang-we,
ル ヤ かちどき あけて

a - - -le - lu - ia: non__ più__ mor-te
A - - -le - lu - ya. Na__ zao__ zi - si
ハ レ ル ヤ み名をた

né do-lo - re, a - - - le - lu - ia.
teng - we___ A - - - le - lu - ya.
たえよ ハ レ ル ヤ

2. Nella fede e nell'amore / annunciamo la salvezza / e per questa umanità / nuovi cieli e terra nuova.

M. Piatti

2. Ukombozi timamu / Umetimu kwa damu, / Mshindi asifiwe, / Yu hai kwa milele.

3. Jiwe, lindo, muhuri, / Vi wapi? na kaburi? / Kifo hakimuweki, / Ametoka peponi.

4. Yu hai Mtukufu, / Cha kifo hatuhofu! / Alitufia sisi, / Tuwe mahuru nasi.

2. 十字架をしのび　　ハレルヤ、
　　死にて死にかち　　ハレルヤ。
　　生きていのちを　　ハレルヤ、
　　ひとにぞたもう　　ハレルヤ。

3. 主の死によりて　　ハレルヤ、
　　すくいはなりぬ　　ハレルヤ。
　　あまつつかいと　　ハレルヤ、
　　ともにぞうたわん　ハレルヤ。

1. اَلْمَسِيحُ الْيَوْمَ قَامَ هَلِلُويَا ۰ فَائِزًا بِالظَّفَرِ هَلِلُويَا ۰ بَعْدَ حَرْبٍ وَصِدَامْ هَلِلُويَا ۰ مَعْ عَدُ وَالْبَشَرِ هَلِلُويَا

2. شَوْكَةُ الْمَوْتِ مَضَتْ هَلِلُويَا ۰ وَانْتَهَى هَوْلُ الْجَحِيمْ هَلِلُويَا ۰ مُدَّةُ الْحَرْبِ انْقَضَتْ هَلِلُويَا ۰ بِخَلَاصٍ لِلْأَثِيمْ هَلِلُويَا

3. قُمْتَ فِي عَرْشِ الْقَضَاءِ هَلِلُويَا ۰ شَافِعًا بِالْمُعْتَدِينْ هَلِلُويَا ۰ فَاتِحًا بَابَ السَّمَاءِ هَلِلُويَا ۰ لِرُجُوعِ الشَّارِدِينْ هَلِلُويَا

4. فَلْنُرَنِّمْ بِانْتِصَارْ هَلِلُويَا ۰ وَهْتَافٍ وَسُرُورْ هَلِلُويَا ۰ وَلْنَعِشْ بِالْإِنْتِظَارْ هَلِلُويَا ۰ لِرَجَا يَوْمِ النُّشُورْ هَلِلُويَا

Ibrahim Baz el Haddad

181

95

C. V. Stanford 1852 - 1924

1. We know that Christ is raised and dies no more____:
1. Le blé qui lève au creux de nos sil - lons____
1. Wir wis - sen: Chri - stus lebt und stirbt für uns____.

em - braced by fu - tile death he broke its hold____,
et porte en lui le poids de nos mois - sons____
Der Tod ver - lor sein Spiel für al - le - zeit____.

and man's des - pair he turned to bla - zing
est lourd aus - si d'es - poirs pour d'au - tres
In Freu - de, Herr, ver - wan - delst du die

joy____; Al - - le - lu - ia!
dons____. Al - - lé - lu - ia!
Angst____. Al - - le - lu - ja.

2. We share by water in his saving death: / this union brings to being one new cell, / a living and organic part of Christ: / Alleluia!

3. The Father's splendour clothes the Son with life: / the Spirit's fission shakes the Church of God: / baptized we live with God the Three in One: / Alleluia!

4. A new Creation comes to life and grows / as Christ's new body takes on flesh and blood: / the universe restored and whole will sing: / Alleluia!

John B. Geyer 1964

2. Le blé broyé moulu comme un martyr / deviendra pain. Rompu, il peut nourir / il a passé l'épi pour s'accomplir. / Alléluia!

3. Le blé du Christ semé au Golgotha / y mûrira, sera broyé en croix / et deviendra le Pain d'Eucharistie. / Alléluia!

4. Le Christ en nous, qui lutte et souffre encore / n'a pas fini de traverser la mort: / mais nous attend vainqueur, sur l'autre bord. / Alléluia!

5. L'amour du Christ, comme un levain nouveau / a fait rouler la meule du tombeau / et déferler sur nos l'Esprit et l'Eau. / Alléluia!

6. A prix d'amour le ciel nous est offert: / un Père enfin nous tend ses bras ouverts: / la mort absurde est morte, et clos l'enfer. / Alléluia!

Louis Arragon 1972

2. Wir haben teil an Christi Tod für uns, / befreit sind wir zum Leben in der Welt / und fürchten nichts, denn er ist unser Freund. / Alleluja.

3. Des Vaters Licht bist du, Sohn, leuchte uns. / Komm Geist und bring die Kirchen auf den Weg. / Dann leben wir, Gott, Vater, Sohn und Geist. / Alleluja.

4. Was gestern war, wird morgen nicht mehr sein: / Dein Frieden kommt zur Welt und schafft sie neu. / Und alle Völker singen dir ihr Lied: / Alleluja.

Friedrich Karl Barth 1972

96

Jean Langlais 1957

Dieu, nous a - vons vu ta
God, your glo - ry we have
Herr, wir ha - ben dich er -

gloire en ton Christ, plein de grâce et de vé - ri -
seen in your Son, full of truth, full of heav'n-ly
kannt in dem Sohn vol - ler Gna - de und Wahr -

té, en lui fais nous vi - vre, pleins de
grace: in Christ make us live___, his love shine
heit. In ihm laß uns le - ben vol - ler

cha - ri - té et le mon - de ver - ra les
on our face, and the na - tions shall see in
Lie - be, und die Welt___ wird sehn die

fruits de ta vic - toi - - re. 1. Le Sei -
us the tri - umph you have won. 1. In the
Früch - te dei - nes Sie - - ges. 1. Gott der

gneur a je - té la pa - role au sil - lon. Il
fields of this world his good news he has sown, and
Herr warf sein Wort auf das A - cker - feld. Er

a se - mé la graine. Il at - tend la mois - son.
sends us out to reap till the har - vest is done.
sä - te aus das Korn, daß zur Ern - te es wächst.

2. Le Seigneur a passé comme un feu dévorant. / Il a lancé la braise. Il attend nos sarments.

3. Le Seigneur s'est livré pour la Pâque en son Corps; / il a rompu le pain. Il attend notre mort.

4. Le Seigneur a foulé le raisin sur la Croix, / il a rempli la coupe, il attend notre joie.

5. Le Seigneur a construit un Royaume nouveau, / il a taillé le pierre. Il attend nos travaux.

Didier Rimaud 1957

2. In his love like a fire that consumes he pass'd by; / the flame has touched our lips; let us shout, 'Here am I!'

3. He was broken for us, God-forsaken his cry, / and still the bread he breaks: to ourselves we must die.

4. He has trampled the grapes of new life on his Cross; / now drink the cup and live: he has filled it for us.

5. He has founded a kingdom that none shall destroy; / the corner-stone is laid. Go to work: build with joy!

Refrain: Sir Ronald Johnson 1964
Verses: Brian Wren 1964

2. Gott der Herr ging vorüber wie lodernde Glut. / Er rührt die Lippen an und erwartet die Frucht.

3. Gott der Vater gab sich selbst an dem Kreuz in den Tod. / Er brach sein Brot für uns, daß wir sterben mit ihm.

4. Gott der Herr hat das Kreuz sich zur Kelter gemacht, / füllt uns den Kelch mit Wein, wartet, daß wir uns freun.

5. Gott der Herr hat sein Reich neu gebaut für die Welt. / Der Eckstein ist gelegt. Arbeit wartet auf uns!

Ursula Trautwein 1972

97

Paris Antiphoner 1681

1. Christ is the world's light; he_____ and none
1. Christ, Roi du mon - de, toi, le Maître u -
1. Chri - stus, das Licht der Welt, welch ein Grund zur

o - ther; born in our dark - ness, he be-came our
ni - que, né tel un hom - me, tu es no - tre
Freu - de! In un - ser Dun - kel kam er als ein

bro - ther. If we have seen___ him, we have
frè - re: voir ton vi - sa - ge c'é - tait
Bru - der. Wer ihm be - geg - net, der sieht

seen the Fa - ther: Glo - ry to God on high!
voir le Pè - re. Gloire et lou - ange à toi!
auch den Va - ter. Eh - re sei Gott, dem Herrn.

2. Christ is the world's peace: / he and none other; / no man can serve him / and despise his brother. / Who else unites us / one in God the Father? / Glory to God on high!

3. Christ is the world's life, / he and none other; / sold once for silver, / murdered here, our Brother– / he, who redeems us, / reigns with God the Father: / Glory to God on high!

4. Give God the glory, / God and none other; / give God the glory, Spirit, Son and Father; / give God the glory, / God in man my brother: / Glory to God on high!

F. Pratt Green 1968

186

2. Christ, paix du monde, / toi douceur unique / celui qui t'aime / doit aimer son frère; / lie nous ensemble / dans l'amour du Père. / Gloire et louange à toi.

3. Christ, vie du monde, / toi, l'espoir unique! / Seul, dans l'angoisse, / tué par tes frères, / toi, qui nous sauves / règne avec le Père! / Gloire et louange à toi.

4. A Dieu la gloire, / Dieu, le Père unique! / A toi la gloire, / Homme-Dieu, mon frère. / A Dieu la gloire, / Esprit Fils et Père / Gloire et louange à Dieu!

G. de Lioncourt 1972

2. Christus, das Heil der Welt. / Welch ein Grund zur Freude! / Weil er uns lieb hat, / lieben wir die Brüder. / Er schenkt Gemeinschaft / zwischen Gott und Menschen. / Ehre sei Gott, dem Herrn.

3. Christus, der Herr der Welt. / Welch ein Grund zur Freude! / Von uns verraten, / starb er ganz verlassen. / Doch er vergab uns / und wir sind die Seinen. / Ehre sei Gott, dem Herrn.

4. Gebt Gott die Ehre. / Hier ist Grund zur Freude! / Freut euch am Vater. / Freuet euch am Sohne / Freut euch am Geiste: / denn wir sind gerettet. / Ehre sei Gott, dem Herrn.

Friedrich Karl Barth, S. Leonhardt und O. Schulz 1972

98

Refrain

Dominique Ombrie 1963

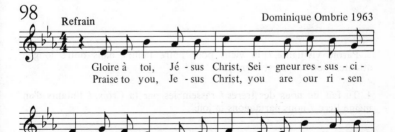

Gloire à toi, Jé - sus Christ, Sei - gneur res - sus - ci -
Praise to you, Je - sus Christ, you are our ri - sen

té, tu nous don - nes la vie; Gloire à toi, Jé - sus
Lord; you have giv'n us new life: Praise to you, Je - sus

Christ, tu viens nous li - bé - rer; tu es notre U - ni - té.
Christ, you came to set us free; you are our U - ni - ty.

1. Tu es la vraie lu - miè - re jail -
2. Vic - toi - re qui dé - li - vre des
1. The cloud of cha - os parts_____ riv'n
2. Your Pas - sion gives new life_____ to

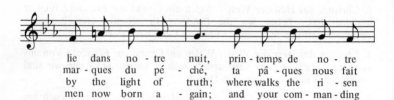

lie dans no - tre nuit, prin - temps de no - tre
mar - ques du pé - ché, ta pâ - ques nous fait
by the light of truth; where walks the ri - sen
men now born a - gain; and your com - man - ding

ter - re c'est toi qui nous con - duis.
vi - vre en vrais res - sus - ci - tés.
Lord_____ old earth re - news her youth.
touch _____ e - ra - ses sin's deep stain.

3. Parole vivifiante, / tu viens pour notre faim; / dans notre longue attente, / ton corps est notre pain.

4. Tu fais de nous des frères / rassemblés par ta Croix. / Enfants d'un même Père, / nous partageons ta joie.

5. Merveille de ta grâce, / tu viens nous libérer. / Qu'en ton amour se fasse, / Seigneur, notre unité.

Dominique Ombrie 1963

3. You, God's life-giving Word / still come our minds to feed, / to waiting wanderers still / you give the living Bread.

4. Your friends are drawn to you / where you are lifted up, / one family of God, / one faith, one joy, one hope!

5. Amazing love! You came / to set your people free. / Now may this love call forth / your people's unity.

Erik Routley 1972

99

Psalmodia Evangelica 1789

1. Je - sus shall reign wher - e'er the sun does
1. Nous te chan-tons, Res - sus - ci - té, ton
1. Je - zus zal heer - sen waar de zon gaat

his suc - ces - sive___ jour - neys run; his
jour se lè - ve sur l'hu - ma - ni - té, tu
om de gro - te___ aar - de om, de

king - dom stretch from shore to___ shore, till
sors vain - queur de l'ombre des tom - beaux, so -
maan zijn lich - te ba - nen___ trekt, zo -

moons shall wax and wane no more.
leil vi - vant des temps nou - veaux.
ver het vers - te land zich strekt.

2. People and realms of every tongue / dwell on his love with sweetest song, / and infant voices shall proclaim / their early blessings on his name.

3. Blessings abound where'er he reigns; / the prisoner leaps to lose his chains; / the weary find eternal rest, / and all the sons of want are blest.

4. Let every creature rise and bring / peculiar honours to our King; / angels descend with songs again, / and earth repeat the long amen.

Isaac Watts 1719

2. Tout l'univers remonte au jour / capable enfin de t'appeler 'Amour'. / Un chant nouveau pour les enfants perdus: / le nom de Dieu nous est rendu.

3. Tu as ouvert pour tous les tiens / en grand la porte du très vieux Jardin / où Dieu convie les hommes pour la joie / sous l'Arbre immense de ta Croix.

4. Vous qui dormez, réveillez-vous, / la nuit émet le signe de l'Epoux. / Il vient chercher le peuple des croyants, / 'Amen' de gloire au Dieux vivant.

Daniel Hameline 1972

2. Het lied in alle talen zal / zijn liefde loven overal, / en uit de kindermond ontspringt / de lofzang die zijn naam omringt.

3. Zijn rijk is volle zaligheid, / wie was gevangen wordt bevrijd, / wie moe was komt tot rust voorgoed, / wie arm was leeft in overvloed.

4. Laat loven al wat adem heeft / de koning die ons alles geeft. / O aarde om dit nieuw begin / stem met het lied der englen in.

J. W. Schulte Nordholt 1968

The Holy Spirit and the Word of God
Der Heilige Geist und das Wort Gottes
Le Saint-Esprit et la Parole de Dieu

100a

Vatican plainsong

1. Ve - ni Cre - a - tor___ Spi - ri - tus,
1. Come, O Cre - a - tor___ Spi - rit, come,
1. Oh! Ven, Es - pí - ri - tu___ Cre - a - dor,

men - tes tu - o - rum___ vi - si - ta
and make with - in our___ hearts thy home;
vi - si - ta nues - tro___ co - ra - zón.

im - ple___ su - per - na___ gra - ti - a
to us___ thy___ grace___ ce - les - tial give,
Tú lo___ cre - as - te___: llé - na - lo

quae___ tu___ cre - as - ti peç - to - ra.
who___ of___ thy___ breath - ing move and live.
del___ fue - go___ de___ tu san - to a - mor.

2. Accende lumen sensibus / infund'amorem cordibus, / infirma nostri corporis / virtute firmans perpeti.

3. Hostem repellas longius, / pacemque dones protinus; / ductore sic te praevio, / vitemus omne noxium.

4. Per te sciamus da Patrem, / noscamus atque Filium, / teque utriusque Spiritum / credamus omni tempore.

9th century

2. Our senses with thy light inflame, / our hearts to heavenly love reclaim; / our bodies' poor infirmity / with strength perpetual fortify.

3. Our mortal foe afar repel, / grant us henceforth in peace to dwell; / and so to us, with thee for guide / no ill shall come, no harm betide.

4. May we by thee the Father learn / and know the Son, and thee discern, / who art of both and thus adore / in perfect faith for evermore.

Robert Bridges 1899

2. Auxiliador benéfico, / supremo don de nuestro Dios, / raudal de luz purísima, / y espiritual consolación!

3. Tus santos dones místicos / son rayos del eterno sol. / Los labios mueva, férvidos, / tu celestial inspiración.

4. A Dios el Padre muéstranos, / y al Hijo, eterno Redentor; / con ellos, Santo Espíritu, / recibe nuestra adoración.

100b

Kempten ca. 1000 /
Wittenberg 1524 / Mainz 1947

1. Komm, Schöp - fer Geist, kehr bei uns ein, und laß
1. Viens, ô Saint Es - prit cré - a - teur, mettre en
1. Ya sing - gah, Kha - lik, Roh Ku - dus, hing - gap -
1. きたれや み た ま よ み 民

uns dei - ne Woh - nung sein; er - füll die Her - zen,
tout homme un nou - veau cœur. Tu veux de nous si
i - lah cip - ta - an - Mu: cu - rah - kan - lah a -
の て て ろ に て よ な き め

dein Ge - bild, mit dei - nen Him - mels - ga - ben mild.
dif - fé - rents for - mer un seul___ peu - ple saint.
nu - ge - rah, di h ha - ti ka - mi di - am - lah!
ぐ み を そ そ が せ た ま え や

2. Ein Tröster kommt zu uns herab, / du bist des Höchsten höchste Gab', / der Lebensquell', die Liebessonn', / der Seele Salbung, Lieb und Wonn'.

3. Gib uns'rer Leuchte klaren Schein, / flöß Liebesglut den Herzen ein! / Stärk unsern Mut, daß er besteh' / des schwachen Leibes Not und Weh.

4. Den Vater und den Sohn, o lehr / sie uns erkennen immer mehr. / Du heil'ger Geist, in alle Zeit / sei'n uns're Herzen dir geweiht.

Anonymous

2. Viens, Saint-Esprit consolateur, / illuminer nos profondeurs; / tu sais nos élans, nos secrets, / reste avec nous à jamais.

3. Tu répands tes dons les meilleurs, / l'amour, la joie et la douceur / que tu nous accordes des cieux / ô Saint-Esprit généreux.

Fr. Pierre–Etienne 1972

2. Ingatan kami t'rangilah / dan hati pun nyalakanlah; teguhkanlah yang tak betah, / kuatkan kami yang lemah.

3. B'ri damai, b'ri sejahtera, / kuasa jahat halaulah / dan pimpin kawan dombaMu / menjauh angkara penyemu.

4. B'ri kami makin mengenal / Bapa dan Anak yang kekal: / Pemancar kasih menerus, / penuhi kami, Roh Kudus.

Yayasan Musik Gerejani 1973

2. なぐさめぬしなる　　　　とうときみたまよ、
　　あふるるいずみと　　　　湧きいでたまえや。

3. ななえのたまもの　　　　さずくるみたまよ、
　　もえたつほのおと　　　　はたらきたまえや。

4. まなこにひかりを、　　　こころになさけを、
　　からだにちからを　　　　ゆたかにたまえや。

5. 御父と御子とを　　　　　さやかに知らしめ、
　　ときわにさかえを　　　　うけさせたまえや。

101

Modern form of 14 th century
German melody

1. Nun bit - ten wir den Hei - li - gen Geist
1. O Ho - ly Spirit, hear us as we pray;
1. Toi, Saint Es - prit, lu - miè - re qui viens,
1. Chie - dia - mo al - lo Spi - ri - to San - to
1. Ro - ga - mos al buen Con - so - la - dor

um den rech - ten Glau - ben al - ler - meist, daß er
keep our faith re - newed from day to day. Free us
clar - té qui des - cends dans no - tre nuit, seul tu
la mas - si - ma e ve - ra fe - de, per - ché in
nos con - ce - da gra - cia, fe y fer - vor; el nos

uns be - hü - te an un - serm En - de, wenn wir heim -
from the cha - os of night and deep - ness; in our life
nous é - clai - res, toi seul nous par - les, toi l'Es - prit
nos - tra fi - ne fe - del ci guar - di, al par - ti -
dé su a - yu - da, su ma - no fuer - te nos am - pa -

fahrn aus die - sem E - len - de. Ky - ri - e - leis.
and death cheer and keep __ us. Lord, have mer - cy.
du Père et l'Es - prit du Fils; tu es Sei - gneur.
re dal nos - tro e - si - lio. Ky - rie, e - leis.
re en la an - gus - tia y la muer - te. Ten pie - dad, Se - ñor.

2. Du wertes Licht, gib uns deinen Schein, / lehr uns Jesus Christ kennen allein, / daß wir an ihm bleiben, dem treuen Heiland, / der uns bracht hat zum rechten Vaterland. / Kyrieleis.

3. Du süße Lieb, schenk uns deine Gunst, / laß uns empfinden der Liebe Glut, / daß wir uns von Herzen einander lieben / und im Frieden auf einem Sinn bleiben. / Kyrieleis.

Martin Luther 1524

2. Uproot and teach us by your restless love, / help us to share all that we are and have, / that with strong affection, in truth and doing, / we may love all men, peace pursuing. / Lord, have mercy.

3. You plead our cause, and by your gift of peace / life is from the fear of death released. / How we need your presence, O gift from heaven, / all our words and deeds to enliven. / Lord have mercy.

Fred Kaan 1968, 1972

2. Toi, Saint-Esprit qui donnes la foi, / qui nous remplis d'amour et d'espoir; / seul tu nous éclaires, toi seul nous guides, / car avec le Père et avec le Fils / tu es Seigneur.

3. Toi, Saint-Esprit, présence de Dieu / dans l'épreuve ou le bonheur des jours; / seul tu nous éclaires, tu nous révèles / dans l'amour du Père et la paix du Fils / ta joie, Seigneur.

H. Capieu 1950

2. O luce santa, dona splendore / per vedere Cristo soltanto; / chè restiam con lui, il Salvatore; / ci conduce a vera patria. / Kyrie, eleis.

3. Concedi il tuo favore, dolce amore, / accendi in noi la fiamma santa; / fa' che ci amiamo gli uni gli altri, / in tua pace e in mente unica. / Kyrie, eleis.

Inni della Riforma

2. Amor sin par, danos tu favor, / llénanos de fervoroso amor, / para que hermanado tu pueblo entero / marche en paz por el mismo sendero. / Ten piedad, Señor.

3. Consuelo fiel, poderoso Dios, / de maldad y afrentas líbranos. / Contra el enemigo cruel y malvado, / sé, al fin, nuestro fuerte abogado. / Ten piedad, Señor.

Albert Lehenbauer (1891–1955)

102

Ralph Vaughan Williams 1906

1. Come down, O Love di - vine, seek thou this soul__ of mine, and vi - sit it with thine own ar - dour__ glow - ing; O Com - for - ter, draw near, with - in my heart ap - pear, and kind - le it, thy ho - ly flame be - stow - ing.

1. O Got - tes - lieb', er - schein und nimm die See - le ein, ent - flam - me sie mit dei - nem rei - nen__ Glü - hen. O na - he er - den - wärts, Geist, Trö - ster in dies Herz, laß al - le mü - de Halb - heit dar - aus__ flie - hen.

1. Des - cends, Es - prit de Dieu, et de tes dons__ pré - cieux veuille a - pai - ser nos peu - reu - ses pri - è - res. Es - prit con - so - la - teur, vi - si - te no - tre coeur, fais - y bril - ler ta cé - les - te lu - miè - re.

2. O let it freely burn, / till earthly passions turn / to dust and ashes in its heat consuming; / and let thy glorious light / shine ever on my sight, / and clothe me round, the while my path illuming.

3. Let holy charity / my outward vesture be, / and lowliness become mine inner clothing; / true lowliness of heart, / which takes the humbler part, / and o'er its own shortcomings weeps with loathing.

4. And so the yearning strong, / with which the soul will long / shall far outpass the power of human telling; / for none can guess its grace, / till he become the place / wherein the Holy Spirit makes his dwelling.

R. F. Littledale 1867

2. Entbrenn' es ohne Maß / zu hellem Brand, bis daß / der Erde Sucht wie Asche sich verloren. / Dein göttlich helles Licht / erleuchte mein Gesicht / und weise mir den Weg zu deinen Toren.

3. Gib heil'ge Milde mir / stets zu Gewand und Zier / und Demut mach zu meines Herzens Kleide, / damit ich immerdar / bleib falschen Stolzes bar / und, wo er durchbricht, ihn mit Schmerz bestreite.

4. Kein Menschenwort mehr kann / erzählen, wie sich dann / die Seele läßt von deiner Sehnsucht treiben. / Denn was hülf' all ihr Ruhm, / würd' sie nicht Eigentum / dir, Heil'ger Geist, d'rin du kannst wohnen bleiben.

Erwin Kleine 1950

2. Brûle nos passions, / que nos affections / soient terre et cendre au regard de ta grâce, / que toute vérité / brille de ta clarté, / que toute paix de ta paix soit la trace.

3. Viens en nous susciter / la sainte charité, / qui nous sera vêtement et parure, / et ce cœur humble et doux / qui nous fasse à genoux / servir le Christ et pleurer nos souillures.

4. Descends, Esprit divin, / car tout langage est vain / pour dire notre amère et grande histoire. / Seul ton vivant amour / nous gardera toujours / dans la douceur, l'allégresse et la gloire.

H. Capieu 1950

103

H. R. Siemoneit 1964

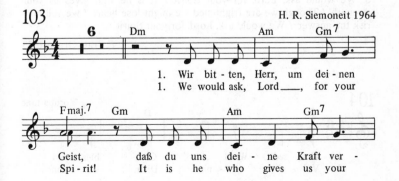

1. Wir bit - ten, Herr, um dei - nen Geist, daß du uns dei - ne Kraft ver -
1. We would ask, Lord___, for your Spi - rit! It is he who gives us your

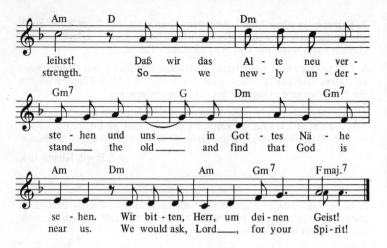

leihst! Daß wir das Al - te neu ver-
strength. So____ we new - ly un - der-

ste - hen und uns____ in Got - tes Nä - he
stand____ the old____ and find that God is

se - hen. Wir bit - ten, Herr, um dei - nen Geist!
near us. We would ask, Lord____, for your Spi - rit!

2. Wir bitten, Herr, um deinen Geist, / daß du uns deine Kraft verleihst! /
Wir wollen nicht nur Fragen nennen, / wir möchten auch die Antwort
kennen. / Wir bitten, Herr, um deinen Geist!

3. Wir bitten, Herr, um deinen Geist, / daß du uns deine Kraft verleihst! /
Auch wenn wir fürchten zu versagen, / so laß uns doch die Antwort
wagen. / Wir bitten, Herr, um deinen Geist!

Dieter Trautwein 1964

2. We would ask, Lord, for your Spirit! / It is he who gives us your
strength. / We don't want just to ask the questions, / we want to know
the answer. / We would ask, Lord, for your Spirit!

3. We would ask, Lord, for your Spirit! / It is he who gives us your
strength. / Though we are frightened we might lose heart, / we still may
risk the answer. / We would ask, Lord, for your Spirit!

F. Pratt Green 1973

104

Yoruba tune

1. Bles - sed Word of God, bles - sed
1. Voi - ci ve - nir Dieu, lais - sons

198

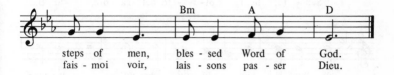

Word of God, light of the fal - ter - ing
steps of men, bles - sed Word of God.

pas - ser Dieu; ou - vre mes yeux, Jé - sus;
fais - moi voir, lais - sons pas - ser Dieu.

2. Holy Word of God, / holy Word of God, / drawing our hearts up to God above, / holy Word of God.

3. Sweetest Word of God, / sweetest Word of God, / message of love coming down from heav'n, / sweetest Word of God.

4. Word of sins forgiven, / word of sins forgiven, / word of salvation's redeeming love, / word of sins forgiven.

5. Word of truth and life, / word of truth and life, / teaching of Jesus, our way and guide, / word of truth and life.

6. Joyous Word of God, / joyous Word of God, / leading us all to the joys of heav'n, / joyous Word of God.

A. M. Jones 1969

2. Voici venir Dieu, / laissons passer Dieu, / viens m'appeler, Jésus: je suis sourd, / laissons passer Dieu.

3. Voici venir Dieu, / laissons passer Dieu, / relève-moi, Jésus: conduis-moi / laissons passer Dieu.

4. Voici venir Dieu, / laissons passer Dieu, / marche avec moi, Jésus: je suis seul / laissons passer Dieu.

5. Voici venir Dieu, / laissons passer Dieu, / éclaire-moi, Jésus: il fait noir, / laissons passer Dieu.

6. Voici venir Dieu, / laissons passer Dieu, / viens me parler, Jésus: sois ma voix / laissons passer Dieu.

Nicole Berthet 1972

105

Jean van der Cauter 1965

1. Es - prit, toi qui gui - des tous les hom - mes, gar - de -
1. Good Spi - rit of God, guide of your chil - dren, keep them
1. San - to, tu lo Spi - ri - to del Pa - dre, tu che

les pour la gloi - re du Pè - re; u - nis -
all for the glo - ry of the Fa - ther; keep them
par - li nel cuo - re dell' uo - mo, che ra -

les dans ton peu - ple de la ter - re; con - duis -
all in the love of one an - oth - er; lead them
du - ni dai con - fi - ni della ter - ra o - gni

les par la rou - te qui mè - ne au Roy - au - me.
all in the quest for the ho - nour of the King - dom.
uo - mo che cer - ca la Stra - da del Re - gno,

Gui - de - nous sur les rou - tes de la ter - re,
Be our guide through this pil - gri - mage of li - ving,
tu ci gui - di sul - le stra - de della ter - ra

con - duis - nous vers les hom - mes, nos frè - res.
turn us each to his bro - ther in self - gi - ving.
ver - so l'uo - mo che è nos - tro fra - tel - lo.

200

2. Esprit, toi qui souffles sur le monde, / brûle-nous de ta flamme si claire; / purifie tous nos gestes de misère; / conduis–nous où la grâce du Christ surabonde. / Guide-nous sur les routes de la terre, / conduis-nous vers les hommes, nos frères.

3. Esprit, toi que donnes la justice, / donne-nous de combattre la haine; / force-nous à défendre ceux qui peinent, / conduis-nous vers les pauvres qui sont ton Eglise. / Guide-nous sur les routes de la terre, / conduis-nous vers les hommes, nos frères.

Didier Rimaud 1965

2. Pure Spirit of God, fresh wind of blessing, / let your fire in its energy inflame us; / let your healing from misery reclaim us; / lead us all where the faithful Christ's grace are confessing. / Be our guide through this pilgrimage of living, / turn us each to his brother in self-giving.

3. Great Spirit of God, source of all justice, / in your war against hatred keep us faithful; / in protecting the poor keep us watchful; / in our search for the household of peace still protect us. / Be our guide through this pilgrimage of living, / turn us each to his brother in self-giving.

Erik Routley 1972

2. Santo, tu lo Spirito di vita, / tu che passi nel cuore del mondo, / che rinnovi come fuoco creatore / ogni uomo chiamato all'amore di Cristo, / tu ci guidi sulle strade della terra / verso l'uomo che è nostro fratello.

3. Santo, tu lo Spirito di pace, / tu che scendi sui popoli in guerra, / che difendi con forza e con giustizia / ogni uomo ferito dall'odio dell'uomo, / tu ci guidi sulle strade della terra / verso l'uomo che è nostro fratello.

Eugenio Costa 1973

106

Old Japanese melody

1. 世 の な か に　　ふ み ち ょ う
1. In this world a-bound scrolls of wis-dom
1. Hom - me, ton es-prit pense at - tein - dre
1. Gro - ße wei - te Welt, Zahl der Klu - gen

ふ み は　　お お け れ ど
num - ber - less, but the pu - rest truth
l'in - fi - ni, mais la Vé - ri - té
rie - sen - groß. Nur die Wahr - heit selbst,

ま こ と の ふ み は　　み ふ み な
in the Word of God is found; this the book that
par le Verbe est ré - vé - lée; il é - clai - re
fin - dest du nicht ü - ber - all. Gibt ein Buch, das

り け り み ふ み な り　　け り
points the way trod by the sa - ges___ long a - go.
le che - min vu par les sa - ges du monde an - cien.
zeigt den Weg. Geh' zu den Al - ten___, fra - ge sie.

2. いにしえの　聖徒のふみし
　　　そのあとも。
　さやかにしめす　ふみやゝてのふみ。

3. くりかえし　またくりかえし
　　　ひもとけど、
　つきぬはかみの　まことなりけり。

4. うえもなき　まことのみちの
　　　かしこさは、
　ふみてのちてそ　しるべかりけり。

2. Study as we may, never can we grasp thereby / all the depth of truth; we must ever watch and pray, / walking on the holy way trod by the sages long ago.

Esther Hibbard 1962

202

2. Il ne suffit pas de la science d'ici bas, / toute Vérité par le Verbe est révélée; / prions Dieu sur le chemin pris par les sages du monde ancien.

* 3. Seigneur notre Dieu, Seigneur, notre seul enjeu, / toute Vérité par ton Verbe est révélée; / O Lumière du chemin vu par les sages du monde ancien.

G. de Lioncourt 1972

*omettre cette strophe en chantant simultanément.

2. Forsche immerzu, kommst ja doch nicht selber drauf. / Nach der Wahrheit selbst mußt du auf die Suche geh'n. / Geh' den Weg, den Gott dir zeigt. Geh' zu den Weisen, frage sie.

Barth-Schulz-Leonhardt 1973

107

Erik Routley 1972

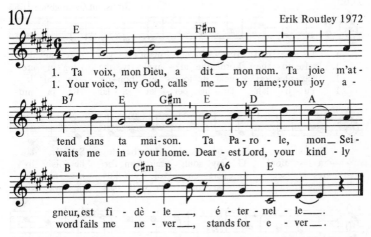

1. Ta voix, mon Dieu, a dit __ mon nom. Ta joie m'at -
1. Your voice, my God, calls me __ by name; your joy a -

tend dans ta mai-son. Ta Pa - ro - le, mon __ Sei -
waits me in your home. Dear - est Lord, your kind - ly

gneur, est fi - dè - le ____, é - ter - nel - le ____.
word fails me ne - ver ____, stands for e - ver __.

2. Ta mort, Jésus, m'a délivré. / Tu vis en moi ressuscité. / Ta Parole, mon Seigneur / est vivante, agissante.

3. Esprit d'amour, redis ce mot / qui crée en moi un cœur nouveau. / Ta Parole, mon Seigneur, / est lumière et prière.

Claude Rozier 1957

2. Your death, my Jesus, sets me free; / your life has risen again in me. / Dearest Lord, your vital word / activates me, captivates me.

3. Spirit of love, repeat that sign / which makes anew this heart of mine. / Dearest Lord, now is your word / shining o'er me, praying for me.

F. Pratt Green 1972

The Church – Its Worship and Praise
Die Kirche – Gottesdienst und Lobpreisung
L'Eglise – Adoration et Louange

108

Stralsund Gesangbuch 1665

1. Lo - be den Her - ren, den mäch - ti - gen Kö - nig der
1. Praise to the Lord! the al - migh - ty, the King of cre -
1. Peu - ples, cri - ez de joie et bon - dis - sez d'al - lé -
1. Pu - ji - lah Tu - han, per - ka - sa - lah Ra - ja mu -

Eh - ren! Mei - ne ge - lie - be - te See - le, das
a - tion! O my soul, praise him, for he is thy
gres - se: Le Père en - voie son Fils ma - ni - fes -
li - a! Se - ge - nap ha - ti dan ji - wa - ku,

ist mein Be - geh - ren. Kom - met zu Hauf! Psal - ter und
health and sal - va - tion! All ye who hear, now to his
ter sa ten - dres - se; ou - vrons les yeux: il est l'i -
pu - ji - lah Di - a! Him - pun ber - kaum! Gaumbus, ke -

Har - fe, wacht auf! Las - set den Lob - ge - sang hö - ren!
tem - ple draw near, serve him in glad a - do - ra - tion!
ma - ge de Dieu! Pour que cha - cun le con - nais - se!
ca - pi, ber - gaung! Ang - kat lan pu - ji - pu - ji - an!

2. Lobe den Herren, der alles so herrlich regieret, / der dich auf Adelers Fittichen sicher geführet, / der dich erhält, / wie es dir selber gefällt. / Hast du nicht dieses verspüret?

3. Lobe den Herren, der deinen Stand sichtbar gesegnet, / der aus dem Himmel mit Strömen der Liebe geregnet. / Denke daran, / was der Allmächtige kann, / der dir mit Liebe begegnet!

4. Lobe den Herren, was in mir ist lobe den Namen. / Lob ihn mit allen, die seine Verheissung bekamen. / Er ist dein Licht; / Seele, vergiss es ja nicht. / Lob ihn in Ewigkeit! Amen!

Joachim Neander 1650-1680

2. Praise to the Lord! Who o'er all things so wondrously reigneth, / shielding thee gently from harm and from fainting sustaineth; / hast thou not seen / how thy desires have been / granted in what He ordaineth?

3. Praise to the Lord! Who doth prosper thy work and defend thee, / surely his goodness and mercy here daily attend thee; / ponder anew / what the Almighty can do, / if with His love He befriend thee!

4. Praise to the Lord! Oh let all that is in me adore Him! / All that hath life and breath come now with praises before Him! / Let the Amen / sound from His people again, / gladly for aye we adore Him.

C. Winkworth 1858

2. Loué soit notre Dieu, Source et Parole fécondes; / ses mains ont tout créé pour que nos cœurs lui répondent; / par Jésus Christ il donne l'être et la vie / pour que sa Vie surabonde.

3. Loué soit notre Dieu, dont la splendeur se révèle / quand nous buvons le vin pour une terre nouvelle; / en Jésus – Christ le monde passe aujourd'hui / vers une gloire éternelle.

4. Peuples, battez des mains et proclamez votre fête: / le Père accueille en lui ceux que son Verbe rachète; / par l'Esprit Saint en qui vous n'êtes plus qu'un, / que votre joie soit parfaite!

Didier Rimaud 1970

2. Pujilah Tuhan; segala kuasa padaNya! / Sayap kasihNya yang aman mendukung anakNya! / Tiada terp'ri / yang kepadamu dib'ri! / Adakah itu kausangka?

3. Pujilah Tuhan yang dapat dan mau melakukan / jauh melebihi doamu dan yang kaurindukan! / Ingat teguh: / Dia berkuasa penuh! / KasihNya 'kan kautemukan!

4. Pujilah Tuhan, manusia, batin-jasmani; mahluk bernafas semua, iringilah kami! / Bumi penuh / s'ri mulia Allah kudus! / Dunia, sahutlah: Amin!

Yayasan Musik Gerejani 1973

1. Al - ma, ben - di - ce al Se - ñor, Rey po - ten - te de
1. Lode all' Al - tis - si - mo, lode al Sig - nor del - la
1. Njoo - ni tum - si - fu - ni Mung - u A - li - ye Mwen -
1. 讚美上主、全能神明、宇宙萬有

glo - ria; De sus mer - ce - des es - té vi - va en
glo - ria! Al re dei se - co - li for - za, o -
ye - zi, Mfal - me wa po - po - te mbing - u - ni
君王; 我靈頌主、因主永遠、是

ti la me - mo - ria. Oh des - per - tad, ar - pa y sal -
no - re, vit - to - ria! Can - ta - te a lui, tut - ti accla -
na du - ni - a - ni. Kwa - sau - ti kuu wo - te wam -
你救贖健康: 兄弟姊妹、都來靠

te - rio en - to - nad Him - nos de ho - nor y vic - to - ria!
ma - te con noi; cie - lo e ter - ra es - ul - ta - te!
si - fu Mung - u, Kum - pi - gi - a mfal - me shang - we.
近主胸懷、歡然向主恭敬讚揚。

2. Alma, bendice al Señor, que a los orbes gobierna. / Y te conduce paciente con mano paterna; / te perdonó, / de todo mal te libró, / porque su gracia es eterna.

3. Alma, bendice al Señor, de tu vida la fuente, / que te creó, y en salud te sostiene clemente; / tu defensor / en todo trance y dolor; / su diestra es omnipotente.

4. Alma, bendice al Señor y su amor infinito; / con todo el pueblo de Dios su alabanza repito: / Dios, mi salud, / de todo bien plenitud, / seas por siempre bendito!

Fritz Fliedner 1845–1901

206

2. Lode all'Altissimo, re dell'immenso creato: / con ali d'aquila tutti i suoi figli ha portato. / Ci guiderà, / ed ogni uomo saprà / quanto è grande il suo amore.

3. Lode all'Altissimo, che a noi dal cielo ha parlato / e per gli uomini l'unico Figlio ha donato. / Morto per noi, / Cristo ci chiama con lui / oltre il peccato e la morte.

4. Lode all'Altissimo, Padre di grazia infinita, / che dona agli umili pace, benessere, vita. / Dio regnerà: / e tutto a lui canterà / gloria nei secoli! Amen!

E. C. - G. S.

2. Njooni tumsifuni Mungu anayetawala / vyote vizuri akuongozaye na wewe. / Waruka juu / kama kwa nguvu ya tai, / ukiongozwa na Mungu.

3. Njooni tumsifuni Mungu aliyetulinda, / atubariki kwa pendo atupa riziki. / Ni mwenyezi, / atutendea makuu, / anatupenda kwa kweli.

4. Njooni tumsifuni Mungi, tumsifu kwa nyimbo, / kama Daudi imbeni na mashangilio. / Tusisahau / ndiye nuru ya roho. / Tumsifu hata milele.

2. 讚美上主、如此奇妙、統治世間萬物、展開恩翼、如此溫柔、將你時常保護：你豈不見、有求皆蒙主恩典、主聲應你、指示方針？

3. 讚美上主、扶你護你、使你作工順利、上主好意、上主慈恩、一定天天跟你：仔細思量、全能的主愛深長、做你朋友、何等福氣。

4. 讚美上主！讓我整個心靈讚美上主！但願天下凡有血氣、同來稱揚上主！屬主的民、重新一致說「阿們、」歡然恭敬讚揚上主。（阿們。）

109 Psalm 116 (117)

Kölner Gesangbuch 1623

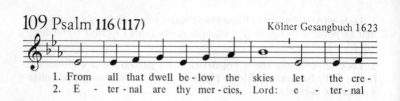

1. From all that dwell be - low the skies let the cre -
2. E - ter - nal are thy mer - cies, Lord: e - ter - nal

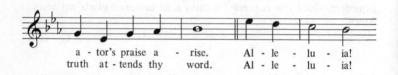

a - tor's praise a - rise. Al - le - lu - ia!
truth at - tends thy word. Al - le - lu - ia!

Al - le - lu - ia! Let the Re - deem - er's
Al - le - lu - ia! Thy praise shall sound from

Name be sung through ev' - ry land in
shore to shore, till suns shall rise and

ev' - ry tongue. Al - le - lu - ia, Al - le - lu - ia,
set no more. Al - le - lu - ia, Al - le - lu - ia,

Al - le - lu - ia, Al - le - lu - ia, Al - le - lu - ia.
Al - le - lu - ia, Al - le - lu - ia, Al - le - lu - ia.

Isaac Watts 1719

110

Johann Crüger 1647

1. Nun dan - ket al - le Gott mit Her - zen,
1. Now thank we all our God, with heart and
1. Lou - ons le Cré - a - teur, chant - ons à

Mund und Hän - den. Der gro - ße Din - ge tut an
hands and voi - ces, who wond - rous things hath done, in
Dieu lou - an - ges! Et joi - gnons no - tre voix au

uns und al - len En - den, der uns von Mut - ter -
whom his world re - joi - ces; who from our mo - ther's
con - cert des saints an - ges! Dès les bras ma - ter -

leib und Kin - des - bei - nen an, un -
arms hath blessed us on our way with
nels il nous a pro - té - gés et

zäh - lig viel zu gut, und noch jetz und ge - tan.
count-less gifts of love, and still is ours to - day.
jus - qu'au der - nier jour, il est no - tre ber - ger.

2. Der ewigreiche Gott / woll uns in unserm Leben / ein immer fröhlich Herz / und edlen Frieden geben / und uns in seiner Gnad / erhalten fort und fort / und uns aus aller Not / erlösen hier und dort.

3. Lob, Ehr und Preis sei Gott / dem Vater und dem Sohne / und Gott dem Heilgen Geist / im höchsten Himmelsthrone, / ihm, dem dreieinen Gott, / wie es im Anfang war / und ist und bleiben wird / so jetzt und immerdar.

Martin Rinckart, 1636, Ecclus 50.
22-4 and Gloria

2. O may this bounteous God / through all our life be near us, / with
ever joyful hearts / and blessed peace to cheer us, / and keep us in his
grace, / and guide us when perplexed, / and free us from all ills / in this
world and the next.

3. All praise and thanks to God / the Father now be given, / the Son,
and Him who reigns / with them in highest heaven, / the one eternal
God, / whom earth and heaven adore; / for thus it was, is now, / and
shall be evermore.

Catherine Winkworth 1858

2. Loué soit notre Dieu! / Que notre vie entière / tous nous vivions
joyeux / sous le regard du Père, / qu'il nous tienne en sa grâce / et nous
guide toujours, / nous garde du malheur / par son unique amour.

3. De ce Dieu trois fois saint / qui règne dans la gloire, / chrétiens
empressons-nous / de chanter la victoire; / son Royaume est aux cieux /
où, plein de majesté, / il règne, seul vrai Dieu, / de toute éternité.

F. du Pasquier 1950

Johann Crüger 1647

1. Lou - ve - mos ao Se - nhor, ra - dian - tes
1. De bo - ca y cor - a - zón a nues - tro

d'a - le - gri - a: Pro - vem do seu a - mor fa -
Dios can - te - mos, pues dió - nos ben - di - ción, sa -

vo - res ca - da di - a! A nós seus peque - ni -
lud, vi - da y con - sue - lo. Tan só - lo a su bon -

nos, vem seu a - mor guian - do, ce -
dad de - be - mos nues - tro ser; con

les - tes dons, di - vinos, a to - dos dis - pen - sando!
su fi - de - li - dad nos guar - da por do - quier.

2. Oh! que tão bom Senhor / domine nossa vida, / Ihe inspire paz e amor / E a faça mais querida! / Quem anda em sua graça / repousara seguro / – enquanto a vida passa – / sem mêdo do futuro!

3. Louvemos ao Senhor / ao Deus augusto e trino: / – Pai, O Salvador, / O Espirito Divino! / Deus uno e verdadeiro, / eterno, onipotente! / Adore-o mundo inteiro, / agora e eternamente!

Isaac N. Salum 1941

2. Dios, rico sin igual, / dénos en cada día / un corazón filial / y lleno de alegría. / Consérvenos la paz / su brazo protector; / nos lleve a ver su faz / en la patria mejor.

3. Dios Padre, mi loor / se eleva hasta tu trono; / Jesus, mi Redentor, / tu salvacion pregono; / espíritu de amor, / accepta la oración / que eleva con fervor / mi grato corazón.

Fritz Fliedner 1845–1901

1. 今當齊來謝主、以心、以手、以聲音、主既完成奇事、世人歡頌主聖名；我從初生時起、蒙主福佑到今、昔受無窮之愛、今猶慰藉溫存。

2. 但願恩慈之主、時常伴我到終身、常將快樂平安、鼓勵安慰我中心；導我脫離疑惑、拯我避免憂驚、無論今生來世、使我蒙主宏恩。

3. 我將感謝頌揚、敬獻父、子、與聖靈、三位本同一體、在天執掌大權衡；獨一永生上主、天人叩拜同心、昔在、今在、永在、千秋萬古永恆。阿們。

111

Kölner Gesangbuch 1623

1. All crea-tures of our God and King, lift
1. Got - tes Ge - schöp - fe kommt zu Hauf! Laßt
1. Vous cré - a - tu - res du Sei - gneur, chan -
1. Oh, cri - a - tu - ras del Se - ñor, can -

up your voice and with us sing Al - le -
brau - sen hoch zum Him - mel auf, Hal - le -
tez tou - jours en son hon - neur, Al - lé -
tad con me - lo - dio - sa voz: Al - le -

lu - ia, Al - le - lu - ia! Thou burn - ing sun
lu - ja, Eu - er Lo - ben! Du Son - ne hell
lu - ia, Al - lé - lu - ia! Car c'est lui seul
lu - ya, Al - le - lu - ya! Ar - dien - te sol

with gol - den beam, thou sil - ver moon with
mit gold - nem Strahl, Mond leuch - tend hoch vom
qu'il faut lou - er. Il donne au so - leil
con tu ful - gor; Oh, lu - na de sua -

soft - er gleam, Al - le - lu - ia, Al - le - lu - ia!
Him - mels - saal, Hal - le - lu - ja, Hal - le - lu - ja!
sa clar - té, Al - lé - lu - ia, Al - lé - lu - ia!
ve es - plen - dor: Al - le - lu - ya, Al - le - lu - ya!

O____ praise Him, O____ praise Him, Al - le - lu - ia!
Singt ihm Eh - re! Singt ihm Eh - re! Hal - le - lu - ja!
Ren - dez gloi - re! Ren - dez gloi - re! Al - lé - lu - ia!
A - la - bad - le! A - la - bad - le! Al - le - lu - ya!

2. Thou rushing wind that art so strong, / ye clouds that sail in heav'n along, / Alleluia, Alleluia! / Thou rising morn, in praise rejoice, / ye lights of evening, find a voice, / Alleluia, Alleluia! / O praise Him, O praise Him, Alleluia!

3. Thou flowing water, pure and clear, / make music for thy Lord to hear, / Alleluia, Alleluia! / Thou fire so masterful and bright, / that givest man both warmth and light, / Alleluia, Alleluia! / O praise Him, O praise Him, Alleluia!

4. Dear mother earth, who day by day / unfoldest blessings on our way, / Alleluia, Alleluia! / The flowers and fruit that in Thee grow, / let them His glory also show, / Alleluia, Alleluia! / O praise Him, O praise Him, Alleluia!

5. And ye all men of tender heart, / forgiving others, take your part, / Alleluia, Alleluia! / Ye, who long pain and sorrow bear, / praise God and on Him cast your care, / Alleluia, Alleluia! / O praise Him, O praise Him, Alleluia!

6. And thou most kind and gentle Death, / waiting to hush our latest breath, / Alleluia, Alleluia! / Thou leadest home the child of God, / and Christ our Lord the way hath trod, / Alleluia, Alleluia! / O praise Him, O praise Him, Alleluia!

7. Let all things their Creator bless, / and worship Him in humbleness, / Alleluia, Alleluia! / Praise, praise the Father, praise the Son, / and praise the Spirit, Three in One, / Alleluia, Alleluia! / O praise Him, O praise Him, Alleluia!

W. H. Draper, about 1913

2. Du Sturm, der durch die Welten zieht, / du Wolke, die am Himmel flieht, / Halleluja, Halleluja! / Du Sommers junges Morgenrot, / du Abendschein, der prächtig lobt, / Halleluja, Halleluja! / Singt ihm Ehre! Singt ihm Ehre! Halleluja!

3. Ihr Quellen all, lachende Flut, / laßt eurem Lauf dem Schöpfer gut, / Halleluja, Halleluja! Du Feuers Flamme auf dem Herd, / daran der Mensch sich wärmt und nährt, / Halleluja, Halleluja! / Singt ihm Ehre! Singt ihm Ehre! Halleluja!

4. Du, Mutter Erde gut und mild, / daraus uns lauter Segen quillt, / Halleluja, Halleluja! / Ihr Blumen bunt, ihr Früchte treu, / die Jahr um Jahr uns reifen neu, / Halleluja, Halleluja! / Singt ihm Ehre! Singt ihm Ehre! Halleluja!

5. Ihr Herzen, drin die Liebe wohnt, / die ihr den Feind verzeihend schont, / Halleluja, Halleluja! / Ihr, die ihr traget schweres Leid, / es Gott zu opfern still bereit, / Halleluja, Halleluja! / Singt ihm Ehre! Singt ihm Ehre! Halleluja!

6. Du, der empfängt in letzter Not, / den Odem mein, O Bruder Tod, / Halleluja, Halleluja! / Führ Gottes Kinder himmelan, / den Weg, den Jesus ging voran! / Halleluja, Halleluja! / Singt ihm Ehre! Singt ihm Ehre! Halleluja!

7. Ihr Kreaturen, eint zum Chor, / niedrig wie hoch, zu Gott empor, / Halleluja, Euer Loben! / Vater und Sohn und Heilgem Geist, / dreieinig, heilig, hochgepreist, / Halleluja, Halleluja! / Sei die Ehre! Sei die Ehre! Halleluja!

Karl Budde 1929

2. Dieu, sois loué pour le soleil, / pour ce grand frère sans pareil, / Alléluia, Alléluia! / Et pour la lune et sa lueur, / pour chaque étoile notre sœur, / Alléluia, Alléluia! / Rendons gloire, rendons gloire, Alléluia!

3. Loué sois-tu pour frère vent, / pour le ciel pur, pour tous les temps, / Alléluia, Alléluia! / L'eau qui nous vient de toi, Seigneur, / nous est une humble et chaste sœur, / Alléluia, Alléluia! / Rendons gloire, rendons gloire, Alléluia!

4. Loués sois-tu pour sire feu, / vivant, robuste, glorieux, / Alléluia, Alléluia! / La terre, en maternelle sœur, / nous comble de ses mille fleurs, / Alléluia, Alléluia! / Rendons gloire, rendons gloire, Alléluia!

5. Heureux les artisans de paix, / leur nom soit béni à jamais, / Alléluia, Alléluia! / Ceux qui ont souffert et pâti, / ils te remettent leurs soucis, / Alléluia, Alléluia! / Rendons gloire, rendons gloire, Alléluia!

6. Loué sois-tu pour notre mort, / elle prendra nos pauvres corps, / Alléluia, Alléluia! / Tu acceuilleras dans les cieux, / ceux qui t'ont obéi, ô Dieu, / Alléluia, Alléluia! / Rendons gloire, rendons gloire, Alléluia!

7. Dieu trois fois saint, nous te louons, / nous te chantons, nous t'adorons, / Alléluia, Alléluia! / Gloire au Père et louange au Fils, / et loué soit le Saint-Esprit, / Alléluia, Alléluia! / Rendons gloire, rendons gloire, Alléluia!

J.-J. Bovet 1950

2. Viento veloz, potente alud, / nubes en claro cielo azul: / Aleluya! Aleluya! / Suave, dorado amanecer; / tu manto, noche, al extender: / Aleluya! Alabadle! / Alabadle! Alabadle! Aleluya!

3. Oh, fuentes de agua de cristal, / a vuestro Creador cantad: / Aleluya! Aleluya! / Oh, fuego, eleva tu loor. / Tú que nos das luz y calor: / Aleluya! Alabadle! / Alabadle! Alabadle! Aleluya!

4. Pródiga tierra maternal, / que frutos brindas sin cesar. / Aleluya! Aleluya! / Rica cosecha, bella flor, / Magnificad al Creador; / Aleluya! Alabadle! / Alabadle! Alabadle! Aleluya!

5. Hombres de tierno corazón, / que paz buscáis y dáis amor: / Aleluya! Aleluya! / Los que sufreis de pena cruel, / vuestro dolor confiadle a El: / Aleluya! Alabadle! / Alabadle! Alabadle! Aleluya!

6. Muerte, tan dulce y sin temor / para quien sigue al Salvador: / Aleluya! Aleluya! / Hacia el hogar nos llevas tú, / que nos prepara el Rey Jesús: / Aleluya! Alabadle! / Alabadle! Alabadle! Aleluya!

7. Con humildad y con amor / cante la entera creación: / Aleluya! Aleluya! / Al Padre, al Hijo Redentor, / y al Eternal Consolador: / Aleluya! Alabadle! / Alabadle! Alabadle! Aleluya!

José Miguez-Bonino 1950

112

Abel Nkuinji 1970

1. Tout est fait pour la gloi-re de Dieu, A-
2. La vie c'est pour la gloi-re de Dieu, A-
3. Le culte est pour la gloi-re de Dieu, A-
4. Le prin-temps pour la gloi-re de Dieu, A-
5. L'of-frande est pour la gloi-re de Dieu, A-

men! A-men!
men! A-men!
men! A-men!
men! A-men!
men! A-men!

1.-5. Tout dé-pend de ce que tu en fais. A-men! A-men! A-men_! A-men__! A-men__! Tout est fait pour la gloi-re de Dieu, A-men! A-men!

215

113

Dieter Hechtenberg 1969

1. Singt das Lied der Freu-de ü-ber Gott!
1. Sing for joy! Sing prai-ses to the Lord!

Lobt ihn laut, der euch er-schaf-fen hat!
Praise his name, the Fa-ther of us all!

Preist ihn, hel-le Ster-ne, lobt ihn, Son-ne, Mond,
Praise him, shin-ing pla-nets, praise him, moon and sun,

auch im Welt-all fer-ne sei-ne Eh-re wohnt.
praise him, far-thest spa-ces, a-toms one by one.

Singt das Lied der Freu-de ü-ber Gott!
Sing for joy! Sing prai-ses to the Lord!

2. Singt das Lied der Freude über Gott! / Lobt ihn laut, der euch erschaffen hat! / Preist ihn, ihr Gewitter, Hagel, Schnee und Wind. / Lobt ihn alle Tiere, die auf Erden sind. / Singt das Lied der Freude über Gott!

3. Singt das Lied der Freude über Gott! / Lobt ihn laut, der euch erschaffen hat. / Stimmt mit ein, ihr Menschen, preist ihn Gross und Klein, / seine Hoheit rühmen soll ein Fest euch sein! / Singt das Lied der Freude über Gott.

4. Singt das Lied der Freude über Gott! / Lobt ihn laut, der euch erschaffen hat. / Er wird Kraft uns geben, Glanz und Licht wird sein, / in das dunkle Leben leuchtet hell sein Schein: / Singt das Lied der Freude über Gott.

Dieter Hechtenberg 1969

2. Sing for joy! Sing praises to the Lord! / Praise his name, the Father of us all! / Praise him, rolling thunder, hail and wind and snow, / praise him, ev'ry creature, moving fast or slow. / Sing for joy! Sing praises to the Lord!

3. Sing for joy! Sing praises to the Lord! / Praise his name, the Father of us all! / Join in, every nation, praise him great and small, / join the celebration! He is Lord of all! / Sing for joy! Sing praises to the Lord!

4. Sing for joy! Sing praises to the Lord! / Praise his name, the Father of us all! / He will send his spirit, day will break on night, / He will give us power, freedom, love and light! / Sing for joy! Sing praises to the Lord!

Ivor Jones 1972

114

1. Se - ka - i no to - mo to te o
1. Here, O Lord, thy ser - vants ga - ther, hand we
1. Dei - ne Knech - te hier ver - ei - net, ste - hen
1. O Jé - sus voi - ci tes frè - res, se te -

tsu - na - gi, Ju - ji - ka no mo - to ni
link with hand: look - ing t'ward our Sa - viour's cross
Hand in Hand, schau - en auf das Kreuz des Her - ren,
nant la main, re - gar - dant la croix du mon - de,

ta - tsu wa - re - ra, Ka - mi no mi - ku -
joined in love we stand. As we seek the realm of
der uns all ver - band. Be - tend ste - hen wir
si - gne de la vie. Pour con - naî - tre ton Ro -

ni o me - a - te to shi, Shu Ie - su no
God we u - nite to pray: Je - sus, Sa - viour
vor dir und ru - fen dir zu: Je - su, Hei - land,
yau - me nous for - mons le cri: O Jé - sus, con -

mi - chi o su - su - mi - yu - kan.
guide our steps for you are the Way.
geh vor - an ! Un - ser Weg bist du.
duis nos pas , toi le seul che - min!

2. Kuni to kotobaba wa kotonaredo, / Kokoro wa onaji Shu no tamu zo. / Kuraki jidai no nozomi naru, / Shu Iesu no makoto hiromeyukan.

3. Uchuu no himitsu saguru tomo, / tokiwa no heiwa nas tooshi. / Tsukare itameru hitobito ni. / Shu Iesu no inochi wakachiyukan.

4. Michi to makoto to inochi naru, / Shu Iesu o tsune no aogitsutsu, / ai ni motozuku tsugi no yo o, / chukara o awase kizukiyukan.

Toko Yamaguchi 1958

2. Many are the tongues we speak, scatter'd are the lands, / yet our hearts are one in God and his love's demands. / Ev'n in darkness hope appears calling age and youth: / Jesus, Teacher, dwell with us, for you are the Truth.

3. Nature's secrets open wide, changes never cease; / where, O where can weary men find the source of peace? / Unto all those sore distressed, torn by endless strife, / Jesus, healer, bring your balm, for you are the Life.

4. Grant, O Lord, an age renewed, filled with deathless love; / help us as we work and pray, send us from above / truth and courage, faith and power needed in our strife: / Jesus, Christ, you are our Way, you our Truth, our Life.

E. M. Stowe 1958 altd.

2. Viele Sprachen sprechen wir, leben weit verstreut, / doch in unsren Herzen wohnet immer gleiche Freud'. / Herr, du rufst die Jung und Alten, lädst uns alle ein. / Wahrheit ist dein Angebind': Hilf uns wahr zu sein.

3. Voller Wunder ist die Erde, zeiget deine Macht. / Doch wie solln wir Frieden finden mitten in der Nacht? / Dank, daß du zu unsrer Hilfe sandtest Jesus Christ, / der nun Heiland, Hoffnung, Herr, unser Leben ist.

4. Mach durch deiner Liebe Kräfte uns zum Dienst bereit. / Hilf uns wachen, hilf uns beten, gib in dieser Zeit / Wahrheit, Mut und starken Glauben, Kraft zu tun dein Wort, / der du Weg und Wahrheit bist, Leben hier und dort.

Erich Griebling 1969

2. Tant de peuples, tant de langues! Nous entendrons-nous? / Mais un Père qui nous aime fonde notre amour. / Tant de langues. Mais la même pousse en nous ce cri: – / O Jésus, habite en nous, toi la Vérité!

3. Notre monde se rénove: tout est merveilleux ... / Mais pourquoi parmi les hommes tant de malheureux, / tant de guerres, de détresses ... Où trouver la paix? / O Jésus, guéris tout homme, toi qui es la Vie!

4. Fais revivre tous les âges par ton seul Esprit! / Fais renaître à l'espérance notre humanité, / Dieu jeunesse, Dieu courage, force d'unité! / Jésus Christ, tu es Chemin, Vie et Vérité.

Claude Rozier 1972

115

Norwegian folk song

1. Her - re Gud, ditt   dy - re navn og   ae - re
1. Might-y God, to   thy dear name be   gi - ven
1. Her - re Gott, deins teu - ren Na - mens Eh - re

o - ver ver - den høit i akt skal vae - re,   og
high-est praise in all the earth and hea - ven.   All
sin - gen Er - de und des Him - mels Hee - re.   Ob

al - le sje - le, de   tret - te trae - le, alt
souls dis - tressed___, all   men op - pressed___, their
Sor - gen quä - len die   mü - den See - len, den -

220

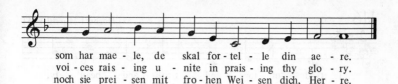

som har mae - le, de   skal for - tel - le din ae - re.
voi - ces rais - ing u - nite in prais - ing thy glo - ry.
noch sie prei - sen mit fro - hen Wei - sen dich, Her - re.

2. Gud er Gud, om alle land lå øde, / Gud er Gud, om alle mann var døde. / Om slekter svimler Blandt Stjernestimler / i høie himler Utallig vrimler Guds grøde.

3. Høie hall og dype dal skal vike. / Jord og himmel falle skal tillike. / Hvert fjell, hver tinde skal brått forsvinne, / men opp skal rinne, som solen skinne Guds rike!

Perrer Dass 1640–1707

2. God is God, tho' all the earth lay wasted; / God is God, though all men death had tasted. / While nations stumble, in darkness fumble, / by stars surrounded countless aboundeth God's harvest.

3. Highest hills and deepest vales shall vanish, / earth and heaven both alike be banished, / as in the dawning of ev'ry morning, / the sun appeareth so glorious neareth God's kingdom.

Eivind Berggrav 1951/2

2. Gott bleibt Gott, ob alle Welt versänke, / Gott bleibt Gott, ob Kreatur ertränke. / Was auch auf Erden Asche mag werden, / In lichten Hallen dort oben schallen dir Lieder.

3. Hohe Berg und tiefe Täler weichen, / Erd und Himmel fallen solln desgleichen. / Die stolzen Zinnen wie Rauch zerrinnen, / Doch fest wird stehen und nie vergehen dein Name.

Eivind Berggrav 1951/2

116

Herbert Murrill 1951

1. God of love and truth and beau - ty,
1. Dieu très haut qui fais mer - veil - le,
1. Gott der Lie - be, Wahr - heit, Schön - heit,

Hal - low'd be thy name; fount of or - der,
Bé - ni soit ton nom! Dieu vi - vant qui
Hei - lig sei dein Name! Quell für Le - ben,

law and du - ty, Hal - low'd be thy name.
fait lar - ges - se, Bé - ni soit ton nom!
Recht und Frei - heit, Hei - lig sei dein Name!

As in heav'n thy hosts a - dore thee, and their
Comme au ciel t'a - dorent les an - ges, et sans
Wie die En - gel Lob dir ge - ben, mit ver -

fa - ces veil be - fore thee, so on earth, Lord,
fin chan - tent lou - an - ge, nous aus - si pri -
hüll - tem Ant - litz be - ben, laß uns, Herr, hier

we im - plore thee, Hal - low'd be thy name.
ons sur ter - re, Bé - ni soit ton nom!
vor dir le - ben: Hei - lig sei dein Name!

2. Lord, remove our guilty blindness, / Hallowed be thy name; / show thy heart of lovingkindness, / Hallowed be thy name. / By our hearts' deep-felt contrition, / by our minds' enlighten'd vision, / by our wills' complete submission, / Hallow'd be thy name.

3. In our worship, Lord most holy, / Hallow'd be thy name; / in our work, however lowly, / Hallow'd be thy name; / in each heart's imagination, / in the Church's adoration, / in the conscience of the nation, / Hallow'd be thy name.

Timothy Rees 1922

2. Dieu vainqueur de nos ténèbres, / Béni soit ton nom! / Dieu penché sur nos faiblesses, / Béni soit ton nom! / Ton amour est notre espérance, / Ta bonté nous rend l'innocence, / De toi seul nous vient la lumière: / Béni soit ton nom!

3. Dieu très saint qui nous libères, / Béni soit ton nom! / Dieu fidèle en tes promesses, / Béni soit ton nom! / Ton Eglise adore en silence / et proclame la délivrance, / de nos cœurs monte une prière: / Béni soit ton nom!

Sœur M-C. Sachot 1972

2. Herr, nimm weg die Schuld, die blendet! / Heilig sei dein Name! / Zeig', was du uns zugewendet. / Heilig sei dein Name ! / Durch des Herzens tiefe Reue, / durch des Geistes wache Treue, / durch Gehorsam stets aufs neue: / Heilig sei dein Name!

3. Wenn wir, Herr, dein Wort befragen – / Heilig sei dein Name! / und am Arbeitsplatz uns plagen: / Heilig sei dein Name! / Wo ein Mensch vor dir sich findet, / wo die Kirche Lob verkündet, / wo ein Volk Recht auf dich gründet: / Heilig sei dein Name!

Auguste Sann 1972

117

Olajida Olude 1964

1. Je - su, a fé pa - dé o L'o - jọ___ Re
1. Je - sus, we want___ to meet on this___ your
1. Je - sus, wir freu - en uns an die - sem
1. O Jé - sus, nous___ voi - ci! nous ve - nons

t'a - jọ mí - mọ́ A sì y'i - te Re ka o
ho - ly day. We ga - ther round___ your throne
dei - nen Tag. Wir stehn um dei - nen Thron
à___ tes pieds! O Jé - sus nous___ voi - ci!

L'o - jọ___ Re t'a - jọ mí - mọ́ I - wọ
on this___ your ho - ly day. You___ are
an die - sem dei - nem Tag. Du___ un -
nous ve - nons à___ tes pieds! Tu___ nous___

ọ - rẹ wa ọ - run A - du - rà wa
___ our heav' - nly friend: our___ prayers are
- ser gro - ßer Freund, hö - re was wir
___ vois ras - sem - blés pour chan - ter et

mbọ wa o, Bo - 'ju - wo e - mi
on their way, look___ on___ our___
ernst ge - meint. Sieh in un - ser Herz___
pour pri - er, et tu dai - gne - ras nous

wa l'o - ni L'o - jọ___ Re t'a - jọ mí - mọ́.
souls this day: on this___ your ho - ly day.
und Den-ken an die - sem dei - nem Tag.
é - cou - ter. C'est ton___ jour, ô___ Sei - gneur!

2. L'erù l'a kunlè ki O, L'Ojo Re t' àjo mímó; / A sì fe k' Iwo ko 'ni L' Ojo Re t' àjo mímó; / Gbà wa là, s' okàn wa d' otun Sàkoso 'se sin yi o, / Bus' èso 'Gbàgbo wa, dakun L' Ojo Re t' àjo mímó.

3. Jesù, a de, bùkun ni l' Ojo Re t' àjo mímó. / F' ayò 'segun Re fun ni, L' Ojo Re t' àjo mímó / Atilà nihin j' èbùn Re, Kà wa ye fun yè, nihín / A fe okàn bi ti Kristì L' Ojo Re t' àjo mímó.

4. L' okàn kan, k' a son l' èye L' Ojo Re t' àjo mímó; / Okan 'lora kò dara, L' Ojo Re t' àjo mímó; / F' Em' Igbàgbo so ni d' òtun Bùkun waasù nihin; / Gbà a nlo, sìn wa lo, Oluwa K' a je Tìre, Tire lai, se.

Olajida Olude 1964

2. We greet you on our knees on this your holy day, / and would be taught by you on this your holy day. / Save us and make us new: lead and guide our songs of praise: / Make the seed of faith to grow, we pray, on this your holy day.

3. Your blessing, Lord, we seek on this your holy day; / give joy of victory on this your holy day. / Through grace alone are we saved; in your flock may we be found; / let the mind of Christ abide in us on this your holy day!

4. Our minds we dedicate on this your holy day; / heart and soul consecrate on this your holy day. / Holy Spirit, make us whole; bless the worship in this place, / and as we go from it, lead us, Lord: we are yours evermore.

Biodun Adebesin and Austin Lovelace 1966

2. Anbetend knien wir an diesem deinem Tag, / daß Gott uns selbst belehr an diesem deinem Tag. / Das Herz bereite du deinem grossen Lobe zu; / lass den Glauben ständig wachsen an diesem deinem Tag.

3. Herr, segne du dein Volk an diesem deinem Tag. / Schenk' Siegesfreunde uns an diesem deinem Tag. / Durch Gnade gib uns Mut. Halte uns in deiner Hut. / Deine Liebe in uns wohne an diesem deinem Tag.

4. Herr, nimm erneut uns hin an diesem deinem Tag; / Herz und Verstand sei dein an diesem deinem Tag. / Dein Geist mach' uns gesund, sei uns nah zu jeder Stund. / Überall, wohin wir gehen, gehören wir zu dir.

Otmar Schulz 1972

2. Tu connais nos péchés! O Jésus, prends pitié! / Tu connais nos péchés! O Jésus, prends pitié! / Mets en nous un cœur pur. / Remplis-nous du Saint-Esprit, / que la foi rayonne dans nos vies! C'est ton jour, ô Seigneur!

3. Bénis-nous, Dieu puissant! Bénis-nous, Christ vivant! / Bénis-nous, Dieu puissant! Bénis-nous, Christ vivant! / Seul Sauveur, seul ami, compte-nous parmi les tiens! / Accompagne-nous dans nos chemins! C'est ton jour, ô Seigneur!

4. Ame et corps, nous voici! Nous voulons te servir! / Ame et corps, nous voici! Nous voulons te servir! / Fais de nous tes témoins dans l'amour et dans la foi. / Donne-nous la paix qui vient de toi! C'est ton jour, ô Seigneur!

Edmond Pidoux 1972

118

Refrain

Melody from Sri Lanka

226

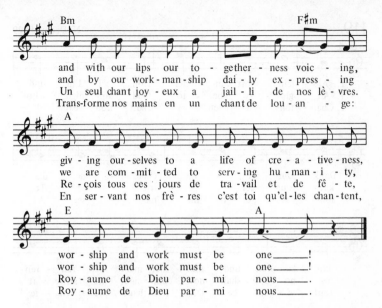

and with our lips our to - gether - ness voic - ing,
and by our work - man - ship dai - ly ex - press - ing
Un seul chant joy - eux a jail - li de nos lè - vres.
Trans-forme nos mains en un chant de lou - an - ge:

giv - ing our - selves to a life of cre - a - tive - ness,
we are com - mit - ted to serv - ing hu - man - i - ty,
Re - çois tous ces jours de tra - vail et de fê - te,
En ser - vant nos frè - res c'est toi qu'el - les chan - tent,

wor - ship and work must be one_____!
wor - ship and work must be one_____!
Roy - aume de Dieu par - mi nous_____.
Roy - aume de Dieu par - mi nous_____.

3. Called to be partners with God in creation, / honouring Christ as the Lord of the nation, / we must be ready for risk and for sacrifice, / worship and work must be one!

4. Bringing the bread and the wine to the table, / asking that we may be led and enabled, / truly united, to find a new brotherhood, / worship and work must be one!

5. Now in response to the life you are giving, / help us, O Father, to offer our living, / seeking a just and a healing society, / worship and work must be one!

Fred Kaan 1972

3. Voici nos mains pour que vienne ton règne. / Voici nos deux mains pour que change la terre: / Remplis de ta force d'amour tous nos gestes, / Royaume de Dieu parmi nous.

4. Voici le pain et le vin sur la table: / Fais de nous Seigneur le ferment dans la pâte / Le sel d'une vie fraternelle, amicale, / Royaume de Dieu parmi nous.

5. Prends nous la main quand nos forces s'épuisent. / Père, que ta main aujourd'hui nous conduise / Là où nous verrons se lever ta justice, / Royaume de Dieu parmi nous.

N. Berthet 1973

119

N. Decius 1529

1. Al - lein Gott in der Höh' sei Ehr und
1. All glo - ry be to God on high, who
1. Chan - tons à Dieu ce chant nou - veau, di -

Dank für sei - ne Gna - de, dar -
hath our race be - friend - ed! To
sons sa gloi - re im - men - se. A

um, daß nun und nim - mer - mehr uns rüh - ren
us no harm shall now come nigh, the strife at
tout vi - vant ce Dieu très haut pré - sen - te

kann___ kein Scha - de. Ein Wohl - ge -
last___ has en - ded. God sho - weth
son___ al - lian - ce: Un cœur ou -

falln Gott an uns hat; nun ist groß Fried ohn
his good - will to men, and peace shall reign on
vert: le Fils li - vré! Un vent de joie: l'Es -

Un - ter - laß, all Fehd hat nun ein En - de.
earth a - gain; O thank him for his good - ness!
prit don - né! Ren - dons à Dieu sa grâ - ce!

228

2. Wir loben, preisn, anbeten dich; / für deine Ehr wir danken, / dass du, Gott Vater ewiglich / regierst ohn alles Wanken. / Ganz ungemessn ist deine Macht, / fort g'schieht, was dein Will hat bedacht: / wohl uns des feinen Herren!

3. O Jesu Christ, Sohn eingeborn, / deines himmlischen Vaters, / Versöhner der', die warn verlorn, / du Stiller unsers Haders, / Lamm Gottes, heilger Herr und Gott: / nimm an die Bitt von unsrer Not, / erbarm dich unser aller.

4. O Heilger Geist, du höchstes Gut, / du alterheilsamst' Tröster, / vor Teufels Gwalt fortan behüt, / die Jesus Christ erlöset / durch grosse Martr und bittern Tod; / abwend all unsern Jammr und Not! / Darauf wir uns verlassen!

N. Decius 1480–1529

2. We praise, we worship thee, we trust / and give thee thanks for ever, / O Father, that thy reign is just / and wise and changes never. / Thy boundless power o'er all things reigns, / done is whate'er thy will ordains: / well for us that thou reignest!

3. O Jesus Christ, thou only Son / of God, thy heavenly Father, / who didst for all our sins atone / and thy lost sheep dost gather; / thou Lamb of God, to thee on high / from out our depths we sinners cry – / have mercy on us, Jesus!

4. O Holy Ghost, thou precious Gift, / thou comforter unfailing, / o'er Satan's snares our souls uplift / and let thy power availing / avert our woes and calm our dread: / for us the Saviour's blood was shed; / we trust in thee to save us.

C. Winkworth 1863

2. Honneur à toi, Premier Vivant! / à toi la gloire, ô Père! / Louange à toi dans tous les temps, / Seigneur de ciel et terre! / Ta voix murmure 'viens au Jour!': / ton cœur nous dit: / 'je suis l'Amour!' / Aimez-vous tous en frères.

3. Jésus, au prix du sang versé, / tu dis l'amour du Père: / O viens, seigneur du plein été, / nous prendre en ta lumière, / délivre-nous de tout péché; / enseigne-nous à tout donner; / rénove enfin la terre.

4. Esprit de Dieu, vivant Amour, / refais nos vies nouvelles. / Engendre-nous, mets-nous au jour; / maintiens nos cœurs fidèles. / Réveille-nous de notre nuit; / Ranime en nous le feu de Vie, / O Feu de joie nouvelle.

C. Rozier 1973

120

1. Bo - že___ Ot - če___, bud' poch - vá -
1. Dank, Gott___, daß du___ nach dunk - ler
1. Dear Fa - ther, God___, we rise to
1. O Dieu, no - tre Pè - re, qui es aux

len, žes nám___ dal ten - to dneš - ní -
Nacht den neu - en Tag___ hast licht___ ge -
say: your name___ be praised for this___ new
cieux, u - ni - que Sei - gneur, in - vi - sible à nos

den, dob - rém___ zdra - ví___ u - hlí - da -
macht. Be - schütz___ uns, Herr___, vor je - dem
day. For health___ and strength our pray - ers to
yeux, en toi tou - te vie en - ra - ci - ne sa

ti ó rač___ nám u - že do - bré dá - ti.
Schad, und bleib___ bei uns___ mit dei - ner Gnad!
lift: grant ev - r'y good___ and per - fect gift!
joie, et tous les che - mins font re - tour vers toi.

2. Bože Synu, tě žádáme, / at'v tento den to konáme, / co by se Tobě líbilo / a nám spasitelné bylo.

3. Bože Duchu, chrăn od zlého, / potěš v żarmutku každého, / a když přijde poslední den, / pojmiž nás všech k sobě, Amen.

Jiri Záboinik, 1608–72

2. Du, Gottes Sohn, Herr Jesu Christ, / schenk uns, was für uns nützlich ist, / und gib uns Kraft, an diesem Tag / zu tun, was dir gefallen mag.

3. O Heil'ger Geist, steh du uns bei, / von allem Übel uns befrei; / tröst, die da sind in Angst noch hier, / und endlich nimm uns einst zu dir.

Erich Griebling, 1969

2. O God the Son, we pray of you, / may all we plan and say and do / be ever welcome in your sight, / be done to your and our delight.

3. O Spirit God, preserve from fear / all those who fret and sorrow here; / and when the day of days arrives, / with fadeless glory crown our lives.

J. J. Vajda, 1969

2. Seigneur Jésus-Christ, Fils du Dieu vivant, / Tu viens parmi nous et ta Croix nous apprend. / Que Dieu se fait nôtre en payant sa vie, / capable d'aimer jusqu'à en mourir.

3. Esprit du Seigneur qui nous est donné, / tu guides nos cœurs au Royaume caché, / tu rends leur saveur aux paroles du Christ: / un monde était mort, et voilà qu'il vit!

D. Hameline, 1972

121

Elena G. Maquiso 1961

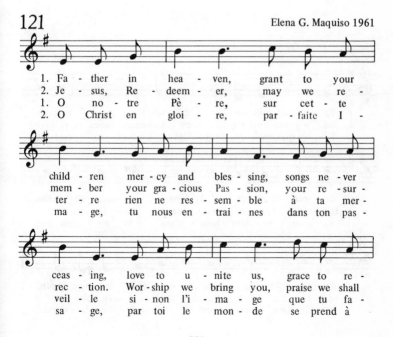

1. Fa - ther in hea - ven, grant to your child - ren mer - cy and bles - sing, songs ne - ver ceas - ing, love to u - nite us, grace to re -
2. Je - sus, Re - deem - er, may we re - mem - ber your gra - cious Pas - sion, your re - sur - rec - tion. Wor - ship we bring you, praise we shall

1. O no - tre Pè - re, sur cet - te ter - re rien ne res - sem - ble à ta mer - veil - le si - non l'i - ma - ge que tu fa -
2. O Christ en gloi - re, par - faite I - ma - ge, tu nous en - trai - nes dans ton pas - sa - ge, par toi le mon - de se prend à

231

deem us,   Fa - ther in   hea - ven,   Fa - ther our   God.
sing you   Je - sus, Re - deem - er,   Je - sus our   Lord.
çon - nes   cré - ant les   hom - mes   pour qu'ils soient tiens.
vi - vre,   tu tiens le   Li - vre   du Der - nier   Jour.

3. Spirit descending, / whose is the blessing – / strength for the weary, /
help for the needy, / sealed in our sonship / yours be our worship – /
Spirit unending, / Spirit adored.

D. T. Niles, 1961

3. Esprit qui veilles / en nos épreuves, / tu viens construire / la Cité
neuve, / par ta présence / tout recommence / dans l'espérance / des
Cieux Nouveaux.

D. Hameline, 1972

122

Martin Luther 1483 - 1546

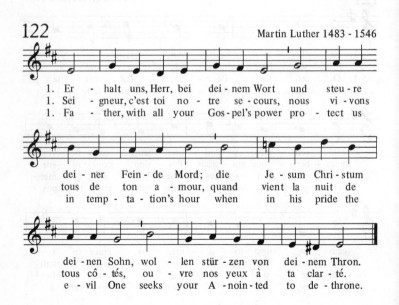

1. Er - halt uns, Herr, bei dei - nem Wort und steu - re
1. Sei - gneur, c'est toi no - tre se - cours, nous vi - vons
1. Fa - ther, with all your Gos - pel's power pro - tect us

dei - ner Fein - de Mord; die Je - sum Chri - stum
tous de ton a - mour, quand vient la nuit de
in temp - ta - tion's hour when in his pride the

dei - nen Sohn, wol - len stür - zen von dei - nem Thron.
tous cô - tés, ou - vre nos yeux à ta clar - té.
e - vil One seeks your A - noin - ted to de - throne.

2. Beweis dein Macht, Herr Jesu Christ, / der du Herr aller Herren bist, / beschirm dein arme Christenheit, / dass sie dich lob in Ewigkeit.

3. Gott, Heilger Geist, du Tröster wert, / gib deim Volk ein'rlei Sinn auf Erd, steh bei uns in der letzten Not, / g'leit uns ins Leben aus dem Tod.

Martin Luther 1524

2. O toi Jésus notre Seigneur, / accorde-nous le grand bonheur / de partager le même pain, / nous réjouir à ton festin. /

3. O viens sur nous, toi Saint-Esprit, / donner ce que Dieu a promis. / Rassemble-nous pour le louer / et le servir en vérité. /

F. Levrier 1972

2. Our King of glory, Jesus Christ, / power in obedience manifest, / defend your church in dangerous days / and liberate us for your praise.

3. Spirit by Christ's atonement given / to bring together earth and heaven / in us, between us, silence strife, / and lead us out of death to life.

Erik Routley 1973 (last line, Catherine Winkworth)

The Church – Its Experience and Faith
Die Kirche – Leben und Glaube
L'Eglise – Expérience et Foi

123

Traditional Irish melody

1. Be thou my_ Vi - sion, O_ Lord of my heart;
1. Qu'en toi je_ vi - ve, Sei - gneur bien ai - mé.
1. Herr mei - nes_ Her - zens, gib_ du auf mich acht!

all else but nought to me save that thou art;
O sour - ce vi - ve, de fé - li - ci - té,
Oh - ne dich bleib ich in Ne - bel und Nacht!

thou my_ best thought in the day and the night___,
qu'à toi_ je_ pen - se le jour et la nuit___,
Oh - ne_ dich sind die Ge - dan - ken ver - wirrt_.

wak - ing and sleep - ing, thy_ pre - sence my light.
car ta clé - men - ce tou - jours me bé - nit!
Sei ge - gen - wär - tig, mein Hei - land und Hirt!

2. Be thou my wisdom, be thou my true Word; / thou ever with me, and I with thee, Lord; / thou my great Father, and I thy true Son: / thou in me dwelling, and I with thee one.

3. Be thou my breastplate, my sword for the fight: / thou my whole armour, and thou my true might; / thou my soul's shelter, and thou my strong tower: / raise thou me heavenward, great power of my power.

4. Riches I heed not nor man's empty praise, / thou mine inheritance now and always; / thou and thou only the first in my heart; / sovereign of heaven, my treasure thou art.

5. High King of heaven, thou heaven's bright sun, / grant me its joys, after vict'ry is won; / heart of my own heart, whatever befall, / be thou my Vision, O ruler of all.

Mary Byrne 1905, here altered as in BBC Hymn Book 1951

2. Dieu, ta sagesse rayonne sur moi; / le mal me presse, toujours garde-moi; / père, fais grâce, pardonne à ton fils, / montre ta face, vis en mon esprit.

3. Lorsque je ploie sois mon ferme appui, / donne ta joie, sois mon sûr abri, / ma forteresse, mon seul bouclier, / de la détresse tu sais me garder.

4. Fuir la richesse les propos flatteurs, / dans l'allégresse servir le Seigneur: / mon bien suprême c'est lui, mon Sauveur, / car si je l'aime, il vit dans mon cœur.

5. A toi la gloire, Seigneur notre Dieu, / car ta victoire nous ouvre les cieux. / Fais, ô bon Maître, toujours, en tous lieux, / à tous connaître ton nom glorieux.

F. du Pasquier 1950

2. Ewige Weisheit, Wahrhaftiges Wort! / Heiliger Vater, mein Herr hier und dort! / Hilf uns zur Kindschaft und eine die Welt, / die mit sich selber in Feindschaft zerfällt.

3. Gib uns die Würde, die jeder verlor! / Führ uns zur Heimat und öffne das Tor; / Zuflucht gewähre dem, den du befreit! / Herr, mein Erretter, mein Schutzherr im Streit!

4. Kostbar ist, König, was du uns getan! / Mit neuen Augen seh'n wir es jetzt an. / Leer ist dagegen was Menschen erdacht, / Reichtum und Ehre vergehn über Nacht.

5. Herrscher der Himmel, bei dem aller Krieg / unter dem Wort sich verwandelt in Sieg! / Herr meines Herzens, wie gern bin ich dein! / Ohne dich wär' ich verwirrt und allein.

Helga Rusche 1950

1. Oh Dios de mi al - ma, sé___ tú mi vi - sión,
1. Deus de minh' al - ma sê___ mi - nha vi - são,
1. て て ろ み の 世 に あ れ ど

na - da te a - par - te de mi co - ra - zón,
na - da te a - fas - te do meu ço - ra - ção;
み ち び き の ひ か り な る

no - che___ y día pien - so yo___ en ti___,
na - es - cu - ri - dã - o di - a a bril - har___
主 を あ お ぎ 雨 の よ も

y tu pre - sen - cia es___ luz pa - ra mi.
tu - a pre - sen - ça me___ ve - nha gui - ar!
た か ら か に は め う た わ ん

2. Sabiduría sé Tú de mi ser; / quiero a tu lado mi senda correr; / como tu hijo tenme, Señor, / siempre morando en un mismo amor.

3. Sé mi escudo, mi espada en la lid; / mi única gloria, mi dicha sin fin; / del alma amparo, mi torreón; / a las alturas condúceme oh Dios.

4. Riquezas vanas no anhelo, Señor, / ni el hueco halago de la adulación; / tu eres mi herencia, Tú mi porción, / rey de los cielos, tesoro mejor.

5. Oh Rey de gloria, del triunfo al final, / déjame el gozo del cielo alcanzar; / alma de mi alma, dueño y Señor, / en vida o muerte sé tú mi visión.

F. J. Pagura 1960

2. Sabedoria sê tu de meu ser; / quero ao teu lado meus dias viver. / Vem tu meu Pai, comigo habitar; / contigo eu quero do amor desfrutar.

3. Sê meu escudo e espada ao lutar, / sê meu deleite, sê glória sem par, / sê proteção, amparo e poder, / que nas álturas eleve o meu ser.

4. Vàs riquezas e glórias daqui, / certa é a herança doada por ti; / tu, em meu ser, somente eu porei / como o primeiro, e o único Rei.

5. Rei soberano, chegando o final / dá-me as delicias da glória eterna; / reina em meu ser, e em meu coração / seja o teu brilho de tudo a visão.

J. Costa 1971

2. まこととなるみことばはよ、
   まよえるをひきかえし、
   めぐみもて子よと呼び、
   わがうちに住みたもう。

3. 富も名もなにかあらん、
   わがうちの宮にます
   あがないの主イエスてそ、
   まさりたるたからなれ。

4. 世のちからせまれども、
   死に勝ちし主によれば、
   やすらけきよろこびは
   わがむねにみちあふる。

124

Chinese melody

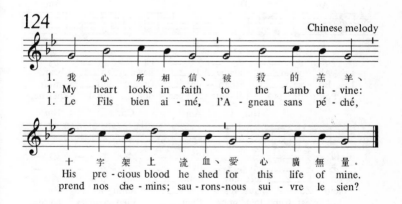

1. 我　心　所　相　信、被　殺　的　羔　羊、
1. My　heart　looks　in　faith　to　the　Lamb　di-vine:
1. Le　Fils　bien　ai-mé,　l'A-gneau　sans　pé-ché,

十　字　架　上　流　血、愛　心　廣　無　量。
His　pre-cious blood　he shed for　this　life　of　mine.
prend　nos　che-mins;　sau-rons-nous　sui-vre　le　sien?

2. 我心所仰望、聖子主耶穌、罪惡有他救渡、跌倒有他
   扶。

3. 我心所敬愛、基督耶穌名、他能使我服務、建立我德
   行。

4. 我有信望愛、我有主耶穌、我有全副軍裝、忠勇做門
   徒。（阿們。）

2. My heart waits in hope / to the Lamb divine: / sure are his promises, / they encompass me.

3. My heart dwells in love / by the Spirit blest; / he heals my sicknesses, / sets my soul at rest.

4. All faith, hope and love / are by Jesus given, / on earth to give us strength / and his peace in heaven.

Frank W. Price 1965

2. Sa gloire humiliée, / son cœur transpercé, / montrent la voie; saurons- / nous prendre sa croix?

3. Tandis qu'il passait, / la crainte en secret / nous a saisis, saurons- / -nous perdre nos vies?

4. O! Viens dans nos cœurs, / esprit du Seigneur, / don sans retour, pour qu'en / nous règne l'amour

Soeur Marie-Pierre Faure 1972

125

12th century Japanese melody

1. Ah what shame I have to bear, for I left my home to pur - sue an empty dream, spent my life in vain!

1. Bö - se Schan - de fiel auf mich; mein Zu - haus ver - spielt. Rann - te lee - ren Träu - men nach. Ziel - los war der Weg.

1. Point de pro - di - gue sans par - don qui le cherche, nul n'est trop loin pour Dieu: Vien - nent les lar - mes où le Fils re - naît, joie du re - tour au Père.

2 ならわぬわざの 牧場守、
草のいおりの おきふしに、
ひとのなさけの うすごろも、
うき世の風ぞ 身にはしむ。

3 破れしたもとに おく露も、
父のめぐみを しのばせて、
まよいの夢も 覚めにけり。
いざふるさとへ かえりゆかん。

2. In this hut I sleep and wake, / taking care of swine: / no one has pity on me: / loud blows the chilly wind.

3. Tatter'd sleeves are wet with dew / when I think of home. / Waking from my foolish dreams, / to my home I'll go.

Esther Hibbard 1962

2. Auf der Straße sitze ich, / keiner dreht sich um, / keiner hilft mir, kümmert sich, / bin allein mit mir.

3. Unter Fremden friere ich, / wär ich nur daheim! / Jäh zerfiel das Kartenhaus. / Nehmt ihr mich noch auf?

F. K. Barth, S. Leonhard und O. Schulz 1972

2. Point de blessure que sa main ne guérisse, / rien n'est perdu pour Dieu: / vienne la Grâce où la vie reprend, / flamme jaillie des cendres.

3. Point de ténèbres sans espoir de lumière, / rien n'est fini pour Dieu: / vienne l'aurore où l'amour surgit, / chant d'un matin de Pâques.

Soeur Marie-Pierre Faure 1972

1 思之慚 愧 不 能 當! 離父 我彷徨，
繁華夢 裏 久 奔忙，沉醉 心如狂。

2 牧豕本 非 我 善長； 倦眠 茅草房，
世人憐 恤 薄 衣裳，難敵 朔風狂。

3 袖間露 點 渾 如 滌，觀之 念父愛，
黃昏將 過，日 將 來，我今 決意歸。

126

Johann Crüger 1653

1. Je - su mei - ne Freu - de, mei - nes Her - zens
1. Je - sus, price - less trea - sure, source of pu - rest
1. Dieu mon al - lé - gres - se, viens, par ta jeu -
1. Cris - to mi a - le - grí - a, pan del al - ma

Wei - de, Je - su mei - ne Zier, ach, wie
plea - sure, tru - est friend to me, long my
nes - se, ra - fraî - chir ma vie: Dieu mon
mí - a, siem - pre fiel a mi. Có - mo

lang, ach lan - ge ist dem Her - zen ban - ge,
heart has pan - ted, till it well nigh fain - ted,
al - lé - gres - se, viens, par ta jeu - nes - se,
he bus - ca - do, cuan - to me he an - gus - tia - do,

und ver - langt nach dir. Got - tes Lamm, mein
thirs - ting af - ter thee. Thine I am, O
ra - fraî - chir ma vie. Vois l'eau vi - ve
se - dien - to de Ti! Siem - pre tu - yo

Bräu - ti - gam, au - ßer dir soll mir auf
spot - less Lamb, I will suf - fer nought to
qui s'en - fuit, le dé - sert et l'a - ven -
he de ser, na - da an - he - lo en es - te

Er - den nichts sonst lie - ber wer - den.
hide thee, ask for nought be - side thee.
tu - re, si tu ne m'as - su - re.
mun - do, si - no so - lo a Ti_____.

240

2. Unter deinem Schirmen / bin ich vor den Stürmen / aller Feinde frei. / Laß von Ungewittern / rings die Welt erzittern, / mir steht Jesus bei. / Ob's mit Macht gleich blitzt und kracht, / wenn gleich Sünd und Hölle schrecken, / Jesus will mich decken.

3. Weicht, ihr Trauergeister; / denn mein Freudenmeister, / Jesus tritt herein. / Denen, die Gott lieben, / muß auch ihr Betrüben / lauter Freude sein. / Duld' ich schon hier Spott und Hohn, / dennoch bleibst auch du im Leide, / Jesus meine Freude.

J. W. Franck 1653

2. In thine arms I rest me; / foes who would molest me / cannot reach me here. / Though the earth be shaking, / ev'ry heart be quaking, / God dispels our fear; / sin and hell in conflict fell / with their heaviest storms assail us: / Jesus will not fail us.

3. Hence, all thoughts of sadness! / for the Lord of gladness, / Jesus, enters in. / Those who love the Father, / though the storms may gather, / still have peace within. / Yea, whate'er we here must bear, / still in Thee liest purest pleasure, / Jesus, priceless treasure!

Catherine Winkworth 1863

2. Dieu mon espérance, / viens, par ta puissance, / réveiller ma vie: / Dieu mon espérance, / viens, par ta puissance, / réveiller ma vie: / vois le temps qui m'a détruit, / la victoire des ténèbres, / si tu ne m'éclaires.

3. Dieu notre impatience, / viens, par ton silence, / apaiser nos vies: / Dieu notre impatience, / viens par ton silence, / apaiser nos vies: / sois un chant pour notre cri, / compagnon qui nous devance, / Dieu notre impatience.

Claude Rozier 1972

2. A sun amor me entrego, / y a Satán no temo, / no puede dañar. / Aunque el mundo tiemble / mi temor ardiente / Jesús calmará. / El dolor puede atacar / y el pecado asaltarme, / el no ha de fallarme.

3. Cuando la tristeza / llame a mi puerta, / Cristo, alégrame. / Si tú estás conmigo, / mi aflicción olvido; / ténme junto a Ti. / Y aunque gima de dolor, / cantará el alma mía, / Cristo, mi alegría.

Roberto E. Ríos

1. Ye - sus, sum - ber su - ka, Kau - lah ku - rin - du - kan,
1. Ye - su mpen - zi wa - ngu u - fu - ra - hi - sha - ye
1. わ が よ ろ て び な ぐ さ め な る

Kau hi - as - an - ku! Sam - pai ka - pan, Tu - han,
mo - yo kwa kwe - li. Ta - ngu si - ku nying - i
さ か え の 主 わ が て ろ は

ha - ti ke - ri - sau - an me - nan - ti - kan - Mu?
ni - na ha - ja kub - wa na - we, Bwa - na - ngu.
ひ さ し く 主 を 待 ち の ぞ む

Dom - ba Hu, Peng - an - tin - ku, tia - da ha -
Ndi - we mpen - zi wa - ngu mkuu, we - we pe -
主 に ま さ り て あ い す

rap lain ku - pu - nya di se - lu - run du - nia!
ke ya - ko mpon - ya ha - pa du - ni - a - ni.
る わ が 友 て の 世 に な し

2. Dalam lindunganMu / aku tak terganggu / rusuh penyerbu. / Biar bergemuruh / langit-bumi runtuh, / Yesus kawanku! / Mau pecah gelora bah, / mau neraka mengejutkan: / Yesus mel uputkan!

3. Surut, momok duka! / Raja t'rang dan suka, / Yesus, yang menang! / Kaum kekasih Tuhan, / buanglah keluhan: / g'lapmu jadi t'rang! / Di tengah cemoh-cela / Kau tetap, pun dalam duka, / Yesus, sumber suka!

Yayasan Musik Gerejani 1973

2. Wewe mlinzi wangu / waondoa shida / zinitesazo. / Mwovu aogofye / vyote viteteme / Yesu yu kwangu. / Huzuni ikizidi, / vyote vikiharibika / Yesu anishika.

242

3. Roho ya huzuni / nenda zako mbali, / Yesu yuaja. / Yesu akiwapo, /
hata shida zote / hazinishindi. / Watu wakinitesa / hawawezi kunitenga /
na mwokozi wangu.

2. 主のいませば　世のあらしも　なにかあらん。
　　地はさくとも　主はわが身と　ともにあらん。
　　つみのちから　われに迫まるとも　恐れあらじ。

3. 主はてよなき　わがよろこび　宝なれ。
　　世のさかえに　まどわされて　なびくまじ。
　　なやみも死も　われを主イエスより　はなすをえじ。

4. とく失せ去れ、　うきとおそれ　主はきまさん。
　　主にありては　くるしみさえ　幸となる。
　　迫めと恥の　おそいきたるとも　われやすけし。

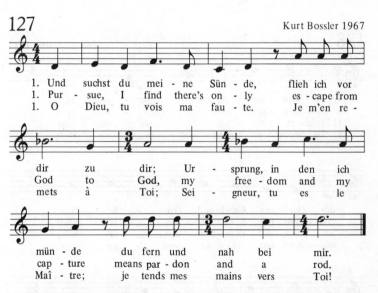

127　　　　　　　　　　　　　　　　Kurt Bossler 1967

1. Und suchst du mei - ne Sün - de, flieh ich vor
1. Pur - sue, I find there's on - ly es - cape from
1. O Dieu, tu vois ma fau - te. Je m'en re -

dir zu dir; Ur - sprung, in den ich
God to God, my free - dom and my
mets à Toi; Sei - gneur, tu es le

mün - de du fern und nah bei mir.
cap - ture means par - don and a rod.
Maî - tre; je tends mes mains vers Toi!

2. Wie ich mich wend und drehe, / geh ich von dir zu dir; / die Ferne
und die Nähe / sind aufgehoben hier.

3. Von dir zu dir mein Schreiten, / mein Weg und meine Ruh, / Gericht
und Gnade, beides, / bist du, bist immer du.

Schalom Ben-Chorim 1931

2. In restless haste my journey / affords no changing view; / the route on which I hurry / begins and ends with you.

3. My start and destination, / my patron and my guest; / you are my Judge and Saviour; / you are my toil and rest.

Ivor Jones 1972

2. Tant ma douleur est grande, / plus de repos pour moi; / toi seul, Seigneur, me sauves: / pitié, pardonne-moi!

3. O Toi qui est Tendresse, / ne m'abandonne pas; / vers Toi; Seigneur, je marche: / tu affermis mes pas!

Sœur Ancelle 1972

128

Johann Walter 1541

1. All Mor - gen ist ganz frisch _ und neu
1. Each mor - ning with its new - born light
1. Fraîche et nou - vel - le cha - que jour
1. De trouw en goed - heid van _ de Heer

des Her - ren Gnad und gro - ße Treu,
pro - claims the Lord of life _ is great!
Ta grâce, ô Dieu, dure à _ ja - mais,
ver - schijnt ons el - ke mor - gen weer,

sie hat kein End den lan - gen Tag,
His faith - ful - ness will have no end;
Of - frant, fi - dèle, à notre a - mour
en blinkt en blijft als dauw zo fris,

drauf	je -	der	sich	ver -	las -	- sen	mag.
to	him	our	songs	of	praise	as -	cend.
un	sûr	a - bri	de	cal -	- me	paix.	
zo -	lang	het	dag	op	aar -	- de	is.

2. Drum steht der Himmel Lichter voll, / daß man zum Leben sehen soll / und es mög schön geordnet sein, / zu ehren Gott, den Schöpfer dein.

3. So hat der Leib der Augen Licht, / daß er dadurch viel Guts ausricht / und seh auf Gott zu aller Frist / und merk, wie er so gnädig ist.

4. O Gott, du schöner Morgenstern, / gib uns, was wir von dir begehr'n: / zünd deine Lichter in uns an, / laß uns an Gnad kein Mangel han.

5. Treib aus, o Licht, all Finsternis, / behüt uns, Herr, vor Ärgernis, / vor Blindheit und vor aller Schand / und beut' uns Tag und Nacht dein' Hand.

6, Zu wandeln als am lichten Tag, / damit was immer sich zutrag, / wir steh'n im Glauben bis ans End' / und bleiben von dir ungetrennt.

Johannes Zwick (1496–1542)

2. The gift of light that fills the sky / helps us to see and choose our way; / then let us order our affairs / in praise of him who for us cares.

3. Lord, let our eyes, the body's light, / be drawn to what is good and right / and to yourself, the source of life, / our hope in fear, our peace in strife.

4. You, Lord of all creation, are / as brilliant as the morning star; / light in our hearts your holy flame / and make us fit to bear your name.

5. Dispel the darkness from our days / and free us from all bitterness, / from haughty mind and blinded sight, / and lead us forward day and night.

6. To walk as in the light of day, / be steadfast always, come what may, / we turn in faith to you, our Friend, / and pray: sustain us to the end.

Fred Kaan 1972

2. Le Ciel rayonne de clarté / pour que nous puissions voir, Seigneur, / notre pêché, ta sainteté / et chantions notre Créateur!

3. Ainsi la clarté de nos yeux / peut nous guider en ces bas lieux, / mais nous tournant vers les hauts cieux / nous connaissons ta grâce, ô Dieu.

4. Seigneur, étoile du matin, / exauce-nous dans ta bonté; / allume en nous, brûlante enfin, / la clarté de ta vérité.

5. Dissipe en nous l'obscurité; / garde-nous de haine et courroux, / d'aveuglement, de dureté, / tends nuit et jour ta main vers nous!

6. Or pour marcher dans le plein jour / nous restons fermes dans la foi / puis, nous haussant vers ton amour, / vivons sans fin tout près de toi.

Pauline Martin 1951

2. O God, Gij schone morgenster, / Gij stralend licht, blijf ons niet ver. / Zet door uw liefde ons hart in gloed. / Geef dat het U nooit missen moet.

3. Drijf uit, o licht, wat duister is, / bewaar ons hart voor ergernis, / voor blinde ijver, zonde en schuld. / Verlicht ons, houdt- U niet verhuld.

4. Opdat wij wandlen als bij dag / en, kome wat er komen mag, / vaststaan in het geloof, o Heer, / van U verlaten nimmermeer.

Ad. den Besten

129

Orlando Gibbons 1623

1. Forth in thy name, O Lord, I go, My dai-ly
1. In dei-nem Na-men, o mein Herr, ich täg-lich
1. Quand je m'en vais à mon tra-vail, Vers Dieu je

la-bour to pur-sue; Thee, on-ly thee, re-solved
mei-ne Ar-beit tu; ich hab da-bei nur dich
lance un cri de foi En re-gar-dant les hom-

to know, In all I think or speak or do.
im Sinn in al-lem Den-ken, Re-den, Tun.
mes___ Pres-ser le pas sous l'hor-lo-ge.

2. The task thy wisdom hath assigned / O let me cheerfully fulfil; / in all my works thy presence find, / and prove thy good and perfect will.

3. Thee may I set at my right hand, / whose eyes my inmost substance see, / and labour on at thy command / and offer all my works to thee.

4. Give me to bear the easy yoke, / and every moment watch and pray, / and still to things eternal look, / and hasten to thy glorious day.

5. For thee delightfully employ / whate'er thy bounteous grace hath given, / and run my course with even joy, / and closely walk with thee to heaven.

Charles Wesley 1749

2. Das Werk, das du mir zugedacht, / laß fröhlich mich erfüllen heut. / In allem Tun sei du mir nah. / Zeig deinen guten Willen mir.

3. Zur Rechten will ich sehen dich, / der du mein Innerstes stets schaust; / will arbeiten auf dein Geheiß, / geweiht sei dir mein ganzes Tun.

4. Hilf mir, zu tragen, Herr, dein Joch / und laß mich wachend, betend sein. / Richt meinen Blick zur Ewigkeit, / bring bald herbei den großen Tag.

5. Für dich mit Freuden ich setz' ein, / was deine Gnade mir einst gab. / Mein Leben ich mit Freuden führ. / Dicht folge ich zum Himmel dir.

E. Schaller 1972

2. Sur les chantiers je vois bâtir / un monde neuf où vit l'Esprit / que Dieu répand sur terre / depuis la Pâque nouvelle.

3. Sous le soleil je vois mûrir / l'épi qui monte pour le fruit / au cœur de ceux qui donnent / un peu d'amour à tout homme.

4. Comme une vigne au pied des monts, / fleurit l'espoir du vigneron / dont le couteau émonde / les belles branches fécondes.

5. Quand mon travail sera fini / et que viendra sur moi la nuit, / entre les mains du Père / j'achèverai ma prière.

J. Martin 1973

130

Lòh I - tò b. 1936

(國) 1. 主 祢 託付 我 工作、 勤 勉
(台) 1. 主 祢 交代 我 工程、 我 盡
1. 'Light and salt' you called your friends, 'on the
1. Je le sais bien, ton a - mour m'in - vite

不 敢 蹉 跎、 無 奈 世 上
力 在 打 併、 若 是 此 世
hill your ci - ty: let your light shine
et me don - ne cœur, mais au long de

太 騷 擾、 令 人 心 煩 意 燥、
間 聲 音、 過 頭 多 攪 擾 心、
out for men, skill and peace and pi - ty.'
ce par - cours qu'il me faut ga - gner pour toi;

那 時 我 心 願 寧 靜、 敞 開
彼 時 我 心 愛 定 定、 集 中
But if salt has lost its taste, and the
je n'ai plus con - fiance en moi car je

心 門 聆 聽、 在 我 每 日
注 神 來 聽、 對 日 日 當
light its fu - el, and the ci - ty
sais mon peu d'ar - deur tout au long de

248

工　作　中、　聽　主　聲　來　跟　　從。
做　工　程、　主　在　指　示　之　　聲。
shuts its gates, whence can come re - new - al?
ce par-cours qu'il— me faut ga - gner, Sei - gneur.

國語音

2. 我正服務此世中、恐流俗與世同、雖然不嫌世路艱、
謀生受苦難免、懇求天父伸聖手、扶持免受引誘、保
守主民百忙中、時刻與主相通。

3. 世上生活不單純、容易跌倒沈淪、有時明知是不義、
尚且難得逃避、或許權勢迫我行、辜負我主聖名、願
我勇敢又清廉、做為世上光塩。

4. 人間事物愈繁雜、人與人難融洽、每逢難事心困擾、
何處供我商討、懇求我主做橋樑、使人互相體諒、祢
是救主世無雙、審判世上君王。

台語音

2. 今我於工作中間、驚了只趁世間、雖無嫌境遇艱苦、
當為生活奔波、懇求天父伸聖手、扶持免受引誘、給
我於無閒中間、也搞住主平安。

3. 世間生活無單純、容易跌落沈淪、有時明知是不義、
尚且難得閃避、有時權勢迫我行、辜負我主尊名、願
我勇敢和清廉、成做世間光塩。

4. 社會辦事愈複雜、人人愈難和合、要緊事情當參詳、
却無路可商量、願主做仲保機能、使人做事和平、祢
是世界主人翁、審判地上君王。

2. Each in his own place receives / gospel, guidance, duty: / daily bread
and daily work, / t'ward the Kingdom's beauty. / Yet the world's
distracting scene / mocks our lofty vision. / Life's complexities confuse /
conscience and decision.

3. Men dispute and nations fight / each all virtue claiming; / your disciple
errs and falls, / false opinion framing. / Judge me, Lord, and plead my
cause, / light and truth now send me; / lead me in your righteousness /
chasten and befriend me.

Paraphrase by Erik Routley
(Not for simultaneous singing)

2. Je le sais bien, tu m'as dit / que l'espoir nous est donné, / mais l'étape d'aujourd'hui / me conduit en plein désert: / je suis seul pour le concert, / abattu, abandonné, / car l'étape d'aujourd'hui / m'a conduit en plein désert.

3. Je le sais bien, avant moi, / sur la croix, cloué pour nous, / un Autre a connu le poids / du silence et du mépris: / il n'est pas de paradis entre les murs de nos jours, / un Autre a connu le poids / du silence et du mépris.

4. Je le sais bien, la fadeur / de ce monde attend mon sel, / et je sais que ma lueur / peut briller dans notre nuit. / Si le sel s'est affadi / comment le salerons-nous, / si ce n'est pas toi, Seigneur, / qui nous donne ton Esprit?

D. Hameline 1972

131

Hungarian melody 1744

1. Pa - ra - di - csom - nak te szép é - lö fà - ja,
1. There in God's gar - den stands the Tree of wis - dom
1. Du schö - ner Le - bens - baum des Pa - ra - die - ses,

O, ke - gyes Jé - zus, is - ten - nek Bà - rà - nya,
whose leaves hold forth the hea - ling of the na - tions,
gü - ti - ger Je - sus, Got - tes Lamm auf Er - den.

te vagy lel - künk - nek i - gaz Meg - vàl -
Tree of all know - ledge, Tree of all com -
Du bist der wah - re Ret - ter uns - res

tó - ja,   sza - ba - di - tó - ja.
pas - sion,   Tree of all beau - ty.
Le - bens,   un - ser Be - frei - er.

2. Ertünk egyedül szörnyü kint szenvedtél, / megfeszittetvén töviset viseltél, / mi büneinkért véreddel fizettél, / megölettettél.

3. Edes Jézusunk, szenteld meg lelkünket, / hogy megbocsàssuk mi is a bünöket / mindeneknek, kik ellenük vétettek / es elestenek.

4. Adjad, hogy mi is értük könyörögjünk, / téged követvén szivböl esedezzünk, / hogy sok szentekkel tehozzàd mehessünk, / idvezülhessünk.

5. A pàlyafutàst mi is elvégezvén, / lelkünket anjànlhassuk szent kezedbe, / mint megvàltottak mondhassuk nagy szépen / eletünk végében:

6. Hála légyen a mennybeli Istennek, / ki megvàltója a bünös embernek, / es megszerzöje szent békességünknek, / idvességünknek.

Pécselyi Kiràly Imre +1961 körül

2. Its name is Jesus, name that says, 'Our Saviour!' / There on its branches see the scars of suffering; / see where the tendrils of our human selfhood / feed on its life-blood.

3. Thorns not its own are tangled in its foliage; / our greed has starved it; our despite has choked it. / Yet look, it lives! Its grief has not destroyed it, / nor fire consumed it.

4. See how its branches reach to us in welcome; / hear what the voice says, 'Come to me, ye weary! / Give me your sickness, give me all your sorrow. / I will give blessing.'

5. This is my ending; this my resurrection; / into your hands, Lord, I commit my spirit. / This have I searched for; now I can possess it. / This ground is holy!

6. All heaven is singing, 'Thanks to Christ, whose Passion / offers in mercy healing, strength and pardon. / All men and nations, take it, take it freely!' / Amen! My Master!

Erik Routley 1973

2. Nur unsretwegen hattest du zu leiden, / gingst an das Kreuz und trugst die Dornenkrone. / Für unsre Sünden mußtest du bezahlen / mit deinem Leben.

3. Lieber Herr Jesus, wandle uns von Grund auf, / daß allen denen wir auch gern vergeben, / die uns beleidigt, die uns Unrecht taten, / selbst sich verfehlten.

4. Für diese alle wollen wir dich bitten, / nach deinem Vorbild laut zum Vater flehen, / daß wir mit vielen Heilgen zu dir kommen / in deinen Frieden.

5. Wenn sich die Tage unsres Lebens neigen, / nimm unsren Geist, Herr, auf in deine Hände, / daß wir zuletzt von hier getröstet scheiden, / Lob auf den Lippen:

6. Dank sei dem Vater, unsrem Gott im Himmel, / er ist der Retter der verlornen Menschheit, / hat uns erworben Frieden ohne Ende, / ewige Freude.

Dieter Trautwein u. Vilmos Gyöngyösi

132

Y. L. Yang 1931

1. A - rise_____, a - rise my soul_____ and praise give to_____ the Lord of nights_____ and
2. Search thou_____ the world from end_____ to end; where is_____ there such an - oth - er
3. Thou art_____ the wea - pon, He_____ the hand; all pur - po - ses His mind_____ has

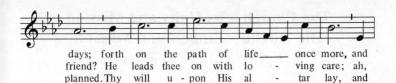

days; forth on the path of life _____ once more, and
friend? He leads thee on with lo - ving care; ah,
planned. Thy will u - pon His al - tar lay, and

God _____ the glo - ri - ous _____ a - dore.
fol - low thou Him ev' - ry - where.
go _____ thou forth with Him _____ to - day.

Nicol Macnicol

253

The Church – Its Unity and Mission
Die Kirche – Einheit und Mission
L'Eglise – Unité et Mission

133

Nj. R. Sutisno

1. We who bear the hu - man name are like
1. Wer den Men - schen - na - men trägt, gleicht den

flow - ers of the field; with - out sta - tus,
Blu - men auf dem Feld: oh - ne Gel - tung,

with - out fame, tram - pled down and made to
oh - ne Rang, oft zer - tre - ten, hin - ge -

yield, un - pro - tect - ed and ex - posed to the
mäht, un - ge - schützt und aus - ge - setzt ei - nem

scorch - ing wind that blows. Let all the
Wind, der al - les dörrt. Laßt doch die

world now blos - som as a field!
Welt jetzt blü - hen wie ein Feld!

2. Even Solomon of old, (said our Lord the man of peace) / with his glory and his gold could not match the flowers' grace. / We are weak, but we recall how the mighty men must fall. / Let all the world now blossom as a field.

3. We are people of the field, crowding Asia's city streets. / We are people called to build a community of peace. / We remember as we toil hope is springing from the soil. / Let all the world now blossom as a field.

Masao Takenaka and Fred Kaan 1972

2. Auch ein Mann wie Salomo, sagte Jesus unser Herr, / übertraf mit Ruhm und Gold nicht der Blumen Herrlichkeit. / Wir sind schwach, doch uns ist klar: Wer der Macht vertraut, verliert. / Laß doch die Welt jetzt blühen wie ein Feld!

3. Wir sind Volk von diesem Feld, Asiens Städte füllen wir. / Wir sind Volk, das bauen soll eine Welt, die Frieden kennt. / Wir erfahr'n, wenn wir uns müh'n, wie die Hoffnung um uns wächst. / Laßt doch die Welt jetzt blühen wie ein Feld!

Dieter Trautwein 1973

134

Orlando Gibbons 1623

1. E - ter - nal Ru - ler of the cease - less round
1. Toi qui con - nais tous les che - mins des cieux,
1. Du ew' - ger Herr - scher uns - res Wel - ten - rund,

of circl - ing pla - nets sing - ing on their way;
où tu con - duis les as - tres ray - on - nants,
Pla - ne - ten sin - gen dir auf ih - rer Bahn,

guide of the na - tions from the night pro - found in -
tu veux gui - der les peu - ples si nom - breux de
die Völ - ker lei - test du nach dei - nem Plan bis

to the glo - ry of the per - fect day; rule
la nuit sombre à ton so - leil le - vant. Viens
in das hel - le Licht der letz - ten Stund. Re -

in our hearts, that we may ev - er be
nous mon - trer dans tou - te sa splen - deur
gie - re auch in uns, daß al - le - zeit

guid - ed and strength - ened and up - held by thee.
ta vé - ri - té, lu - miè - re de nos cœurs.
ge - lei - tet und ge - stärkt wir sind be - reit.

2. We are of thee, the children of thy love, / the brothers of thy well-beloved Son; / descend, O Holy Spirit, like a dove / into our hearts, that we may be as one: / as one with thee, to whom we ever tend; / as one with him, our brother and our friend.

3. We would be one in hatred of all wrong, / one in our love of all things sweet and fair, / one with the joy that breaketh into song, / one with the grief that trembleth into prayer, / one in the power that makes the children free / to follow truth, and thus to follow thee.

4. O clothe us with thy heavenly armour, Lord, / thy trusty shield, thy sword of love divine; / our inspiration be thy constant word; / we ask no victories that are not thine: / give or withhold, let pain or pleasure be; / enough to know that we are serving thee.

J. W. Chadwick 1864

2. Par ton amour, nous sommes tes enfants, / et par ton Fils des frères bien-aimés. / O Saint-Esprit, esprit du Dieu vivant, / conduis nos cœurs ensemble à l'unité, / liés à toi, Seigneur et souverain, / comme à ce frère au bord de nos chemins.

3. Tu nous feras, d'un seul et même cœur, / haïr le mal et rechercher le bien, / chanter la joie à l'heure du bonheur, / prier ensemble à l'heure du chagrin, / toujours unis quand il faudra lutter pour la justice et pour la vérité.

4. Toi seul, ô Dieu, tu peux nous affermir / et nous donner les armes de la foi, / et nous voulons ensemble te servir, / aller au monde et le gagner à toi. / Non pas, Seigneur, à nous de décider, / mais qu'il soit fait selon ta volonté.

Edmond Pidoux 1972

2, Wir sind ja dein, sind dir wie Kinder gleich, / weil wir Geschwister seines Sohnes sind. / Komm Herr, und mach uns deines Geistes Kind, / mach uns die Einheit, die uns zu dir zieht / und Frieden, der, wo Christus ist, geschieht.

3. Wir wollen einig sein, dem Bösen feind, / eins in der Liebe aller guten Ding', / eins, daß die Freude aus uns sing', / eins im Gebet, wenn unser Nächster weint, / eins, daß man sieht: wir dürfen Kinder sein – / wer deiner Wahrheit folgt, ist immer dein.

Auguste Sann 1972

135

Sven-Erik Bäck 1970

1. Se här byg - ges   Ba - bels torn   sla - var
1. See them build - ing   Ba - bel's tower: slaves   the
1. Seht, sie bau - en   Ba - bels Turm.   Skla - ven

bär dess ste - nar   där   up - pe   glöm - mer
stones are carry - ing: here   no   man   cares for
tra - gen Stei - ne.   Von   Brü - dern   wis - sen

man sin bror
bro - ther man: (1 - 3) ky - ri - e - lei - son.
sie nichts mehr.   (4 - 7) Hal - le - lu - ja.

2. Vägen uppåt leder bort / mänskan blir en främling / och bröd lös vid sin broders bord / kyrieleison.

3. Brodersordet har vi glömt / ratat som en byggsten / man slängt i gräset nedanför / kyrieleison.

4. Någon finner den till slut / ser att en förkastad / är hörnsten till Guds berg och hus / halleluja.

5. På vårt eget tungomål / vi en dag hör talas / om broderskapet nerifrån / halleluja.

6. Himmelriket stormar in / över alla gränser / och vinden blåser vart den vill / halleluja.

7. Babels torn skall falla snart / nedanför där växer / Guds vete och hans broderskap / halleluja.

Olov Hartman 1970

2. Far astray that upward road, / man, become a stranger, / goes hungry at his brother's board: / Kyrieleison.

3. 'Brotherhood', forgotten word / down the grassy hillside / rejected from that building lies. / Kyrieleison.

4. Men one day will find it there / and will recognize it / as keystone of God's hill and house. / Hallelujah!

5. Then their cry will rise, and we, / each in his own language / shall hear of brotherhood once more, / Hallelujah!

6. Mighty wind of heaven's rule, / storming every barrier / will blow for ever where it wills, / Hallelujah!

7. So shall Babel come to nought. / Where it stood shall flourish / the harvest of God's brotherhood. / Hallelujah.

Caryl and Ruth Mickletem 1972

2. Weg nach oben – Weg ins Nichts. / Menschen werden Fremde / und brotlos an des Bruders Tisch. / Kyrieleison.

3. Bruder – dieses Wort von Gott / haben wir verworfen, / als wär's ein Baustein, der nicht taugt. / Kyrieleison.

4. Einer endlich findet ihn, / sieht, daß ein Verworfner / der Eckstein ist zu Gottes Haus. / Hosianna.

5. In der eignen Sprache Klang / hören wir bezeugen: / von unten Bruderschaft entsteht. / Halleluja.

6. Und der Sturm des Himmelreichs / bricht durch alle Grenzen. / Der Wind weht, wo und wann er will. / Halleluja.

7. Babels Turm fällt bald in Schutt. / Schon beginnt zu wachsen / auf Gottes Feld die Bruderschaft. / Halleluja.

Markus Jenny 1971

136

Refrain   Christopher Coelho 1972

Di - vi - ded our path-ways, and hea - vy our
Ge - trennt sind die We - ge, und schwer ist die
Nos che - mins ont creu - sé des fos - sés pro -

guilt;   bur-den'd, un - see - ing, we grope for the
Schuld.   Blind und be - la - stet suchen ta - stend wir
fonds;   er - rant, in - cer - tains, nous cher-chons la

one way.   Far from our home, O Fa - ther, we
den Weg.   Weit von zu - haus', o Va - ter, wir
rou - te   vers toi, mon Dieu, d'un seul cœur nous

call out – 'Heal us, for - give us: bring us
ru - fen: Hei-le uns, ver - gib uns,   bring uns
cri - ons: Par - don! Prends pi - tié!   Ras - sem -

to - ge - ther in Je - sus your Son!'
zu - sam - men in Jesus, dei - nem Sohn.
ble nous tous 'en ton Fils Jé - sus.

1. Holy Father, keep those you have   gi - ven
1. Heiliger Vater, erhalte sie in deinem Namen,   den du

260

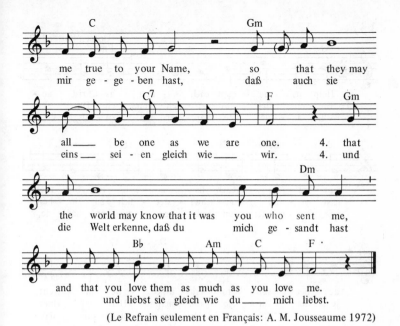

me true to your Name, so that they may
mir ge - ge - ben hast, daß auch sie

all___ be one as we are one. 4. that
eins___ sei - en gleich wie___ wir. 4. und

the world may know that it was you who sent me,
die Welt erkenne, daß du mich ge - sandt hast

and that you love them as much as you love me.
und liebst sie gleich wie du___ mich liebst.

(Le Refrain seulement en Français: A. M. Jousseaume 1972)

2. Father, may they be one in us as you are in me and I am in you, / so that the world may come to believe it was you who sent me.

3. I have given them the glory that you gave to me, / that they may all be one as we are one.

4. With me in them and you in me may they be so completely united, / that the world may know that it was you who sent me, / and that you love them as much as you love me.

John 17 and Christopher Coelho 1972

2. Auf daß sie alle eins seien in uns gleichwie du Vater in mir und ich in dir, / damit die Welt glaube, du habest mich gesandt.

3. Und ich habe ihnen gegeben die Herrlichkeit, die du mir gegeben hast, / daß auch sie eins seien gleichwie wir.

4. Ich in ihnen und du in mir, auf daß sie vollkommen eins seien, / und die Welt erkenne, daß du mich gesandt hast / und liebst sie gleichwie du mich liebst.

Otmar Schulz

137

Doreen Potter 1974

1. Help us ac - cept each o - ther as Christ ac -
1. Ein - an - der auf - zu - neh - men, wie Du es
1. Elk - an - der te aan - vaar - den zo - als Gij

cept - ed us; teach us as sis - ter, bro - ther
hast ge - tan; ge - schwi - ster - lich zu le - ben,
ons aan - vaardt: één huis - ge - zin op aar - de,

each per - son to em - brace. Be pre - sent,
je - der für je - der - mann — Herr, sei hier
de an - der al - les waard — help ons dat

Lord a - mong us and bring us to be - lieve we are our -
ge - gen - wär - tig und leg' uns stän - dig nah: wir, von Dir
waar te ma - ken en geef ons te ver - staan: wij le - ven

selves ac - cept - ed and meant to love and live.
auf - ge - nom - men, wir sind zum Lie - ben da.
voor de lief - de - Gij hebt het voor - ge - daan.

2. Teach us, O Lord, your lessons, / as in our daily life / we struggle to be human / and search for hope and faith. / Teach us to care for people, / for all — not just for some, / to love them as we find them / or as they may become.

3. Let your acceptance change us, / so that we may be moved / in living situations / to do the truth in love; / to practise your acceptance / until we know by heart / the table of forgiveness / and laughter's healing art.

4. Lord, for today's encounters / with all who are in need, / who hunger for acceptance, / for righteousness and bread, / we need new eyes for seeing, / new hands for holding on: / renew us with your Spirit; / Lord, free us, make us one!

Fred Kaan 1974

2. Lehr uns im Alltagsleben / ohn' Unterlass, o Herr, / nach Menschlichkeit zu streben, / sei auch Dein Tag noch fern. / Lehr uns den Menschen lieben, / Adam aus Staub und Erd', / wie immer er vorhanden / ist und noch werden wird.

3. Verändert ist das Leben, / denn Du, Herr, nahmst uns an, / damit von all den Deinen / die Wahrheit wird getan. / Dies hilf uns einzuüben, / bis jeder innehat / die Tafel der Vergebung, / des Lachens Heilungskraft.

4. Für jegliche Begegnung / mit allen, die in Not / nach Aufnahme sich sehnen, / Gerechtigkeit und Brot, / brauchen wir neue Augen / und Arme stark und weit: / ihn, der ja alles neu macht, / uns einigt und befreit!

C. Michael de Vries 1974

2. Heer, wil ons onderwijzen / wanneer wij uur na uur / ons best doen mens te wezen, / de rug tegen de muur. / Leer ons om mensen geven, / om Jan en alleman, / om Jezuswil om Adam / en wat hij worden kan.

3. Gij breekt ons uit het schema, / veranderd is de tijd: / aanvaarding is het thema, / liefd' en waarachtigheid. / Help ons te repeteren / „zeventig zevenmaal", / 't binnenste buiten keren: / Een lach is liefdestaal.

4. Om allen te ontwaren / vertwijfeld in hun nood, / die hunkren naar aanvaarding, / gerechtigheid en brood, / geef, Heer, ons nieuwe ogen, / geef ons vasthoudendheid,/Gij, die de wereld nieuw maakt, / verenigt en bevrijdt!

C. Michael de Vries

138

Lucien Deiss 1971

Un   seul Sei - gneur,   u - ne seu - le   foi,   un
We   have one Lord,   we have one___   faith,   we

seul bap - tê - me,   un   seul Dieu et   Pè -   re!
have one bap - tism,   one   God and one   Fa -   ther.

1. Ap - pe - lés   à   gar - der   l'u - ni -
1. Called to   keep___   the   u -   ni -

té   de   l'Es - prit   par   le   lien   de   la
ty   of   the   Spirit   in   the   bond___   of

paix,   nous chan - tons   et   nous pro - cla - mons___.
peace,   let   us   sing!   let   the whole world   hear___!

2. Ap - pe - lés   à   for - mer   un   seul Corps   dans un
2. Called to   build___   in   love___   one   bo - dy   in

seul Es - prit___,   nous chan - tons et   nous pro - cla -   mons__.
one___ Spi - rit,   let   us   sing; let   the whole world   hear___.

264

3. Ap - pe - lés à par - ta - ger u - ne
3. Called to share in ex - pec - ta - tion one

seule es - pé - ran - ce dans le Christ, nous chan -
liv - ing hope in Je - sus Christ, let us

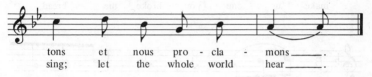

tons et nous pro - cla - mons_____.
sing; let the whole world hear_____.

E: Erik Routley 1972

265

139a

Peter Cutts 1965

1. Lord Christ, the Fa - ther's migh - ty Son, whose
2. To make us one your prayers were said, to

work u - pon the cross was done
make us one you broke the bread,

all men to re - ceive, make all our scat -
for all to re - ceive; its pie - ces scat -

ter'd chur - ches one, that the world may be - lieve.
ter us in - stead: how can o - thers be - lieve?

3. Lord Christ, forgive us, make us new! / What our designs could never do / your love can achieve. / Our prayers, our work, we bring to you, / that the world may believe.

4. We will not question or refuse / the way you work, the means you choose, / the pattern you weave; / but reconcile our warring views / that the world may believe.

Brian Wren 1965

139b

Doreen Potter 1971

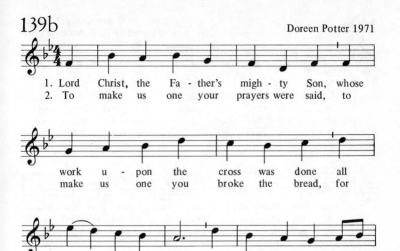

1. Lord Christ, the Fa-ther's migh-ty Son, whose
2. To make us one your prayers were said, to

work u-pon the cross was done all
make us one you broke the bread, for

men __ to re-ceive, make all our scat-ter'd __
all __ to re-ceive; its piec-es scat-ter __

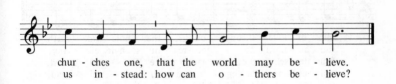

chur-ches one, that the world may be-lieve.
us in-stead: how can o-thers be-lieve?

3. Lord Christ, forgive us, make us new! / What our designs could never
do / your love can achieve. / Our prayers, our work, we bring to you, /
that the world may believe.

4. We will not question or refuse / the way you work, the means you
choose, / the pattern you weave; / but reconcile our warring views / that
the world may believe.

Brian Wren 1965

140a

American folk hymn
adapted by H. T. Burleigh 1941

1. In___ Christ there is no___ East or West, in
1. Gens de tous pa - ys, du___ sud au nord, vous
1. In___ Chri - stus ist nicht_ Ost noch West, nicht
1. O - rien - te ni oc - ci - den - te hay, en
1. O - rien - te, O - es - te___, Nor - te, Sul, ñao

him no South or___ North, but___ one great fel - low-
ê - tes in - vi - tés: De___ l'ouest à l'est, du
Sü - den o - der___ Nord, nur___ ei - ne gro - ße
Cris - to y su___ bon - dad, in - clui - da en su a -
há em - ti___, Se - nhor: Só___ há, por to - do o

ship of love through - out___ the whole wide earth.
sud au nord, ac - cour-rez du mon-de en - tier.
Brü - der - schaft, die___ gan - ze Er - de - fort.
mor es - tá la en - te - ra hu - ma - ni - dad.
mun-do ir - maos, U - ni - dos___ pe - lo___ a - mor.

2. In him shall true hearts everywhere / their high communion find, / his service is the golden cord / close-binding all mankind.

3. Join hands, then, brothers of the faith, / whate'er your race may be; / who serves my Father as a son / is surely kin to me.

4. In Christ now meet both East and West, / in him meet South and North, / all Christlike souls are one in him, / throughout the whole wide earth.

John Oxenham 1924

2. Le Seigneur Jésus nous a donné / le monde à réunir: / allons-nous laisser se déchirer / le plus grand de ses désirs?

3. Des cités, des champs, des monts, des bourgs, / venez vous rassembler: / il n'y a qu'un grand réseau d'amour / à travers le monde entier.

4. Donnons-nous la main, les blancs, les noirs, / chantons d'un même cœur: / notre Père a mis en nous l'espoir / qu'annonçait Jésus Sauveur.

Nicole Berthet

2. Die wahren Herzen finden all / in ihm die heil'ge Statt; / er ist es, der das goldne Band / um sie geschlungen hat.

3. Drum, Glaubensbrüder, schließt den Bund / welch Stamm euch auch gesandt! / Wer meinem Vater dient als Sohn, / ist wahrlich mir verwandt.

4. In Christus eint sich Ost und West / und eint sich Süd und Nord, / die Seelen sein sind eins in ihm / die ganze Erde fort.

M. Liesegang 1924

2. En Dios los fieles al Señor, / su comunión tendrán / y con los lazos de su amor / al mundo ligarán.

3. De razas no haya distinción, / obreros de la fe! / El que cual hijo, sirve a Dios, / hermano nuestro es.

4. Oriente y occidente en él / se encuentran, y su amor / las almas une, por la fe, / en santa comunión.

J. R. de Balloch

2. Da terra os crentes corações / em ti vêm-se abrasar, / Enquanto em doce comunhão, / vêm todos enlaçar.

3. De toda raça, tôda côr, / vós, crentes, ecultai. / Dai mãos, pos quer-vos bem Jesus: Servis a Deus, o Pai.

4. Em Cristo congregados, pois, / ó povos, vinde unir / de vossas almas o louvor / que aos ceus fareis subir.

França Campos 1952

140b

A. R. Reinagle 1836

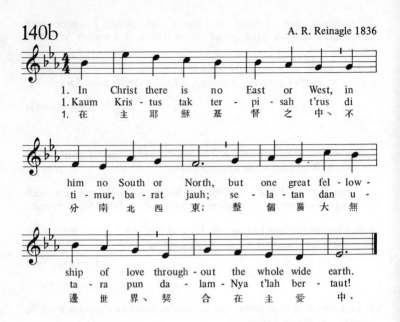

1. In Christ there is no East or West, in
him no South or North, but one great fel - low -
ship of love through - out the whole wide earth.

1. Kaum Kris - tus tak ter - pi - sah t'rus di
ti - mur, ba - rat jauh; se - la - tan dan u -
ta - ra pun da - lam - Nya t'lah ber - taut!

1. 在 主 耶 穌 基 督 之 中、不
分 南 北 西 東; 整 個 廣 大 無
邊 世 界、契 合 在 主 愛 中。

2. In him shall true hearts everywhere / their high communion find, / his service is the golden cord / close-binding all mankind.

3. Join hands, then, brothers of the faith, / whate'er your race may be; / who serves my Father as a son / is surely kin to me.

4. In Christ now meet both East and West, / in him meet South and North, / all Christlike souls are one in him, / throughout the whole wide earth.

John Oxenham 1924

2. OlehNya kita bertemu / di Tubu yang kudus: / pengabdianNya adalah / pengikat seterus.

3 Berganding tangan, kaum iman / di mana-mana pun: / tetaplah kau anggotaNya / mengabdi bertekun.

4. Semua bangsa satulah / di dalam Penebus / dan yang tadinya bercerai / berdamailah terus!

Yayasan Musik Gerejani 1973

2. 在主愛中、眞誠的心、到處相愛相親; 基督精神、如環如帶、契合萬族萬民。

3. 信主弟兄、不分國族、同來攜手歡欣、同為天父孝順兒女、契合如在家庭。

4. 在主耶穌基督之中、連合南北西東; 信主之靈、結成一體、契合在主愛中。 (阿們。)

١. اَلْكُلُّ فِي الْمَسِيحِ لاَ ۰ شَرْقٌ وَلاَ غَرْبُ ۰ بِوِحْدَةٍ شَامِلَةٍ ۰ قُوَامُهَا الْحُبُّ

٢. أُخُوَّةٌ بَيْنَ الشُّعُوبِ ۰ وَشِرْكَةٌ عُلْيَا ۰ تَسْمُوبِهَا كُلُّ الْقُلُوبِ ۰ عَنْ عَرْضِ الدُّنْيَا

٣. خِدْمَتُهُ تَرْبُطُنَا ۰ بِأَوْثَقِ الرِّبَاطِ ۰ كَسِلْكٍ تِبْرٍ نَاظِمٍ ۰ عِقْدًا بِلَا انْفِرَاطْ

٤. هَيَّا اعْقِدُوا الْأَيْدِي إِذَنْ ۰ يَامَعْشَرَ الْإِيمَانْ ۰ أَنْ نَخْدُمَ الْآبَ مَعًا ۰ إِذْ كُلُّنَا إِخْوَانْ

Elias Marmura

141

Doreen Potter 1970

1. Ga - thered here___ from ma - ny na - tions, one in
1. Wir sind hier___ aus vie - len Län - dern, eins im
1. De par - tout___ sur cet - te ter - re, nous voi -

wor - ship and in - tent, let us for___ the
Dank___ und eins im Ziel. Laßt uns drum___ in
ci___ pour t'a - do - rer. En toi seul___ ton

days that face us all our hopes___ to God pre -
die - sen Ta - gen Hoff - nung set - zen nur auf
peuple es - pè - re, toi seul peux___ nous ras - sem -

sent___, that our com - mon life may
ihn ___. Steh' Er uns___ in al - lem
bler ___. En Christ, nous___ tous som - mes

be___ full of joy___ and___ tru - ly free.
bei ___, daß die Ein - heit___ sicht - bar sei.
frè - res, don - ne - nous___ ton___ u - ni - té.

272

2. May the spring of all our actions / be, O Lord, your love for man; / may your word be seen and spoken / and your will be clearly done. / Help us, who your image bear, / for the good of each to care.

3. Give us grace to match our calling, / faith to overcome the past; / show us how to meet the future, / planning boldly, acting fast. / Let the servant-mind of Christ / in our life be manifest.

4. Now ourselves anew committing to each other and to you, / Lord, we ask that you will train us / for the truth we have to do; / that the world may soon become / your great city of shalom.

F. H. Kaan 1972

2. Deine Liebe zu den Menschen / treibe uns zu Taten an, / die der Welt dein Wort verkünden, / daß dein Wille sei getan. / Hilf uns, deinem Bilde gleich, / mitzubau'n an deinem Reich.

3. Gib uns Kraft, dir nachzufolgen. / Altes wird durch Hoffnung neu. / Zeig uns Wege in die Zukunft, / neues wagend ohne Scheu. / Nur im Dienst bezeugt ein Christ / ihn, der aller Diener ist.

4. Herr, wir preisen deine Treue / und erneuern unsren Bund. / Unser Tun und unser Reden / mache deine Wahrheit kund. / So wird bald die Welt zur Stadt, / die Schalom zum Wappen hat.

Konrad Raiser und C. M. de Vries 1972

2. Que ton amour pour les hommes / s'exprime en nos actions, / que ta parole résonne / jusqu'au cœur des nations, / pour que bientôt l'heure sonne, / de notre libération.

3. Rends-nous aptes à la tâche / que tu places devant nous. / Pour avancer sans relâche, / vers le but dirige-nous. / Pour que le monde entier sache / ce que Christ a fait pour tous!

4. Tu nous veux à ton service, / et ton service est concret: / lutter contre l'injustice, / témoigner de tes bienfaits. / Pour qu'en tout lieu chacun puisse / t'adorer, Dieu de la paix!

Etienne de Peyer 1972

142

Rolf Schweizer 1967

1. Herr, du hast dar-um ge-be-tet, daß wir
1. Lord, you of-fered to the Fa-ther prayers that

sol-len ei-nes sein. Hilf du sel- -ber
we might all be one. To that u- -ni-

uns zur Ein-heit, denn die Kir-che ist ja dein.
ty now lead us: let the Fa-ther's will be done.

2. Dein Reich ist nicht unsre Kirche, / unsre Konfession allein, / nein, dein Reich, Herr, ist viel größer. / Brich mit deinem Reich herein.

3. Laß den Brüdern uns begegnen, / die in andern Kirchen stehn / und sich dort, wie wir es hier tun, / mühen, deinen Weg zu gehn,

4. die mit andern Stimmen loben / deinen großen Namen, Christ, / der für sie, wie auch für uns, Herr, / Name ohnegleichen ist.

5. Laß uns zueinander stehen, / ganz so, wie es dir gefällt, / daß dein Reich in Wahrheit komme, / Herr, in unsre müde Welt.

Otmar Schulz 1967, 1971

2. For our church is not your Kingdom: / this your word may teach us still. / No, your kingdom, Lord, is greater: / reconcile us to your will.

3. Lord, we long to join our brethren / whom our rival laws restrain, / but who study just as we do / Christ's own standards to maintain.

4. Lord, we long to share their worship / who prefer another form, / but whose anthems, just as ours do, / take Christ's glory as their norm.

5. Lord, we long to stand beside them / in fulfilment of your plan, / that by true faith shall your kingdom / bring reality to man.

Ivor Jones 1968, 1971

143

Melchior Vulpius 1609

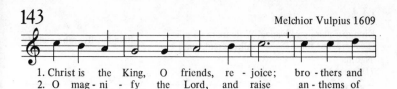

1. Christ is the King, O friends, re - joice; bro - thers and
2. O mag - ni - fy the Lord, and raise an - thems of

sis - ters with one voice make all men know he
joy and ho - ly praise for Christ's brave saints of

is your choice. Al - le - lu - ia_____!
an - cient days. Al - le - lu - ia_____!

Al - le - lu - ia_____! Al - le - lu - ia!
Al - le - lu - ia_____! Al - le - lu - ia!

3. O Christian women, Christian men, / all the world over, seek again, / the Way disciples followed then. / Alleluia!

4. Christ through all ages is the same: / place the same hope in his great name; / with the same faith his word proclaim. / Alleluia!

5. Let Love's unconquerable might / your scattered companies unite / in service to the Lord of light. / Alleluia!

6. So shall God's will on earth be done, / new lamps be lit, new tasks begun, / and his whole Church at last be one. / Alleluia!

Bishop G. K. A. Bell 1883–1959

144

Kiongozi mara ya kwanza. Wote mara ya pili
(Leader, first time;   All, second time)

Ihandzu-Ilyamba melody

Ngoma
(Drum)

1. Tu - me - po - ke - a   ne - e - ma;
1. We have from the Lord re - ceived grace,

tu - i - mbe   so - te   kwa   sha - ngwe.
ex - tol   his   mer - cies   for   ev - er.

Kiongozi mara ya kwanza; Wote mara ya pili
(Leader, first time;   All, second time)

Ngoma
(Drum)

Mu - ngu   Ba - ba   ka - mpe - le - ka
His   Spi - rit   he   sent   to   our   race,

Ro - ho   M - fa - ri - ji   wa - ke.
from whom no   one   us   can   se - ver.

Refrain after all verses:

Kiongozi   Wote
(Leader)   (All)

Ngoma
(Drum)

Ee - ndu - gu,   fu - ra - ha   ku - bwa
Tu - na - o   sa - sa   u - we - za
O   Chris - tians, ours   is   joy   in - deed,
And   po - wer   in   both   word   and   deed

276

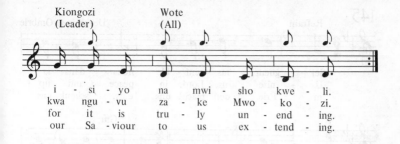

i	- si	- yo	na	mwi	- sho	kwe	- li.
kwa	ngu	- vu	za	- ke	Mwo	- ko	- zi.
for	it	is	tru	- ly	un	- end	- ing.
our	Sa	- viour	to	us	ex	- tend	- ing.

2. Njoo, Roho Mtakatiju, utujaze nguvu zako; / tuende kwa watu wetu, tutangaze neema yako.

3. Ee Roho Mtakatifu, uliye Mwanga wa kweli, / Twapenda kukusukudu, kwandi u pamoja nasi.

4. Ahadi ya Yesu Kristo, hakika imetimizwa; / Twaimarishwa mioyo, tuishuhudie neema.

5. Baba Mungu, naye Mwana, naye Roho Mtakatifu, / Mungu wa Utatu, Mmoja, milele tutakusifu.

Zakarias D. Mzengi

2. O Spirit of truth and of light, dispel deceit and all darkness. / Make truer and clearer our sight to recognize sin's dread starkness.

3. Come Spirit, abide in our heart, transform our weakness to power. / That to others we may impart word of your grace every hour.

4. The promise which Christ gave mankind has been fulfilled to perfection. / He sent us His Spirit; we find in Him sure hope and protection.

5. God Almighty, Father and Son, and Holy Spirit all-knowing, / distinct yet united as One, accept the praise we're bestowing.

Howard S. Olson

145

Refrain   Dominique Ombrie

Sei - gneur, ras - sem - ble nous dans la
U - nite us, Lord, in peace and up -
Im Frie - den mach' uns eins, schenk uns

paix de ton a - mour. 1. Nos fau - tes nous sé -
hold us with your love. 1. Our faults di - vide and
dei - ne Lie - be, Herr! 1. Es trennt uns uns - re

pa - rent, ta grâ - ce nous u - nit; la joie de
hin - der; your grace can make us one; we won - der
Sün - de, doch dei - ne Gna - de eint. Dein Sieg ist

ta vic - toi - re é - clai - re no - tre nuit.
at your ris - ing, your light is like the sun.
uns - re Freu - de, er - leuch - tet uns - re Nacht.

2. Tu es notre espérance / parmi nos divisions; / plus haut que nos
offenses / s'élève ton pardon.

3. Seigneur, vois la misère / des hommes affamés. / Partage à tous nos
frères / le pain de l'unité.

4. Heureux le cœur des pauvres / qui cherchent l'unité! / Heureux dans
ton royaume / les frères retrouvés.

5. Fais croître en notre attente / l'amour de ta maison; / l'Esprit dans le
silence / fait notre communion.

6. Ta croix est la lumière / qui nous a rassemblés; / O joie de notre terre, / tu nous a rachetés.

7. La mort est engloutie, / nous sommes délivrés: / qu'éclate en nous ta vie, / Seigneur ressuscité!

Dominique Ombrie

2. You are our expectation / in loneliness and pain; / your healing and your pardon / are greater than our sin.

3. Lord, look upon the starving / and set the captive free. / Share out among our brothers / the bread of unity.

4. How happy are the people / who strive to be at one, / who learn to live as brothers, / who lay their hatred down.

5. O Lord, whose silent spirit / enlightens and endows, / make us in faith receptive / and help us love your house.

6. Your cross will draw together / the circle of mankind; / in you shall all the people / their true communion find.

7. Death can no longer hurt us, / triumphant is your word. / Let life now grow and blossom, / O Jesus, risen Lord!

Fred Kaan 1972

2. Du, Herr, bist unsre Hoffnung / in der Zerrissenheit. / Wir haben dich beleidigt, / trotzdem verzeihst du uns.

3. Herr, sieh, die Menschen leiden / am Hunger, der sie quält. / Teil aus an unsre Brüder / das Brot der Einigkeit.

4. Preist glücklich alle Armen / die auf der Suche sind! / Preist glücklich alle Menschen / die zu Dir heimgekehrt!

5. Laß in uns allen wachsen / die Liebe für dein Reich! / Dein Geist wirkt in der Stille / Gemeinschaft unter uns.

6. Dein Kreuz wirft helle Strahlen / die haben uns vereint. / O Glück, weil du die Erde / uns wieder lieben lehrst!

7. Der Tod ist jetzt verschlungen, / wir Menschen sind befreit! / Durchdringe unser Leben, / du auferstand'ner Herr!

Marlies Flesch-Thebesius 1972

146

Martin Luther 1483 - 1546

1. Ein fe - ste Burg ist un - - ser Gott,
1. A safe strong - hold our God___ is still,
1. C'est un rem - part que no - - tre Dieu,

ein gu - te Wehr und Waf - - - fen.
a tru - sty shield and wea - - - pon.
une in - vin - cible ar - mu - - - re.

Er hilft uns frei aus al - - ler Not,
He'll help us clear from all___ the ill
No - tre dé - li - vrance en _____ tout lieu,

die uns jetzt hat be - trof - - - fen.
that hath us now o'er - ta - - - ken.
no - tre dé - fen - se sû - - - re.

Der alt___ bö - se Feind, mit Ernst er es
The an - - cient prince of hell hath ris'n with pur -
L'en - ne - - mi con - tre nous re - dou - ble de

jetzt meint, groß Macht und viel List sein grau - sam Rü -
pose fell; strong mail of craft and power he wea - reth in
cour - roux: Vai - ne co - lè - re! Que pour - rait l'ad -

stung ist, auf Erd ist nicht seins - glei - - chen.
this hour, on earth is not his fel - - low.
ver - saire? L'E - ter - nel dé - tour - ne___ ses coups.

2. Mit unsrer Macht ist nichts getan, / wir sind gar bald verloren; / es streit't für uns der rechte Mann, / den Gott selbst hat erkoren. / Fragst du nun, wer der ist? / Er heißt Jesus Christ, / der Herr Zebaoth, und ist kein andrer Gott; / das Feld muß er behalten.

3. Und wenn die Welt voll Teufel wär / und wollt uns gar verschlingen, / so fürchten wir uns nicht so sehr, / es soll uns doch gelingen. / Der Fürst dieser Welt, / wie sauer er sich stellt, / tut er uns doch nichts; / das macht, er ist gericht't; / ein Wörtlein kann ihn fällen.

4. Das Wort sie sollen lassen stahn / und kein Dank dazu haben; / er ist bei uns wohl auf dem Plan, / mit seinem Geist und Gaben. / Nehmen sie uns den Leib, / Gut, Ehre, Kind und Weib, / laß fahren dahin; / sie habens kein Gewinn; / das Reich muß uns doch bleiben.

Martin Luther 1529

2. With force of arms we nothing can, / full soon were we down-ridden; / but for us fights the proper Man, / whom God Himself hath bidden. / Ask ye, who is this same? / Christ Jesus is His name, / of Sabaoth the Lord, / sole God to be adored; / 'tis He must win the battle.

3. And were this world all devils o'er, / and watching to devour us, / we lay it not to heart so sore; / not they can overpower us. / And let the prince of ill / look grim as e'er he will, / he harms us not a whit; / for why? his doom is writ; / a word shall quickly slay him.

4. God's word, for all their craft and force, / one moment will not linger, / but, spite of hell, shall have its course; / 'tis written by His finger. / And, though they take our life, / goods, honour, children, wife, / yet is their profit small; / these things shall vanish all, / the city of God remaineth.

Thomas Carlyle 1831

2. Seuls, nous bronchons à chaque pas, / notre force est faiblesse; / mais un héros, dans les combats, / pour nous lutte sans cesse. / Quel est ce défenseur? / C'est toi, divin Sauveur, / Dieu des armées, / tes tribus opprimées / connaissent leur libérateur.

3. Que les démons forgent des fers / pour accabler l'Eglise, / ta Sion brave les enfers, / sur son rocher assise. / Constant dans son effort, / en vain, avec la mort, / Satan conspire: / pour briser son empire, / il suffit d'un mot du Dieu fort.

4. Dis-le, ce mot victorieux, / dans toutes nos détresses; / répands sur nous du haut des cieux / tes divines largesses. / Qu'on nous ôte nos bien, / qu'on serre nos liens, / que nous importe! / Ta grâce est la plus forte, / et ton royaume est pour les tiens.

H. Lutteroth (1802–1892)

1. Cas - ti - llo fuer - te - es nues - tro Dios,
1. Cas - te - lo for - te é nos - so Deus,

de - fen - sa y buen es - cu - do,
es - pa - da e bom es - cu - do,

con su po - der____ nos li - bra - rá
com seu po - der____ de - fen - de os seus,

en to - do tran - ce a - gu - do.
em to - do o tran - se a - gu - do.

Con fu - ri - a y con a - fán a - có - sa - nos
Com fú - ria____ per - ti - naz Per - se - gue Sa -

Sa - tán: por ar - mas deja ver as - tu - cia y gran
ta - nás, Com â - ni - mo cru - el; as - tu - to e mui

po - der, cual él no hay en la ti - er - ra.
re - bel. I - gual não há na ter - ra.

282

2. Nuestro valor es nada aqui, / con él todo es perdido; / mas con nosotros luchará / de Dios el escogido. / Es nuestro Rey Jesús, / el que venció en la cruz, / Señor y Salvador, / y siendo el solo Dios, / el triunfa en la batalla.

3. Y si demonios mil están / prontos a devorarnos, / no temeremos, porque Dios / sabrá como ampararnos. / Que muestre su vigor / Satán, y su furor! Dañarnos no podrá, / pues condenado es ya / por la Palabra Santa.

4. Esa palabra del Señor, / que el mundo no apetece, / por el Espíritu de Dios / muy firme permanece. / Nos pueden despojar / de bienes, nombre, hogar, / el cuerpo destruir, / más siempre ha de existir / de Dios, el Reino eterno.

J. B. Cabrera (1837–1916) revisado por F. J. Pagura 1960

2. A fôrça de homem nada faz, / sòzinho, está perdido; / mas nosso Deus socorro traz, / em seu Filho escolhido. / Sabeis quem é? Jesus, / o que venceu na cruz, / Senhor dos altos Céus; / e, sendo, o próprio Deus, / triunfa na batalha.

3. Se nos quisessem devorar / demônios não contados, / não poderiam dominar, / nem ver-nos assustados. / O principe do mal, / com seu plano infernal, / já condenado está; / vencido cairá / por uma só palavra.

4. De Deus o verbo ficará, / sabemos com certeza, / e nada nos perturbará / com Cristo por defesa. / Se temos de perder / familia, bens, prazer, / se tudo se acabar / e a morte nos chegar, / com êle, reinaremos!

E. J. von Hafe (Revisão do Hinário Evangélica 1962)

Another version of the tune is in the Full Score edition.

1. اَللهُ مَلْجَاءُ لَنَا ٠ وَقُوَّةٌ طُولَ الْمَدَى ٠ وَهْوَ لَنَا فِي ضِيقِنَا ٠ عَوْنًا شَدِيدًا وُجِدَا ٠ إِلهُنَا الْمُعِين ٠ حِصْنٌ لَنَا حَصِين ٠ وَمَلْجَاءٌ أَمِين ٠ تَرْجُوهُ مُؤْمِنِينْ ٠ لِذَاكَ نَحْيَا آمِنِينْ

2. اَللهُ فِي وَسَعِلِنَا ٠ دَوْمًا فَلَنْ نُزَعْزَعَا ٠ يُعِينُنَا اللهُ الْعَلِي ٠ لِلنَّصْرِ يَأْتِي مُمْرِعًا ٠ إِلهُنَا الْمُعِين ٠ حِصْنٌ لَنَا حَصِين ٠ وَمَلْجَاءٌ أَمِين ٠ نَرْجُوهُ مُؤْمِنِينْ ٠ لِذَاكَ نَحْيَا آمِنِين

3. اللهُ أَعْطَى صَوْتَهُ ، مِنْ عَرْشِهِ الْأَسْمَى الْعَظِيمْ ، يَسْحَقُ قُوَّاتِ الْعِدَى ،
وَيَسْكُبُ الْمُقَا وِمِينْ ، إِلهُنَا الْمُعِينْ ، حِصْنٌ لَنَا حَصِينْ ، وَمَلْجَاءٌ
أَمِينْ ، نَرْجُوهُ مُؤْمِنِينْ ، لِذَاكَ نَحْبَا آمِنِينْ

4. رَبُّ الْجُنُودِ مَعَنَا ، وَهُوَ لَنَا دَوْمًا مُعِينْ ، إِلهُنَا السَّامِي الْقَوِّي ،
مَلْجَأُنَا فِي كُلِّ حِينْ ، إِلهُنَا الْمُعِينْ ، حِصْنٌ لَنَا حَصِينْ ، وَمَلْجَاءٌ أَمِينْ ،
نَرْجُوهُ مُؤْمِنِينْ ، لِذَاكَ نَحْبَا آمِنِينْ

Asaad el Rassy

147

Thomas John Williams 1869 - 1944

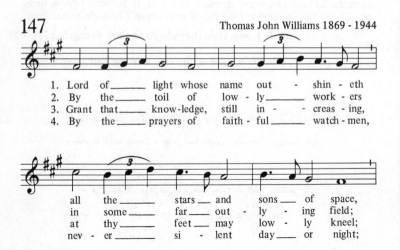

1. Lord of _____ light whose name out - shin - eth
2. By the _____ toil of low - ly _____ work - ers
3. Grant that _____ know-ledge, still in - - creas - ing,
4. By the _____ prayers of faith - ful _____ watch - men,

all the _____ stars _ and sons _ of space,
in some _____ far - out - ly - ing field;
at thy _____ feet _ may low - ly kneel;
nev - er _____ si - lent day _ or night;

deign to_____ make us thy co___ work\-ers
by the_____ cour\-age where the_____ ra\-diance
with thy_____ grace our tri\-umphs___ hal\-low,
by the_____ cross of Je\-sus_____ bring\-ing

in the_____ king\-dom of_____ thy grace;
of the_____ cross___ is still___ re\-vealed;
with thy_____ cha\-ri\-ty_____ our zeal;
peace to_____ men___, and heal\-ing light;

use us_____ to ful\-fil thy_____ pur\-pose
by the_____ vic\-to\-ries of_____ meek\-ness,
lift the_____ na\-tions· from the_____ sha\-dows
by the_____ love that pass\-eth_____ know\-ledge,

in the_____ gift of Christ thy_____ Son:
through re\-proach and suf\-fering_____ won:
to the_____ glad\-ness of the_____ sun:
mak\-ing_____ all thy chil\-dren_____ one:

1.\-4. Fa\-ther_____, as in high\-est_____ hea\-ven,

so on_____ earth___ thy will___ be done.

Howell Elvet Lewis 1916

285

148a

Geistlich Böhmische Brüder 1566

1. Son - ne der Ge - rech - tig - keit, ge - he
1. Sun of Righ - teous - ness_____, a - rise now, to -

auf zu uns - rer Zeit; brich in dei - ner Kir - che an,
day in our___ own skies; in your Chur-ch's dawn - ing be

daß die Welt es se - hen kann, er - barm dich, Herr.
that one light by which men see. Have mer - cy, Lord!

2. Weck die tote Christenheit / aus dem Schlaf der Sicherheit; mache deinen Ruhm bekannt / überall im ganzen Land / Erbarm dich, Herr. /

3. Schaue die Zertrennung an, / der kein Mensch sonst wehren kann; / sammle, grosser Menschenhirt, / alles, was sich hat verirrt. / Erbarm dich, Herr.

4. Tu der Völker Türen auf, / deines Himmelreiches Lauf / hemme keine List noch Macht, / schaffe Licht in dunkler Nacht. / Erbarm dich, Herr.

5. Gib den Boten Kraft und Mut, / Glaubenshoffnung, Liebesglut; / laß viel Früchte deiner Gnad / folgen ihrer Tränensaat. / Erbarm dich, Herr.

6. Laß uns deine Herrlichkeit / ferner sehn in dieser Zeit / und mit unsrer kleinen Kraft / üben gute Ritterschaft. / Erbarm dich, Herr.

7. Kraft, Lob, Ehr und Herrlichkeit / sei dem Höchsten allezeit, / der, wie er ist drei in ein, / uns in ihm läßt eines sein. / Erbarm dich, Herr.

vv. 1, 6 Christian David 1690–1851

vv. 2, 4, 5 Christian Gottlob Barth 1799–1862

vv. 3, 7 Christian Nehring 1671–1725

arranged by Otto Riethmüller 1889–1938

2. Wake dead Christianity, sleeping / in complacency; / may it listen to you, Lord,/ turn again and trust your Word. / Have mercy, Lord. /

3. See your Church by troubles rent / men were helpless to prevent; / gather, Shepherd of us all, / those who stumble, stray and fall. / Have mercy, Lord.

4. Open wide your people's doors; / may no guile, no earthly powers, / do your Kingdom harsh despite. / Lord, create in darkness light. / Have mercy, Lord.

5. Give your servants from above / faith and courage, hope and love; / let rich harvests there be grown / where they have in ,sorrow sown. / Have mercy, Lord.

6. Let us see your glory now / as about the world we go; / with our little strength increase / whatsoever makes for peace. / Have mercy, Lord.

7. Every honour, glory, praise, / shall the Highest have always; / so that in the Three-in-One / we ourselves shall be at one.

F. Pratt Green 1971

148b

Geistlich Böhmische Brüder 1531

Son - ne der Ge - rech - tig - keit, ge - he auf
Sun of Righ - teous - ness, a - rise now to - day

zu uns - - rer Zeit; brich in dei - ner Kir -
in our own skies; in your Chur - ch's dawn -

che an, daß die Welt es se - hen kann.
ing be that one light by which men see.

149

Martin Shaw 1875 - 1958

1. God is___ work-ing his pur-pose out
1. Dieu est à l'œuvre en cet â - ge,
1. Os seus in-ten-tos___ cum-pre Deus
1. Los de - si - gnos de nues-tro Dios

as___ year suc - ceeds to year;
les___ temps sont les der - niers.
no de - cor - rer dos a - nos.
cum-pli - en - - dose es - tan:

God is___ work - ing his pur - pose out
Dieu est à l'œuvre en cet â - - ge,
Ele e - xe - cu - ta o seu que - rer
el Es - pi - ri - tu del Señ - or

and the time is___ draw - ing near.
son___ jour va___ se le - ver!
le - - van - do a - van - te os pla-nos.
no___ de - ja___ de ob - rar:

Near - er and near - er draws the time, the
Ne dou-tons pas du jour___ qui vient, la
Eis, a - pro - xi - ma - se o fi - nal! Bem
hor - as y sig - los sin___ ce - sar, al

288

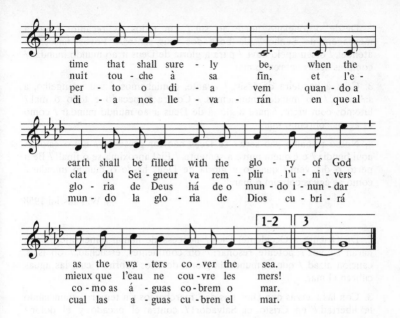

time that shall sure - ly be, when the
nuit tou - che à sa fin, et l'e -
per - to o di - a vem quan - do a
di - a nos lle - va - rán en que al

earth shall be filled with the glo - ry of God
clat du Sei - gneur va rem - plir l'u - ni - vers
glo - ria de Deus há de o mun - do i - nun - dar
mun - do la glo - ria de Dios cu - bri - rá

as the wa - ters co - ver the sea.
mieux que l'eau ne cou - vre les mers!
co - mo as á - guas co - brem o mar.
cual las a - guas cu - bren el mar.

2. What can we do to work God's work, / to prosper and increase / the brotherhood of all mankind, / the reign of the Prince of Peace? / What can we do to hasten the time, / the time that shall surely be, / when the earth shall be filled with the glory of God / as the waters cover the sea.

3. March we forth in the strength of God / with the banner of Christ unfurled, / that the light of the glorious Gospel of truth / may shine throughout the world; / fight we the fight with sorrow and sin / to set their captives free, / that the earth shall be filled with the glory of God / as the waters cover the sea.

A. C. Ainger 1894

2. Quelle est la tâche des hommes / que Dieu vient rassembler, / afin de bâtir le Royaume / du Prince de la Paix? / Que peut-on faire pour hâter / ce jour tant espéré / où l'Eclat du Seigneur va remplir l'univers / mieux que l'eau ne couvre les mers?

3. Que notre marche s'éclaire / au signe de Jésus! / Lui seul peut sauver notre terre / où l'homme n'aime plus; / il faut défendre l'exploité / ouvrir au prisonnier, / et l'Eclat du Seigneur va remplir l'univers / mieux que l'eau ne couvre les mers!

Didier Rimaud 1972

2. Desde o longíquo norte ao sul, / em todos os recantos, / sai a mensagem do Senhor / da boca dos seus santos. / Povos, nações, ó atendei, / o seu apelo ouvi, / para a glória de Deus ir ao mundo inundar / como as águas cobrem o mar.

3. Com a bandeira de Jesus, / avante, caminhemos; / seu evangelho, a salvaçao, / ao mundo anunciemos. / Contra o pecado e todo o mal / lutemos com vigor, / para a glória de Deus ir ao mundo inundar / como as águas cobrem o mar.

4. Nosso trabalho váo será / se Deus não for presente. / Ele o esforço aqui bendiz / e é quem nutre a semente. / Eia! aproxima-se o final! / Bem perto o dia vem / quando a glória de Deus há-de o mundo inundar / como as águas cobrem o mar.

J. W. Faustini 1958

2. De Oriente a Occidente, Dios / no cesa de llamar / mensajeros que harán su voz / potente resonar: / oh continentes, escuchad, / oh islas, canción alzad, / que al mundo la gloria de Dios cubrirá / cual las aguas cubren el mar.

3. Con las fuerzas que Dios nos da / marchemos sin temor; / anunciando la libertad / en Cristo el Salvador: / contra el pecado y el dolor / debemos con el luchar, / que al mundo la gloria de Dios cubrirá / cual las aguas cubren el mar.

4. Nuestras obras son vanidad / sin el favor de Dios; / la cosecha en su mano está / el es Rey y Señor: / pero se acerca el tiempo ya / y nada lo detendrá, / en que al mundo la gloria de Dios cubrirá / cual las aguas cubren el mar.

F. J. Pagura

150

P. E. Ruppel 1965

Semichorus: 2 voices in Canon

Gleich - wie   mich   mein
As   my   heaven - ly

Va - ter ge - sandt hat, so sen - de ich euch ___ .
Fa - ther has sent me, so I am send - ing you ___ .

1.+2. { Er hat mich ge - sandt zu pre - di - gen den Ge-
{ und ich sen - de euch zu pre - di - gen den Zer-

1.+2. { He has sent ___ me to tell ___ those in pri - son
{ I am send - ing you to tell ___ the op - press'd and

fan - ge - nen, daß sie los sein ___ sol - len.
schla - ge - nen, daß sie frei sein ___ sol - len.
that their cap - ti - vi - ty is ___ o - ver.
poor that their night of sor - row is end - ed.

The Holy Communion and the Last Things
Das Heilige Abendmahl und die letzten Dinge
La Sainte-Cêne et les Choses Dernières

151

Johann Crüger 1598 - 1662

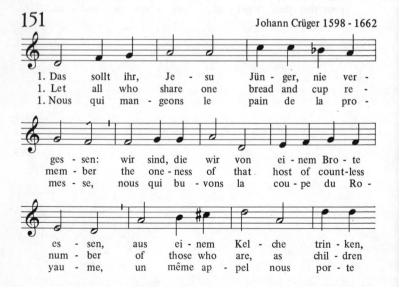

1. Das sollt ihr, Je - su Jün - ger, nie ver -
1. Let all who share one bread and cup re -
1. Nous qui man - geons le pain de la pro -

ges - sen: wir sind, die wir von ei - nem Bro - te
mem - ber the one - ness of that host of count-less
mes - se, nous qui bu - vons la cou - pe du Ro -

es - sen, aus ei - nem Kel - che trin - ken,
num - ber of those who are, as chil - dren
yau - me, un même ap - pel nous por - te

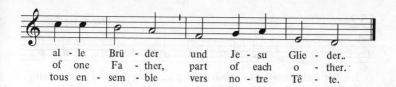

al - le   Brü - der   und   Je - su   Glie - der..
of one   Fa - ther,   part   of each   o - ther.
tous en - sem - ble   vers   no - tre   Tê - te.

2. Wenn wir wie Brüder beiander wohnten, / Gebeugte stärkten und der Schwachen schonten, / dann würden wir den letzten heilgen Willen / des Herrn erfüllen.

3. Ach dazu müsse seine Lieb uns dringen! / Du wolltest, Herr, dies grosse Werk vollbringen, / daß unter einem Hirten eine Herde / aus allen werde.

Based on a hymn by J. A. Cramer 1723-88

2. If only we would learn to live as brothers, / put faith to practice, truly care for others, / then we would do the will of Him who sends us, / whose love attends us.

3. Use for yourself our highest and profoundest, / so that, O Lord, with all men who surround us, / we may enjoy a world in Christ united, / so long awaited.

Fred Kaan 1972

2. En recevant le don du Christ aux hommes, / nous accueillons l'élan de son offrande; / que cet élan nous guide à la rencontre / de tous nos frères.

3. Graine de froment et grappes de la vigne / sont rassemblés dans le pain et la coupe; / ainsi, Jésus, c'est toi qui nous rassembles / dans ton Eglise.

Frère Pierre-Yves 1972

293

152

French carol melody

1. Let all mor - tal flesh keep __ si - lence and with
1. Lors - que les mor - tels, en si - len - ce fré - mi -
1. Schwei - get al - le, die ihr __ sterb - lich nun in
1. Lo mor - tal es - té en si - len - cio Y se

fear and trem - bling __ stand; pon - der noth - ing
ront de crain - te par - tout; lors - que fi - ni -
Ehr - furcht vor ihm __ steht; denn mit Hän - den
a - cal - le con te - mor; na - da hu - ma - no

earth - ly __ mind - ed, for with bless - ing
ra l'es - pé - ran - ce, nos yeux s'ou - vri -
vol - ler __ Se - gen Chri - stus durch die
con - si - de - re, pues con ben - di -

in his __ hand Christ our Lord to earth des -
ront tout à coup, nous ver - rons le Christ en
Rei - hen __ geht, reich - lich zu be - schen - ken
ción y a - mor Cris - to nues - tro Dios des -

cen - deth, our full ho - mage to de - mand.
gloi - re re - ce - voir l'hom - ma - ge de tous.
je - den, der um sei - nen Se - gen fleht.
cien - de ex - i - gien - do to - do ho - nor.

2. King of kings, yet born of Mary, / as of old on earth he stood, / Lord
of lords, in human vesture / – in the Body and the Blood – / he will give
to all the faithful / his own Self for heavenly food.

3. Rank on rank the host of heaven / spreads its vanguard on the way, / as the Light of light descendeth / from the realms of endless day, / that the powers of hell may vanish / as the darkness clears away.

4. At his feet the six-winged seraph: / cherubim with sleepless eye, / veil their faces to the Presence, / as with ceaseless voice they cry, / 'Alleluia, Alleluia, / Alleluia, Lord most high.'

G. Moultrie, from the Greek Liturgy of St James

2. Roi du monde, né de Marie, / qui fus autrefois un enfant, / Seigneur qui vécus notre vie, / homme par le corps et le sang / tes Frères humains t'implorent, / sauve-les encore du néant.

3. Lorsque danseront les atomes, / et que surgira l'Absolu, / Fais-nous place dans ton Royaume, / range-nous parmi tes élus. / Le Mal à jamais s'efface, dans le grand soleil du salut.

4. Nous verrons la foule des anges / soutenir les pieds du Sauveur. / Et tous les vivants crient louange / devant l'Eternel créateur; / les ressuscités proclament / leur Alléluia au Seigneur.

G. de Lioncourt 1972

2. König aller Königreiche, / einst für uns als Mensch geborn, / hast aus lauter Lieb und Güte / uns zu deinem Reich erkorn. / Gib uns ewge Speise heute, / die wir wärn ohn' dich verlorn.

3. Licht vom Licht, zu uns gekommen, / aus der Welt der Ewigkeit, / mach die Macht des Bösen schwinden, / weichen alle Dunkelheit. / Zünde an in uns dein Feuer, / mach uns selbst zum Dienst bereit.

4. Und am Ende dieser Tage / lade uns zum Festmal ein. / Laß uns mit der Schar der Deinen / in dein Lob dann stimmen ein: / Halleluja, halleluja, / Gott sei Preis, ihm Ehr' allein!

Erich Griebling 1969

2. Rey de reyes que en lo antiguo / vino al mundo a morar / y en humana vestidura, / si, de carne y sangre, a andar, / ha de darse a los fieles / a sí mismo por manjar.

3. Van las huestes celestiales / su vanguardia a desplegar, / y la Luz de luz desciende / de aquel reino eternal, / el poder del mal ahuyenta, / las tinieblas al clarear.

4. A sus pies los serafines, / sus vigilias al guardar, / cúbrense de la Presencia / sin dejar de aclamar: / 'Aleluya, Aleluya, / Aleluya, Rey sin par.'

Pablo D. Sosa 1959

1. Em silêncio toda carne, / com temor e devoção / abandone reverente / todo pensamento vão; / nosso Deus à terra desce / tributailhe adoração!

2. Rei dos reis, da Virgem, filho / entre nós ele habitou, / Deus em corpo e sangue humano / Deus-Senhor que se humilhou. / Os seus filhos alimenta, / ele disse: 'O Pão eu Sou.'

3. Hostes celestiais preparam / o caminho do Senhor / ao descer a Luz das luzes / do seu Reino de esplendor. / Quem tombou seu inimigo / extinguia a treva e a dor.

4. Vigilantes anjos voam / ao redor do Criador / e cobrindo as suas faces / cantam o eternal louvor: / 'Aleluia, Aleluia! / Ao supremo Deus Senhor!'

J. Costa 1960

1. 凡有血氣、皆當靜默、敬畏謙恭同肅立；毋思絲毫世
俗事物、因主基督臨世界、親手分賜天福神恩、接受
我衆恭敬拜。

2. 王之王兮、聖母誕生、血肉為體掩神光、主之主兮、
仍在下方、今日依然恩澤長、自願將其聖身寶血、賜
與信者作天糧。

3. 千萬天軍、排列成行、前隊先鋒一路長、周圍環繞光
之光兮、親從永晝天堂降、消滅地獄可怖權威、推開
黑暗、揚眞光。

4. 西拉冰兮、伏主足下、基路冰兮常警醒、雨翅遮面、
大聲讚美、頌歌騰響門庭震、阿勒盧亞、阿勒盧亞、
阿勒盧亞、主至聖。阿們。

1. 生けるもの凡て　おののきてもたせ、
世の思い棄てて　ひたすらにあおけ、
かみの御子は　くだりたもう
このきよき日にぞ。

2. きみの君なれど　マリヤより生れ、
うまぶねの中に　産声をあげて、
おのが身をば　あたえたもう
つみびとのために。

296

3. とてしえの光　　暗き世にてりて、
　　み使は御子を　　かしてみて崇む。
　　いざわれらも　　はめうたわん
　　　　いとたかき君を。

1. يَا إِلَهِي اَسْمَعْ صُرَاخِي ۰ وَاَصْغَ يَا رَبِّي إِلَيَّ ۰ مِنْ صَمِيمِ الْقَلْبِ أَدْعُو ۰
حِينَمَا يُغْشَى عَلَيَّ ۰ يَا إِلَهِي اَسْمَعْ صُارَخِي ۰ وَاَصْغَ يَا رَبِّي إِلَى

2. أَنْتَ تَهْدِينِي لِصَخرٍ ۰ هُوَ مِنِّي أَرْفَعُ ۰ كُنْتَ لِي مَلْجَأ أَيمانٍ ۰ مِنْ
عَدُوٍّ وَيَنْفَزَعُ ۰ يَا إِلَهِي اَسْمَعْ صُرَاخِي ۰ وَاَصْغَ يَا رَبِّي إِلَى

3. بُرْجُ قُوَّةٍ لِضُعْفِي ۰ أَنْتَ مِنْ وَجْهِ الْعِدَى ۰ مِنْ جَنَاحَيْكَ بِسِتْرٍ ۰
أَحْتَمِيَ طُولَ الْمَدَى ۰ يَا إِلَهِي اَسْمَعْ صُرَاخِي ۰ وَاَصْغَ يَا رَبِّي إِلَى

4. لِاَسْمِكَ الْقُدُوسِ أُهْدِي ۰ كُلَّ تَسْبِيحِ الْحَيَاهِ ۰ وَأَنِّي يَوْمًا فَيَوْمًا ۰
كُلَّ نَذْرٍ لِلْوَفَاةْ ۰ يَا إِلَهِي اَسْمَعْ صُرَاخِي ۰ وَاَصْغَ يَا رَبِّي إِلَى

Nasef el Yazgi

297

153

Negro Spiritual early 19th century

1. Let us break bread to-geth-er on our knees;
1. Par - ta - geons tous le pain qui nous u - nit;
1. La tua ma - no, Si - gno - re, ci da - rà
1. De ro - di - llas par-ta-mos hoy el pan,
1. み ま え に われ ら つ ど い

let us break bread to-geth-er on our knees:
re - ce - vons à ge-noux Dieu, no - tre vie!
ques - to pa - ne, di - vi - so qui fra noi.
De ro - di - llas par-ta-mos hoy el pan;
と も に わ か つ み 糧 を

Refrain

When I fall on my knees, with my face to the
Quand je tombe à ge - noux, le vi - sage au so -
Quando ca - do in gi - noc-chio e vol - go lo sguar -
De ro - di - llas es-toy, con el ros-tro al na -
世 の 光 なる 主 の て と

ris - ing sun, O Lord, have mer - cy on me.
leil le - vant, Oh Sei - gneur, don - ne ton Pain.
do a te, Si - gnor, pi - e - tà di me.
cien - te sol, ¡ Oh, Dios, a - piá - da - te de mi!
は も て し ゅ く し た ま え

2. Let us drink wine together on our knees; / let us drink wine together
on our knees: / when I fall on my knees, / with my face to the rising
sun, / O Lord, have mercy on me.

3. Let us praise God together on our knees; / let us praise God together
on our knees: / when I fall on my knees, / with my face to the rising
sun, / O Lord, have mercy on me.

Negro Spiritual, early 19th century

2. Partageons tous le vin qui nous unit; / recevons à genoux Dieu, notre vie! / Quand je tombe à genoux, / le visage au soleil levant, / Oh, Seigneur, donne ton Vin!

3. Partageons tous l'Amour qui nous unit; / recevons à genoux Dieu, notre vie! / Quand je tombe à genoux, / le visage au soleil levant, / Oh, Seigneur, donne l'Amour.

Marc Ginot 1972

2. La tua mano, Signore, ci darà / questo vino, versato qui per noi. / Quando cado in ginocchio / e volgo lo sguardo a te, / Signor, pietà di me.

3. La tua mano, Signore, ci darà / questa gioia, perché tu sei con noi. / Quando cado in ginocchio / e volgo lo sguardo a te, / Signor, pietà di me.

Eugenio Costa

2. Compartamos la copa en gratitud, / compartamos la copa en gratitud; / de rodillas estoy, / con el rostro al naciente sol, / ¡Oh Dios, apiádate de mi!

3. De rodillas loemos al Señor, / de rodillas loemos al Señor; / de rodillas estoy, / con el rostro al naciente sol, / ¡Oh Dios, apiádate de mi!

F. J. Pagura

1. De joelhos partamos nosso pão, / de joelhos partamos nosso pão. / Se de joelhos estou / contemplando o nascer do sol, / Senhor, tem pena de mim.

2. De joelhos tomemos vinho, irmãos, / de joelhos tomemos vinho, irmãos. / Se de joelhos estou / Contemplando o nascer do sol, / Senhor, tem pena de mim!

3. De joelhos louvemos nosso Deus, / de joelhos louvemos nosso Deus. / Se de joelhos estou / Contemplando o nascer do sol, / Senhor, tem pena de mim!

J. W. Faustini 1969

2. み招きにこたえつつ
あずかるさかずきをも、
世の光なる主のことばもて
しゅくしたまえ。

3. みわざをたたえうたい、
みまえにつどう民を、
世の光なる主のことばもて
しゅくしたまえ。

154

Alfred M. Smith 1941

1. Come, ri - sen Lord, and deign to be our
1. Komm, Herr des Le - bens, sei du un - ser
1. Ain - si tu viens, Sei - gneur, pour être à

guest; nay, let us be thy guests, the feast is
Gast und laß auch uns bei dir als Gä - ste
nous. L'a - mour de Dieu nous fixe un ren - dez -

thine: thy - self at thine own board make ma - ni -
sein. Mach' sel - ber dich an die - sem Tisch be -
vous: Voi - ci le pain, la coupe en - tre tes

300

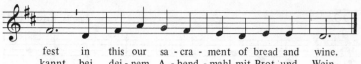

fest	in	this	our	sa - cra - ment	of	bread	and	wine.
kannt	bei	dei - nem	A - bend - mahl	mit	Brot	und	Wein.
mains.	Jé - sus	va	nous ai - mer	jus - qu'à	la	fin.

2. We meet, as in that upper room they met; / thou at the Table blessing yet dost stand: / 'This is my Body', so thou givest yet: / faith still receives the cup as from thy hand.

3. One body we, one body who partake, / one church united in communion blest; / one name we bear, one bread of life we break, / with all thy saints in earth and saints at rest.

4. One with each other, Lord, for one in thee, / who art one Saviour and one living head; / then open thou our eyes, that we may see; / be known to us in breaking of the bread.

G. W. Briggs 1875–1958

2. Wie bei den Jüngern in der letzten Nacht / bist du am Tisch und sagst den Segen dann: / 'Dies ist mein Leib', so reichst du uns das Brot. / Und Glaube nimmt den Kelch der Liebe an.

3. Ein Leib, so nehmen wir das eine Brot, / als eine Kirche zu uns selbst befreit. / Du, Christus, leihst uns deinen Namen aus / wie allen Glaubenden zu ihrer Zeit.

4. Eins miteinander sind wir, eins in dir, / der du noch Hoffnung für uns alles hast. / Herr, öffne unsre Augen, daß wir seh'n / wie du zugleich uns Geber bist und Gast.

Wolfgang Derreth 1972

2. A notre Table, en signe de ta mort, / on redira, 'Mangez, voici mon corps'. / Tes propres mots sont ici prononcés, / 'Voici mon sang, amis, prenez, buvez.'

3. Ton Corps, c'est nous, en toi remodelés; / un même Nom, le tien, nous est donné. / Tu fais de nous un peuple pour ta Paix / qu'un même Esprit anime désormais.

4. Tu vis pour nous, vivons aussi pour toi, / mais notre cœur hésite dans sa foi, / sur le chemin, en l'étranger d'un soir, / reviens, Seigneur, pour nous apprendre à voir.

D. Hameline 1972

155

Lee H. Bristol 1971

1. As the dis - ci - ples when thy Son had
1. Wie einst die Jün - ger nach dem Ab - schied

left them____, met in a love - feast joy - ful -
Je - su____ ein Fest der Lie - be und der

ly con - vers - ing____, all the stor'd mem' - ry
Wie - der - ho - lung____ des letz - ten Mah - les

of the Lord's last Sup - per____, fond - ly re -
ih - res Her - ren mach - ten____ und sei - ner

hears - ing; so may we here who ga - ther
harr - ten, so wol - len wir uns hier in

now in friend - ship____, seek for the spi - rit
Freund-schaft sam - meln____, und wie die Chri - sten

of those ear - lier chur - ches____; wel- com - ing him who
je - ner er - sten Stun - de____ für ihn be - reit sein,

stands and for an en - trance___ pa - tient- ly search - es.
daß er Ein - laß fin - de___ bei sei - nen Brü - dern.

2. As when their converse closed and supper ended, / taking the bread and wine, they made thanksgiving, / breaking and blessing thus to have communion / with Christ the living; / so may we here, a company of brothers, / make this our lovefeast and commemoration / that in his Spirit we may have more worthy / participation.

3. And as they prayed and sang to thee rejoicing, / here in the nightfall they embraced and parted, / in their hearts singing as they journeyed homeward, / brave and truehearted; / so may we here, like grain that once was scattered, / over the hillside, now one bread united, / led by the Spirit, do thy work rejoicing, / lamps fill'd and lighted.

Percy Dearmer 1931

2. Wie sie einst, dankend für die guten Gaben / des Wortes und des Brots und der Gemeinschaft, / das Zeichen tauschten der gewissen Nähe / des Auferstand'nen. / So wollen wir, Genossen seiner Liebe, / an ihn gedenkend auch sein Mahl begehen / und seinem Geist uns öffnen im Vertrauen, / daß er uns eine.

3. Wie sie mit Liedern deinen Namen priesen, / bevor zum Abschied sie die Hand sich boten / und neuen Muts an ihre Arbeit gingen / in deiner Freude. / So wollen wir, wie Korn aus tausend Äckern / im Brot vereinigt vielen Leben spendet, / der Liebe Arbeit willig auf uns nehmen, / von Dir geleitet.

Ernst Lange 1972

156

Urdu melody

1. Je - sus the Lord said: 'I am the Bread, the
1. Il nous a dit: c'est moi le vrai pain, Le
1. Je - sus, der Herr, sprach: „Ich bin das Brot, das

Bread of Life for man - kind am I, the
pain pour la vie é - ter - nel - le; le
Brot des Le - bens für je - der - mann, das

Bread of Life for man - kind am I, the
pain pour la vie é - ter - nel - le, le
Brot des Le - bens für je - der - mann, das

Bread of Life for man - kind am I.'
pain pour la vie é - ter - nel - le.
Brot des Le - bens für je - der - mann."

Je - sus the Lord said: 'I am the Bread___, the
Il nous a dit: c'est moi le vrai pain___; le
Je - sus, der Herr, sprach: „Ich bin das Brot ___, das

Bread of ___ Life ___ for man - kind am I.'
pain pour la vie ___ é - ter - nel - le.
Brot des ___ Le - bens für je - der - mann."

304

2. Jesus the Lord said: 'I am the Door, / the Way and the Door for the poor am I.'

3. Jesus the Lord said: 'I am the Light, / the one true Light of the world am I.'

4. Jesus the Lord said: 'I am the Shepherd, / the one Good Shepherd of the sheep am I.'

5. Jesus the Lord said: 'I am the Life, / the Resurrection and the Life am I.'

Dermott Monahan 1962

2. Il nous a dit: c'est moi le chemin / la route qui mène au Royaume.

3. Il nous a dit: c'est moi la lumière / la seule lumière du monde.

4. Il nous a dit: c'est moi le berger / le bon berger qui vous guide.

5. Il nous a dit: c'est moi la vraie vie / la vie qui renaît éternelle.

J. Gelineau 1972

2. Jesus, der Herr, sprach: Ich bin die Tür, / der Weg und die Tür für die Armen.

3. Jesus, der Herr, sprach: Ich bin das Licht, / das einzig wahre Licht für die Welt.

4. Jesus, der Herr, sprach: Ich bin der Hirt, / der eine gute Hirt für die Schafe

5. Jesus, der Herr, sprach: Ich bin das Leben, / die Auferstehung und das Leben.

Otmar Schulz 1972

157

Su Yin-Lan 1934

1. The bread of life for all men bro - ken!
1. En sou - ve - nir de sa ten - dres - se,
1. Du bist das Brot für uns ge - ge - ben,

He drank the cup on Gol - go - tha.
Voi - ci le Pain li - vré pour_ nous.
Du bist der Wein, un - ser Le - ben.

His grace we trust, and spread with rev' - rence
Signe é - ter - nel de son Ro - yau - me,
Dein Wort sagt uns, die dies Brot neh - men:

this ho - ly feast, and this re - mem - ber.
A - mour of - fert à tous les hom - mes.
„Das sollt ihr tun, mir zum Ge - dächt - nis."

2. With godly fear we seek thy presence; / our hearts are sad, people distressed. / Thy holy face is stained with bitter tears, / our human pain still bearest thou with us.

3. O Lord we pray, come thou among us, / lighten our eyes, brightly appear. / Immanuel, heaven's joy unending, / our life with thine for ever blending.

W. R. O. Taylor

2. En souvenir de ses souffrances, / voici le Sang versé pour nous. / Signe éternel de son passage, / amour vivant pour tous les âges.

3. Que le soleil de sa présence / redonne vie au monde entier. / Reste avec nous car le jour tombe, / feu dans la nuit, clarté du monde.

Claude Rozier 1972

2. Die Last der Welt und uns'rer Seelen, / wollen wir dir, Herr, befehlen. / Du rufst uns zu, wenn wir uns quälen: / „Kommt her zu mir, all ihr Beladenen".

3. Zieh' ein bei uns mit deiner Wahrheit. / Wo Schatten ist, bring du Klarheit. / Dein Kreuz und Sieg ist unsre Freiheit. / „Ich bin bei euch, immer und ewig."

Konrad Raiser 1972

1. 救世之身、為眾生擘開、在骷髏地、痛飲苦杯；蒙恩信眾、奉命常紀念、敬設聖筵、追憶當年。

2. 吾眾今朝、虔誠來入覲、國難民愁、遍心創痕；仰瞻聖容、看血淚千行、人間苦痛、主仍擔當。

3. 懇求臨格、在我們中間、開我心目、昭現妙身；以馬內利、天福永無邊、與主合一、同享永生。阿們。

158

Stanley L. Osborne 1971

1. As we break the bread and taste the life of
1. Bre - chen wir das Brot und schmek - ken Kraft vom

V. 1–3

wine, we call to mind our Lord, Man of all
Wein: Mensch, ge - denk des Herrn, denn___ er ist

V. 4

time. world, scat - tered as grain.
dein! als___ Saat ge - - streut.

2. Grain is sown to die; it rises from the dead, / becomes through human toil our common bread.

3. Pass from hand to hand the living love of Christ! / Machine and man provide bread for this feast.

4. Having shared the bread that dies to rise again, / we rise to serve the world, scattered as grain.

Fred Kaan 1968

2. Kornsaat, die erstirbt, steht wieder auf vom Tod, / durch unsre Arbeit, gemeinsam Brot.

3. Geh von Hand zu Hand, sag, daß uns Gott nicht läßt. / Durch Menschenhände kommt Brot zum Fest.

4. Ist das Brot verzehrt, soll's auferstehn erneut. / Wir sind gesendet, als Saat gestreut.

Dieter Trautwein 1972

159

Dieter Trautwein 1967

1. Herr,   du   bist   an   vie - len   Ti - schen
1. Lord,   you   are   at   ma - ny   ta - bles

ein - ge - la - den und zu Gast.   Und auch bei
an   in - vi - ted, ho - noured guest.   E - ven   of

de - nen,   die sich selbst ge - nü - gen,   wird kei - ner
those, Lord,   who are self - suf - fi - cient   you let none

dir   zur   Last. Tei - le   mit   uns ___ das Mahl,
bear   you   down. Come, share the   meal ___ with us,

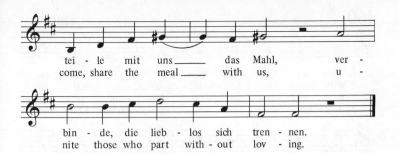

tei - le mit uns_____ das Mahl, ver -
come, share the meal_____ with us, u -

bin - de, die lieb - los sich tren - nen.
nite those who part with - out lov - ing.

2. Herr, du bist an vielen Tischen / eingeladen und zu Gast. / Sprichst auch mit denen, / die sonst nichts erwarten / als neuer Tage Last. / Teile mit uns das Mahl, / teile mit uns das Mahl, / gib Glanz in die Augen der Müden.

3. Herr, du bist an vielen Tischen / eingeladen und zu Gast. / Kommst auch zu Menschen, / die sich dir versagen. / Frommtun ist dir verhaßt. / Teile mit uns das Mahl, / teile mit uns das Mahl, / daß wir deinem Angebot trauen.

4. Herr, du bist an vielen Tischen / eingeladen und zu Gast. / Sorgst dann als Gastherr, / daß wir uns ertragen, / einer des andern Last. / Teile mit uns das Mahl, / teile mit uns das Mahl, / jetzt hier und an all unsren Tischen.

Dieter Trautwein 1967

2. Lord, you are at many tables / an invited, honoured guest. / You also speak, Lord, / to those who see nothing / except tomorrow's cares. / Come, share the meal with us, / come, share the meal with us, / give light to the eyes of the weary.

3. Lord, you are at many tables / an invited, honoured guest. / You come to people / who do without you. / False piety you hate. / Come, share the meal with us, / come, share the meal with us, / then, Lord, we shall trust what you offer.

4. Lord, you are at many tables / an invited, honoured guest. / But as our Host, Lord, / you make sure we carry / each other's load of cares. / Come, share the meal with us, / come, share the meal with us, / here, now, and at each of our tables.

F. Pratt Green 1973

160

Grenoble Antiphoner 1753

1. Now let us from this ta - ble rise re -
2. With minds a - lert, up - held by grace, to
1. Nun laßt uns von dem Mahl auf - stehn, ganz
2. In wa - chem Sinn und fri - scher Kraft be -

newed in bo - dy, mind and soul; with
spread the Word in speech and deed, we
neu ge - stärkt an Leib und Geist. Weil
wei - sen Mund und Hand ver - eint: Wir

Christ we die and live a - gain, his
fol - low in the steps of Christ, at
Chri - stus un - ge - teilt sich gab, wird
fol - gen Chri - stus Schritt um Schritt sind

self - less love has made us whole.
one with man in hope and need.
un - ser gan - zer Mensch ge - speist.
je - dem nah, der lacht, der weint.

3. To fill each human house with love, / it is the sacrament of care; / the work that Christ began to do / we humbly pledge ourselves to share.

4. Then give us courage, Father God, / to choose again the pilgrim way, / and help us to accept with joy / the challenge of tomorrow's day.

Fred Kaan 1968

3. Es zeigt die Liebe überall: / so weit reicht Jesu Sakrament! / Das Werk, das Christus einst begann, / verbindet Leben, das sich trennt.

4. Drum gib uns Mut, du Herr des Mahls, / zu wählen deine neue Welt. / Hilf uns zu einem ganzen Ja, / das jeden neuen Tag sich stellt.

Dieter Trautwein 1973

161

La Forme des Prières, Strasbourg 1545

1. Fa - ther, we thank thee who hast plant - ed
1. Chri - stus, wir tra - gen dei - nen Na - men.

Thy ho - ly name with - in our hearts.
Präg ihn in uns - re Her - zen ein.

Know - ledge and faith and life im - mor - tal
Glau - ben, Er - kennt - nis, ew - ges Le - ben,

Je - sus thy Son to us im - parts.
laß auch in uns - rem All - tag sein.

2. Thou, Lord, didst make all for thy pleasure, / didst give man food for all his days, / giving in Christ the bread eternal; / thine is the power, be thine the praise.

3. Watch o'er thy Church, O Lord, in mercy, / save it from evil, guard it still, / perfect it in thy love, unite it, / cleansed and conformed unto thy will.

4. As grain, once scattered on the hillsides, / was in the broken bread made one, / so from all lands thy Church be gathered / into thy kingdom by thy Son.

F. Bland Tucker 1940

2. Gib, Herr, was wir zum Leben brauchen, / gib deinen Frieden auch dazu / und laß uns mit dem Bruder teilen; / entlarve bei uns fromme Ruh'.

3. Bewahre deine Kirche heute / vor Spaltung, Neid und Heuchelei. / Vereine uns durch deine Liebe. / Mach uns zum Dienst für andre frei.

4. Wie Korn gesät auf einen Acker / in einem Brot beisammen ist, / so sammelst du aus allen Völkern / dir deine Kirche, Jesus Christ.

F. K. Barth, S. Leonhard, O. Schulz 1972

162

Sven-Erik Bäck 1959

1. Du som gick fö - re oss längst in i ån - ge - sten
1. You, Lord, who chose to share and shoul - der man's des - pair,
1. Du, der du vor uns gingst hin - ein in tief - ste Angst,

hjälp oss att fin - na dig Her - re, i mör - kret.
be where your peo - ple are in fear and dark - ness.
hilf uns zu fin - den dich, Herr, in dem Dun - kel.

2. Du som bar all vår skuld in in förlåtelsen / du är vårt hjärtas fred
Jesus, för evigt.

3. Du som med livets bröd går genom tid och rum / giv oss för varje dag
Kristus, det brödet.

4. Du som går före oss ut i en trasig värld / sänd oss med fred och bröd
Herr, i världen.

Olov Hartmann 1968

2. Lord, you who went before, counting our sins no more, / peace to our
hearts restore; be with us always.

3. You, who with living bread fill the earth far and wide, / each day this
bread provide, Christ, at our table.

4. You, Lord, who went ahead into a world of dread, / send us with
peace and bread to all your people.

Fred Kaan 1972

2. Der du die Sünden trugst und gabst Vergebung uns, / bist unsres
Herzens Trost, Jesus, für immer.

3. Der du des Lebens Brot mitführst durch Zeit und Raum, / gib uns an
jedem Tag, Christ, von dem Brot.

4. Du, der voraus uns geht in unsre wunde Welt, / schick uns mit Brot
und Heil, Herr, zu den Menschen.

Helli Halbe 1972

163

Philipp Nicolai 1599

1. „Wa - chet auf", ruft uns die Stim - - me,
1. 'Sleep - ers wake!' with ti - dings thril - - ling,
1. O Si - on, O peuple im - men - - se,
1. Des - per - tad! que ya nos lla - - ma

der Wäch - ter sehr hoch auf der Zin - ne,
the watch - men all the air are fil - ling,
de - bout! voi - ci ta dé - li - vran - ce!
el guar - da fiel con su pro - cla - ma:

„wach auf, du Stadt Je - ru - sa - lem."
'a - rise, Je - ru - sa - lem, a - rise!'
Tu vas con - naî - tre ton Sau - veur.
Des - pier - ta! Pue - blo de Da - vid!

Mit - ter - nacht heißt die - se Stun - - de,
Mid - night strikes! No more de - lay - - ing,
Ton Sei - gneur vers toi s'a - van - - ce;
Es lle - ga - da ya la ho - - ra

sie ru - fen uns mit hel - lem Mun - de:
'the hour has come', we hear them say - - ing,
il veut t'u - nir à sa puis - san - - ce
que lla - ma con su voz so - no - - ra:

313

„Wo seid ihr klu - gen Jung - frau - en?"
'where are you all, you vir - gins wise?'
dans tout l'é - clat de sa splen - deur.
Pru - den - tes vír - gen - es sa - lid!

Wohl - auf, der Bräut - gam kommt, steht auf,
The Bride - groom comes in sight; raise high
Jé - sus re - vient pour toi: en - tends
La lam - para en - cen - ded, y al fiel

die Lam - pen nehmt! Hal - le - lu - ja!
your torch - es bright. Al - le - lu - ia!
chan - ter sa voix. Al - lé - lu - ia!
Es - po - so ved. Al - le - lu - ya!

Macht euch be - reit zu der Hoch - zeit;
The wed - ding song swells loud and strong:
Voi - ci ton Roi, voi - ci ta joie;
pres - to a - cu - did al a - da - lid!

ihr müs - set ihm ent - ge - gen - gehn!
go forth and join the fes - tal throng.
que son a - mour soit tout pour toi!
Con jú - bi - lo a sus bo - das id.

2. Zion hört die Wächter singen, / das Herz tut ihr vor Freuden springen, / sie wachet und steht eilend auf. / Ihr Freund kommt vom Himmel prächtig, / von Gnaden stark, von Wahrheit mächtig, / ihr Licht wird hell, ihr Stern geht auf. / Nun komm, du werte Kron, / Herr Jesu, Gottes Sohn! / Hosianna! / Wir folgen all zum Freudensaal, / und halten mit das Abendmahl.

3. Gloria sei dir gesungen, / mit Menschen und mit Engelzungen, / mit Harfen und mit Zimbeln schön. / Von zwölf Perlen sind die Tore / an deiner Stadt, wir steh'n im Chore / der Engel hoch um deinen Thron. / Kein Aug hat je gespürt, / kein Ohr hat mehr gehört / solche Freude. / Des jauchzen wir und singen dir / das Halleluja für und für.

Philipp Nicolai 1599

2. Sion hears the watchmen shouting, / her heart leaps up with joy undoubting, / she stands and waits with eager eyes. / See her Friend from heav'n descending, / adorned with truth and grace unending! / Her light burns clear, her star doth rise. / Now come, thou precious crown, / Lord Jesus, God's own Son, / Hosanna! / Let us prepare to follow there, / where in thy supper we may share.

3. Every soul in Thee rejoices; / from men and from angelic voices / be glory given to Thee alone! / Now the gates of pearl receive us, / thy presence never more shall leave us, / we stand with Angels round Thy throne. / Earth cannot give below / the bliss Thou dost bestow. / Alleluia! / Grant us to raise to length of days / the triumph-chorus of Thy praise.

F. C. Burkitt 1906

2. Gloire à toi, clarté vivante, / Esprit d'amour, ô joie ardente, / qui nous unis en Jésus-Christ. / Gloire à toi, Sauveur des hommes / qui nous apprend comment on nomme / la Vie qui nous donne toute vie! / Déjà parait le jour / du règne de l'Amour; / taris les pleurs, / enfuie la mort, chassé le froid, / nous chanterons: Alléluia!

Claude Rozier 1970

2. Escuchando a los vigías / despierta Sión con alegría; / levántase a recibir / al que es fuerte y poderoso, / a su leal y tierno Esposo / que desde el cielo ha de venir. / Corona eres tú, / Eterno Rey, Jesus! / Cantando va / todo mortal / al sin igual / festín del Reino Celestial.

3. Gloria sea a ti cantando / por querubines, entonando / con arpas de sonora voz. / Doce perlas en la entrada / que nos conduce a la morada, / mansión de paz de nuestro Dios. / Jamás el ojo vió, / Ningún oido oyó / de un coro / tal igual cantar. / Id sin tardar, / eternos himnos a entonar.

Fritz Fliedner y Nicolás Martinez

315

1. Das a - mei - as o vi - gi - a,
1. On - do - ke - ni! tu - na - i - twa
1. 'Ba - ngun - lah!', se - ru su - a - ra

em ró - seo des - pon - tar do di - a,
na wa - lin - zi wa juu mna - ra - ni:
pe - nga - wal, ting - gi di me - na - ra,

voz cla - ri - nan - te faz ou - vir:
Ye - ru - sa - le - mu, am - ka - wee!
'Ye - ru - sa - lem, hai ba - ngun - lah!'

Que Si - ão es - te - ja a - ten - ta,
Ni u - si - ku wa ma - na - ne,
Ma - lam jauh! Wak - tu - nya ti - ba!'

a ho - ra, vê - de, se a - pre - sen - ta,
yu - a - ja Bwa - na wa a - ru - si,
De - ngar se - ru - an yang meng - im - bau:

de o pla - no e - ter - no se cum - prir.
wa - na - wa - li wa - ko wa - pi?
'Hai pu - t'ri Si - on, ja - ga - lah!'

O Vir - gens de Si - ão, ao al -
Am - ke - ni u - pe - si, ka - zi -
Jem - put Peng - an - tin - mu! Si ap -

to o co - ra - ção! Al - le - lu - ia!
wa - she - ni taa. Ha - le - lu - ya!
kan lam - pu - mu. Ma - ra - na - ta!

As por - tas já an - dai, cor - rei!
Fu - a - te - ni a - ru - si - ni
Be - ri - as - lah 'kan pes - ta - Nya

Eis que é che - ga - do o gran - de Rei!
kwen - da kum - po - ke - a Bwa - na!
Dan song - song Di - a se - ge - ra!

2. Atendei, levai, prudentes, / acesas luzes resplendentes. / Alegra-te, ó Jerusalém! / Entre nuvens fulgurantes, / com céus e terra, jubilantes / ao teu encontro o Esposo vem! / Tesouro para os seus, / gracioso dom de Deus, / Aleluia! / Pois nos atrai, com grande amor. / Contigo iremos, ó Senhor!

3. Encha os céus, inunde a terra, / a glória que seu nome encerra. / Vós órgãos e harpas ressonai! / Na cidade esplendorosa / não cesse a festa jubilosa / em torno ao sólio do Deus Pai. / Jamais se contemplou, / sequer se imaginou, / tanta glória! / A ele, pois, com gratidão, / louvor e eterna adoração!

J. M. da Mota Sobrinho 1961

2. Sioni anasikia, / moyo waruka kwa furaha, / yu macho, anaondoka. / Mponya wake anashuka / mbinguni mwenye utukufu, / aleta mwanga wa kweli. / Taji yake yaja / na mwana wa Mungu. / Hosiana! / Twafuata kwenye shangwe / tukale karamu yake.

3. Waimbiwa nyimbo nzuri / kwa misemo ya watu wote / na ya malaika mbinguni. / Tukifika mjini kwako / kwenye milango ya malulu / tutakuimbia nasi. / Furaha kama hii / haijasikiwa / duniani. / Nasi sasa tunaimba, / tunakusifu, ee Bwana.

2. Sion sadar 'kan berita, / hatinya lonjak bergembira, / terbangun dia bergesa. / Mempelai nun sudah datang, / penuh karunia, kebenaran: / t'rang hari agung merekah! / Ya Tuhan, marilah! / MahkotaMu baka! / Hosiana! / Kami serta masuk pesta / jamuan yang bahagia!

3. ,Gloria! k'lak kita nyanyi / teriring gambus dan kecapi, / malaikat dan manusia! / Ada duab'las gapura, / terbuat dari mutiara, / menyambut bangsa dunia! / Di kota yang kudus / gembira menerus / tak bertara! / Bersoraklah: Haleluya! – / sekarang dan selamanya!

Yayasan Musik Gerejani 1973

Another version of the tune is in the Full Score edition.

164

Gustav Holst 1906

1. From glo - ry to glo - ry ad - vanc - ing, we
2. Thanks - giv - ing and glo - ry and __ wor - ship and
1. Le jour s'est le - vé sur ter - re! Par - tout
2. Sur les hauts che - mins qui mè - nent vers la

praise thee, O Lord; thy name with the Fa - ther and
bless - ing and love; one heart and one song have the
re - naît la joie! l'Es - prit que Dieu nous a don -
ci - té de paix un peu - ple chan - te son es -

Spi - rit be ev - er a - dored. From __
saints up - on earth and a - bove. Ev - er
né ré - veil - le no - tre foi: Pleins de
poir de voir s'ou - vrir le ciel: Le Sei -

strength un - to strength we go for - ward on
more __, O Lord, to thy ser - vants thy
for - ce nous mar - chons vers la lu - mi -
gneur nous ac - cueil - le - ra en é - ten -

318

Si - on's high - way, to ap - pear be - fore
pre - sence be nigh; ev - er fit us by
è - re d'en haut! De nos voix nous ac -
dant sur nos corps ses mains plei - nes du

God in the ci - ty of in - fi - nite day.
ser - vice on earth for thy ser - vice on high.
cla - mer - ons le Sei - gneur des temps nou - veaux!
sang ver - sé pour dé - trui - re tou - te mort.

From the Greek Liturgy of St. James, 4th century
(E) C. W. Humphreys 1906

(F) J. Martin 1973

165

Claude Rozier

1. Puis - sance et gloi - re de l'Es - prit: heu - reux les
1. Your power and glo - ry, Ho - ly Ghost, as - sure the

vrais mar - tyrs ____! La chair dont Dieu les
mar - tyrs' prize ___; their flesh, re - sem - bling

a pé - tris en lui pour - ra sur - gir _____.
Christ the most in him, re - new'd can rise ____.

2. Pareil aux grains qui sont broyés / pour être notre pain, / leur Corps se joint au Corps brisé / qui s'offre par nos mains.

3. Leur sang se mêle au Sang sauveur / qui lave nos péchés, / ils sont l'amour du même Cœur / qui nous a tant aimés.

4. Heureux qui donne sans compter / jusqu' à sa propre chair! / Il trouve en Dieu sa liberté, / visage découvert.

5. La chair es vaine sans l'Esprit / et cendre dans la mort. / Par votre Croix, Seigneur, survit / la gloire de nos corps.

6. Dans vos martyrs, c'est vous qu'on tue, / mais vous qu'on glorifie; / car votre Eglise en eux salue / la force de l' Esprit.

7. Le grain survit dans la moisson, / au jour de votre Jour. / La vie, la mort n'ont plus de nom / au règne de l'Amour.

Claude Rozier

2. Like wheat grain, crushed to make our bread, / and kneaded for our good, / their broken bodies join their Head, / our sacramental food.

3. Their blood is shed with him and part / of him, for sin's amends; / their love is fed from Jesus' heart, / who died to save his friends.

4. How blest are they who count no cost, / when flesh and courage fail! / They find in God the life they lost, / see him without a veil.

5. Apart from Spirit, flesh is vain, / it turns to dust in death. / Your way, O Lord, through cross and pain / is Spirit's life and health.

6. Each martyr killed is Jesus slain, / and, Lord, your glorious hour; / your Church discerns in all their pain / the Spirit's conquering power.

7. Their life and death are but the loam / that feeds, in Jesus' way, / the seeds that live when harvest's home / on Love's triumphant Day.

Emily Chisholm 1951

Liturgical Material · Liturgische Gesänge
Matériel Liturgique

Byzantine 15th century
tr. and arr. D. E. Conomos

166

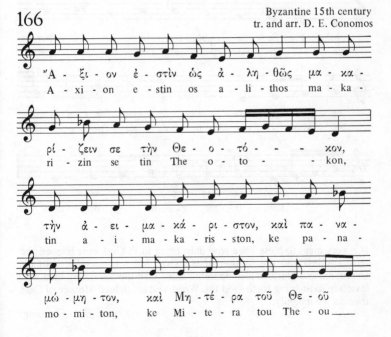

"Α - ξι - ον ἐ - στὶν ὡς ἀ - λη - θῶς μα - κα -
A - xi - on e - stin os a - li - thos ma - ka -

ρί - ζειν σε τὴν Θε - ο - τό - - - κον,
ri - zin se tin The - o - to - - - kon,

τὴν ἀ - ει - μα - κά - ρι - στον, καὶ πα - να -
tin a - i - ma - ka - ris - ton, ke pa - na -

μώ - μη - τον, καὶ Μη - τέ - ρα τοῦ Θε - οῦ
mo - mi - ton, ke Mi - te - ra tou The - ou___

ἡ - - - - μῶν, Τὴν Τι - μι - ω - τέ - ραν
i - - - mon. Tin Ti - mi - o - te - - ran

τῶν Χε - ρου - βὶμ καὶ ἐν - δο - ξο - τέ - ραν
ton khe - rou - vim ___ ke en - tho - xo - te - ran

ἀ - συγ - κϛ - - - τως τῶν Σε - ρα - φεὶμ,
as - sing - kri - - - tos ton se - ra - fim,

τὴν ἀ - δι - α - φθό - ρως, Θε - ὸν Λό - γον
tin a - di - af - tho - ros, The - on Lo - gon

τε - κοῦ - - σαν, τὴν ὄν - τως Θε - ο - τό -
te - kous - san, tin on - tos The - o - to -

- - κον, σὲ με - γα - λύ - νο - μεν.
- - kon, se me - ga - li - no - men.

It is very meet to bless Thee who didst bring forth God, ever blessed and
most spotless and the Mother of our God. More honourable than the
Cherubim, and glorious incomparably more than the Seraphim, thou who
inviolate didst bring forth God the Word, and art indeed Mother of God,
thee do we magnify.

(not to be sung)

322

Il est digne et juste en vérité de te bénir, Mère de Dieu, toujours bienheureuse et toute immaculée et la Mère de notre Dieu, plus vénérable que les Chérubins et plus glorieuse que les Séraphins, toi qui sans perdre ton intégrité as conçu Dieu le Verbe, tu es vraiment la Mère de Dieu, nous chantons ta gloire. (à ne pas chanter)

Wahrhaft würdig ist es, dich seligzupreisen, Gottesgebärerin, allzeit Selige und Makellose und Mutter unseres Gottes! Geehrter als die Cherubim und unvergleichlich herrlicher als die Seraphim, unversehrt hast du das göttliche Wort geboren: du wahrhaft Gottesgebärerin, sei hochgepriesen! (nicht singen)

167a

Kievan melody

До - стой - но есть я - ко во - ис - ти - ну

бла - жи - ти Тя Бо - го - ро - ди - цу,

при - сно - бла - жен - ну - ю и пре - не - по -

роч - ну - ю, и Ма - терь Бо - га на - ше - го

Честней - шу - ю Хе - ру - вим, и слав - ней -

шу - ю без срав - не - ни - я Се - ра - фим,

без ис - тле - ни - я Бо - га Сло -
ва рож - дшу - ю, су - щу - ю Бо -
го - ро - ди - цу Тя ве - ли - ча - ем.

167b

It is ve - ry meet to bless thee who didst
bring forth God, ev - er bless - ed and most spot -
less and the Moth - er of our God. More hon -
our - a - ble than the che - ru - bim, and glo -
rious in - com - pa - ra - bly more than the se -

ra - phim, thou who in - vi - o - late didst bring

for th God the Word, and art in - deed Moth -

er of God, thee do we mag - ni - fy.

168

Traditional Serbian melody

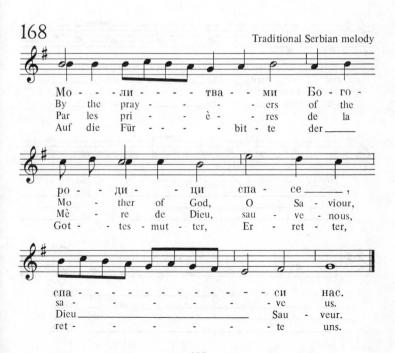

Mo - ли - тва - ми Бо - го -
By the pray - ers of the
Par les pri - è - res de la
Auf die Für - bit - te der

ро - ди - ци спа - се ,
Mo - ther of God, O Sa - viour,
Mè - re de Dieu, sau - ve - nous,
Got - tes - mut - ter, Er - ret - ter,

спа - си нас.
sa - ve us.
Dieu Sau - veur.
ret - te uns.

325

Traditional Serbian melody

Те - бе по - ем, те - бе бла - го - сло - вим,
We sing____ thee, we bless_____ thee,
Nous te chan - tons, nous__ te bé - nis - sons,
Dir sin - gen wir, dich prei - sen wir____, Herr,

те - бе бла - го - да - рим Го - спо - ди:
we give_____ thanks to thee, O Lord,
nous te ren - dons grâ - ce, Sei - gneur,
wir____ dan - ken dir, wir dan - ken dir,

и ____ мо - лим - ти - сја_____,
and we pray to thee_____,
et nous te pri - - - ons_____,
und wir be - ten____ zu____ dir,

Бо - - - - - - - - бе, Бо - - -
О_____, О____
ô_____; ô____
О_____, О____

- - - - - - же_____ наш.
_____ our____ God.
_____ no - tre Dieu.
_____ Gott.

326

Traditional Roumanian melody

Pre Ti - ne___ Te___ lā - u - dăm,
pre Ti - ne___ bi - ne___ Te___
cu - vîn - tăm. Ti - e îți mul - țu -
mim__, Doam - ne și ne ru - găm___ Ti - e,
Dum - ne - ze - u - lui___ no - - stru.

We sing Thee, we bless Thee, we give thanks to Thee, O Lord, and we pray to Thee, our God.

English paraphrase, not to be sung

Nous te chantons, nous te bénissons, nous te rendons grâce, Seigneur, et nous te prions, ô notre Dieu.

Paraphrase française, à ne pas chanter

Dir singen wir, dich preisen wir, Herr, wir danken dir, und wir beten zu dir, unser Gott.

Deutsche Paraphrase, nicht singen

171

Byzantine 15th century
tr. and arr. D. E. Conomos

Πᾶ - σα πνο - ή_____ αἰ - νε - σά - τω
Pas - sa pno - i_____ e - nes - sa - to

τὸν __ Κύ - - - ρι - - - ον. Αἰ - νεῖ -
ton ki - - - ri - - - on. E - ni -

τε τόν Κύ - - - - ρι - - -
te ton ki - - - - ri - -

ον __, ᾿Αλ - - λη - λού - - ϊ - - α
on __, al - li - lou - - i - - a.

Let everything that hath breath praise the Lord. Praise the Lord. Alleluia.

English paraphrase, not to be sung.

172

Byzantine 15th century
tr. and arr. D. E. Conomos

Χρι - στός ἀ - νέ - στη ἐκ νε - κρῶν, θα - νά - τω
Chri - stos a - ne - sti ek ne - kron, tha - na - to

θά - να - τον πα - τή - - σας, καί τοῖς ἐν τοῖς
tha - na - ton pa - ti - - sas, ke tis en tis

328

μνή - μα - σι ζω - ήν χα - ρι - σά - με - νος.
mni - ma - si zo - in ha - ri - sa - me - nos.

Christ is risen from the dead, trampling down death by death, and to those in the tombs hath he given life.

English paraphrase, not to be sung

Le Christ est ressuscité des morts, par sa mort il a triomphé de la mort, il nous délivre du tombeau pour nous donner la vie.

Paraphrase française, à ne pas chanter

Christ ist erstanden von den Toten, im Tode bezwang Er den Tod, schenkt denen die entschlafen ewiges Leben.

Deutsche Paraphrase, nicht singen

173

Byzantine 15th century
tr. and arr. D. E. Conomos

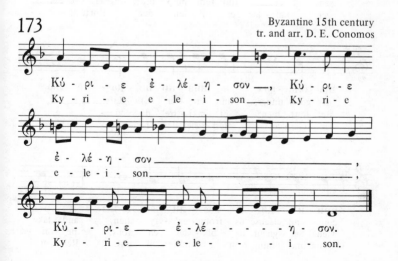

Κύ - ρι - ε ἐ - λέ - η - σον —, Κύ - ρι - ε
Ky - ri - e e - le - i - son —, Ky - ri - e

ἐ - λέ - η - σον _____ ,
e - le - i - son _____ ,

Κύ - ρι - ε ____ ἐ - λέ - - - η - σον.
Ky - ri - e ____ e - le - - - i - son.

174

Russian Orthodox Chant

Царю небесный утешителю
O heav-en-ly King, the Com-for-ter Spi-
O Roi cé-les-te, Con-so-la-teur, Es-
O Him-mels Kö-nig, un-ser Trö-ster, du

душе истиный иже везде-
rit of truth_____ who fill-est all_____
prit de vé-ri-té, qui es par-tout pré-
Geist der Wahr-heit, all-ge-gen-wär-ti-

сый и вся исполня-яй сокрови-
things, who art in all pla-ces; O treas'-ry
sent et___ qui rem-plis tout; Tré-sor_____
ger, al-les er-fül-len-der Hort; al-

ще благих и жизни по-да-те-лю
of good things, and giv-er of Life_____,
de tout bien et maî-tre de vi-e,
ler Gü-ter Herr-scher des Le-bens,

прииди и все-ли-ся в ны и о-
come and cleanse us from ev'-ry stain, and take
viens, Sei-gneur, ha-bi-ter en nous, pu-ri-
komm und nimm Woh-nung bei uns. Rei-ni-

330

чи - сти ны от вся - ки - я скве - - ны
up thine a - bode in us, O God_____
fie - nous de tou - te les souil - lu - - res,
ge uns von Schand' und al - lem Scha - den;

и спа - си Бла - же ду - ши на - - ша.
and save our souls O Ho - ly_____ One!
E - ter - nel, viens sau - ver nos â - - mes.
o Gott, er - ret - te uns' - re See - len.

175

Traditional Bulgarian chant

Svya - ti Bo - - - zhe_____,
Ho - ly God_____,
Dieu____ Saint_____,
Hei - li - ger Gott_____,

Svya - ty Kryep - - - - ky,
Ho - ly, Might - - - - y,
Saint___, fort_____ - y,
Hei - li - ger, star - - - - ker,

Svya - ty Bez - smer - tny_____,
Ho - ly, Im - mor - tal_____,
Saint ___, Im - mor - tel_____,
Hei - li - ger, un - sterb - - li - cher,

331

po - mi - - - - lui___ nas.
have__ mer - cy up - on_____ us.
aic____ pi - tié__ de_____ nous.
er - bar - me__ dich__ un - - - ser.

176

Russian Orthodox Liturgy

Во цар - - стви - и тво - ем по - мя -
Re - mem - ber thy ser - vants, Lord, when com -
Sou - viens - toi de nous, Sei - gneur, au jour
Ge - denk____ an uns, o Herr, wenn du

ни нас Гос - по - ди. Бла - жен - - ни
est thy glo - rious reign. Bless - ed____ are
où tu ré - gne - ras! Heu - reux____ sont
bist in dei - nem Reich! Se - lig____ sind

ни - щи - и ду - хом я - котех есть
the poor in spi - rit; For the heavenly
en Dieu les pau - vres; car c'est pour eux
die geist - lich Ar - men; denn das Himmelskö -

цар - ство не - - бес - но - е.
King - - - dom is theirs.
que s'ouvri - - - ront les cieux.
nig - - - reich ist ihr.

2. Блаженни плачущии яко тии утешаться. / Блаженни кротции яко тии наследят землю. / Блаженни алчущшии и жаждущшии правды яко тии насытятся. / Блаженни милостивии яко тии помилованы будут. / Блаженни чистии сердцем яко тии Бога узрят. / Блаженни миротворцы яко тии сынове Божии нарекутся. / Блаженни изгнанны правды ради яко тех есть царство небесное. / Блаженни есте егда поносят вас и изженут и рекут всяк зол глагол на вы лжуще Мене ради. / Радуйтеся и веселитеся яко мзда ваша многа на небеси.

2. Blessed are they that do mourn; / for their Lord shall wipe away their tears. Blessed in Him are the meek; / for their heritage shall be the earth. Blessed are they that seek righteousness; / in that great day their thirst shall be quenched. / Blessed are they that show mercy; / for God shall be merciful unto them. Blessed are the pure in heart; / for in that day shall they see their God. Blessed are they that make peace; / for they shall be called children of God. Blessed those who suffer for Him; / the righteous own the Kingdom of Heav'n. Blessed ye whom men revile; / this world shall persecute you for me. Rejoice, be ye glad in God; / for in Heaven great is your reward.

M. M. Gowen, 1949

2. Heureux aussi ceux qui pleurent, / Dieu de sa main, essuiera leurs yeux. Heureux sont les débonnaires, / le monde, un jour, reconnaîtra leur loi. Heureux dans leur faim les justes, / les temps viendront où ils n'auront plus faim. Heureux fils de la promesse, / pitié à qui exerça la pitié. Heureux ceux dont l'âme est pure, / dans sa clarté ils connaîtront leur Dieu. Heureux dans la paix céleste / ceux qui, sur terre, ont procuré la paix. Heureux ceux qui, pour Christ, souffrent, / car le Royaume des cieux est à eux. Heureux ceux que l'on outrage. / Celui qu'ils ont servi les bénira. Vous tous, tressaillez de joie, / la récompense est grande dans les cieux.

J. Vincent 1930

2. Selig sind, die da Leid tragen; / denn sie sollen reich getröstet werd'n. Selig sind die sanften Mutes; / denn der Erde Reich fällt ihnen zu. Selig, die hungern und dürsten nach Gerechtigkeit; / sie werden satt. Selig sind alle Barmherz'gen; / denn auch ihnen wird Barmherzigkeit. Selig sind, die reines Herzens; / denn sie werden Gottes Antlitz schau'n. Selig sind, die Frieden machen; / Kinder Gottes wird ihr Name sein. Selig, die verfolget werden um Gerechtigkeit; / das Reich ist ihr. Selig ihr, wenn man euch schmähet; / fälschlich Übles spricht um meinetwill'n; Da freut, freut euch überschwenglich; / In den Himmeln wart't eu'r grosser Lohn.

H. Laepple 1930

177

Traditional Roumanian

A - li - lu - i - a___, A - li - lu - i-
- a, A - li - lu - i - a.

178

Coptic Orthodox

Thok__ te ti - gom__ nem pi - o - ou nem pi-
Thine__ be the pow'r__ and the glo - ry and the

smou nem pi - a - ma - hi sha_____ e-
praise__ and do - mi - nion, ev - er-

neh, a - min: Em - ma - nu - il pen - ou - ty pen - ou-
more, A - men: Em - ma - nu - el our God and e'er our__

ro__ Thok te ti - gon__ nem pi - o - ou nem pi-
King__ Thine be the pow'r and the glo - ry and the

smou nem pi - a - ma - hi sha - e - neh, a-
praise__ and do - mi - nion ev - er - more, A-

334

min: pa - chois__ Je - sos__ pi - Kris - tos__
men: O Je - sus__ Christ, Mas - ter, Lord__,

pa - so - tir en - a - ga - thos. Thok te ti -
Righ - teous Sav - iour, just and true, Thine be the

gom__ nem pi - o - ou nem pi - smou nem pi - a -
pow'r__ and the glo - ry, and the__ praise__ and do -

ma - hi sha - e - neh__, a - min.
mi - nion, ev - er - more__, A - men.

ΘⲰⲔ ⲦⲈ ϮϪⲞⲘ ⲚⲈⲘ ⲠⲓⲰⲞⲨ ⲚⲈⲘ ⲠⲓⲤⲘⲞⲨ ⲚⲈⲘ ⲠⲓⲀⲘⲀϨⲒ ϢⲀ
ⲈⲚⲈϨ, ⲀⲘⲎⲚ: ⲈⲘⲘⲀⲚⲞⲨⲎⲖ ⲠⲈⲚⲚⲞⲨϮ ⲠⲈⲚⲞⲨⲢⲞ, ΘⲰⲔ ⲦⲈ
ϮϪⲞⲘ ⲚⲈⲘ ⲠⲓⲰⲞⲨ ⲚⲈⲘ ⲠⲓⲤⲘⲞⲨ ⲚⲈⲘ ⲠⲓⲀⲘⲀϨⲒ ϢⲀ ⲈⲚⲈϨ,
ⲀⲘⲎⲚ: ⲠⲀϬⲞⲒⲤ ⲒⲎⲤⲞⲨⲤ ⲠⲒⲭⲢⲒⲤⲦⲞⲤ ⲠⲀⲤⲰⲦⲎⲢ Ⲛ̄ⲀⲄⲀΘⲞⲤ,
ΘⲰⲔ ⲦⲈ ϮϪⲞⲘ ⲚⲈⲘ ⲠⲓⲰⲞⲨ ⲚⲈⲘ ⲠⲓⲤⲘⲞⲨ ⲚⲈⲘ ⲠⲓⲀⲘⲀϨⲒ
ϢⲀ ⲈⲚⲈϨ ⲀⲘⲎⲚ.

179

Coptic Orthodox

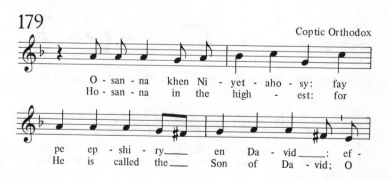

O - san - na khen Ni - yet - a - ho - sy: fay
Ho - san - na in the high - est: for

pe ep - shi - ry____ en Da - vid____: ef -
He is called the____ Son of Da - vid; O

es ma - ro - ot en - je fith - ni - yo: khen e -
bless - ed is He, He who com - eth ___ in the

fran em - ep - chois en - te ___ ni - gom.
name ___ of Him, the ___ Lord ___ of ___ Hosts.

Ef - ez - mo e - ron en - jef - no - ty:
O may God e - ver bless His sons and

ten - naz - mo èp e - fran eth - o - wab ___: en -
may we e - ver bless ___ His ho - ly name ___:

si - yo ni - ven e - re pef - ez - mo: Na -
His prais - es e - ver - more re - sound: Through all

sho - pi ef - nin e - vol ___ khen - ron.
time and through ___ e - ter - ni - ty.

Ef - ez ma rot en - je Ef - yot nem Ep - shi - ry:
O may we laud the Fa - ther and the ___ Son and

336

nem Ep - hev - ma___ eth - o - wab___: ti et-ri-
al - so laud the___ Ho - ly Spi - rit, three in___

yas as - gik e - vol: ten - o - osht em - mos ten-
One and___ One in___ three: we a - dore and glo - ri -

ti - o - nas Ky - ri ye - lei - son, Ky - ri -
fy___ thy___ name. Ky - ri - e - lei - son, Ky - ri -

ye - lei - son_____, Ky - ri___ ye - lei - son.
e - lei - son_____, Ky - ri - e - lei - son.

ΩCANNA ϦEN NHETϬOCI: ΦAI ΠE ΠϢHPI Ν̄ΔAYIΔ:
Ϥ̄ⲤⲘAⲢⲰOYT Ⲛ̄Ⲭ€ ΦHEΘNHOY: ϦEN ΦPAN Μ̄ΠϬOIC Ν̄ΤE
ⲚⲒⲬⲞⲘ ⲤⲈⲤⲘⲞⲨ ⲈⲢⲞⲚ Ⲛ̄ⲬⲈ ΦⲚⲞⲨϯ ⲦⲈⲚⲤⲘⲞⲨ ⲈⲠⲈϤⲢⲀⲚ
ⲈⲐⲞⲨⲀⲂ: Ⲛ̄ⲤⲎⲞⲨ ⲚⲒⲂⲈⲚ ⲈⲢⲈ ⲠⲈϤⲤⲘⲞⲨ: ⲚⲀϢⲰⲠⲒ ⲈϤⲘⲎⲚ
ⲈⲂⲞⲖ ϦⲈⲚ ⲢⲰⲚ. Ϥ̄ⲤⲘⲀⲢⲰⲞⲨⲦ Ⲛ̄ⲬⲈ ΦⲒⲰⲦ ⲚⲈⲘ ΠϢⲎⲢⲒ: ⲚⲈⲘ
ⲠⲒⲠⲚⲈⲨⲘⲀ ⲈⲐⲞⲨⲀⲂ: ϯⲦⲢⲒⲀⲤ ⲈⲤⲬⲎⲔ ⲈⲂⲞⲖ: ⲦⲈⲚⲞⲨⲰϢⲦ
Μ̄ⲘⲤ ⲦⲈⲚϯⲰⲞⲨ ⲚⲀⲤ ⲔⲨⲢⲒⲈ ⲈⲖⲈⲎⲤⲞⲚ ⲔⲨⲢⲒⲈ ⲈⲖⲈⲎⲤⲞⲚ ⲔⲨⲢⲒⲈ
ⲈⲖⲈⲎⲤⲞⲚ

180

Gallican ancien

Ky - ri - e e - le - i - son, Chri - ste e -

le - i - son, Ky - ri - e e - le - i - son.

181

J. Berthier

Gloire à Dieu, Paix aux hom - mes, Joie du
Praise to God! Peace to all men, joy to
Lob sei Gott, Fried den Men - schen, freu dich,

Fine

ciel sur la ter - re. 1. Pour tes mer-veil - les,
earth comes from hea - ven! 1. For all your won - ders,
Him - mel und Er - de. 1. Für dei - ne Wun - der,

Sei - gneur Dieu, ton peu - ple te rend grâ - ce.
O Lord God, your peo - ple come to thank you.
Herr und Gott, bringt Dank dein Volk und preist dich.

A - mi des hom - mes, sois bé - ni pour ton
Our gra - cious friend, we bless your name, for your
Freund der __ Men - schen, sei ge - lobt, daß dein

rè - gne qui vient! A toi les chants de
King - dom which comes! To you we bring our
Reich zu uns kommt. Dir klin - gen uns - re

D. C.

fê - te par ton fils bien ai - mé, dans l'Es - prit.
prai - ses through the love of the Son and of the Spirit.
Lie - der den Geist dei - nes Sohns, der __ uns hilft.

2. Sauveur du monde, Jésus-Christ, / écoute nos prières. / Agneau de Dieu,
Vainqueur du mal, / sauve-nous du péché. / Dieu saint, splendeur du
Père, / Dieu vivant, le Très Haut, le Seigneur.

2. The world's redeemer, Jesus Christ, / receive the prayer we bring you. / O Lamb of God, you conquered death; / now have mercy on us. / Most Holy Jesus, Son of God: / living Lord of all worlds, our Lord God!

Erik Routley 1972

2. Retter der Welt Herr Jesus Christ, / erhöre unsre Bitten: / Lamm, das trägt der Menschen Schuld, / rette uns aus dem Tod! / O heiliger Gott Vater, / der du lebst in dem Sohn, und dem Geist.

Ursula Trautwein 1972

182 From Psalm 47 and Rev. 5

J. Gelineau et
M. Chappuis

O - mnes gen - tes plaud -i - te ma - ni -
All__ you peo - ple cheer__ with voice __ and
Ihr Men - schen al - le ju - belt mit Hand __ und

bus Ju - bi - la - te De - -
hands and re - joice__ in God __ the
Mund und freut euch__ in Gott __ dem

Fine

o in vo - ce ex - ul - ta - ti - o - nis.
Lord with shouts __ of ex - ul - ta - tion!
Herrn mit Lob - ge - sang__ und Lie - dern.

Semichorus

O - mnes__ gen - tes plau - di - te
Bless - ing and ho - nour and glo - ry and
Se - gen und Eh - re und Herr - lich - keit

ma - ni - bus: rex ma - gnus su - per o - mnem
po - wer, all bless - ing and ho - nour and
und Ge - walt, ja Se - gen und Eh - re und

ter - ram____ sub - je - cit____ po - pu - los
glo - ry and pow'r be un - to him____
Herr - lich - keit und Ge - walt ge - hö - ren nur

no - bis pe - di - bus no - stris spe - ciem
that __ sits on the throne and to the
ihm, der auf____ dem Thron sitzt und dem

D. C. al fine

Ja - cob quam ___ di - le - xit!
Lamb for e - ver and e - ver!
Lamm zu al - - len Zei - ten.

(E) arranged by David S. Goodall
(D) Ursula Trautwein 1972

183

D. Rimaud

A toi le rè - gne! A toi la puis -

sance et la gloi - re pour les siè - cles des siè - cles!

340

184 Refrain after spoken verses

J. Gelineau 1971

Je ___ crois ___ mais aug - men - te ma ___ foi ___!
I be - lieve ___, Lord, in - crease ___ my ___ faith ___!
Herr, ich glau - be, dar - um stär - ke mei - nen Glau - ben!
Yo ___ cre - o, pe - ro au - men - ta mi ___ fe ___.

1. Je crois en Dieu le Père tout-puissant, / créateur du ciel et de la terre.

2. Je crois en Jésus-Christ, / son fils unique, notre Seigneur, / qui est né de la Vierge Marie, / a souffert la passion, été enseveli, / est ressuscité d'entre les morts / et qui est assis à la droite du Père.

3. Je crois en l'Esprit Saint, / à la sainte Eglise universelle, / à la communion des saints, / à la remission des péchés, / à la resurrection de la chair, / et à la vie éternelle.

185

Vatican XVII

San - ctus ___, San - ctus ___, San - ctus Do - mi -

nus De - us Sa - ba - oth. Ple - ni sunt

cae - li et ter - ra glo - ri - a tu - a.

Ho - san - na in ex - cel - sis. Be - ne - di - ctus

341

qui ve - nit in no - mi - ne Do - mi - ni.

Ho - san - - na in ex - cel - sis_____.

186 Jubilate

John Erickson 1971

All peo - ple on earth sing to the Lord!
Ihr Men - schen der Welt, sin - get dem Herrn!

For he is our God.
Er ist un - ser Gott,

Joy! joy! joy! joy! joy! joy!
freut euch heut! freut euch heut!

His____ truth is____ love.
Lie - be zeigt er für uns!

Gloria

Glo - ry to the Fa - ther_____ and to the Son___
Eh - re sei dem Va - ter_____ und auch dem Sohn_

_____ and to the Ho - ly Spi - rit; as in the be -
_____ und auch dem Hei - li - gen Geist, wie es war im

gin - ning, so now__ and for e - ver. A - men.
An - fang, jetzt und__ al - le Zeit__. A - men.

(D) Ursula Trautwein 1972

The four phrases of this JUBILATE may be sung as a canon, or they may
be performed aleatorically. In the latter case four groups should be
formed, perhaps in different parts of the room. At the signal to begin,
each group sings one of the phrases over and over again, beginning
pianissimo, rising to fortissimo. The organ or other instruments should
begin to improvize under the singing when it has been going for a
minute or two, and should build up to a decisive chord, fortissimo, which
is then abruptly released. This is the signal for the whole congregation to
take up the GLORIA which follows.

Anmerkung:
Die vier Sätze von JUBILATE können als Kanon gesungen oder
aleatorisch gebracht werden. In letzterem Falle sollten vier Gruppen
gebildet werden, möglichst in verschiedenen Teilen des Raumes. Beim
Zeichen zum Beginn singt jede Gruppe einen Satz immer wieder, indem
sie pianissimo beginnt und fortissimo endet. Die Orgel oder andere
Instrumente sollten nach einer oder zwei Minuten zu improvisieren
beginnen und auf einen abschließenden Akkord fortissimo abrupt enden.
Dies ist das Zeichen für die ganze Gemeinde, das nachfolgende GLORIA
zu singen.

187

John Erickson 1971

Ho - ly, Ho - ly, Ho - ly Lord, God of pow'r___ and might, heav'n and earth are full___ of your glo - ry. Ho - san - na in the high - est! Bless - ed is He who comes in the name___ of the Lord. Ho - san - na in the high - est!

Rounds and Canons · Rundgesänge und Kanons
Canons

188

Herbert Beuerle 1967

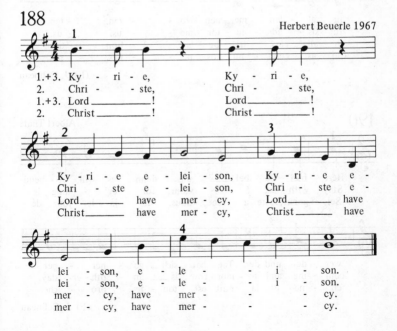

1.+3. Ky - ri - e,   Ky - ri - e,
2.   Chri - ste,   Chri - ste,
1.+3. Lord_____!   Lord_____!
2.   Christ_____!   Christ_____!

Ky - ri - e   e - lei - son,   Ky - ri - e   e -
Chri - ste   e - lei - son,   Chri - ste   e -
Lord_____   have   mer - cy,   Lord_____   have
Christ_____   have   mer - cy,   Christ_____   have

lei - son,   e - le -   -   i - son.
lei - son,   e - le -   -   i - son.
mer - cy,   have   mer -   -   -   cy.
mer - cy,   have   mer -   -   -   cy.

189

Adam Gumpelzhaimer 1559 - 1625

Neig dein Ohr zu mir, mein Gott, und
Au - di, Do - mi - ne, et mi - se -
Bow thine ear to me, have mer - cy
Prends pi - tié de nous, é - cou - te

sei mir gnä - dig, Herr Je - su, hilf mir
re - re me - i, do - mi - ne Je - su,
on thy ser - vant, Lord Je - sus help me
nos pri - è - res, Sei - gneur Jé - sus, toi

in al - len mei - nen Nö - - ten. - ten.
tu sis ad - iu - tor me - - us. - us.
in all my tri - bu - la - - tion. - tion.
qui as con - nu nos pei - - nes. - nes.

(F) J. Gelineau

190

Albert Thate

Herr, blei - be bei___ uns, denn es will A - bend
Stay with us, Sa - viour, for ev' - ning is
Sei - gneur, reste a - vec nous, dé - jà le jour dé -

wer - den, und der Tag hat sich___ ge - nei - get.
com - ing and to - mor - row is___ an - oth - er day.
cli - ne et la nuit est tou - te pro - che.

(F) J. Gelineau

346

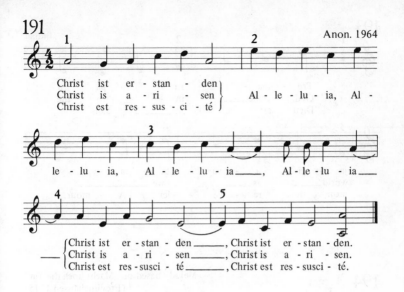

191 Anon. 1964

Christ ist er - stan - den ⎱
Christ is a - ri - sen ⎬ Al - le - lu - ia, Al -
Christ est res - sus - ci - té ⎰

le - lu - ia, Al - le - lu - ia___, Al - le - lu - ia___

⎧ Christ ist er - stan - den___, Christ ist er - stan - den.
⎨ Christ is a - ri - sen___, Christ is a - ri - sen.
⎩ Christ est res - susci - té___, Christ est res - susci - té.

192 Tétouom

Jé - sus-Christ est né, il est né au - jourd'-hui!

last time

Jé - sus-Christ est né, il est né au-jourd'-hui! -jourd'-hui!

Jé - sus-Christ est né, il est né au - jourd'-hui.

347

193

Indian

Pre - ma - - ru - - pa to
God came____ in - - to the
Dieu est ve - nu____ dans le

ja - gi a - va - ta - ra - là.
world____ as ____ love____.
mon - de ré - vé - ler l'A - mour.

194

Melody based on „Macht hoch die Tür"
(Freylinghausen 1715)

Er ist die rech - te Freu - - den -
The cloud - less sun of joy____ he
De toi dé - cou - le tou - - te

sonn, bringt mit sich lau - ter Freud__
is, who bring - eth pure de - light__
paix, à toi re - tour - ne tou - -

und Wonn: ge - lo - bet sei mein Gott!
and bliss: e - ter - nal praise to God!
te joie: lou - é sois - tu, mon Dieu!

Georg Weissel 1590 - 1635
(F) J. Gelineau
(E) Catherine Winkworth 1863

195

Lee Hastings Bristol 1970

The Lord is my shep - herd, my guard - -
Der Herr ist mein Hir - te, mein Hü - -

ian, my guide. What - so - ev - er I want he doth
ter, mein Licht, und bei ihm bin ich si - cher, denn

sure - ly pro - vide. Ev - er since I was
er hält mich fest. Er hat mich seit dem

born ___, it is he ___ that hath crowned the
Ta - ge, an dem ___ ich ge - born, um -

life that he gave me with bless - ings all round.
ge - ben mit Gü - te und Schutz ü - ber - all.

Lee Hastings Bristol, Jr.
Deutsch: Ursula Trautwein 1972

196

Herman Stern 1943

Dan - ket dem Herrn und lob - singt sei - nem Na - men!
Thanks be to God and all praise to his Name ___!
Gloire au Sei - gneur! et que vien - ne son Rè - gne.

(F) J. Gelineau

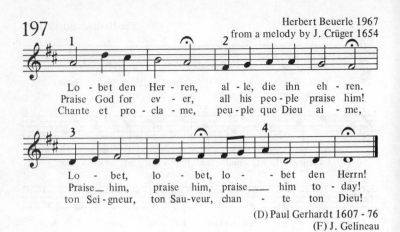

197

Herbert Beuerle 1967
from a melody by J. Crüger 1654

Lo - bet den Her - ren, al - le, die ihn eh - ren.
Praise God for ev - er, all his peo - ple praise him!
Chante et pro - cla - me, peu - ple que Dieu ai - me,

Lo - bet, lo - bet, lo - bet den Herrn!
Praise_ him, praise him, praise_ him to - day!
ton Sei - gneur, ton Sau-veur, chan - te ton Dieu!

(D) Paul Gerhardt 1607 - 76
(F) J. Gelineau

198

Hermann Stern

Sin - get und spie - let dem Herrn_ in
Sing_____ and re - joice_____ in the Lord in your

eu - ren_ Her - zen, sin - get und spie - let.
hearts with thanks-giv - ing, sing_____ and re - joice in him.

199

Gerd Watkinson 1955

Herr, un - ser Herr - scher, wie herr - lich ist
O Lord, our Mas - ter, how ex - cel - lent
Dieu, no - tre Maî - tre, ton nom est grand,

350

dein_ Na - me in al - len Lan - den.
is your' name_____ in all the world _.
ton_ nom est saint, par tout l'u - ni - vers.

(F) J. Gelineau

Two Parting Blessings · Schlußsegen
Deux Bénédictions

200 An Indian Blessing

Gazar

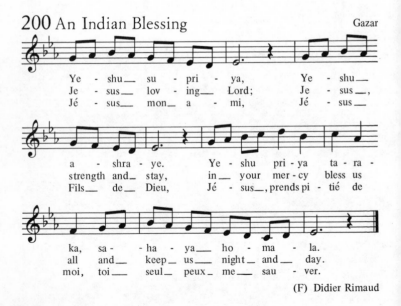

Ye - shu__ su - pri - ya,   Ye - shu__
Je - sus__ lov - ing__ Lord;   Je - sus __,
Jé - sus__ mon__ a - mi,   Jé - sus __

a - shra - ye.   Ye - shu pri - ya ta - ra -
strength and__ stay,   in __ your mer - cy bless us
Fils__ de__ Dieu,   Jé - sus__, prends pi - tié de

ka, sa - -ha - ya__ ho - ma - la.
all and__ keep_ us__ night_ and __ day.
moi, toi__ seul_ peux_ me__ sau - ver.

(F) Didier Rimaud

येशू सुप्रिय येशू आश्रया   येशू प्रिय तारका सहाय हो मला

352

201 An Israeli Blessing

To be sung antiphonally

A Ge - he ein in dei - nen Frie - den!
A Go in peace, and God be with you:
A Quand va - cil - lent tes pau - piè - res

B Schla - fe dei - nen gu - ten Schlaf!
B Sleep in peace, God hold you fast!
B Dieu t'ac - cueil - le dans la paix!

A Ruh dich aus nach dei - ner Ar - beit,
A Take your ease from dai - ly du - ty;
A Quand som - meil - le no - tre ter - re

B und ge - seg - net sei die Nacht!
B af - ter la - bour, rest at last!
B Dieu é - veil - le l'u - ni - vers!

A Mond - licht fließt her - ab vom Him - mels - zelt,
A Moon - light shares a glimpse of hea - ven's mirth,
A Le ciel est beau et la lu - ne luit!

B und der Tau glänzt auf un - serm Feld.
B dew - fall fresh - ens flow - ers of earth.
B sur ton re - pos pas - se la nuit.

353

A Preist den Tag und die Nacht!
A Thank God for day and night.
A O nuit veil - le sur nous!

B Preist die Nacht und den Tag!
B Thank God for dark and light.
B O nuit, Mè - re du jour!

A & B together

Preist die Son - ne, prei - set die Er - de,
For the Sun and for all things liv - ing
Nuit de la foi! nuit de la Pâ - que,

preist den Herrn al - ler Wel - ten.
to their Lord prais - es giv - ing! A - men! A - men!
tu en - fan - tes la gloi - re!

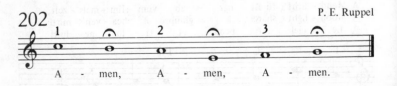

202   P. E. Ruppel

A - men, A - men, A - men.

354

Index of Sources · Quellenregister
Index des références

Those texts marked CD III have been specially prepared for the present edition of *Cantate Domino*. The editors and publishers would like to thank all those who have given permission for the inclusion of material. Every effort has been made to trace copyright holders but in some cases this proved impossible and in others no reply has been received. If for these reasons or through inadvertence any rights have been overlooked we express our regrets and our readiness to make the necessary correction in subsequent editions.

Alle mit CD III gekennzeichneten Texte wurden neu für die vorliegende Ausgabe von *Cantate Domino* erstellt. Herausgeber und Verlag danken allen, die für dieses Buch Ihre Abdruckerlaubnis gegeben gaben. Wir haben uns bemüht, die jeweiligen Urheber herauszufinden, in einigen Fällen aber vergebens. Wenn aus diesem Grunde oder aus unbeabsichtigten Versehen die Erlaubnis nicht eingeholt wurde, möchten wir uns entschuldigen. Wir sind selbstverständlich bereit, die entsprechende Ergänzung in künftigen Ausgaben hinzuzufügen.

Les textes qui sont marqués CD III ont été spécialement écrits pour cette édition du *Cantate Domino*. Rédacteurs et éditeurs veulent exprimer ici leur reconnaissance à tous ceux qui ont bien voulu donner leur accord pour l'insertion de leurs œuvres. Nous nous sommes efforcés de trouver les personnes qui détiennent les droits de chaque cantique, mais dans certains cas cela n'a pas été possible alors que dans d'autres aucune réponse n'a été reçue. Si pour ces raisons ou par inadvertance la permission a été omise, nous nous en excusons ici; nous sommes prêts à rectifier cette omission dans les éditions ultérieures.

Abbreviations / Abkürzungen / Abréviations

M: Melody / Melodie / Melodie
O: Original / Original / Original
Q: Sources / Quellen / Sources
T: Text / Text / Texte
© Copyright

Languages / Sprachen / Langues

a = Afrikaans / afrikaans / africain
arab = Arab / arabisch / arabe
bul = Bulgarian / bulgarisch / bulgare
chin = Chinese / chinesisch / chinois
d = German / deutsch / allemand
e = English / englisch / anglais
f = French / französisch / français
fin = Finnish / finnisch / finnois
grie = Greek / griechisch / grec
hind = Hindi / hindi
indo = Indonesian / indonesisch / indonésien
j = Japanese / japanisch / japonais
lat = Latin / lateinisch / latin

nie	=	Dutch / niederländisch / néerlandais
no	=	Norwegian / norwegisch / norvégien
p	=	Portuguese / portugiesisch / portugais
rum	=	Rumanian / rumänisch / roumain
rus	=	Russian / russisch / russe
s	=	Spanish / spanisch / espagnol
schw	=	Swedish / schwedisch / suédois
serb	=	Serbian / serbisch / serbe
su	=	Swahili / suaheli / swahili
tsch	=	Czech / tschechisch / tchêque
un	=	Hungarian / ungarisch / hongrois
yor	=	Yoriba / Yoruba / yoruba

Publishers / Verlage / Editeurs

BE	=	Bosse-Edition, Regensburg
BHV	=	Burckhardthaus-Verlag, Gelnhausen
BV	=	Bärenreiter-Verlag, Kassel, Basel, Tours, London
ChVH	=	Christophorus-Verlag Herder
CMC	=	Commission Musique et Chant, Paris
CMSN	=	Centre de Musique Sacrée de Nevers
CNPL	=	Centre de Nationale Pastorale Liturgique, Paris
EdC	=	Editions du Cerf, Paris
E.R.	=	Erik Routley
F.J.P.	=	F.J. Pagura
F.K.	=	Fred Kaan
GVH	=	Gütersloher Verlagshaus, Gütersloh
HV	=	Hänssler-Verlag, Neuhausen-Stuttgart
L.H.B.	=	Lee Hastings Bristol
LWF	=	Lutheran World Federation, Genève
OUP	=	Oxford University Press, London
P.G.	=	F.Pratt Green
SEFIM	=	Secrétariat des Editeurs de Fiches Musicales, Paris
StB	=	Stainer & Bell, London
Grail	=	Grail Publications, Nottingham
VMB	=	Verlag Merseburger, Berlin
VSG	=	Verlag Singende Gemeinde, Wuppertal
VV	=	Voggenreiter-Verlag, Bonn-Bad Godesberg
WCC	=	World Council of Churches, Genève

Sources / Quellen / Sources

BfG	=	Bausteine für den Gottesdienst
CD I	=	Cantate Domino I, 1. Auflage 1924
CD II	=	Cantate Domino II, 2. Auflage 1951
CD III	=	Cantate Domino III, 3. Auflage 1974
CN	=	Cantico Nuevo
EKG	=	Evangelisches Kirchengesangbuch
HoF	=	Hymns of Faith, Baptist Publications, Beirut
Ld	=	Laudamus
PP	=	Pilgrim Praise
VE	=	Venite Exultemus
VP	=	Vingt-quatre Psaumes et un cantique

1 All people that on earth do dwell

T:(O:e) William Kethe, (f) Roger Chapal, (d) Cornelius Becker·David Denicke, (i) E. Costa, (s) F.J. Pagura, (su) *Nyimbo* (Standart), (indo) Yayasan Musik Gerejani, (j) *Sanbika* 1955 – M: *Octante-trois Psaumes*, Geneva 1551 – © T:(f) CNPL, (i) E. Costa – Q: CD II, T:(f,i,indo) CD III

2 Our God, our help in ages past

T:(O:e) Isaac Watts, (f) G. de Lioncourt, (d) Theodor Werner, (s) F.J. Pagura, (indo) Yayasan Musik Gerejani, (arab) Amin Faris, (su) *Tenzi za Rohoni*, (j) *Sanbika* 1955 – M: William Croft – © T:(f) CNPL, (d) LWF – Q: CD II, (f, indo) CD III, (d) Ld, (s) CN, (arab) HoF

3 Let us, with a gladsome mind

T:O:e) John Milton, (f) S. Bidgrain, (d) Johann Christoph Hampe, (s) F.J. Pagura, (p) Jorge Cesar Mota, (chin) CD II, (j) *Sanbika* 1955 – M: Chinese traditional chant – © T:(d,s,p) WCC Q: CD II, (s,p) VE

4 Comme un cerf altéré brame

T:(O:f) Roger Chapal, (e) Erik Routley, (i) G. Sobrero, (s) M. Gutierrez Marin / F.J. Pagura, (indo) Yayasan Musik Gerejani – M: *Octante trois Psaumes*, Geneva 1551 – © T:(f) CMC, (e) E.R., (i) G. Sobrero, (s) F.J.P. – Q: (e,i) CD III, (s) CN

5 Que tout mon cœur soit dans mon chant

T:(O:e) Robert Bridges, (f) Roger Chapal – M: *Pseaulmes cinquante de David*, Lyon, 1547 – © T:(f) CMC, (e) OUP – Q:(e) *Yattendon Hymnal*

6 Entonnons un nouveau cantique

T:(O:f) Roger Chapal, (e) Erik Routley – M: *Octante-trois Psaumes*, Geneva 1551 – © T:(f) CMC, (e) E.R. – Q: (e) CD III

7 Happy is he who walks in God's wise way

T:(O:thai) C. Kingshill, (e) Erik Routley – M: Thai Traditional Melody – © T:(thai) Christian Literature Department of the Church of Christ in Thailand, (e) E.R. – Q:(thai) *Thai Hymnal,* (e) CD III

8 Lord, how majestic is your name

T:(O:e) Fred Kaan, (f) Claude Rozier, (d) Dieter Trautwein, M: Margot Toplis – © M: Margot Toplis, T:(e) St.B, (f) CNPL, (d) BV – Q: T:(e) PP, M, T:(f,d) CD III

9 Herrasta veisaa kieleni

T:(O:fin) Julius Krohn, (e) E.E. Ryden / Toivo Harjunpää, (d) Käthe Siegfried, (f) D. Hameline – M: Finnish Traditional Melody – © T:(d,e) LWF, (f) CNPL – Q: T:(d,e) Ld, (f) CD III

10 Herr, deine Güte reicht so weit

T:(O:d) Gerhard Valentin, (e) Emily Chisholm – M: Rolf Schweizer – © (M+T,d,e) HV – Q: M+T(d) BfG, (e) CD III

11 Misaora an' i Zanahary

T:(O:) Psalm 102(103), (e,d) U.S. Leupold – M: Malagasy Melody – © T:(e,d) LWF – Q: M+T:(e,d) Ld

12 Praise, praise the Lord all you sisters

T:(O:e) Barry Chevannes, (d) Ursula Trautwein – M: Barry Chevannes – © M+T(e) Barry Chevannes (d) BV – Q:(e) Manuscript collection by Barry Chevannes (d) CD III

13 Praise the Lord!

T:(O:e) Psalm 113,1-2/Marjorie Jillson, (f) Claude Rozier, (d) Heinz Werner Zimmermann – M: Heinz Werner Zimmermann –© M+T:(e,d) Concordia Publishing House, (f) CNPL Q: (f) CD III

14 By the Babylonian rivers we sat down

T:(O:e) Ewald Bash, (f) Daniel Hameline, (d) Barth·Leonhard·Schulz – M: Latvian melody – © M+T:(e)

American Lutheran Church, Minneapolis, (f) CNPL, (d) BV – Q: M + T: (e) *Songs for today*, (f,d) CD III

15 All things that are praise God

T:(O:e) Brian Foley, (f) P. de la Tour du Pin, (d) Dieter Trautwein – M: Elisabeth Poston – © M + T:(e) Faber Music, London, (f) CNPL, (d) BV Q: M + T:(e) *New Catholic Hymnal*, (f,d) CD III

16 Das ist ein köstlich Ding

T:(O:d) Psalm 91 (92), (e) Emily Chisholm – M: Rolf Schweizer – © M + T:(d,e) HV – Q: M + T:(d) BfG, (e) CD III

17 Ich will dir danken, Herr

T:(O:d) Paul-Ernst Ruppel, (e) Ivor Jones – M: Paul-Ernst Ruppel – © M + T:(d) VSG (e) Ivor Jones, London – Q: M + T:(d) Eigentum VSG (e) CD III

18 O praise the King of heaven

T:(O:e) E. Maweleva Tembo, (f) Claude Rozier – M: Malawi wedding song – © M + T:(e) The Overton Institution Livingstonian Mission, Malawi, (f) CNPL – Q: M + T:(e) *Tunes from Nyasaland*, (f) CD III

19 O Seigneur notre Dieu

T:(O:f-Antiphon) Joseph Samson – M: Joseph Gelineau – © M + T:(f) EdC – Q: VP

20 Le Seigneur est mon berger

T:(O:f) de la Bible de Jerusalem – M: Joseph Gelineau – © M: SEFIM Q: VP

21 Au Seigneur la terre et sa plénitude

T:(O:f) Psalm 23 (24) – M: Joseph Gelineau – © M: SEFIM – Q: VP

22 Your word, O Lord, is a lamp to my feet

T:(O:e) Psalm 118 (119), (f) Claude Rozier, M: Christopher Coelho – © M: Christopher Coelho, T:(e) The Grail, England, (f) CNPL – Q: T:(e) The Grail Translation, (f) CD III

23 Remember me, O Lord

T:(O:e) Psalm 24 (25), (f) Joseph Gelineau – M: Christopher Coelho – © M: Christopher Coelho, T:(e) The Grail, England, (f) CNPL Q:(f) CD III

24 Bénis le Seigneur, ô mon âme

T:(O:f) de la Bible de Jerusalem, (e) Grail – M: Antiphon: J. Langlais, Psalmodie: Joseph Gelineau – © M: SEFIM, T:(e) The Grail, England – Q: *Cinquante-troi Psaumes et quatre cantiques*

25 Louez le Seigneur, tous les peuples

T:(O:f) Joseph Samson, (e) The Psalms · Erik Routley – M: Joseph Samson – © M + T:(f) EdC, (e) The Grail – Q:(e) The Psalms, a version for singing

26 Des profondeurs, je crie vers toi

T:(O:f) Psalm 129 (130), (e) The Grail – M: Joseph Gelineau – © M: SEFIM – Q: VP

27 Rendez grâce au Seigneur car il est bon

T:(O:f) Psalm 135 (136) – M: Joseph Gelineau – © M: SEFIM – Q: VP

28 Ummai vazhtuvom ummai potruvom

T:(O:tamil) Psalm 150 – M: Charles Mani – © Charles Mani, O.F.M.

29 God of grace and God of glory

T:(O:e) Harry Emerson Fosdick, (d) Sabine Leonhard – M: Henry Purcell – © T:(e) Dr. Elinor Fosdick·Downs, New York, (d) BV – Q:(d) CD III

30 It's a long, hard journey

T:(O:e) Nick Hodson, (d) Gerhard Valentin – M: Nick Hodson – © M + T:(e) The Liturgical Conference, USA, (d) BV – Q:(d) CD III

31 Take the dark strength of our nights

T:(O:e) John Hoad – M: Doreen Potter – © M: Doreen Potter, T:(e) John Hoad – Q: CD III

32 Die ganze Welt hast du uns überlassen

T:(O:d) Christa Weiß, (e) John B. Geyer, (f) Marc Ginot - M: Hans Rudolf Siemoneit - © M: GVH T:(d) BE, (f) CNPL - Q: M+T:(d) *Neue geistliche Lieder*, (f) CD III

33 'Vi ville dig se', så grekerna bad

T:(O:schw) Anders Frostenson, (e) Fred Kaan, (d) Helli Halbe - M: Sven Johanson - © M+T:(schw) AB Ansgar, Stockholm, (e) Fred Kaan, (d) BV - Q: M+T:(schw) *71 psalmer och visor*, (e,d) CD III

34 'Am I my brother's keeper?'

T:(O:e) John Ferguson, (f) Claude Rozier, (d) Ernst Lange - M: Reginald Barrett-Ayres - © Q: M+T:(e) *Dunblane Praise*, (f,d) CD III

35 Nesta grande cidade vivemos

T:(O:p) João Dias de Araujo, (s) F.J. Pagura, (e) Fred Kaan, (f) Sœur M.-C. Sachot, - M: J.W. Faustini - © J.W. Faustini, (e) F.K. (f) CNPL - Q: M+T:(p) *Os Céus Proclamam*, (s,e,f) CD III

36 Can I see the suffering crowd

T:(O:e) S. Wilfred Hodge - M: Doreen Potter - © M: Doreen Potter, T:(e) S. Wilfred Hodge - Q: CD III

37 When I needed a neighbour

T:(O:e) Sydney Carter, (f) Nicole Berthet, (schw) Anders Frostenson - M: Sydney Carter - © M+T:(e) StB, (f) CNPL, (schw) AB Ansgar - Q: M+T:(e) Celebration series, (f) CD III

38 Sing we of the modern city

T:(O:e) Fred Kaan, (d) Dieter Trautwein - M: Doreen Potter - © M+T:(e) StB, (d) BV Q: M+T:(e) PP, (d) CD III

39 Sing we a song of high revolt

T:(O:e) Fred Kaan, (f) Marie-Pierre Faure, (d) Dieter Trautwein - M: Doreen Potter - © M: Doreen Potter, T:(e) StB, (f) CNPL, (d) BV - Q: T:(e) PP, (f,d) CD III

40 All who love and serve your city

T:(O:e) Erik Routley, (f) Claude Rozier - M: Philibert Jambe-de-Fer - © T:(e) StB, (f) CNPL - Q: *Dunblane Praises II*

41 O God of earth and altar

T:(O:e) G.K. Chesterton, (f) G. de Lioncourt, (s) S. Jerez - M: English traditional © T:(e) OUP, (f) CNPL - Q: CD III

42 Turn back, O man

T:(O:e) Clifford Bax, (d) Auguste Sann, (f) Roger Chapal, (s) F.J. Pagura - M: *Octante-trois Psaumes*, Geneva 1551 - © T:(e) D. Peters & Co, London, (d) BV, (f) CMC, (s) F.J.P. - Q: M+T:(e) *Songs of Praise*, (d,f,s) CD III

43 Now join we to praise the Creator

T:(O:e) Fred Kaan, (d) Dieter Trautwein, (f) Claude Rozier - M: Geoffrey Laycock - © M: Faber Music, T:(e) StB, (d) BV (f) CNPL - Q: M+T:(e) *New Catholic Hymnal* (d,f) CD III

44 Tron sig sträcker efter frukten

T:(O:schw) Anders Frostensin, (e) Fred Kaan, (f) Père Lorigiola, (d) Helli Halbe - M:Gustaf Bjarnegård - © M+T:(schw) AB Ansgar (e) F.K. (f) CNPL, (d) BV - Q: M+T:(schw) *71 psalmer och visor*, (e,f,d) CD III

45 God who spoke in the beginning

T:(O:e) Fred Kaan, (f) Daniel Hameline, (d) Dieter Trautwein - M: Erik Routley - © M+T:(e) StB, (f) CNPL, (d) BV Q: M+T:(e) PP, (f,d) CD III

46 Père du premier mot

T:(O:f) Didier Rimaud, (e) Caryl Micklem, (d) Ursula Trautwein - M: Joseph Gelineau - © M+T:(f) SEFIM, (e) Caryl Micklem (d) BV Q: T(d) CD III

47 Singet dem Herrn ein neues Lied

T:(O:d) Paulus Stein, (e) F. Pratt Green, (f) E. Pidoux - M: Rolf Schweizer - © M+T:(d,e) HV, (f) CNPL - Q: M+T:(d) BfG, (e,f) CD III

48 Von guten Mächten wunderbar geborgen

T:(O:d) Dietrich Bonhoeffer, (e) F. Pratt Green, (f) F. Frié - M: Joseph Gelineau - © M: SEFIM, T(d) Kaiser-Verlag, München (e) OUP (f) CNPL - Q: M+T:(e,f) CD III

49 Guds kärlek är som stranden

T:(O:schw) Anders Frostenson, (e) Fred Kaan, (f) Nicole Berthet, (d) Ernst Hansen, (s) F.J. Pagura - M: Lars Åke Lundberg - © M+T:(schw) AB Ansgar, (e) Fred Kaan, (f) CNPL, (d) BHV, (s) F.J.P. - Q: M+T:(schw) 71 psalmer och visor, (e,f,d,sj CD III

50 When in his own image

T:(O:e) Fred Kaan, (d) Ursula Trautwein, (f) Didier Rimaud - M: James Carley - © M+T:(e) StB, (d) BV (f) D. Rimaud - Q: M+T:(e) PP, (d,f CD III

51 De aarde is vervuld

T:(O:nie) W. Barnard, (f) Daniel Hameline, (e) Fred Kaan - M: Fritz Mehrtens - © M+T:(nie) Nederlandse Kerk, (f) CNPL, (e) F.K. - Q: M+T:(nie) 102 Gezangen, (f,e) CD III

52 De Heer heeft mij gezien

T:(O:nie) Huub Oosterhuis, (e) Redmond Mc Goldrick - M: Bernard Huijbers - © M+T:(nie) B. Huijbers, Hilversum, (e) Seabury Press - Q: M+T(nie) Liturgischen Gezangen, (e) Prayers, Poems + Songs

53 Veni, veni Emmanuel

T:(O:lat), (e) J.M. Neale, (f) Frère Pierre-Yves, (s) F.J. Pagura, (p) Isaac N. Salum, (arab) Dr. Walter Skollio, (su) Nyimbo za Dini, (j) Sanbika 1955 - M: French melody - © T:(f) CNPL - Q: CD III

54 Viens pour notre attente

T:(O:f) Dominique Ombrie, (e) F. Pratt Green, (d) M. Flesch-Thebesius - M: Dominique Ombrie - © M+T:(f) CNPL, (e) OUP (d) BV - Q: T:(e,d) CD III

55 Lord Christ when first thou cam'st

T:(O:e) Walter Russell Bowie, (d) Gerhard Valentin, (f) G. de Lioncourt - M: J. Lindemann - © T:(e) Abingdon Press, Nashville, (d) BV (f) CNPL - Q: M+T:(e) Hymns for Church and School 1964, (d,f) CD III

56 Die Nacht ist vorgedrungen

T:(O:d) Jochen Klepper, (f) Armand Ory, (e) F. Pratt Green - M: Johannes Petzold - © M+T:(d) BV, (f) CNPL, (e) OUP - Q: M+T:(d) Neue Weihnachtslieder, (f,e) CD III

57 Bendito el Rey que viene

T:(O:s) F. J. Pagura, (e) F. Pratt Green, (f) J.F. Frié (d) Arthur Blatezky - M: Homero Perera - © M+T:(sj Methopress (h. La Aurora), (e) OUP (f) CNPL, (d) BV - Q: M+T:(s) CN, (e,f,d) CD III

58 Corde natus ex parentis ante mundi

T:(O:latein), (e) R.F. Davis, (f) J. Martin - M: Piae Cantiones 1582 © T:(f) CNPL

59 When he comes back

T:(O:e) Malcolm Stewart, (d) Konrad Raiser - M: Malcolm Stewart - © M+T:(e) Chapman Ltd, London, (d) BV - Q: M+T:(e) Gospel Songs for Today, (d) CD III

60 Kommt Gott als Mensch in Dorf und Stadt

T:(O:d) Dieter Trautwein, (e) Fred Kaan - M: Gottfried Neubert und Seminargruppe - © M+T:(d) BHV, (e) F.K. - Q: M+T:(d) Schalom, (e) CD III

61 Wer kann mir sagen, wo Jesus Christus geboren ist?

T:(O:d) Kurt Rommel, (e) Emily Chisholm, (f) Nicole Berthet - M: Gerd

Watkinson – © M+T:(d) BHV, (e) Emily Chisholm, (f) CNPL – Q: M+T:(d) *Schalom*, (e,f) CD III

62 My soul doth magnify the Lord

T:(O:e) D.T. Niles – M: Maluku Popular Tune – © T:(e) P. Niles, Princeton – Q: *EACC Hymnal*

63 Aujourd'hui dans notre monde

T:(O:f) Didier Rimaud, (e) F. Pratt Green, (d) Ursula Trautwein – M: C. Geoffray – © T:(f) SEFIM, (e) OUP, (d) BV Q: M: *Cantiques et psaumes*, T:(e,f,d) CD III

64 Tout le ciel s'emplit d'une joie nouvelle

T:(O:f) Claude Rozier, (e) F. Pratt Green, (d) Ursula Trautwein – M: traditionelle d'Auvergne – © M+T:(f) EdC, (e) OUP (d) BV Q: M: *Cantiques et psaumes*, T:(e,f) CD III

65 Adeste fediles laeti triumphantes

T:(O:lat), (e) F. Oakeley, (d) anon., (f) Claude Rozier, (s) Juan B. Cabrera, (i) E. Costa, (j) *Sanbika* 1955, (arab) Khalil Assad Ghobrial – M: J.F. Wade – Q: CD II

66 Herr, laß uns hören

T:(O:d) Dieter Trautwein / Kurt Rommel, (e) F. Pratt Green — M:Hans Rudolf Siemoneit / Dieter Trautwein – © M+T:(d) BHV – Q: M+T:(d) *Schalom*, (e) CD III

67 Jeesus saapui Kapernaumiin

T:(O:fin) Juhani Forsberg, (e) Emily Chisholm, (d) Dieter Trautwein – M: Juhani Forsberg – © M+T:(fin) Juhani Forsberg, (e) Chisholm (d) BHV – Q: T:(d) *Schalom*, (e) CD III

68 Show us your ways, O Lord

T:(O:e) Psalm, (f) Joseph Gelineau – M: William Llewellyn – © M: OUP, T:(f) CNPL Q: M+T:(e) *Hymns for Celebration*, (f) CD III

69 Han satte sig ner på stranden

T:(O:schw) Anders Frostenson, (e) Fred Kaan, (f) Edouard Kressmann, (d) Helli Halbe – M: Roland Forsberg – © M+T:(schw) AB Ansgar, (e) F.K., (f) CNPL, (d) BV – Q: M+T:(schw) *71 psalmer och visor*, (e,f,d) CD III

70 Main prema hun prema

T:(O:hind) Bantam Ram Banda, (e) Erik Routley (d) Konrad Raiser – M: J.R. Chandran – © M: BV, T:(e) E.R., (d) BV Q: T:(hind) *Masihi Sangeet*, (e,d) CD III

71 Son of the Father, Jesus Lord

T:(O:e) Fred Kaan, (f) Nicole Berthet – M:Sri Lanka – © T:(e) Fred Kaan, (f) CNPL – Q: M+T:(e) *New Songs of Asian Cities*, (f) CD III

72 Därför att Ordet bland oss bor

T:(O:schw) Anders Frostenson, (e) Fred Kaan, (f) Armand Ory, (d) Helli Halbe – M: Carl Nielson – © M+T:(schw) AB Ansgar, (e) F.K., (f) CNPL, (d) BV – Q: M+T:(schw) *71 psalmer och visor*, (e,f,d) CD III

73 Wir sind nicht irgendwer

T:(O:d) Dieter Trautwein, (e) F. Pratt Green, – M: Gerhard Kloft – © M+T:(d,e) BHV – Q: M+T:(d) *Schalom* (e) CD III

74 Zolang er Mensen zijn op aarde

T:(O:nie) Huub Dosterhuis, (f) Marie-Claire Sachot (d) Dieter Trautwein, (e) Fred Kaan – M: Tera de Marez Oyens – © M+T:(nie) Nederlandse Hervormde Kerk, (f) CNPL, (d) BHV, (e) F.K. – Q: M+T:(nie) *102 Gezangen*, (d) *Schalom*, (f,e) CD III

75 This is my commandment

T:(O:e) 1. Cor. 13 / John 15 (f) Joseph Gelineau – M: J.B. Fernandes – © M: J.B. Fernandes, T:(f) CNPL – Q: T:(f) CD III

76 Todos saberão que somos de Christo

T:(O:p) John 13, (e) Helena Scott, (f) Joseph Gelineau - M: José Alves - © M: José Alves, T:(f) CNPL, (e) Helena Scott Q: T:(f) CD III

77 Prova de amor maior não há

T:(O:p) John 15 (e) Helena Scott, (f) J.F. Frié - M: José Weber - © M: José Weber, T:(f) CNPL (e) Helena Scott - Q:(f) CD III

78 Par la Croix qui fit mourir

T:(O:f) Didier Rimaud, (e) F. Pratt Green - M: Joseph Gelineau - © M + T:(f) SEFIM, (e) OUP - Q: CD III

79 What wondrous love is this

T:(O:e) American folk hymn, (f) Claude Rozier, (d) Dieter Trautwein - M: American folk hymn - © T:(f) CNPL, (d) BV

80 My song is love unknown

T:(O:e) S. Crossman, (d) Erich Griebling - M: John Ireland - © M: Dr. John Ireland (Norah Kirby, Steyning), T:(d) LWF - Q: T:(d)

81 De såg ej dig, blott timmermannens son

T:(O:schw) Anders Frostenson, (e) Fred Kaan, (f) G. de Lioncourt, (d) Helli Halbe - M: Verner Ahlberg - © M + T:(schw) AB Ansgar, (e) F.K., (f) CNPL, (d) BV - Q: M + T:(schw) Passionspsalmer, (e,f,d) CD III

82 O Haupt voll Blut und Wunden

T:(O:d) Paul Gerhardt, (e) J.W. Alexander, (f) Henri Capieu, (i) E.C.-G.S., (s) Isaac Salum, (arab) George Khoury, (su) Nyimbo za Kikristo, (chin) P'u T'ien Sung Tsan - M: H.L. Hassler - © T:(f) CNPL - Q: EKG

83 When I survey the wondrous Cross

T:(O:e) Isaac Watts, (f) Daniel Hameline, (d) Wilhelm Horkel, (s) W.T.T. Milham, (arab) Salim Abdel Ahad (indo) Yayasan Musik Gerejani, (su) Tenzi za Rohoni, (j) Sanbika, 1955 - M: E. Miller - © T:(f) CNPL Q: CD II

84 Gelobt sei Gott im höchsten Thron

T:(O:d) Michael Weisse, (e) C.A. Alington, (f) Frère Pierre-Yves - M: Melchior Vulpius - © T:(f) CNPL, (e) The Proprietors of Hymns Ancient + Modern, Worthing - Q: T:(f,e) CD III

85 He is King of kings

M + T:(O:e) Negro Spiritual Q: M + T: American Negro Songs and Spirituals

86 Notre Dieu Sauveur est Jésus Seigneur

T:(O:f) Abel Nkuinji, (e) Erik Routley - M: Traditional Melody from Cameroun - © T:(f) Abel Nkuinji, (e) E.R. -

87 Bwana Yesu kafufuka

T:(O:su) Joas Kijugo, (e) Erik Routley, (f) Nicole Berthet - M: Jaos Kijugo - © M + T: (su) Jaos Kijugo, (e) E.R., (f) CNPL - Q: T:(e,f) CD III

88 Mfurahini, Halleluya

T:(O:su) Bernhard Kyamanywa, (e) Howard S. Olson, (d) U.S. Leupold - M: Tanzanian Melody - © M + T:(su,e,d) LWF - Q: M + T:(su,e,d) Ld

89 Cristo vive, fuera el llanto

T:(O:s) Nicolas Martinez, (e) Fred Kaan, (d) Arthur Blatezky, (f) J.F. Frié - M: Pablo D. Sosa - © M + T:(s) Methopress Ltd., Buenos Aires, (e) F.K., (d) BV, (f) CNPL - Q: M + T:(s) CN, (e,f,d) CD III

90 Spread the news that our world is redeemed

T:(O:persisch) Hassan Dehqani-Tafti, (e) Lewis Johnson, (f) G. Comment - M: Persian Melody - © T:(persisch) Hassan Dehqani-Tafti (f) CNPL - Q: M + T:(persisch) Persian Hymnbook, (e,f) CD III

91 Christ ist erstanden

T:(O:d) 13. Jahrh. (e) E. Miles Coverdale, - M: 13. Jahrh. - Q: EKG

92 Christ lag in Todesbanden

T:(O:d) Martin Luther, (e) R. Massie, (f) H. Capieu - M: Martin Luther - © T:(f) Capieu - Q: M + T:(d) EKG, (f) CD III

93 A toi la gloire, O Ressuscité

T:(O:f) Edmund Bury, (e) F. Pratt Green, (d) Johanna Meyer, (i) Mario Piatti - M: Georg Friedrich Händel - © T:(f) WCC (e) OUP - Q: CD I

94 Christ the Lord is ris'n today

T:(O:e) Charles Wesley, (f) Nicole Berthet, (d) Emil Schaller Gruppe, (s) J.B. Cabrera, (i) M. Piatti, (arab) Ibrahim Raz el Haddad, (su) *Tenzi za Rohoni*, (j) *Sanbika* 1955 - M: Lyra Davidica - © T:(f) CNPL, (d) BV - Q: (d,f) CD III

95 We know that Christ is raised

T:(O:e) John B. Geyer, (f) Louis Arragon, (d) Fr. Karl Barth - M: C.V. Stanford - © M+T:(e) StB, (f) CNPL, (d) BV Q: T:(f,d) CD III

96 Dieu, nous avons vu ta gloire

T:(O:f) Didier Rimaud, (e) Brian Wren (Refrain von Sir Ronald Johnson), (d) Ursula Trautwein - M: Jean Langlais - © M+T:(f) SEFIM, (e) OUP, (d) BV - Q: T:(d) CD III

97 Christ is the world's light

T:(O:e) F. Pratt Green, (f) G. de Lioncourt, (d) Barth·Leonhardt·Schulz - M: Paris Antophoner - © T:(e) OUP, (f) CNPL, (d) BV - Q: T:(e) *Songs of Praise*, (f,d) CD III

98 Gloire à toi, Jésus Christ

T:(O:f) Dominique Ombrie, (e) Erik Routley - M: Dominique Ombrie - © M+T:(f) CNPL (e) E.R. -

99 Jesus shall reign where'er the sun

T:(O:e) Isaac Watts, (f) Daniel Hameline, (d) Johann Christoph Hampe, (nie) J.W. Schulte-Nordholt - M: *Psalmodia Evangelica* - © T:(f) CNPL

100 Veni Creator Spiritus

T:(O:lat) 9th century, (e) Robert Bridges, (f) Fr. Pierre-Etienne, (d,s) anonym, (indo) Yayasan Musik Gerejani, (j) *Sanbika* 1955 - M: Vatican Plainsong - © T:(f) CNPL, (e) OUP - Q: CD II

101 Nun bitten wir den Heiligen Geist

T:(O:d) Martin Luther, (e) Fred Kaan, (f) M. Capieu, (s) Albert Lehenbauer, (i) *Inni della Riforma* - M: from 14th century - © T:(e) F.K. (f) WCC - Q: M+T:(d) EKG

102 Come down, O'Love divine

T:(O:e) R.F. Littledale, (d) Erwin Kleine, (f) H. Capieu - M: Ralph Vaughan Williams - © M: OUP, T:(d,f) WCC - Q: M: *English Hymnal*, T:(d,f) CD II

103 Wir bitten, Herr, um deinen Geist

T:(O:d) Dieter Trautwein, (e) F. Pratt Green - M: Hans Rudolf Siemoneit - © M: GVH, T:(d,e) BHV - Q: M+T:(d) *Schalom*, (e) CD III

104 Blessed word of God

T:(O:e) A.M. Jones, (f) Nicole Berthet - M: Yoruba tune - © T:(e) Lutterworth Press, (f) CNPL - Q: M+T:(e) *Africa Praise*, (f) CD III

105 Esprit, toi qui guides tous les hommes

T:(O:f) Didier Rimaud, (ej Erik Routley, (i) Eugenio Costa - M: Jean van der Cauter - © M+T:(f) SEFIM, (e) E.R. - Q: F:(e,i) CD III

106 In this world abound T:(O:j) Saichiro Yuya, (e) Esther Hibbard, (f) G. de Lioncourt, (d) Barth·Leonhard·Schulz - M: Old Japanese Melody - © M+T:(e) Church of Christ, Tokio, (f) CNPL, (d) BV Q: M+T:(e) *Hymns of the Church*, (f,d) CD III

107 Ta voix, mon Dieu a dit mon nom

T:(O:f) Claude Rozier, (e) F. Pratt Green - M: Erik Routley - © M: E.R., T:(f) CNPL (e) OUP - Q: T:(e) CD III

108 Lobe den Herren, den mächtigen König

T:(O:d) Joachim Neander, (e) Catherine Winkworth, (f) Didier Rimaud, (s) Fritz Fliedner, (i) E.C.-GS (indo) Yayasan Musik Gerejani, (su) *Nyimbo za Kikristo*, (chin) P'u T'ien Sung Tsan - M: Stralsunder Gesangbuch - © (f) CNPL - Q: CD I

109　From all that dwell below the skies

T:(O:e) Isaac Watts - M: aus *Kölner Gesangbuch*, 1623 -

110　Nun danket alle Gott

T:(O:d) Martin Rinkhardt, (e) Catherine Winkworth (f) F. du Pasquier, (p) Isaac N. Salum, (s) Fritz Fliedner, (chin) *P'u T'ien Sung Tsan* - M: J. Crüger -Q: CD II

111　All creatures of our God and King

T:(O:e) W.H. Draper, (d) Karl Budde, (f) J.J. Bovet, (s) José Miguez-Bonino - M: aus *Kölner Gesangbuch*, 1623 - © T:(e) Roberton Publications - Q: CD II

112　Tout est fait pour la gloire de Dieu

M+T: Abel Nkuinji - © M+T: Abel Nkuinji Q: *Chantons*, Caméroun

113　Singt das Lied der Freude über Gott

T:(O:d) Psalm 148 / Jörg Zink / Dieter Hechtenberg - M: Dieter Hechtenberg - © ChVH - Q: *111 Kinderlieder zur Bibel*

114　Sekai no tomo to te o tsunagi

T:(O:j) Tokuo Yamaguchi, (e) E.M. Stowe, (d) Erich Griebling, (f) Claude Rozier - M: Isao Koizumi - © M+T:(japan) Church of Christ, Tokyo (e,d) LWF, (f) CNPL - Q: T:(e,d) Ld, (f) CD III

115　Herre Gud, ditt dyre navn og aere

T:(O:no) Perrer Dass, (e) Eivind Berggrav, (d) Eivind Berggrav - M: Norwegian folk song - © M+T:(no,e,d) LWF - Q: M+T:(no,e,d) Ld

116　God of love and truth and beauty

T:(O:e) Timothy Rees, (f) M.-C. Sachot, (d) Auguste Saun - M: Herbert Murrill - © M+T:(e) Mowbrays & Co, Oxford, (f) CNPL, (d) BV Q: M+T:(e) *The Mirfield Mission Hymnbook*

117　Jesu, a fé padé

T:(O:yor) Olajida Olude, (e) Biodun Adebesin / Austin Lovelace, (d) Otmar Schulz, (f) Edmond Pidoux - M: Olajida Olude - © M+T:(yor) Olajide Olude, (f) CNPL, (d) BV - Q: M+T:(yor) *Yoruba Hymns and Carols*, (d,f) CD III

118　Worship the Lord, worship the Father

T:(O:e) Fred Kaan, (f) Nicole Berthet - M: Sri Lanka - © T:(e) Fred Kaan, (f) CNPL, - Q: M+T:(ej *New Songs of Asian Cities*, (f) CD III

119　Allein Gott in der Höh' sei Ehr

T:(O:d) N. Decius, (e) Catherine Winkworth, (f) Claude Rozier - M: N. Decius - © T:(f) CNPL - Q: T:(f) CD III

120　Bože Otče, bud' pochválen

T:(O:tsch) Jiri Zabojnik, (d) Erich Griebling, (e) J.J. Vajda, (f) Daniel Hameline - M: *Paris Antiphoner*, 1681 - © T:(d,e) LWF, (f) CNPL - Q: T:(d,e) Ld, (f) CD III

121　Father in heaven, grant to your children

T:(O:e) D.T. Niles, (f) Daniel Hameline - M: Blene G, Maquiso - © T:(O:e) P. Niles, Princeton, (f) CNPL - Q: M+T:(e) *EACC Hymnal*, (f) CD III

122　Erhalt uns, Herr, bei deinem Wort

T:(O:d) Martin Luther, (f) F. Levrier, (e) Erik Routley - M: Martin Luther - © (f) CNPL, (e) E.R. - Q: M+T:(d) CD II, (f,e) CD III

123　Be thou my Vision

T:(O:e) Mary Byrne, (d) Helga Rusche, (f) F. du Pasquier, (s) F.J. Pagura, (p) J. Costa, (j) *Sanbika* 1955 - M: Traditional Irish Melody - Q: M+T: CD II

124　My heart looks in faith to the Lamb

T:(O:chin) T.C. Chao, (e) Frank W. Price, (f) Marie Pierre Faure - M: Chinese Melody - © T:(e) Dr. Frank W. Price, Lexington, (f) CNPL - Q: M+T:(chin) *P'u T'ien Sung Tsan*, (e) *EACC Hymnal*, (f) CD III

125 Ah what shame I have to bear

T:(O:j) Sogo Matsumoto, (e) Esther Hibbard, (d) Barth·Leonhard·Schulz, (f) Marie-Pierre Faure, (chin) *P'u T'ien Sung Tsan*, - M: 12th century Japanese Melody - © T:(j) Church of Christ, Tokio, (d) BV, (F7 CNPL - Q:(j) *Sanbika* 1955, (d,f) CD III

126 Jesu meine Freude

T:(O:d) J.W. Franck, (e) Catherine Winkworth, (f) Claude Rozier, (s) Roberto E. Rios, (indo) Yayasan Musik Gerejani, (su) *Nyimbo za Kikristo*, (j) *Sanbika Dai-z-hen* 1967 - M: J. Crüger - © T:(f) CNPL - Q: T:(f,s,indo) CD III

127 Und suchst du meine Sünde

T:(O:d) Schalom Ben-Chorim, (e) Ivor Jones, (f) Sœur Ancelle - M: Kurt Bossler - © M+T:(d,e) HV, (f) CNPL - Q: M+T:(d) BfG, (e,f) CD III

128 All Morgen ist ganz frisch und neu

T:(O:d) Johannes Zwick, (e) Fred Kaan, (f) Pauline Martin (nie) Vertailing Ad. den Besten - M: Johann Walter - © T:(e) F.K. Q: T:(e) CD III

129 Forth in thy name, O Lord

T:(O:e) Charles Wesley, (d) Emil Schaller, (f) J. Martin - M: Orlando Gibbons - © T:(d) BV, (f) CNPL - Q: T:(d,f) CD III

130 'Light and salt' you called your friends

T:(O:mandarin) I-to Loh, (e) Erik Routley, (f) Daniel Hameline - M: I-to Loh, © M+T:(mandarine) I-to Loh, © E.R. (f) CNPL

131 Paradicsomnak te szép élö fàja

T:(O:un) Pecselyi Kiraly Imre, (e) E. Routley, (f) Dieter Trautwein·Vilmos Gyöngyösi - M: Kolozsvàr © T:(d) BV

132 Arise, arise my soul

T:(O:e) Nicol Macnicol - M: Y.L. Yang - © T:(e) Winslow, Goldalming, - Q: M+T:(e) *EACC Hymnal*

133 We who bear the human name

T:(O:e) Masao Takenaka/Fred Kaan, (d) Dieter Trautwein - M: Nj.R. Sutisno - © T:(e) F.K. (d) BV Q: M+T:(e) *New Songs of Asian Cities*, (d) CD III

134 Eternal Ruler of the ceaseless round

T:(O:e) J.W. Chadwick, (f) Edmond Pidoux, (d) Auguste Sann - M: Orlando Gibbons - © T:(f) Edmond Pidoux, (d) BV - Q: T:(f,d) CD III

135 Se här bygges Babels torn

T:(O:schw) Olov Hartman, (e) Caryl and Ruth Micklem, (d) Markus Jenny - M: Sven-Erik Bäck - © M+T:(schw) Olov Hartman, (e) Caryl Micklem (d) Theologischer Verlag Zürich - Q: M+T:(schw) *71 psalmers och visor*, (e,d) CD III

136 Divided our pathways

T:(O:e) Christopher Coelho, (d) Otmar Schulz, (f) A.M. Jousseaume - M: Christopher Coelho - © M+T:(e) Christopher Coelho, (d) BV (f) CNPL Q: T:(d,f) CD III

137 Help us accept each other

T:(O:e) Fred Kaan, (d,nie) Michael de Vries - M: Doreen Potter -© M: D.P., T:(e) F.K., (d,nie) M.d.V. Q: CD III

138 Un seul Seigneur, une seule foi

T:(O:f) Lucien Deiss, (e) Erik Routley - M: Lucien Deiss - © M+T:(f) SEFIM, (e) E.R. - Q: T:(e) CD III

139 A Lord Christ, the Father's mighty son

T:(O:e) Brian Wren - M: Peter Cutts - © M+T:(e) OUP - Q: M+T:(e) *Dunblane Praise*

139 B Lord Christ, the Father's mighty son

T:(O:e) Brian Wren - M: Doreen Potter - © M: Doreen Potter, T:(e) OUP - Q: T:(e) *Dunblane Praise*, M: CD III

140 A In Christ there is no East or West

T:(O:e) John Oxenham, (f) Nicole Berthet, (d) M. Liesegang, (s) J.R. de Balloch, (p) Franca Campos - M: American folk hymn by H.T. Burleigh Q: T:(d,s) CD I, (p) Ld, (f) CD III

140 B In Christ there is no East or West

T:(O: indo) Yayasan Musik Gerejani, (arab) Elias Marmura, (chin) *P'u T'ien Sung Tsan* - M: A.R. Reinagle

141 Gathered here from many nations

T:(O:e) Fred H. Kaan, (d) Konrad Raiser, (f) Etienne de Peyer - M: Doreen Potter - © M + T:(e) StB, (d) BV (f) SEFIM - Q: M + T:(e) PP, (d,f) CD III

142 Herr, du hast darum gebetet

T:(O:d) Otmar Schulz, (e) Ivor Jones - M: Rolf Schweizer - © M: HV, T:(d) BHV, T:(e) Jones Q: M + T:(d) *Schalom*

143 Christ is the King, O friends, rejoice

T:(O:e) G.K.A. Bell - M: Melchior Vulpius - © T:(e) OUP - Q: T:(e) *Songs of Praise*

144 Tumepokea neema, tuimbe sote kwa shaugwe

T:(O:su) Zakarias D. Mzengi, (e) Howard S. Olson - M: Ihandzu-Ilyamba Melody - © M + T:(su,e) Lutheran Theological College Makumira, Tanzania

145 Seigneur, rassemble nous dans la paix

T:(O:f) Dominique Ombrie, (e) Fred H. Kaan, (d) Marlies Flesch-Thebesius - M: Dominique Ombrie - © M + T:(f) CNPL, (e) F.K. (d) BV Q: T:(e,d) CD III

146 Ein feste Burg ist unser Gott

T:(O:d) Martin Luther, (e) Thomas Carlyle, (f) H. Lutteroth, (s) J.B. Cabrera rev. F.J. Pagura, (p) E.J. von Hafe rev. *Hinário Evangélica*, (arab) Asaad el Rassy - M: Martin Luther -

147 Lord of light whose name outshineth

T:(O:e) Howell Elvet Lewis - M: Thomas John Williams -

148 Sonne der Gerechtigkeit

T:(O:d) Christian David / Barth / Nehring, (e) F. Pratt Green - M: Geistlich Böhmische Brüder / Neufassung Otto Riethmüller - © für Neufassung: BHV (e) OUP Q: M + T:(d) *Schalom*, (e) CD III

149 God is working his purpose out

T:(O:e) A.C. Ainger, (f) Didier Rimaud, (p) J.W. Faustini, (s) F.J. Pagura - M: Martin Shaw - © T:(f) CNPL, (p) Faustini, (s) F.J.P. - Q: M + T:(e) *Songs of Praise*, (f,p,s) CD III

150 Gleichwie mich mein Vater gesandt hat

T:(O:d) John 20 - M: Paul Ernst Ruppel - © M: HV - Q: M + T:(d) BfG

151 Das sollt ihr, Jesu Jünger, nie vergessen

T:(O:d) J.A. Cramer, (e) Fred Kaan, (f) Pierre Yves - M: J. Crüger - © T:(e) F.K., (f) CNPL - Q: T:(e,f) CD III

152 Let all mortal flesh keep silence

T:(O:e) Liturgy of St. James, (f) G. de Lioncourt, (d) Erich Griebling, (s) Pablo D. Sosa, (p) J. Costa, (arab) Nasef el Vazgi (chin) *P'u T'ien Sung Tsan*, (j) *Sanbika* 1955 - M: French carol melody - © T:(f) CNPL, (d) LWF, (s) WCC - Q: T:(d) Ld, (f) CD III

153 Let us break bread together on our knees

T:(O:e) Negro Spiritual, (f) Marc Ginot, (i) Eugenio Costa, (s) F.J. Pagura, (p) J.W. Faustini, (j) Yoichi Kishimoto, *Sanbika Dai-z-hen* - M: Negro Spiritual - © T:(f) CNPL - Q: T:(f) CD III

154 Come, risen Lord, and deign to be our guest

T:(O:e) G.W. Briggs, (d) Wolfgang

Derreth, (f) Daniel Hameline – M: Alfred M. Smith – © T:(e) OUP, (f) CNPL (d) BV Q: M+T:(e) *Songs of Praise*, (d,f) CD III

155 As the disciples when thy Son had left

T:(O:e) Percy Dearmer, (d) Ernst Lange – M: Lee H. Bristol – © M: L.H.B., T:(e) OUP, – Q: M+T:(e) *Songs of Praise*, (d) CD III

156 Jesus the Lord said

T:(O:e) Dermott Monahan, (f) Joseph Gelineau, (d) Otmar Schulz – M: Urdu melody – © M: har. F.B. Westbrook, T:(f) CNPL, (d) BV – Q: M+T:(e) *EACC Hymnal*, (d,f) CD III

157 The bread of life for all men broken

T:(O:chin) Timothy Tingfang Lew, (e) W.R.O. Taylor, (f) Claude Rozier, (d) Konrad Raiser – M: Su Yin-Lan – © M+T:(chin,e) East Asia Christian Conference, Bangkok, (f) CNPL, (d) BV – Q: M+T:(chin,e) *EACC Hymnal*, (f,d) CD III

158 As we break the bread

T:(O:e) Fred Kaan, (d) Dieter Trautwein – M: Stanley L. Osborne – © M: Stanley L. Osborne, T·(e) StB, (d) BV – Q: *The Hymnbook* of the United and Anglican Church of Canada

159 Herr, du bist an vielen Tischen

T:(O:d) Dieter Trautwein, (e) F. Pratt Green – M: Dieter Trautwein – © M+T:(d) BHV, (e) OUP Q: M+T:(d) *Schalom*, (e) CD III

160 Now let us from this table rise

T:(O:e) Fred Kaan, (d) Dieter Trautwein – M: *Grenoble Antiphoner* – © T:(e) StB, (d) BV Q: T:(d) CD III

161 Father, we thank thee who hast planted

T:(O:e) F. Bland Tucker, (d) Barth·Leonhard·Schulz – M: La Forme

des Prières – © T:(d) BV Q: M+T:(e) Hymnal 1940, (d) CD III

162 Du som gick före oss längst in

T:(O:schw) Olov Hartman, (e) Fred Kaan, (d) Helli Halbe – M: Sven Erik Bäck – © M: Nordiska Musikförlaget, T:(schw) Olov Hartmann, (e) F.K., (d) BV – Q: M+T:(schw) *71 psalmers och Visor*, (e,d) CD III

163 „Wachet auf", ruft uns die Stimme

T:(O:d) Philipp Nicolai, (e) F.C. Burkitt, (f) Claude Rozier, (s) Fliedner/Martinez, (p) J.M. de Mota Sobrinho, (indo) Yayasan Musik Gerejani, (su) *Nyimbo za Kikristo* – M: Philipp Nicolai – © T:(f) CNPL – Q: M+T:(d,e) CD II, (f) CD III

164 From glory to glory advancing

T:(O:e) C.W. Humphreys, (f) J. Martin – M: Gustav Holst – © M+T:(e) OUP, (f) CNPL – Q: M+T:(e) *English Hymnal*, (f) CD III

165 Puissance et gloire de l'Esprit

T:(O:f) Claude Rozier, (e) Emily Chisholm – M: Claude Rozier – © M+T:(d) SEFIM, (e) Chisholm

166 Axion estin os alithos

T:(O:grie) – M: Byzantine 15.-16th century arr. by D.E. Conomos – © M: D.E. Conomos

167 It is very meet to bless thee

T:(O:rus) – M: Kievan Melody

168 By the prayers of the Mother of God

T:(O:serb) – M: Traditional Serbian Melody

169 We sing thee, we bless thee

T:(O:serb), (f) Daniel Hameline – M: Traditional Serbian Melody

170 Pre Tine Te lăudăm

T:(O:rum) – M: Traditional Roumanian Melody

171 Pasa Pnoi enessato

T:(O:grie) – M: Byzantine 15.-16th

century arr. D.E. Conomos - © M: D.E. Conomos

172 Christos anesti ek nekrōn
T:(O:grie) - M: Byzantine 15.-16th century arr. D.E. Conomos - © M: D.E. Conomos

173 Kyrie eleison
T:(O:grie) - M: Byzantine 15.-16th century, arr. D.E. Conomos - © M: D.E. Conomos

174 O heavenly King, the Comforter Spirit
T:(O:rus) - M: Russian Orthodox Chant - Q: CD II

175 Svyati Bozhe, Svyaty Kryepky
T:(O:bul) - M: Traditional Bulgarian chant

176 Remember thy servants, Lord
T:(O:rus), (e) M.M. Gowen, (f) J. Vincent, (d) H. Laepple M: Russian Orthodox Melody - Q: CD II

177 Aliluia, Aliluia
T:(O:rum) - M: Traditional Roumanian

178 Thok te tigom nem pioou
T:(O:Coptic) - M: Coptic

179 Osanna khen Niyetahosy
T:(O:Coptic) - M: Coptic

180 Kyrie eleison, Christe eleison
T:(O:grie) - M:Gallican ancien

181 Gloire à Dieu, Paix aux hommes
T:(O:f), (d) Ursula Trautwein - M: J. Berthier - © M: Editions Fleurus, Paris, T:(f) AELF, (d) BV

182 Omnes gentes plaudite manibus
T:(O:lat), (e) David S. Goodall, (d) Ursula Trautwein - M: Joseph Gelineau © M + T:(d) BV, (e) Goodall

183 A toi le règne
T:(O:f) - M: Didier Rimaud - © M + T:(f) AELF

184 Je crois mais augmente ma foi
T:(O:f) Joseph Gelineau - M: Joseph Gelineau - © M: SEFIM

185 Sanctus Dominus
T:(O:lat) - M: Vatican, XVII Jahrh.

186 Jubilate and Gloria
T:(O:e) John Erickson, (d) Ursula Trautwein - M: John Erickson - © M: JUBILATE: WCC, GLORIA: BV, T:(d) BV - Q: T:(d) CD III

187 Holy Lord
T:(O:e) - M: John Erickson © M: WCC

188 Kyrie eleison
M: Herbert Beuerle - © M: Fidula-Verlag, Boppard und Salzburg - Q: Gnadenquell

189 Neig dein Ohr zu mir, mein Gott
T:(O:d) Adam Gumpelzhaimer, (f) Joseph Gelineau - M: Adam Gumpelzhaimer - © T:(f) CNPL - Q: T:(f) CD III

190 Herr, bleibe bei uns
T:(O:d) Albert Thate, (f) Joseph Gelineau - M: Albert Thate - © M + T:(d) BV, (f) CNPL - Q: Geistliche Zwiegesänge

191 Christ ist erstanden
T + M: 1529·1964

192 Jésus Christ est né, il est né aujourd'hui
T:(O:f) - M: Tétouom - © M: Tétouom, Caméroun

193 Premarupa to jagi avataralà
T:(O:hind) - M: aus Indien

194 Er ist die rechte Freudensonn
T:(O:d) Georg Weissel, (e) Catherine Winkworth, (f) Joseph Gelineau - M: Freylinghausen 1715 - © T:(f) CNPL - Q: EKG, (f) CD III

195 The Lord is my shepherd
T:(O:e) Lee Hastings Bristol, (d) Ursula

Trautwein – M: Lee Hastings Bristol – ©
M + T: (e) Abingdon Press, Nashville, (d)
BV – Q: M + T: (e) *Let the Children sing*,
(d) CD III

196 Danket dem Herrn und lobsingt

T: (O: d) Hermann Stern, (f) Joseph
Gelineau – M: Hermann Stern – ©
M + T: (d) VMB, (f) CNPL

197 Lobet den Herren, alle, die ihn ehren

T: (O: d) Paul Gerhardt, (f) Joseph
Gelineau – M: Herbert Beuerle – © M:
BHV, T: (f) CNPL – Q: M: *Mein Dudelsack*, T: (f) CD III

198 Singet und spielet dem Herrn

T: (O: d) Hermann Stern – M: Hermann
Stern © M + T: VMB

199 Herr, unser Herrscher, wie herrlich

T: (O: d) Gerd Watkinson, (f) Joseph
Gelineau – M: Gerd Watkinson – ©
M + T: (d) VV (f) CNPL – Q: T: (f) CD
III

200 Yeshu supriya, Yeshu ashraye

T: (O: hind), (f) Didier Rimaud – M:
Indian Blessing

201 Gehe ein in deinen Frieden

T: (O: d) – M: An Israeli Blessing – ©
M + T: VV

202 Amen

M: Paul Ernst Ruppel – © M: VMB – Q
Das Monatslied, Heft 1

Topical Index · Verwendungshinweise
Table analytique

God · Gott · Dieu

His Providence and Promises · Seine Vorsehung und seine Verheißungen · Sa providence et ses promesses No / Nr. 2, 9, 10, 11, 24, 27, 43-52, 115

His Creation · Seine Schöpfung · Sa création No. / Nr. 3, 8, 12, 15, 19, 27, 31, 32, 43, 44, 71, 111, 113

His Word · Sein Wort · Sa parole (see also: The Scriptures · siehe auch: Die Heilige Schrift · voir aussi: l'Ecriture No. / Nr. 7, 22, 45, 46

His Reign · Sein Reich · Son règne No. / Nr. 6, 17, 21, 113, 146

The Holy Trinity · Die Heilige Dreifaltigkeit · La sainte trinité No. / Nr. 119-122, 152, 175, 177, 179, 184, 185, 187, 188

Jesus Christ · Jesus Christus · Jésus Christ

His Advent and Incarnation · Seine Ankunft und seine Menschwerdung · Sa venue et son incarnation No. / Nr. 21, 50, 52-65, 152, 165-167, 179, 181, 192, 193

His Ministry and Teaching · Sein Amt und seine Lehre · Son ministère et son enseignement No. / Nr. 33, 37, 66-77, 81, 104, 125, 130, 150, 156

His Passion · Sein Leidensweg · Sa passion No. / Nr. 14, 40, 78-83, 131, 162

His Resurrection · Seine Auferstehung · Sa résurrection No. / Nr. 84-99, 172, 191

His Reign and Glory · Sein Reich und seine Herrlichkeit · Son règne et sa gloire No. /Nr. 79, 81, 93-99, 178

The Holy Spirit · Der Heilige Geist · Le Saint-Esprit

The Gifts of the Spirit · Die Gaben des Heilgen Geistes · Les dons de l'Esprit No. / Nr. 100-105, 144, 174

The Scriptures · Die Heilige Schrift · L'Ecriture No. / Nr. 7, 22, 45, 46, 104, 106, 107

The Church · Die Kirche · L'Eglise

Worship anf Praise · Gottesdienst und Lobpreisung · Louange et adoration No. / Nr. 1, 3, 6, 13, 16, 18, 21, 25, 28, 47, 57, 108-122, 169, 171, 175, 177, 182, 183, 186, 187, 190, 194, 197, 198

Unity and Mission · Einheit und Sendung · Unité et mission No. / Nr. 1, 13, 63, 76, 77, 97-99, 133-150, 164

Penitence · Busse · Pénitence No. / Nr. 60, 136, 139, 148

The Sacraments · Die Sakramente · Les sacrements No. / Nr. 95

The Eucharist · Das Heilige Abendmahl · L'eucharistie No. / Nr. 20, 46, 74, 83, 92, 96, 151-162, 164, 166-187, 195

Morning · Morgen · Matin No. / Nr. 120, 128, 129, 132

Evening · Abend · Soir No. / Nr. 200, 201

The Saints · Die Heiligen · Les saints No. / Nr. 143, 163, 165

Man · Der Mensch · L'homme

The City · Die Stadt · La cité No. / Nr. 29, 35, 38, 39, 40, 41

The Earth · Die Welt · Le monde No. / Nr. 8, 19, 32, 43

Peace · Frieden · Paix No. / Nr. 18, 42, 55, 134, 148

Service and Friendship · Dienst und Freundschaft · Service et fraternité No. / Nr. 30, 32, 34, 36, 37, 38, 43, 45, 49, 50, 59, 61, 66, 70, 75, 133-135, 138, 145, 151, 160

Index of First Lines
Verzeichnis der Liedanfänge
Répertoire selon les premiers mots

373

374